11500

Sadat

With the authors'
compliments and best
~ the.

David Hirst
Beirut, 3 May 1982

also by David Hirst
The Gun and the Olive Branch

Sadat

David Hirst and Irene Beeson

faber and faber

First published in 1981
by Faber and Faber Limited
3 Queen Square London WC1N 3AU
Filmset in Great Britain by
Latimer Trend & Company Ltd, Plymouth
Printed in Great Britain by
The Thetford Press Ltd, Thetford, Norfolk
All rights reserved

British Library Cataloguing in Publication Data

Hirst, David
  Sadat.
  1. Sadat—Anwar el-
  2. Egypt—President—Biography
  I. Title   II. Beeson, Irene
  962′.054′0924   DT107.828.S23

  ISBN 0–571–11690–6

Contents

For Krystyna
in fond remembrance

Prologue

Anwar Sadat, the peace-maker, died at a celebration of war. To his 'victory' in the fourth round of the Arab–Israeli struggle he attributed those subsequent pacific exploits that were to make him, in the West, the most revered statesman of his generation. On 6 October 1973 his army had stormed across the Suez Canal, and it was his habit, every year, to relive those glorious hours at a grandiose military parade.

At 11 a.m. on 6 October 1981 he took his seat on the ornate bronze dais, decorated with impressions of Osiris and other Egyptian gods, in Nasr (Victory) City on the outskirts of Cairo. His new blue-and-gold uniform, the Star of Sinai and the green sash which adorned it and his brown leather knee-boots were all of such splendour that the onlookers, accustomed though they were to his martial finery, gasped audibly. On his right, similarly if not equally resplendent, sat Vice President Husni Mubarak and, on his left, Defence Minister Abdul Halim Abu Ghazala, amid a galaxy of the most eminent and influential in the land. Behind, in a special glassed-in enclosure, was Sadat's wife Jihan and other ladies.

Security was elaborate. Sadat had arrived with eight bodyguards clinging to his limousine. His personal secretary, seated directly behind him, was armed. Republican guards were stationed behind and beside the dais. Paratroopers gazed sternly into the crowd. The troops on parade had been rigorously searched for amunition; that, it was presumed, was the only quarter from which danger might come. Over the years the United States had contributed every possible type of expertise and sophisticated device, at a cost of between $20 and 25 million, to protect the life of the man on whom, more than any other, all their Middle East strategies depended.

11

At 11.05 an *imam* recited verses from the Koran; General Ghazala delivered a short speech thanking the Americans for the new equipment which, interspersed with ageing Russian stock, was about to be unveiled for the first time; Sadat laid a wreath at the pyramid-shaped Tomb of the Unknown Soldier on the opposite side of the parade route; and then the gigantic procession, a full 10 miles long, began to move amid raucous music, the roll of drums, fireworks and the crack of mortars firing little parachutes carrying tiny Egyptian flags and portraits of the President. By 11.40 the first of the mounted troops had filed past, followed by a huge contingent of cadets. Sadat, relaxed and chatting with his neighbours, lit up his beloved pipe. At 12 noon he enthusiastically applauded a spectacular exhibition of free-fall parachuting. Then at 1 p.m., as the ground display began to grow less interesting, the aerobatics began—American Phantoms screaming through the cloudless sky and French Mirages billowing red, blue and green smoke. On the ground sand-and-green Russian lorries, four abreast, were towing heavy Russian field guns; but, with all eyes craning upwards, no one noticed as one of them, nearest to the reviewing stand, came shuddering to a halt.

Inside the cab Lieutenant Khalid Islambouli had put his automatic rifle to the driver's head. He ordered him to brake and leaped to the ground; three of his accomplices were in the back of the lorry. He raced towards the reviewing stand as the others hurled grenades and provided covering fire. It was all over in forty-five seconds, a microcosm, in its meticulous planning and brilliant execution, of the event Sadat was there to commemorate. Indeed, in his last moments it might have seemed to him like a replay, for his benefit, of the storming of the Bar Lev line. For he apparently rose to salute this exuberant display of homage from his 'boys'—as he habitually called his soldiers—as they rushed towards him shouting 'Glory to Egypt!' But he only made himself an easier target for Lieutenant Islambouli, who, without encountering any fire from the bewildered, fleeing security guards, had reached the reviewing stand. Raising his rifle over the parapet, he pumped automatic fire into his President at point-blank range.

In the West there was dismay, outrage and sorrow. In the Arab world there was unrestrained jubilation. In Egypt itself there was complete indifference.

For Washington Sadat's death was a catastrophe, pure and simple. Calling the murder 'an act of infamy, cowardly infamy' which 'fills us with horror', President Reagan was nonetheless confident that, in the 'martyrdom' of this 'good and brave man', the cause of 'peace and humanity' for which he had always lived would endure and triumph. His predecessor, Jimmy Carter, extolled Sadat as the greatest leader he had ever met, who had done more for 'peace on earth' than anyone this century. The pundits and the leader writers were not to be outdone, especially in the United States, where such journals as the *New York Times*, the *Washington Post*, *Time* and *Newsweek* mourned the passing of this 'great man', this 'historic figure', this 'profound, serene fatalist', this 'man of peace', 'vision' and 'courage', the 'beleaguered, valiant, seemingly indispensable Anwar Sadat'. They wondered, fearfully, what the world would be like without him, whether it had witnessed 'a Middle Eastern Sarajevo, the single death-by-terror that unhinges everything'.

In Syria there was dancing in the streets, and Damascus Radio exulted: 'The traitor is dead. . . . it is a victory. . . . our comrades of the Egyptian army have avenged us.' In Beirut the inhabitants fired into the air with the vast panoply of weaponry which they usually directed against each other. In Libya there were accidents galore as drivers careered about the streets, trumpeting their joy. For the Americans such jubilation bordered on the obscene; *Time* magazine called it 'dancing upon the assassinated corpse of one of the world's last great men'.

In Egypt, 43 million people went on with the celebration of *Id al-Adha*, the Feast of the Sacrifice, as if nothing had happened. The streets of Cairo were unusually empty and remained so even on the day of the funeral, four days later. That was an almost exclusively Western occasion. And the West did their slain friend proud. For security reasons President Reagan could not go himself, but, as an unprecedented mark of respect, he invited his three predecessors— Richard Nixon, Gerald Ford and Jimmy Carter—to attend on his behalf. Secretary of State Alexander Haig and Secretary of Defense Casper Weinberger were there too, and so, last but not least, was Sadat's 'good friend' Henry Kissinger. Britain sent Prince Charles, former Prime Minister James Callaghan and the Foreign Secretary, Lord Carrington; from France came President François Mittérand and his predecessor Valéry Giscard d'Estaing; from Germany, Chancellor Helmut Schmidt. Even though it was the Sabbath and, as a strictly observant Jew, he could not use his bullet-proof limousine, Israeli Prime Minister Menachim Begin insisted on paying his last respects to his 'friend' and 'partner in peace'.

But as the funeral of the President of the most powerful and populous Arab country, only one of the twenty-four members of the Arab League was represented by a head of state, Jaafar Numairi of the Sudan. Only two others, Oman and Somalia, sent representatives at all. As for the Egyptian people, in the name of security they were rigorously, deliberately excluded; but even if they had not been, it is likely that only the curious would have shown up, and very few of them. The sentimental, good-natured Egyptian masses, foreign correspondents concluded, did not appear to be missing 'the hero of war and peace'.

Eleven years before, President Nasser had made his last journey through the heart of Cairo amid unforgettable scenes of spontaneous, tumultuous grief and lamentation. Sadat made his through a dusty wasteland on its outskirts. The compact little throng of foreign dignitaries, herded along by bodyguards of a dozen different nationalities, followed the gun-carriage down the same desolate stretch of tarmac that had been used for the military parade. Thousands of policemen guarded them against non-existent crowds. It was a bleak, furtive, almost seedy spectacle. And even before the man they had come to bury had been lowered into a temporary grave at the Tomb of the Unknown Soldier, the presidents, princes and prime ministers were leaving for the airport, conveniently near at hand. Sadat, said French Foreign Minister Claude Cheysson on his return to Paris, had been buried 'without the people and without the army'.

Within minutes of an event that shook the world, continuity was the watchword. Vice President Mubarak stepped more swiftly and more smoothly into Sadat's shoes than Sadat had into Nasser's. The only candidate in a presidential referendum, he secured, according to the official count, a 98·46 per cent vote in his favour. He pledged that he would not 'budge an inch' from his predecessor's path; he reserved his first interview for the Israeli newspaper *Ma'ariv*, assuring it of his unswerving commitment to peace.

Mubarak moved swiftly to show that he was in control. But the means he chose was a measure of the difficulties he faced. He ordered a year-long state of emergency. He would, he said, show 'no mercy' to trouble-makers, whom police were authorized to shoot on sight. Troops were parachuted in to put down an insurrection by Moslem fundamentalists in the southern town of Asyut. There were purges in the army and widespread arrests directed mainly, but not exclusively, against the fundamentalists. The first official version of the assassination was that it had been carried out by a small group of 'fanatics' acting entirely on their own; then the operation was said to have been 'limited' in scope; later it was described as the spearhead of a wider, aborted conspiracy to establish an 'Islamic republic' on the Iranian model.

The Americans expressed their confidence in the new Egyptian leadership. The assassination, said presidential councillor Edwin Meese, 'does not indicate instability any more than the shooting of President Reagan indicates instability in the United States'. But there was a touch of panic all the same. Having lost their most loyal friend, the Americans were determined to show that Mubarak was their man too. The United States, said Meese, would defend Egypt not only from invasion but also from 'internal subversion coming from external sources'. The Sixth Fleet was put on increased alert. Two AWACS surveillance aircraft were dispatched to patrol the Libyan frontier. Joint manoeuvres, already scheduled for November, were to be expanded; the 82nd Airborne Division would be making parachute drops over the Western Desert and B52s would fly in, unload their bombs and, having refuelled in the air, return to their bases in North Dakota. The Russians protested about 'gross pressures on a sovereign state'.

The Israeli Government promptly welcomed Mubarak's assurances. It, too, expressed its confidence that he was firmly in command. But there was no disguising the fact that, if he were not, the final withdrawal from Sinai, scheduled for April 1982, would not take place and that the whole 'peace process' would collapse. Militant settlers stepped up their campaign to 'stop the withdrawal from Sinai'.

The international order which, since his pilgrimage to Jerusalem, Sadat had built and had come to personify is still in place. But that his violent end, so eminently foreseeable, should be regarded as having dealt it such a devastating blow merely illustrates how fragile and unnatural that order has always been. The rejoicing in the Arab world was certainly in poor taste, but it was no more out of place than the official grief and extravagant obituaries in the West. The following pages, completed a few days before Sadat's death, offer an explanation for both reactions.

D. H. and I. B.
November 1981

15

1

The Crossing

The Hero of the Crossing

Tuesday, 16 October 1973. A glorious day for Egypt's President Muhammad Anwar Sadat.

The entire Egyptian people would be hanging upon every word of the speech he was to deliver that afternoon to the People's Assembly. All who could be would be out to cheer him on his way; indeed, long before his motorcade set out from his residence across the Nile, hundreds of thousands had already gathered in the streets. The air was filled with the rhythmic tumult of hands clapping and feet stamping to chants of 'Sadat . . . Sadat . . . Sadat'. Overnight, the route he was to take—Giza Avenue, Kasr el-Nil Bridge, Midan el-Tahrir, Kasr el-Aini Street—had assumed a fairground appearance. Banners slung across the broad thoroughfares of central Cairo acclaimed the 'Leader of the Liberation Struggle', 'The Hero of the Crossing'. His features were everywhere looking benignly down from huge photographs and gaudily painted portraits on walls and hoardings. Flowers, flags and bunting festooned public buildings, private houses, shops, kiosks, buses and trams. The galabiyah-clad multitudes spilled off the pavements into the centre of the street. They crowded on to terraces, windowsills, and rooftops; they scaled every vantage point—statues, lamp posts, palm trees—that could be scaled.

It was three years since the inhabitants of Cairo had laid on one of their exhibitions of spontaneous popular fervour which no other city can equal. The last had been the extraordinary outpouring of grief at the death of President Nasser. They had been three lean, ungrateful years for his successor. He had never really won his people's respect and affection. On the contrary, his stock had fallen so low that, if he made a speech, it only furnished material for those mischievous jokes for which the Egyptians are celebrated; and, as often as not, if crowds gathered in the streets, they would be demonstrating students. Among their rich repertoire of rhyming slogans the cruellest was the one which reminded him of the contrast, in their minds, between himself and the 'immortal leader' whose mantle he had so fortuitously put on: '*Rah al-Wahsh, Gaa al-Gahsh*'; 'Gone is the Giant, the Donkey has taken his place'.

As he passed, upright in his open limousine, resplendent in military uniform, nothing can have rung more sweetly in his ears than the two syllables of his own name, flung at him in the same thunderous, delirious roar as the '*Nasser . . . Nasser . . . Nasser . . .*' which had always greeted the public appearance of his predecessor.

Nasser may have been a 'giant', but it was he who had led the Arabs to catastrophic defeat in the Arab-Israeli war of June 1967. Was it not Sadat who was now leading them to victory? Was it not he who, in alliance with the Syrians, had ordered an all-out attack on Israeli-occupied Sinai; whose daring the Egyptian army had more than vindicated, crossing the Suez Canal and smashing the 'impregnable' Bar Lev line; who was restoring the terribly wounded pride of Egyptians and Arabs everywhere?

'Remember,' exclaimed Moussa Sabri, loyalest of Cairo columnists, in *al-Akhbar* newspaper, 'remember, Arabs, how much he suffered in silence.' As he went on his way to make his historic speech, the Hero of the Crossing beamed radiantly down on the rebellious youths now so vociferously acknowledging their mistake of the past three years.

Operation Badr

The apotheosis of Anwar Sadat had begun on Saturday, 6 October. For the Egyptians it had promised to be just another warm and sunny day. True, they were in the midst of Ramadan, the taxing month during which devout Moslems fast from dawn to dusk. And they were vaguely aware, perhaps, that for the Jews it was Yom Kippur, the Day of Atonement, and that in Israel, on this most sacred of days, life comes to a complete standstill.

At a quarter past two in the afternoon Cairo Radio interrupted its regular programmes to announce that 'at 13.30 hours today the Israeli enemy attacked our forces in the areas of Zafrana and Sukhna in the Gulf of Suez, using several formations of warplanes, while some of its gunboats approached the west coast of the Gulf. Our forces are now confronting the attacking forces.'

A great many of Cairo's citizens missed the announcement. They were either still at work in offices and factories or, struggling through the frantic rush-hour chaos, on their way home to sleep away the rest of the day until the ceremonial salvo at sunset signalled the *Iftar*—the breaking of the fast. There were to be few siestas that afternoon.

Word flew around the city in a flash. Of course, no one could quite believe that this was full-scale war, let alone a war Egypt had begun. Although President Sadat had pledged that if all attempts to achieve a peaceful settlement of the Arab-Israeli conflict failed he would resort to the military alternative, he had said it so often no one took him seriously any more—neither the outside world, nor the Arabs or the Israelis, and certainly not the Egyptians. That, after all, was why the students used to lampoon him as a donkey. At most people imagined it was yet another punitive raid—though an unusually big one—launched by the Israelis, as was their custom, against their Arab neighbours in retaliation for the latest exploit of the Palestinian resistance movement. Nothing infuriated the Israelis more than the hostage-taking operations that the guerrillas, unable to achieve much in Israel itself, aimed against Zionist targets in foreign countries, and they were still smarting at a particularly successful operation which had occurred eight days before.

On 28 September two members of a hitherto unknown organization, the Eagles of the Palestinian Revolution, had seized three Soviet Jewish emigrants on board a train that was taking them from Czechoslovakia to Austria. After eleven hours of negotiation, the Austrian chancellor, Bruno Kreisky, had submitted to the guerrillas' single demand—the closure of the Schoenau transit camp near Vienna through which the *émigrés* had to pass on their way to Israel. The Israeli Prime Minister, Golda Meir, denouncing the Austrian decision as 'the greatest encouragement to terrorism throughout the world', had gone to Vienna in person in a bid to get it reversed. But she had failed. It turned out that the Eagles of the Palestine Revolution was a branch of the Syrian-backed Saiqa guerrilla organization, and in the past few days tension on the Golan Heights was reported to be rising dangerously, with the Syrians bracing themselves for massive Israeli retaliation. Sure enough, five minutes after the Cairo war bulletin there came a similar one from Damascus. 'At 14.00 hours today', it said, 'enemy forces began to attack our advanced positions along the

19

ceasefire lines. Our forces are replying to the sources of fire and silencing them. Formations of enemy planes have tried to penetrate our air space in the northern sector of the front. Our fighters intercepted them. . . .'

Then Cairo Radio switched to martial music and patriotic songs. It broadcast instructions to civil defence organizations 'to prepare for all eventualities'. In every café, shop and home people gathered round their radio sets. The city was tense and hushed—one giant listening post. Confirmation soon came from the enemy camp. On Yom Kippur even the Israeli broadcasting services close down for twenty-four hours. But at 14.40 Israel Radio broke its silence to announce that the Egyptian and Syrian armies had launched a combined offensive on the country's southern and northern fronts. More Egyptian communiqués followed. One said that 'our air force carried out its duty with success and scored hits on enemy positions. All our aircraft, except one, returned safely to base.' Another said that the Egyptians had now shot down eleven enemy aircraft for the loss of ten of their own.

There could no longer be any doubt. This was all-out war, the long-awaited 'fourth round' between Arabs and Israelis. There was a deep, uneasy feeling in Cairo that already events were following the same pattern as before; that, as in 1956 and, above all, in 1967, the enemy had struck first with another of those devastating surprise attacks which, however long the actual hostilities might go on, had already sealed the Arab armies' fate. In 1967, it was recalled, the Israelis had disguised their own pre-emptive strike with a claim that the Egyptian army was marching across their southern frontier, while the first Egyptian war bulletins had claimed the downing of 115 enemy aircraft. And everyone remembered the wild enthusiasm with which those first apparent successes had been greeted. This time there was to be no premature rejoicing. It was in apprehensive calm that people awaited the next communiqué. Number five soon came: 'Our forces succeeded in crossing the Canal at several points and they have now occupied enemy positions. . . . The Egyptian flag has been raised on the east side of the Canal.' Meanwhile, Damascus Radio announced the capture of Mount Hermon. With this news, a mere two hours after the outbreak of fighting, the hush deepened; complete bewilderment reigned. Was it possible? Surely the Egyptian high command had learned the lesson of 1967. Surely it would not deceive the people with such cruel lies yet again. Communiqué number seven, just an hour later, sounded simply incredible: 'Egyptian forces have succeeded in crossing the Suez Canal at all points along the front and have occupied almost all Israeli positions on the eastern side of the Canal.'

For six years the Egyptians had been dreaming of, and dreading, the awful necessity of the Crossing. For six demoralizing years of 'no war, no peace' they had been making sacrifices for the 'inevitable battle' which, it seemed, would never come; a desperately poor and over-populated country had diverted precious resources to the reconstruction of its shattered army or the purchase of costly and sophisticated weapons. Instead of the Crossing, the army had attempted a grinding 'war of attrition', pounding the enemy positions with massive artillery barrages. But the Israelis had countered with retribution on an even greater scale. They had reduced the Canal Zone cities—Port Said, Suez, Ismailia—to a ghostly shambles, blitzed and rubble-strewn. Hundreds had died before the civilian population, a million of them, could be evacuated and absorbed at great economic and social cost into the teeming cities of the Delta. In the early 1970s, newly acquired American-made Phantom bombers enabled the Israelis to reach out beyond the Canal to strike at the Egyptian heartland. In desperation President Nasser begged the Soviet Union to take over Egypt's air defences itself; Russian experts arrived to set up and man a screen of SAM missile sites on the ground and Russian pilots joined Egyptian ones in patrolling Egyptian air space. Then, in the summer of 1972, President Sadat inexplicably expelled 20,000 Soviet 'experts'—seeming to leave the country more vulnerable than ever.

Now, in two laconic sentences, the Egyptians were told that the Crossing had been accomplished. It had taken four hours. Could it be true? What had happened to the 'invincible' Israeli army? General Moshe Dayan, it was not forgotten, had said that for Egypt another war would be 'suicide',[1] and General Ezer Weizmann had warned that if Sadat did attack, the Egyptians 'would take such a trouncing, inside Egypt proper, in their own homes, that the 1967 war would seem like an agreeable memory in comparison'.[2] What of the famous Bar Lev line that General Weizmann had called 'the best line of defence any king or president has had in the history of the Jewish people'? Had not expert Western opinion agreed that, arrogant though the Israeli claims were, they were none the less largely justified? The balance of military power did seem to lie overwhelmingly in their favour. Among the political intelligentsia, students and activists of many persuasions, disbelief jostled with a strong suspicion that this was not really the promised 'war of liberation' at all, but some kind of monstrous military-diplomatic gimmick, the perfect *mise en scène* for a 'battle' staged as a three-act play: Crossing; ceasefire; American-sponsored peace negotiations. They forecast that the 'battle' would soon be over.

But they were wrong. The sheer weight of evidence soon told against them. Not only had the Egyptian army accomplished the Crossing, it was apparently planning to fight on until the whole of Sinai was restored. Everything seemed to suggest that President Sadat was well on the way to achieving what a Beirut newspaper hailed as 'a June war in reverse'.

This time the Arabs *had* struck first, in complete contrast to 1967. Then it had been the Arabs who had cried havoc, the Israelis who had wrought it. With his *ostensible* closure of the Straits of Tiran, President Nasser had handed the Israeli generals the *casus belli* they had been waiting for. And no sooner had he done so than Arab armies had begun—or so it had appeared—to converge on Israel amid a terrible clamour of boastful rhetoric. Cairo's 'Voice of the Arabs' and half a dozen other radio stations had vied with one another in forecasting the dire fate that awaited the enemy. President Nasser had said that 'we are burning like hot coals in expectation of the battle'. According to the Syrian Prime Minister, Dr Yusuf Zu'ayyen, Syria had 'turned into a bastion of steel and fire capable of destroying this imperialist monster'. By contrast, the Israelis had hidden their inner tensions beneath an outward calm, the authentic and dignified reaction of a people who, believing themselves in real peril, were bound together in an unspoken but passionate resolve to ward it off.

This time it was the pre-war Israeli boasting that proved itself, in retrospect, to have been hubris, which got the nemesis it deserved. The generals had all said, and the people believed them, that President Sadat would not even dare to attack. Naturally enough, after the calamity of 1967, the Arabs had been as uncertain of themselves as the Israelis had been cocksure. So the decision to fight, after years of indecision, was a breakthrough in itself—regardless of the consequences. It broke the psychological barrier of fear and inferiority. As Sadat himself subsequently put it: 'It was a thousand times more honourable that I die in this battle, that I am defeated after I have fought and inflicted heavy losses on the enemy—better this than to remain alive, in a cringing posture of no war and no peace . . . with the whole world convinced that we are nothing but a lifeless corpse.'[3]

But the Egyptians were not defeated. In fact their successes quickly surpassed all their commanders' expectations. It was only just. Long before the decision was taken, they had been preparing for Operation Badr (as it was called, after the Prophet Muhammad's first victory) with the same thoroughness that the Israelis had lavished on their master-plan for the destruction of Arab air power in 1967. In addition to such characteristically Egyptian virtues as dogged perseverance, the military planners had also exhibited a flair and versatility more generally associated with the Israelis. Apart from strictly battlefield considerations, which were complex enough, they had to take into account factors ranging from the higher diplomatic, such as the state of international *détente*, to the intricately technical: on which particular night of the lunar cycle would there be enough light for the bridging engineers to see by but not too strong a tidal current through the Canal to hamper them in their vital task? Egypt's secret weapon was also its most original, its simplest and least expensive. Perhaps the most formidable feature of what the Israelis jocularly described as the world's best anti-tank ditch was the steepness and irregularity of its banks. In addition, mounds of sand, 30 to 60 feet high, had been piled up on the Israeli side of the waterway. The Egyptians had to open up in these defences sixty holes 20 feet across, and they had to do it before the Israelis had time to mount a counter-attack against the infantry-held bridgehead which the initial boat crossing would establish.

It was not until May 1972, after all sorts of experiments, that a young officer of the engineers came up with the idea of using water under great pressure. Five months later the West German firm of Magirus Deutz Fire Protection Techniques of Ulm, Bavaria, received an order for no fewer than 100 of its powerful turbine-driven machines capable of pumping 1,000 gallons of water a minute. It was left unexplained why the re-equipping of the Egyptian fire brigades—the official reason given—had suddenly acquired such urgency.

Of the planning of Operation Badr the Egyptian Commander in Chief, General Ahmed Ismail, could say without false modesty: 'It was a great and scientific piece of work of the first order. When our documents are all laid out for historical study, this work will certainly earn its full due of appreciation and will enter the scientific history of war as a model of minute precision and genuine research.'

Operation Badr was also superbly executed. It was not, perhaps, in the same class as Israel's June 1967 airstrike—certainly the most devastating of its kind in the history of warfare—when, in 170 minutes, the Mirages and the Mystères had destroyed, on the ground, more than 300 of some 340 serviceable Egyptian aircraft. It was a masterstroke none the less. For a massive land offensive of this kind, as in a strike from the air, surprise is vital. Yet, involving as it did long and elaborate deployment of troops and weapons, it would be much more difficult to achieve. But the Egyptians and the Syrians achieved it with a completeness which their commanders had not dared to expect.

They owed their success quite as much to their care and ingenuity as to the blinkered complacency of the Israeli command. Their deception plan embodied many elements, perhaps the most cunning of which was its exploitation of enemy psychology. In Jerusalem it was all but axiomatic that countries as diverse as Syria and Egypt could never achieve sufficient unity of purpose to attack on two fronts. Although the outline for such cooperation had already been agreed upon, General Saad Shazly, the Egyptian Chief of Staff, was careful to put on a display of pessimism after a meeting of Arab Chiefs of Staff: 'The presence of some political and military problems', he announced, 'is still obstructing joint action.' Another element in the plan was diversion, of which the Schoenau guerrilla hijack appears to have been a part. If so, it succeeded; for Schoenau obsessed the Israelis to the exclusion of almost everything else and, allowing Syria to voice its fears of Israeli retaliation, gave it the excuse it wanted for an ostensibly defensive build-up.

On the diplomatic front, the Americans and others were impressed by the Arabs' seemingly pacific intentions. In *al-Ahram*, a newspaper carefully scrutinized by Israeli intelligence, the military correspondent reported a few days before Saturday, 6 October that the Commander in Chief had opened a list for those officers who wanted to perform the *Umra*, or lesser Meccan pilgrimage. On the military front proper, the final deployment of troops was made under the reassuring cover of the annual autumn manoeuvres. Conveniently, these had been getting larger each year; the Israelis saw nothing particularly sinister in the fact that, this time, they involved formations of division strength. What the Israelis did not guess, however, was that for every brigade that moved up to the front in the morning only a battalion, a third of the men, returned at night—'to give the impression', General Ismail explained, 'that the forces had been on training duty and come back after finishing it'.[4] The Egyptian high command had reckoned that they would be lucky if the Israelis did not tumble to their intentions by Wednesday, 3 October, at the very latest. But even by zero-hour Israeli front-line troops had not been alerted to the imminence of war. To bring the thirty-one strongpoints and twenty rear posts of the Bar Lev line up to operational strength required at least a brigade—some 4,000 men. On 6 October there were 600 of them, most of them middle-aged businessmen, and many on their last tour of duty before retiring from the reserves. 'It seemed incredible to us', wrote Muhammad Heikal, editor of *al-Ahram*, for by well before Saturday there had been 'nobody in Egypt who could escape the impression that something was impending'.[5]

Even more incredible was the actual Crossing itself. President Sadat watched it all unfold, in three breathtaking hours, in Centre Number Ten, a huge complex of meeting halls, operation rooms, communications centres, map rooms and offices which, approached through a series of great steel doors and long descending corridors, lies deep underground on the sandy outskirts of Cairo. It was the Egyptian military headquarters for the war. Here General Ismail had repaired after his last visit to the Syrian front on 2 October; he was not to see daylight again until he went to hear Sadat make his historic address to the People's Assembly, a fortnight later. On the afternoon of Friday, 5 October, in the presence of the President in full-dress uniform, the staff of Centre Number Ten had taken an oath: 'We pledge to God on this Koran that each of us will give his utmost, even to the last breath in his body, to fulfill the mission with which he is entrusted.' After that the 'bunker' was virtually sealed off from the outside world.

It was a magnificent centre from which to conduct a set-piece campaign and it functioned perfectly for the Crossing. General Ismail was almost mystical about it:

You should have seen this room on Y-Day [6 October] . . . you would have felt then that this room symbolized not only this age but the entire history of Egypt. We were all at our seats. The whole sequence of operations we had planned was displayed in front of us. As messages came from the front we could see the operations progressing before our eyes: such-and-such a task has started, such-and-such a task has been fulfilled. . . . From two o'clock the scene in this room was exciting to the limit. The work was carried on with more precision than anybody could have imagined— efficiently and daringly. There were moments when feelings were shaken to the core, but we did not allow ourselves to be swept by emotion. . . . Our nerves had to remain cool and intact. Any confusion at headquarters would unbalance the entire operation.[6]

The 'tasks' so swiftly and successfully completed had begun at 14.05 hours when, in the first assault wave, 8,000 Egyptian commandos slithered down the west bank of the Canal and launched their rubber dinghies across the waterway. At the same moment 2,000 howitzers and heavy mortars concealed among the sand dunes opened up in four tremendous barrages, while, amid a similar artillery barrage 250 miles to the north, Syrian tanks—a full 700 of them—began their relentless, awe-inspiring advance on Israeli positions on the Golan Heights.

To the puzzlement of the Israelis in their concrete bunkers, almost every commando who came scrambling up the east bank with the aid of rope-and-bamboo ladders was carrying unusually shaped equipment. Some had 'tubes' over their shoulders; others had canvas-covered 'suitcases' in their hands or strapped to their backs. The first wave did not try to capture the bunkers themselves—they left that to the one behind. Their task was to knock out the forward armour which was an integral part of the Bar Lev defences. The tubes they carried were launchers of the Soviet-built bazooka, the RPG-7. The suitcases contained a more sophisticated device: the wire-guided 'Sagger' anti-tank missile. Within minutes, this initial bazooka and missile onslaught, combined with the artillery and tank fire from across the Canal, had silenced almost all the armour the Israelis had deployed on the east bank. Then, while the second commando wave began its assault on the Bar Lev bunkers with grenades, smoke, sub-machine guns and savage hand-to-hand combat, the missile troops loaded up their equipment on to the 'golf trolleys' that had been ferried across the Canal, and fanned out into the desert for nine or ten miles. There they dug in, re-assembled their anti-tank missiles, and produced the third, and most sophisticated, of their new infantry weapons: this was the portable Soviet anti-aircraft missile, the SAM-7.

The task of the missile infantry, Shazly explained later, was 'to hold the ground against counter-attack by tanks and aircraft for a period of from twelve to twenty-four hours while we got our tanks and heavy weapons across'. This was the critical phase of the Crossing. It was then that the Israelis had expected, in such an eventuality, to regain the initiative and thwart the laying of bridges. But with the aid of the most up-to-date Soviet bridging equipment, as well as their Magirus pumps, the Egyptians worked at least twice as fast as the Israelis had thought possible. 'In a period of between six and nine hours', said Shazly, 'our engineering corps carved sixty holes, established ten bridges, and set up fifty ferries.' And by dusk it was clear that the missile infantry were holding off the first Israeli counter-attacks by tank and low-flying aircraft. Under cover of darkness the heavy equipment began to roll across the waterway. By midnight on Saturday, after a mere ten hours of war, 500 tanks were assembled on the east bank, as well as a forward missile defence system. To an astonished Sadat and General Ismail it was as if they had been watching a training exercise. According to Heikal, the Egyptians had been prepared for 26,000 casualties in the initial assault.[7] The commandos suffered 180 dead.[8] The dashing former paratroop commander, General Shazly, waxed even more lyrical than his chief: 'The whole operation was a magnificent symphony played by tens of thousands of men.'[9]

Not only on account of its lightning territorial gains, but also the manner in which they were made, it was indeed a June war in reverse. The Arab soldiers were painfully aware that the Israelis—and much of the world besides—held in contempt not merely their ability to fight with modern weapons, but their ability to fight at all. Israeli 'Arabists' such as Ezra Danine dressed their contempt in pseudo-scientific guise. 'Till this day', he expounded shortly before the war, 'the basic elements of what we and other people call patriotism have not developed among the Arabs. With them, the individual, so to speak, has no inclination to sacrifice his life for the general interest . . . they can pile up arms, brag and scream their heads off, as Sadat does several times a month, but it is all so much vain pretence.'[10] To cite the popular view, the Arabs were cowards who ran away at the first opportunity; furthermore—as Israeli photographs of barefoot Egyptian prisoners captured in 1967 purported to show—they took their boots off the better to run. So, even if the Egyptian army had not accomplished the Crossing, that a valiant attempt had been made would still have done much to restore the Arabs' honour in their own and the world's eyes. Egyptians and Syrians fought with a courage that in the terrifying rout of 1967 they had hardly had a chance to display. Their ordinary Israeli counterparts were better witnesses to that than the self-styled 'experts'. 'After we had destroyed a whole regiment of tanks, they continued to attack us, even though we were in a better position than they. I can assure you that I did not see them run away. I saw them rescue their

27

wounded under heavy fire. All the things we had been told about them—it is rubbish.'[11]

Few contemporary conflicts have been so distorted by public relations as the Arab–Israeli one. Here again, one of the lessons of 1967—that, in this respect, the Arabs were their own worst enemies—seemed to have been well learned. By the third day of the October 1973 war, the Beirut newspaper *L'Orient-Le-Jour* was able to exclaim: 'In forty-eight hours how many victories have we won over ourselves! We have only to listen to our own radios and compare their dignified tone with the hateful racism distilled by Radio Israel to measure the distance we have travelled since 1967. Ahmad Said [a notorious commentator on Cairo's 'Voice of the Arabs'] belongs to the other side this time.'[12]

It was largely true. Israel's war bulletins were not only less accurate than those of the Arabs, they were on occasion demonstrably false; their official commentaries on the progress of the fighting were specious and evasive. And this time, it was the Israeli, not an Arab, broadcasting station which succumbed to bellicose hyperbole such as this: 'We shall turn your days into night and show you the stars at high noon. We shall put your faces and noses in the mud. We shall make the enemy leaders pay dearly for this. We shall break your bones.' It was foolish of Israeli propagandists on the second day of the war to speak of Syrian soldiers shooting one another in their flight from the battlefield, and even more so to speak of Damascus under curfew when all its inhabitants were out on streets, balconies and rooftops watching the dogfights over their city. It was premature, to say the least, to liken President Assad to a 'Nero setting alight his country to watch it burn' at a time when, whatever they had thought of him before, the Syrian people were rallying round him as a wartime leader. An Israeli journalist summed up the feelings of his compatriots, a mixture of anger and stupefaction, in a *bon mot* that became famous: 'The Arabs have learned from Israel how to fight, and we have learned from the Arabs how to lie.' If in Cairo and elsewhere doubts lingered that General Shmuel Gonen, commander of the Sinai front, might not be lying when he said that the Egyptians were still struggling vainly for possession of the east bank of the Canal they were soon dispelled by the films of the Crossing that they were seeing on their own television screens.

For the first time, too, they saw Israeli prisoners paraded before the cameras. They saw thirty-seven inmates of a Bar Lev bunker, haggard, dishevelled, hands on heads, surrendering under UN auspices to Egyptian military police; a bemused Lieutenant Colonel Assaf Yacouri being interviewed about the destruction of the tank battalion he commanded. They saw Israeli wounded being treated in Egyptian hospitals. Hebrew-language programmes broadcast conversations with Israeli prisoners, some of whom were prevailed upon to denounce 'the good-for-nothing leaders who sent us to fight an unjust war'. The prisoners' nightly appearances on the television screens were not just weapons of psychological warfare aimed against the enemy; these bedraggled survivors were living proof that the Israelis were not the race of supermen they sometimes fancied themselves to be—and which the Arabs half-believed they were.

Hardly less gratifying were the exhibitions of captured enemy hardware in the squares of Cairo and Damascus. After previous 'rounds' it had been the Israelis who, in grandiose military parades to mark Independence Day, had displayed their vast array of booty. And scarcely had the 'fourth round' begun than the Arabs heard about the Israeli generals quarrelling among themselves. Last time, comrades all, they had lectured an admiring public about their various campaigns, while, in Egypt, Marshal Abdul Hakim Amer had committed suicide and, under popular pressure, many of his generals had been tried, imprisoned or cashiered. This time, however, they were soon exchanging the most violent insults in the local and international press.

Operation Spark

So much for the Egyptian and Syrian combatants. But there was another, pan-Arab dimension to the 'fourth round'. It was not for nothing that, while General Ismail had called the military plan Operation Badr, President Sadat had code-named the higher political strategy Operation Spark. The spark had precisely the electrifying effect on the Arab world he had anticipated. Other Arab countries, to which the Crossing had come as no less a surprise than it had to Israel, hastened to make their contributions to the war effort. For some, such as Iraq, it was a military contribution; for others, such as Libya, it was the dispatch of weapons. But in relation to Egypt and Syria's initial, minutely prepared *blitzkrieg*, the impact that such improvised contributions, however substantial in themselves, could have on the course of the battle was minor. Far more important, for Sadat's purposes, was that other form of warfare which the Arabs were now, more than ever, in a position to wage.

29

In 1967 the deployment of the famous Arab oil weapon had been a fiasco. It is true that within two days of the outbreak of hostilities most oil-producing countries had drastically reduced output and Saudi Arabia, the biggest of them all, had stopped it altogether. But it had been a decision forced upon King Faisal by the Arab ruler he most cordially detested, by a President Nasser who, as the great champion of pan-Arab revolution, had been doing his utmost, via the Yemeni civil war, to undermine him and his profoundly traditionalist, quasi-theocratic rule. On the eve of the war Nasser had proclaimed that he would not coordinate his strategy with such 'reactionary' monarchs because that would 'mean giving our plans to the Jews and Israel'. Furthermore, it was on the strength of a whopping falsehood that Nasser had expected his adversaries to come to his rescue. In the aftermath of the devastating Israeli airstrike, the Egyptian high command had announced that the United States and Britain had joined the fighting on Israel's side, and that their aircraft had bombarded targets in Egypt and Syria. This was not just a face-saving explanation for a defeat that was already certain; it was an attempt to carry the battle from the military to the economic front. In a fury of demagogic incitement, Cairo Radio called on Arabs everywhere to 'destroy US and British interests'. Anger swept the volatile masses; mobs rampaged through the streets. If the governments did not stop the flow of oil, their people might do it violently for them.

Drastic though the stoppage was, it had little effect. The West had plentiful stocks, military defeat was swift and complete, and President Nasser had suffered a shattering blow to his own prestige. If he entertained any hopes of getting the 'oil Arabs' to prolong the economic war long after the shooting war had stopped, he soon abandoned them.

In 1973 the economic war was as coolly and convincingly waged as the shooting one. It should have been more readily foreseen than the Crossing; yet it took the West almost as much by surprise. King Faisal did not have to be pressed into action this time; he was on the best of terms with Sadat. He had been quietly warning the Americans that they could not forever expect to reap the benefits of Saudi friendship (oil at the price and in the amount they desired) without fulfilling the obligations of that friendship—applying a degree of pressure on their Israeli protégé which alone could make a Middle East settlement possible. There were no bloodcurdling threats or ultimatums. It was with the exquisite courtesy of the indigent, desert-born chieftain he once was that Faisal, Croesus of the modern world, began to turn the screw. His warnings fell on resolutely deaf ears. Few took this very serious man any more seriously than they took Sadat. His patience was great. It was only on 17 October, eleven days after the war had begun, that the Arab oil-producers announced a programme of reprisals against the Western backers of Israel, and seemingly moderate ones at that. There was to be an immediate, 5 per cent cutback in output, followed by further such reductions every month until Israel had withdrawn from all the occupied territories and the rights of the Palestinians had been restored.

Nothing like the total cut-off of 1967, yet it was infinitely more serious. There were already worries about an 'energy crisis'; for in six years the demand for Arab oil had grown faster than all expectations, and nothing had been growing faster than America's share of that demand. True, the Arabs pledged that 'friendly' Western countries would continue to receive their normal supplies. However, such distinctions were very hard to apply, and in reality a sword of Damocles had been raised over the entire industrialized West. The message to America was blunt: get your Israeli protégé to come to its senses, or drive first your European allies and then yourselves into economic recession, crisis, and ultimately total collapse.

The very next day President Nixon formally asked Congress for $2·2 billion in emergency funds to finance the massive airlift of arms to Israel that was already underway. For Faisal, believing that he had had Nixon's word about an impending change in American policy, this was the last straw. He finally lost all patience. He called a *jihad*. Without even consulting other oil-producers, he decreed an immediate, 10 per cent cutback in Saudi output and, five days after that, the suspension of all shipments to the United States. Before the October war Israelis had scoffed at the oil weapon, some even suggesting that, if the Arabs did try to use it, the West had only to leave it to them to stop them. As the self-appointed gendarme of the West, Israel had such an over-weening belief in its own omnipotence that some of its leaders could seriously propose 'the seizure of Arab oilfields to prevent their owners from subjecting the entire world to the tyranny of an anti-Israel front'.[13] Some American politicians shared these amazing delusions, or at least professed to. But, apart from the Crossing itself, nothing did more to puncture them than the oil war now being waged at the instigation of America's stoutest friend in the Arab world.

It was more than just the Arabs whom the Spark was meant to

galvanize. The attitude of the superpowers was transformed. The first of them to which Sadat turned, in the ecstasy of his triumph, was the Soviet Union. A mere two hours after his commandos had gone in, he was on the telephone to the Russian ambassador in Cairo and told him, laughing: 'Vinagradov, my boys are riding on the Bar Lev line; we've crossed the Canal. I want you to telephone our friends in Moscow and tell them my sons are on the eastern bank of the Canal.'[14] The ambassador's job had often been a difficult one—especially when it came to arms supplies and what Sadat held to be the Kremlin's unjustifiable reluctance to furnish them in the quantity and quality he needed—but that day there was no happier man in Cairo than Vladimir Vinagradov. 'It was with your weapons that we made the Crossing,' Sadat had told him—and promptly asked for more.[15] This time the Russians were to have no hesitation in meeting the request.

If the Soviets were naturally delighted at the unexpected success of their 'side' in the Middle East, the West had mixed feelings—but these necessarily included a new respect for the Arabs and the man who had so metamorphosed them. Of course, it did not mean that, overnight, the West had become 'even-handed', still less 'pro-Arab'. But the contrast with 1967 was striking.

Of the 'third round' it could be said that never in the history of warfare had the passions of so many people been engaged by a conflict in which they had no part, and engaged with such unanimity on behalf of one combatant against the other. It had been the Arabs' fearful anti-Zionist rhetoric that had done so much to turn the West against them. Genocide, Munich, the Arab Nazis, Nasser-the-new-Hitler—these, the most emotive slogans in the Western political vocabulary, rang round Europe and America in late May and early June 1967. The Arab reputation reached its nadir when Cairo Radio broadcast those allegations of Anglo-American collusion which came to be known as the Big Lie. 'This monstrous story'—as British Prime Minister Harold Wilson called it—so enraged the British public that his government had difficulty in justifying a position of even ostensible neutrality. In America, the Johnson administration hardly disguised its partisanship, with Under-Secretary of State Eugene Rostow jocularly telling his colleagues: 'Come on, fellows, remember we're neutral in thought, word and deed.' It was with intense satisfaction that they watched the destruction of the Soviet-equipped Egyptian and Syrian armies, which Secretary of State Dean Rusk described as 'quite a victory for the West'.

In 1973 it was clear from the outset that, although the West might deplore Sadat's methods, it could hardly condemn his aims. He was acting within the framework of international legality. He was seeking to achieve by military means what he had failed to achieve by diplomacy—the recovery of the occupied Arab territories. That was consistent with Security Council Resolution 242 of November 1967. For the world community, including the United States, 242 was holy writ. The Europeans were quicker to grasp the legitimacy of Sadat's purpose than the Americans. Geographical proximity, closer historical ties, a more sophisticated public opinion, a sobering awareness of just how dependent they were on Arab oil, all contributed to that. In the past six years there had been a change in European attitudes, a dawning perception in many quarters that Israel, intransigent and expansionist, was the principal obstacle to a Middle East peace. The Crossing suddenly illumined the change. It was like an earthquake. Sadat had wrought a fundamental shift, in the Arabs' favour, of the Middle East balance of power.

But if the Europeans could find moral as well as expedient reasons for adjusting to this new reality, the Americans found it much more difficult. For they had remained obdurately, unswervingly devoted to Israel, which enjoyed a unique place in the affections of the general public and exerted a unique influence on the ruling institutions. It was the object of a bounty—in the shape of arms and economic aid—which no other nation could command. It had a very special relationship with American intelligence agencies. It was hailed as a 'bastion of democracy' in an area that lacked such a thing, an outpost of Western civilization in the struggle against communism. After 1967, attaining the apogee of its strength and self-esteem, Israel barely had to raise its voice in protest against any timid call for 'even-handedness'—as official acknowledgements that there was, after all, an Arab side to the Middle East story were euphemistically known—and the offender fell silent.

When the October war broke out, a dutiful host of American senators, mobilized by the Zionist lobby, chorused their denunciations of Arab 'aggressions'. Recovering from his shock, Secretary of State Henry Kissinger immediately adopted what, on the face of it, seemed an extravagantly pro-Israeli posture even by American standards. In reality, however, his first concern was not to stop the Arab 'aggressors', but to rescue them from what he imagined would be the consequence of their own folly. 'What did you do it for?' he asked the Egyptian Foreign Minister Muhammad Zayyat, then in

New York, 'Israel will mobilize its forces in a couple of days and launch a devastating attack.'[16] Unlike his predecessor in 1967 he did not believe that yet another Israeli military success would be 'quite a victory for the West'. In the short term, there was the danger that the Russians might intervene on the Arabs' side, obliging the Americans to do the same for Israel. In the longer term, yet another Arab rout would make the prospects for a Middle East settlement—and his hoped-for role in achieving it—more remote than ever. For his own purposes, Dr Kissinger well understood the need to forestall Egyptian defeat, but even if defeat had been staring the Egyptians in the face, his means of preventing it would have been worse than defeat itself. After behind-the-scenes representations, the US submitted to the Security Council a draft resolution whereby 'military operations must be halted and the parties involved return to the positions they had occupied before the fighting broke out'.

But defeat was *not* staring the Egyptians in the face. It was simply grotesque. Did the Americans really think, after the Crossing, that the Egyptians were going to re-cross the Canal in the opposite direction, reinstalling Israeli troops in the Bar Lev line? Were Sadat's 'boys' fighting and dying in order to restore Sinai to the enemy? Reports of the American resolution were dwarfed, in the Cairo press of 9 October, by banner headlines announcing the liberation of Kantara East—the second town in Sinai—and the establishment of Egyptian control over a strip of territory running the whole length of the Canal. The night before, the Egyptians had seen their soldiers on television, kissing the sand of Sinai and raising the Egyptian flag where, symbol of their own impotence, the Star of David had flown before. An entire people was fired with patriotic ardour. Men of all ages were clamouring to enlist in the 'people's militia'. Women overwhelmed the Red Crescent with offers of help. There were long queues to donate blood. In such circumstances a ceasefire—any ceasefire—was unthinkable. It was not only the people who thought so, but their leadership too. A well-informed editor, Ihsan Abdul Koddous, assured his readers of that. He reported that the government had

made calculations for all that would be required in a war aimed at the liberation of all occupied land. We took into account the need to carry on for days, weeks, months and years. This means the fighting will continue until a situation is reached in which fighting is no longer necessary. This means we reject any dis-

34

cussion of a ceasefire before the reasons for opening fire are no longer there. . . . I am not expressing my own opinion, or voicing a patriotic cry, but I know that this is the decision that has been taken.[17]

If defying the ceasefire call meant defying the most powerful nation on earth, then so be it. Not to defy it would have been to mock those deep instincts, the need for dignity and self-respect, which had inspired the Crossing in the first place. And, surely, in few nations can such instincts run deeper than in the Arabs, haunted as they are by a sense of their own great past, their great military past. Such patriotism was inextricably intertwined with the religion, Islam, which the Arabs had founded. The code-name Badr was not accidentally chosen. It was on the tenth of Ramadan in the year A.D. 624 (the third year of the Islamic calendar) when the Prophet Muhammad began preparations for the battle of Badr, the first victory in the campaign which culminated, in 630, with his entry into Mecca—and, within a hundred years of his death, brought Arab warriors to the gates of China in the East and, via North Africa and Spain, to France and the heart of Christendom in the West.

Nasser leads the Arabs to defeat and despair

In the wake of the great conquests there arose a brilliant new civilization that encompassed the whole of *Dar al-Islam*, the House of Islam. Many converted peoples shared in its glories, but for the first few centuries it was the original Arab conquerors who, as its ruling class, bound a vast empire together; the Omayyads took Damascus for their capital, the Abbasids Baghdad. In time, however, the unifying ascendancy of the Arabs crumbled beneath a combination of internal convulsions and external challenges. As decadence set in, the Caliphs began to rely on a soldiery levied among robust, non-Arab peoples within the empire, or mercenaries from outside it. Eventually the non-Arabs seized control for themselves. Meanwhile, weakened from within, the heartlands of Arabia fell prey to foreign invasion. The Crusaders established themselves for two centuries in Palestine and the Levant. Baghdad was sacked by Mongol hordes in 1258. Thereafter the Arabs came under many alien, albeit Moslem, rulers, the last and longest-lasting of whom were the Ottoman Turks. During the four hundred years that Constantinople held sway, the decline of the Moslem world, and the

Arabs as a part of it, accelerated disastrously in relation to a European Christendom which was forging triumphantly ahead in all fields of human endeavour. It was in response to this European peril, and the consequent invasion or outright annexation of parts of *Dar al-Islam*, that Arab thinkers, prominent among them the Egyptian Muhammad Abduh, began to reflect on the reasons why a once great nation had fallen so low. At first it was as Moslems that they reacted. But by the turn of the century, in that movement known as the Arab Awakening, they tended more and more to look upon themselves as Arabs. They were inspired both by the new European creed of secular nationalism and by a growing distaste for an Ottoman rule to which they attributed the deplorable backwardness of its subject peoples.

It is from this period of intellectual ferment that the Arabs date their modern history. The ideals to which the Awakening gave birth have informed their actions ever since. The central idea was that of nationhood: there *was* an Arab nation; however diverse its component parts might be, they had certain basic aspirations in common. The closer each worked with the other, the stronger all would be. The Arabs would achieve their renaissance through a fusing of their own cultural heritage with all those forms of progress in which Europe had left them so far behind.

The Arabs' opportunity came with the cataclysm of the First World War, when, under the banner of the Hashemite dynasty, they rose in alliance with Britain against the Ottomans. The Sick Man of Europe, kept artificially alive by imperialist powers jealous of each other's ambitions, finally expired. For the first time since the rise of Islam, the Arabs were masters of their own destiny. They were very backward, very poor and very weak — but they were free. Or so it seemed.

Egypt took no part in the Arab Revolt. In all but name it had long since shaken off Ottoman rule; moreover, since the early nineteenth century it had made such strides in the process of turning itself into a modern state that it was not only far more advanced than the rest of the Arab world, it posed a military threat to the Ottoman Empire itself. All this, however, had been achieved under foreign rule. At the apex was the dynasty founded in 1805 by Muhammad Ali, an Albanian officer of political and military genius, who owed no more than a nominal allegiance to the Sultan. He imported Europeans to furnish the energy, the expertise and the money which he needed for the furtherance of his very personal ambitions. In time, however, largely owing to the extravagance of his successors, the European presence turned into European economic domination and then political control. Britain acquired a 44 per cent share in the Suez Canal from Khedive Ismail, grandson of Muhammad Ali, who was in dire financial straits, and in 1882 it invaded and occupied Egypt. The country was never formally incorporated into the British Empire, remaining, officially, an autonomous vice-royalty under the suzerainty of the Ottoman Sultan. But British authority, exercised through a consul-general from behind the Khedival throne and a screen of Egyptian ministers, was absolute in most things that mattered. The British brought camp-followers in their wake. There was a great increase in the number of foreigners—French, Italians, Greeks, Levantines, Jews—who enjoyed special legal privileges conferred upon them by a system of Capitulations and dominated the economic life of the country alongside a small native élite of land-owners and entrepreneurs.

Although by the end of the First World War Egypt was little affected by the idea of pan-Arabism, there was developing a natural bond of sympathy between it and those parts of the Arab world where the idea had put down strongest roots. For at a time when Egypt was agitating, more and more forcefully, for its own independence, the former provinces of the Ottoman Empire were losing the independence which they had just won, and losing it, moreover, to the very power—plus France—which had promised to help them achieve it.

Thanks to British betrayal, the heady expectations aroused by liberation from the Turks were swiftly and brutally dissipated. In their modern history, the Arabs have known little but humiliation and defeat. But two catastrophes stand out. The first of them was the Sykes-Picot agreement of 1916. In return for the Arabs' contribution to the allied war effort, Britain had undertaken to 'recognize and support' their independence in the Arabian Peninsula, Palestine, Transjordan, Syria and Iraq. But under this secret deal—to which Czarist Russia had originally been a party—Britain and France agreed to divide up the former Ottoman provinces among themselves. It was a new form of colonialism which—under the guise of a 'sacred trust of civilization'—Britain and France imposed on the Arab world. Ironically, the most backward parts of it—what is now Saudi Arabia and Yemen—were to be permitted independent statehood, while the more advanced and mature were to come under 'direct or indirect' foreign rule. Furthermore, the Arabs not only found themselves under foreign rule, they found themselves divided, and subdivided, more arbitrarily than they had been under the Turks. The eastern part of the Arab world known as the Fertile Crescent, formerly treated as a single unit, was now broken down into no less than ten separate entities; the Arab world as a whole consisted of twenty-five of them. And a year after Sykes–Picot came the Balfour Declaration, whereby Britain pledged itself to work for 'the establishment in Palestine of a national home for the Jewish people'. The Declaration insisted that 'nothing shall be done which may prejudice the civil and religious rights of the existing non-Jewish communities of Palestine', but the Arabs rightly sensed from the outset that the Zionists' ultimate aim was to create a Jewish State in a land without Arabs.

The new European order was not imposed without violent resistance. Throughout the 1920s, 1930s and 1940s, as Egypt kept up its own separate struggle, Arabs elsewhere devoted much of their energies to securing that genuine independence which their wartime allies had perfidiously denied them. They assumed that, once this had been achieved, the rest would automatically follow, that all the aspirations fostered by the Arab Awakening — unity and everything that could be subsumed under the general heading of 'progress' — would be fulfilled. For it was the foreign ruler who — while conferring certain benefits of a chiefly technical and administrative nature — thwarted, or seemed to thwart, these aspirations. Within a few years of the end of the Second World War most Arab countries had achieved at least a formal independence and — despite the continued existence of foreign military bases and other forms of neo-colonial influence — they felt themselves in large measure masters of their own destiny. But no sooner was this so than they were shaken by that second catastrophe, the rise of the State of Israel, which they had always feared but never quite believed could actually come to pass. The loss of Palestine in the Arab-Israeli war of 1948 and the uprooting of its inhabitants was an event so distressing that they called it quite simply that, al-Nakba, the Catastrophe. It was the yardstick of their own weakness and debilitation — of the hollowness of their independence in a world where might was right. From then on nothing would so obsess them as the need to redress the wrong done in Palestine. It was not just a matter of restoring the refugees to what was rightfully theirs, it was a matter of dignity. Without the recovery of Palestine, how could there be such a thing as a self-respecting Arab nation?

38

While for Syrians, Jordanians or Iraqis the emotional effect of the Catastrophe was like losing an integral part of themselves, Egyptians, perhaps, were less affected by it. In its geographical location, its economic and political weight, in its language, religion and, in good measure, its culture, Egypt might seem to have been always the natural centre of the Arab world. But Egyptians have also their special sense of separate identity, their own Nile-based unity and cohesion that reaches back beyond the Arab conquest and the conversion to Islam, into the remote antiquity of the Pharaohs. They were late-comers to the ideas of pan-Arabism, and what became to them its logical corollary: that their country should play the leading role in promoting it. But the idea had none the less been gaining ground in the years before the Second World War. Among those for whom it had a particular fascination was a young schoolboy named Gamal Abdul Nasser. 'I remember', he confided later, 'that the first notions of Arab consciousness began to creep into my mind when I was still a secondary school student. I used to come out with my fellow students on a general strike every year on 2 November as a protest against the Balfour Declaration. . . .'[18]

At the time Nasser scarcely knew why he felt this way. But later, in the fire of direct experience, he was to forge those convictions which he elaborates in *The Philosophy of the Revolution*. As a captain in the Sixth Battalion of Infantry, Nasser was wounded in the first Arab-Israeli war at a place called Fallouga. So it was that an episode in the Egyptian campaign subsequently became famous less for its own intrinsic significance than for the brave and distinguished role he had played in it. Throughout the war, and later as a lecturer at staff college, he brooded over the reasons for the collapse of the Arab armies: imperialist plots; the complicity of Arab regimes; corruption; backwardness; but, above all, division. The struggle was indivisible. Defending Palestine was defending Egypt.

When I returned home, after the siege and battles in Palestine were over, the picture left in my mind represented a homogenous whole . . . the same region, the same circumstances, the same factors, even the same forces dominating and directing it. It was clear that Imperialism was the most striking of these forces. . . . Gone are the days when the barbed wire of frontiers marked the confines of states, dividing and isolating them. . . . Is it possible for us to overlook that, around us, lies an Arab Circle, and that this Circle is as much a part of us as we are a part of it, that our history has been merged with it and that its interests are linked with ours? These are actual facts and not mere words.[19]

All that was needed, Nasser mused, was the hero who could perform the great unifying mission. 'I do not know why I always imagine that in this region in which we live there is a role wandering aimlessly about in search of an actor to play it. And I do not know why this role, tired of roaming about in this vast region, should at last settle down, exhausted and weary, on our frontiers beckoning us to move to dress up for it as nobody else can do.'

Nasser and his generation attributed defeat in Palestine to the rottenness of the existing Arab order, to the monarchies, the regimes of the *beys* and *pashas*, the great landowners and feudalists, selfish, frivolous, reactionary, subservient to the Western creators of Israel. 'We were fighting in Palestine but all our thoughts were concentrated on Egypt.' It was in Palestine that 'Kamal-Eddin Hussein once came and sat by my side and, with a wistful look and an absent air, said to me: "Do you know what were Ahmad Abdul Aziz's last words before he died?" "What did he say?" I enquired. In a deep voice and with a still deeper look, Kamal-Eddin Hussein replied: "He said, 'Listen, Kamal, the supreme struggle is in Egypt. . . .' "[20]

The role would find its actor, the 'Arab Circle' its hero in the hero of Fallouga. On 28 July 1952, as the leader of the Free Officers Organization, Colonel Nasser overthrew King Farouk and the monarchy. He had carried 'the battle' to Egypt. This momentous event had been preceded, it is true, by convulsions in Syria which— like those he had brought to pass—had been precipitated by the original earthquake that was the Catastrophe. But though Syria had been the progenitor of pan-Arabism it was Nasser, with all the weight of Egypt at his disposal, who was destined to become its great champion. Like most of his comrades, Nasser was a man of the people who had spent much of his youth in the village, that world of back-breaking toil for absent masters, of tight-packed squalor where men and animals live side-by-side among mud, flies and dank, insanitary canals, the timeless Egypt of the *fellaheen*, the peasants, who, while conquerors came and went, remained immemorially attached to the soil. For the first time in more than two thousand years Egypt was ruled by its own true sons.

There was a massive exodus of the aliens who had thrived, under the *ancien régime*, in the administration, in business and industry. Nasser assumed dictatorial powers. He outlawed all existing political parties, replacing them with a monolith of his own creation. He suppressed free trade unions and professional associations, manipulated the judiciary, pressed newspapers into the service of his revolution. But he did all this with broad popular assent because, if he was taking democratic liberties away, he was doing it, or so it appeared, to promote the highest good for the highest number of people. He declared war on poverty, backwardness and disease. He undertook the land reforms which the *pashas*, through their control of the old parliament, had strenuously resisted. He began a massive programme of state-sponsored industrialization. On the international front he sought to turn formal independence into a real independence, to show the world what some of the world was not yet ready to accept—that Egypt had a sovereign will of its own. He fought against those new forms of hegemony which the old European colonial powers, and the new American superpower, tried to impose on the Arab world. After a brief guerrilla campaign, he negotiated the withdrawal of British troops from their Canal Zone base. He became a pillar of non-alignment; he resisted all attempts to bring Egypt into an anti-Soviet alliance. He would not be dictated to. When the Americans refused to sell him arms without strings attached he turned to the Russians (via Czechoslovakia) instead, and turned to them again when US finance promised for the construction of the Aswan High Dam was withdrawn. And as a supreme act of defiance, he nationalized the Suez Canal.

The British and French governments reacted to this intolerable affront by encouraging Israel to launch an all-out *blitzkrieg* into Sinai. Then, with the ostensible purpose of separating the combatants, they invaded the Canal Zone themselves. But far from bringing the upstart down, as they had hoped, they made him overnight into an all-Arab, as well as just an Egyptian, champion. With the help of President Eisenhower, who forced the evacuation of the chastened British, French and Israelis, Nasser transformed what, in the circumstances, was not dishonourable defeat into overwhelming political victory. He became the idol of the Arab masses everywhere.

In 1958, Syria linked its destiny to Egypt's in the United Arab Republic. It was the first giant stride towards that Arab unity, which, for this post-colonial generation, had become the primary goal of all activity, endowed with a transcendent, almost mystical significance. The tumultuous enthusiasm which swept through Syria at the advent of the union, the delirious throngs who greeted Nasser on his first pilgrimage to Damascus, seemed to indicate that he was about to carry all before him, that in due course other peoples of the region would rise up against their 'reactionary' rulers and join the irresistible tide of Egyptian-led revolution. The uprising against President Chamoun of Lebanon, bastion of Eastern Christendom, followed by General Kassem's overthrow of the Hashemite dynasty in Iraq, mainstay of British influence in the Arab world, brought these expectations to fever pitch.

But the tide running in Nasser's favour had reached its high-water mark. The ramparts of the threatened order, plugged by Western aid, stemmed the flood. In Jordan, the other Hashemite throne, occupied by the young King Hussein, tottered, but did not fall. The British sent troops to prop it up. Chamoun left office, but a landing was made by American Marines to ensure that 'Christian Lebanon' retained its special status essentially intact. In Iraq, General Kassem quickly turned out to be a more resolute adversary of Nasser than the monarchy and its elder statesman, Nuri Said. Then, in 1961, those self-same fickle Syrians who had so ardently entered Egypt's unionist embrace three years before threw it off in a secessionist *coup d'état*. It was a grievous setback for which, Nasser decided, local 'reactionaries' had been as responsible as the Western 'imperialists'. From now on his revolution would have a more radical character. He was still the champion of pan-Arabism, but the prerequisite for unity was a 'socialist transformation' that would pre-empt all 'reactionary' schemes to sabotage it.

Nasser did not have to wait long to regain the initiative in the Arab world. In 1962, intervening in the civil war in Yemen that followed the overthrow of the medieval despotism of the Imams, he dispatched a large part of his army to help the Republicans against the Saudi-assisted Royalists. Yemen became his Vietnam. His army could never subdue the fierce tribesmen in their mountain fastnesses, and the war was a heavy drain on resources that Egypt could ill afford to divert from the 'battle' for development at home. In any case, it was already apparent that, even without such foreign adventures, the July Revolution was not coming up to expectations. The socio-economic plagues of Egypt were daunting enough, and, however impressive an economic growth rate the regime achieved, it was to a great extent automatically cancelled out by the explosive growth in population.

But there were also grave defects within the regime itself. There were those abuses—arbitrary decision-making, sycophancy, the lack of accountability—which flowed inevitably from the concentration of so much power in one man's hands. There was the reliance on a narrow group of army officers, almost all drawn from Nasser's own generation, to fill high positions for which they were not qualified. There were the improvisations and false starts engendered by the absence of a real ideology. Without democracy and public debate such defects were of course masked. And if, for some reason, they were exposed, the people still had Nasser, above and apart from the system he controlled, a kind of demi-god in whose wonder-working powers they were invited to put their faith, which he would surely justify in the fullness of time.

For all the undoubted blows it struck for the people, Nasserism, in its decline, was becoming the victory of myth over reality, of propaganda over performance. In an Arab world where words are so often taken for deeds, it was an easy victory to perpetuate — until June 1967. Nasser called the 'third round' al-Naksa, the Setback, but in reality it was another Nakba, another Catastrophe, and in a sense it was a worse one than before. Far from liberating Palestine, the Arab revolutionary order had now lost more of it, and this time the Western powers, which had indeed been largely responsible for the earlier defeat, could hardly be blamed. If the struggle for Palestine was to have been the yardstick of the success of the revolutionary regimes in modernizing and transforming their societies, it was now in reality the yardstick of their failure.

On 9 June 1967, in a voice choking with emotion, Nasser announced that he was resigning. But hardly had he uttered the word than the multitudes poured into the street to demand its retraction. Nasser's grief was theirs too. If he was responsible, so were they. It was an extraordinary tribute to the place he had won in the hearts of his people. But at the same time it was an extraordinary, if psychologically understandable, exhibition of the lengths to which a people can go in deceiving itself. Reality was so painful that, in their shock and bewilderment, the Egyptians took refuge in the collective illusion that by preserving Nasser, symbol of their dignity, they had somehow salvaged victory from the wreckage of defeat.

President Nasser did survive for another three years. He struggled valiantly, but vainly, against the two enemies which, in the wake of the defeat, strengthened one another. There was the external one: an Israel which now indulged in its traditional retaliatory raids against its neighbours as a kind of sport, as an opportunity to exhibit, before an admiring world, its seemingly inexhaustible military virtuosity. There was the old familiar internal one — poverty, backwardness and disease—which, with yet more resources now diverted from combating it, regained all the ground, and more, that it had lost in the early, triumphant years of the Revolution. Nasser remained the most powerful man in the Arab world; the sheer weight of Egypt, plus his own immense, if declining, prestige ensured that. But his old adversaries, the 'reactionaries', were gaining in strength and self-confidence. They—and not just they—frustrated him at every turn.

Nasser was sick in body and almost broken in spirit when, in September 1970, civil war broke out in Jordan. Though it had begun in a small way before the Arab-Israeli war of 1967, and to some extent precipitated it, Yasser Arafat's Palestinian resistance movement had undergone a dramatic expansion after it. These refugees-turned-guerrillas were proving that the fires of defiance still flickered in a nation seemingly abased. Unable to establish themselves inside Israel or the occupied territories proper, they had found in Jordan, with its large Palestinian population, their most convenient and hospitable base of operations. In 'Black September' 1970 King Hussein unleashed his impatient bedouin troops against this anarchic state-within-his-state. In ten days of fratricidal strife he broke the back of guerrilla power in Jordan. With the half-hearted exception of Syria, the Arabs, fearful of American or Israeli intervention, had abandoned them to their fate.

For Arafat it was the ultimate betrayal by the Arabs of their most sacred cause. It was the spearhead of what he called 'an Arab plot'.[21] Had President Nasser been a party to it? The Palestinians suspected as much. For King Hussein had timed his offensive well. It came two months after Nasser, on 23 July 1970, the eighteenth anniversary of his Revolution, had stunned the Arabs by accepting the peace plan put forward by the American Secretary of State William Rogers.

There had always been a certain ambivalence in the Egyptian position. On the one hand, through its endorsement of UN Security Council Resolution 242, it had implicitly accepted the idea of a peaceful settlement. On the other hand, it had subscribed to the three 'no's' of the 1967 Arab summit conference in Khartoum—no peace, no recognition and no negotiation—and, during 1969, it had formally acknowledged the 'failure' of the search for peace. The acknowledgement came in deference not to the Palestinian resistance movement—wedded to all-out armed struggle as it emerged as a powerful new force on the Arab stage—but to Nasser's old adversary, King Faisal of Saudi Arabia. For one of the ironies of the times was that this arch-conservative among Arab rulers was also their arch-hawk. America's greatest friend was also, when it came to Israel, the greatest opponent of its peace-seeking diplomacy. So, at least, Faisal made out. He would, he said, throw his political and financial weight behind President Nasser only if the Egyptian leader, repudiating peaceful settlements once and for all, committed himself to the military alternative. Nasser was never able to do this with a conviction that satisfied the king— or his incongruous bedfellow, President Boumediène of Algeria, socialist revolutionary, who, like Faisal, nursed an old resentment of domineering Egyptian ways. Faisal and Boumediène both thought Nasser was bluffing, that what he really wanted was a build-up of Arab military strength without an irreversible commitment to using it. Since March 1969 Egypt had been waging its 'war of attrition' across the Canal. This had been proving at least as costly, in human lives, as the 1967 Setback itself but, Faisal being the hard, implacable man that he was, Egypt had to go on fighting it more or less alone, without that stepped-up Arab assistance, that 'mobilization' of all Arab resources, for which Nasser had pleaded.

The acceptance of the Rogers peace plan seemed to run counter to the logic of events; it came at a time when deepening Soviet involvement on the Egyptian side was bringing the 'war of attrition' to new heights of ferocity and when the Palestinian guerrillas really did seem to be achieving the purpose they had set themselves, of rallying the Arab masses behind them in a 'popular liberation war' that would sweep away any ruler who dared to stand in its way. The Arab world seemed to be ripe for great upheavals, and Nasser still the man to harness and direct the forces they would unleash. But then came this bombshell, this acceptance of a peace plan framed by the very superpower whose policies the Egyptians, indeed almost the entire Arab world, were daily assailing as irredeemably prejudiced in Israel's favour.

It was a blatant volte-face, a fundamental change of course. Egypt was turning in upon itself; that pan-Arabism which had been Nasser's great asset was becoming his intolerable liability. It was the beginning of a go-it-alone Egyptian peace-seeking diplomacy, of a process of stage-by-stage solutions to the Middle East problem which, however they might be dressed up, would lead in the end to a separate peace between Israel and the great power of the Arab world. It would leave everybody else in the lurch. That, at least, was how almost everybody else saw it. There had been harbingers enough. True, in public, a reassuring refrain was ever on Nasser's lips: Jordan before Egypt, the Golan before the Sinai. He would never, he swore, be the Pétain of the Arabs.[22] But he protested a little too much, and his protests were accompanied by intimations that, had he so desired, he could have settled Egypt's own problems, via the Americans, long ago.

His speech accepting Rogers' plan contained a new stress on Egyptian, as distinct from Arab, patriotism. It was a theme which, stung by Arab reproaches, the state-controlled newspapers took up in derision of 'those who talk but don't fight. Those who raise their voices, but never their weapons. Those who speak about the front, but keep away from it. All those and others, let us leave them alone to talk and whirl and say what they like. Words don't bring down Phantom jets. Statements don't sap the enemy strength. Press conferences don't liberate enemy territory.'[23] Muhammad Heikal, editor of *al-Ahram* and Nasser's closest confidant, scathingly invited those Arab countries—Iraq, Syria and Algeria—which opposed the Israeli-Egyptian ceasefire to break the ceasefire on other fronts.[24] He inveighed against the 'ignorance and stupidity' of those Arabs who refused to see that it was Egypt which, through its Soviet-assisted 'war of attrition', had *obliged* America to take the diplomatic initiative, Egypt which had *obliged* Israel, for the first time since 1967, to admit the principle of withdrawal from all the occupied territories.[25]

Unlike the Arab states, the Palestinians *were* fighting in their resolute if none-too-effective way, and their condemnations of the American offer and Egyptian acceptance rang more sincerely than those of others. For it was they who would in the end be the principal victims of the coming 'sell-out'. To suggest otherwise, they said, was mere casuistry. They wanted nothing less than 'complete liberation' and they believed that Egypt was trying to set the more pacific instincts of the Palestinians under occupation against the more militant ones of those outside it. It was trying to bribe them with the prospect of half-a-loaf; half-Palestine (or, to be more precise, 23 per cent of it), a mini-state that would be established in the West Bank and Gaza side by side with the Zionist usurper. No one condemned Nasser more fiercely than those Palestinians such as George Habash, leader of the left-wing Popular Front for the Liberation of Palestine, who had once been his devoutest supporters. In its heart, said the Popular Front newspaper, *al-Hadaf*, the Egyptian regime knew that it had taken 'a posture of surrender which it can only hold to with massacres and bloody repression'.

And so it proved—even though it was not the Egyptian regime which carried out the massacres. This was the opportunity that King Hussein of Jordan had been patiently waiting for. Since Nasser had accepted the Rogers peace plan, Hussein would surely be rendering them both a service by cutting its most dangerous opponents down to size. To be sure, Nasser did not want a blood-bath. He seems to have made that clear when Hussein visited him in Egypt on the eve of Black September.[26] But the two leaders also agreed on the need for 'complete coordination' of their peace-seeking strategy. Was not that the green light Hussein needed?

Palestinian suspicions were indeed well-founded. Would Nasser really have gone as far as a separate Israeli-Egyptian peace? Probably not. But that was soon to be an academic question anyway. For, if the emergency summit conference which Nasser convened in Cairo succeeded in putting an end to the massacre, it killed the host. Perhaps it was fitting that Nasser should have died when he did, for Black September spelled the collapse of all that he, the great Arab champion, stood for. Hussein's bedouins were massacring not just Arabs, but Palestinians. They were destroying the very cause which, in the trenches of Fallouga, Nasser had identified as the Arab cause *par excellence*. And inside the conference chamber Colonel Muammar Gadafi of Libya, fiery reminder of Nasser's own younger, uncynical self, was threatening to shoot Hussein, survivor from the pre-revolutionary order now perpetrating a monstrous *lèse-Arabisme* which Nasser himself had helped to encourage. There was no escaping the misery of it all and when, in the midst of a particularly acrimonious exchange, King Faisal suggested that 'perhaps we are all mad', it is small wonder that Nasser seconded him: 'Sometimes, when you see what is going on in the Arab world, Your Majesty, I think this may be so. I suggest that we appoint a doctor to examine us regularly and find out which ones are crazy.'[27]

Racked with pain and fatigue, Nasser kept himself going through the conference and, when it was over, through the succession of ceremonial farewells. But no sooner had he seen off the Sheikh of Kuwait, the last of his guests, than he collapsed and died. It fell to Vice President Anwar Sadat, who had first announced the July Revolution to the world, to announce that his master was no more. It fell to him also to 'complete the path' which Nasser had charted. But if 'the giant' had proved so unequal to the task, what hope could there be for the ordinary mortal emerging from his shadow?

Sadat promises victory and peace

It took the newly installed President Sadat three more demoralizing years to produce his answer: three more years of 'no war, no peace', and his own reduction to the status of Egypt's 'donkey' and the world's officially licensed buffoon. But long before he reached the People's Assembly that afternoon of 16 October 1973, long before he mounted the podium, stood there, rapt, beaming, arms uplifted in acknowledgement of the thunderous applause, embraced the Holy Koran and commenced the greatest speech of his career – long before that he knew that the Crossing had furnished an answer which no one could gainsay. And no one did, even though he had never been so conciliatory – more conciliatory, by far, than his late predecessor, whose speech, delivered from this self-same spot a little over three years before, had precipitated the crisis of Black September. Moreover, at a time when the entire Arab world was not only venting its fury against the United States but, with the oil embargo, was actually translating it into drastic punitive action – at this time it was still the United States to which President Sadat directed the main burden of his conciliatory appeal. He was ready, he told President Nixon, to accept a ceasefire 'on the basis of an immediate Israeli withdrawal under international supervision' from all occupied Arab territories. Once this had been achieved Egypt was ready to attend an international conference under the auspices of the UN, and he himself would 'try to persuade [his] comrades-in-arms, the Arab leaders and representatives of the Palestinian people, to accept such a conference in order to establish, together with the world community, a peace founded on respect for the legitimate rights of all the countries in this region....'[28]

It was the immense prestige conferred by the Crossing that enabled Sadat to make the military breakthrough the foundation for another, altogether more important one – the political, diplomatic and psychological breakthrough that was implicit in this clearly enunciated readiness, and the Arabs' acceptance of it, to end the world's most dangerous conflict. This was indeed an historic turning point. Hitherto it had been axiomatic that the Arabs could not rest until they had liberated Palestine in its entirety. This had been an article of pan-Arab faith. Wrong must be redressed, honour restored. For all Arabs, not just Palestinians, Palestine was as much theirs as Oxfordshire is English, Pennsylvania American. They had been driven out of it, in times of weakness and division, by alien invaders who were no more entitled to it than the Crusaders centuries before them; like the Crusaders, the Zionists would eventually be driven out in their turn. Yet here was the leader of the most powerful Arab state granting Israel title to the land it had usurped. Obviously, this kind of peace would require Israeli concessions—territorial and of other kinds—but in the true historical perspective, it would be the Arabs, not the Israelis, who were making the fundamental concessions. They would be consecrating a pure Zionist gain against a pure Arab loss; it would be an act of historic magnanimity.

It was the immense prestige of the Crossing which made it possible—and the manifest determination to fight on, come what may. This time there would be none of those premature, demeaning ceasefires. Sadat would not fall for such enemy tricks and subterfuges. He would put no trust in 'vague and meaningless promises'. Egypt was ready for a long war, ready to 'pay the price in blood and sweat until we have achieved the goals we have set ourselves'. He had 'unlimited faith in Egypt's armed forces, [its] men and weapons'; and he could have no more gallant allies than the Syrians, who had 'fought like heroes' on the Golan Heights. Addressing the Israeli leaders, he declared that if they thought they could strike in depth he had to warn them that the 'long-range Egyptian missiles, the *Zafir* . . . are on their launching ramps ready to strike into the furthermost corners of Israel'. Addressing the Americans, he assured them that, even now, Egypt was ready for their friendship—'your interests are in the Arab world and not in Israel'—but that, if need be, Egypt would fight both Israel and the Americans combined. 'There are American naval and air lifts bearing new tanks, planes, artillery, rockets and electronic devices. We tell the Americans that this will not frighten us, but we and you have to ask ourselves the question: where to and until when?'[29] In that exalted moment, few Egyptians really cared. All they knew was that, the 'immortal leader' finally forgotten, they were ready to follow his successor, the Hero of the Crossing, almost anywhere he led them.

2
In the Shadow of Nasser

Mit Abul Kom

> . . . I saw Zahran in dreams and reverie, and I wished I were like
> him. I hoped my story would grow into a ballad that would live
> in the hearts of posterity.[1]

To be a hero: this, it seems, had been the ambition of Muhammad
Anwar Sadat since earliest childhood. But he had passed his fiftieth
birthday without fulfilling it, and there must have appeared scant
prospect that he ever would. Before the 1952 Free Officers' Revolu-
tion the most he had achieved was some notoriety, but little glory,
as a conspirator and as the impresario behind political assassina-
tions of a kind that he would later condemn as senseless terrorism.
And though, after the Revolution, he enjoyed the official eminence
which mere proximity to Nasser conferred upon him, the extrava-
gance of the public flatteries which he, in return, heaped upon his
master must have been a measure of his secret pain for, in his
opinion, Nasser had usurped the role which destiny had manifestly
intended for himself.

Zahran, his earliest idol, was a simple peasant, a *fellah* of the Nile
Delta, who had been hanged twelve years before Sadat was born.
In the summer of 1906, near the village of Denshawi, a party of
British officers were out shooting pigeons at the invitation of the
local *omdah*. or headman. All of a sudden a wheat silo caught fire,
apparently struck by a bullet. The villagers went berserk; in the
ensuing mêlée a British captain was killed and two of his comrades
wounded. This was an affront to which the occupying authorities

responded with harsh, exemplary justice—though, technically, it was an Egyptian court which condemned four villagers to death and twelve others to flogging and imprisonment. Zahran was the first to go to the scaffold, erected on the very spot where the incident took place. He died with dignity in the sun-drenched fields of Denshawi. He may have earned only a few lines in the British press, but the Egyptians immediately adopted him as a national hero, and his martyrdom is still commemorated today. The infant Anwar learned the story of Zahran from his mother. She would tell it to him night after night. Listening to her, half-waking, half-sleeping, he would allow his imagination to roam: 'I often saw Zahran and lived his heroism in dreams and reverie—I wished I was Zahran.'[2]

Sadat, too, was 'peasant-born'—as, in later life, he never ceased to recall—in the small village of Mit Abul Kom, not far from Denshawi, some 40 miles north of Cairo in the province of Menufiyeh. In 1918, the year of his birth, Mit Abul Kom was not the showplace which, thanks to its famous son, it is today. It resembled some 4,000 other Egyptian villages, islands of sun-baked mud houses in a sea of rich pasture and crop-land. Sadat's family seems to have been prominent in village life; for he was proud to be known as 'the *effendi*'s son'.[3] In his memoirs, however, he relates that, like the great majority of *fellaheen*, his family was poor. His father, a civil servant, earned a monthly salary of £E16—not bad for the time—but on that he had to support a wife and thirteen children. Throughout his schooldays, the young Anwar lived 'below the poverty line'.[4]

He spent his first seven years in Mit Abul Kom—despite the poverty, years of pure contentment. So, at least, he describes them. His mother was Sudanese, which accounted for his dark complexion, and when she and his father moved to the Sudan, Anwar was taken in charge by his grandmother. For her he professed a deep love and respect; she was 'a haven for everyone . . . a woman with a very strong personality and rare wisdom'[5] He remembers her dashing out of the house when the village crier announced that a boatload of treacle had arrived up the nearby canal. 'We buy a big jar of treacle and return home. I trot along behind her—a small dark boy, barefooted and wearing a long Arab dress over a white calico shirt—my eyes fixed on the treasured jar of treacle.'[6] There was no greater delight, for the little grandson, than to tuck into a dish of this treacle mixed with curdled milk. He also remembers gathering carrots straight from the soil, 'not from the greengrocer'; slipping an onion into the oven when the bread was baking; boy's games . . .

leading the cattle into the fields . . . the smoke rolling down the alley that promised a delicious meal at the end of the day . . . the perfect calm and peace in the hearts of all.

For Sadat, to have been peasant-born was clearly to have been endowed with special qualities that his city-born compatriots lacked. He was brought up on the banks of the Nile 'where man first witnessed the dawn of time'. He conjures up a picture of himself in the role of Man witnessing, if not the birth of time, at least the birth of Egypt. That he was, as it were, the father, rather than the child, of his country and people was revealed to him by his own unusual response to what, after all, is a common enough occurrence in a countryside criss-crossed by irrigation canals. He fell into one of them. He nearly drowned. But, upon being fished out, it was not shock which he experienced, or relief at his narrow escape, it was the sublimely presumptuous realization that 'if I had drowned Egypt would have lost Anwar Sadat'.[7]

This was the earliest, spontaneous manifestation of a conviction that, in later life, he was to enlarge upon without false modesty. In the prologue to his memoirs, *In Search of Identity*, he explains that his own life story is 'at the same time the story of Egypt since 1918 — for so destiny has decreed'. The identity that he sought was both 'his own and that of Egypt. They are one and the same thing.'[8]

Sadat's birth and early years did indeed coincide with momentous events. Another stage in Egypt's struggle for independence — sharpened by the grievous socio-economic legacies of the First World War — was getting under way. It was in 1919 that Saad Zaghloul, a former judge, founded the great Egyptian nationalist party, the *Wafd*, which was to spearhead that struggle for a generation. The following year saw a nationwide, anti-British uprising. It was put down, but the popular movement from which it sprang continued to grow and intermittently erupt until, with the 1952 Revolution, Nasser and his Free Officers threw off the last shackles of foreign domination. Naturally enough, in the tumultuous years of Sadat's childhood, the whole country, down to its smallest hamlet, stirred with pride at the exploits of the great Egyptian patriots, past and present. It was from his grandmother that he first learned of such men as Ahmad Orabi, who, in 1882, had attempted a pathetic military resistance to the British occupation, and Mustafa Kamil and Adham Sharqawi, all fore-runners of Zaghloul and the *Wafd*.

Later his horizons broadened. He was catholic in his choice of heroes. Anyone who sought to restore his country's freedom or dignity, by whatever means, could join his pantheon. When, in 1932, Mahatma Gandhi passed through Egypt on his way to London, the Cairo press was full of reports of the struggle for Indian independence. Sadat was so impressed that he felt compelled to emulate the Indian leader even to the point of removing his clothes, covering himself with an apron and withdrawing with a spindle of his own manufacture to the roof of the family house. He stayed up there for a few days until his father induced him to come down, pointing out that the only thing that this 'passive resistance' would achieve was pneumonia.[9] Another lasting hero of Sadat's was Adolf Hitler. When the Führer marched on Berlin 'to wipe out the consequence of Germany's defeat in World War I', Sadat was so thrilled that he urged his friends to do likewise and march on Cairo from Mit Abul Kom. His exhortations went unheeded. He was twelve years old at the time.[10]

But it was his original hero, Zahran, who always remained closest to his heart; like him, Sadat wanted to achieve immortality, though not, he admits, in quite the same way, for he had no desire to be sentenced to death. His dream was to 'lead a revolution to destroy the British and deliver Egypt from their rule'.[11]

When he was barely more than a toddler, Sadat attended the Koranic school in the village. There he learned to read, write and recite the Holy Book. Later, his grandmother sent him to a Christian school in the neighbouring village of Toukh. And she it was who decided that instead of going to Cairo's al-Azhar University and becoming a teacher of religion—the traditional, highest ambition of every villager—he should, like his father, have a modern, secular education.

In 1925, Sadat's father returned from the Sudan. One of the sanctions imposed by the British following the assassination, the year before, of the British commander of the Egyptian army, Sir Lee Stack, had been the withdrawal of the Egyptian army from the Sudan. The seven-year-old Anwar moved from Mit Abul Kom to Cairo, where the family lived in a small house in Kubri al-Qubbah, near the royal palace of al-Qubbah. He used to pass it every day on his way to school. He recalls how, in fear and trepidation, he and his friends used to steal apricots from the royal orchard. In spite of the earlier fantasies of future greatness, nothing apparently was further from his mind during these poaching expeditions than the thought that 'I would grow up to take part . . . in changing the course of history . . . that I myself would one day cross that awesome wall and sit on the very chair on which King Fuad and subsequently King Farouk, had sat.'[12]

From the Islamic Benevolent Society School where Sadat completed his preparatory and the first two years of his primary education, he went to the Sultan Hussein School in Heliopolis. Here he obtained the General Certificate of Primary Education and, in 1930, he and his elder brother Tal'at went on to the Fu'ad I Secondary School. The rule at the time was that if two brothers were at the school only one was supposed to pay fees, but Anwar failed to secure exemption and his father had to provide for both of them by instalment. An entire month's salary went on the first instalment. The second instalment was never paid. For Tal'at took the money, spent it all 'on God knows what', then came back to announce that he did not wish to pursue his studies.

'Perhaps destiny had decreed this, too,' Sadat observed in his memoirs, for his father could not have afforded to keep both brothers at school, and if Tal'at had not thrown his education away, as the younger brother it would probably have been he who would have had to make the sacrifice.[13] Sadat was always a great believer in portents. The move to Cairo, and his registration at school, had furnished one of the earliest ones. 'How old was I?' he wrote. 'I didn't know at the time. Only later did I realize that significant events in my life coincided with events of public, even historic, significance. So, apparently, destiny has decreed.' On registering at school he had learned that he was born on Christmas Day.[14]

Sadat fared none too well at school. It was only with difficulty that he finally obtained his coveted General Certificate of Education in 1936, at the age of eighteen. It was another of the 'salient events' of his life which 'coincided with historic events'. He was not yet, he concedes, politically mature. Of course, he shared the patriotic emotions of all Egyptians: he took part in demonstrations, chanted slogans, burned trams and called for the removal of ministers and for the restoration of the 1923 Constitution, which granted Egypt a substantial measure of formal independence. But he 'did not even know what that Constitution really was'.[15] High on the list of men he admired at the time was Mustafa Nahas Pasha, who had succeeded Saad Zaghloul at the head of the *Wafd*. Every evening Sadat used to go to al-Khalifa al-Mamun Street to watch Nahas going from his home to the National Assembly and back. He was 'a symbol of the struggle of the entire Egyptian people against the British'.[16] The 'historic event', this time, was the treaty which

Nahas concluded with the British. The treaty, a landmark in Egypt's emancipation from foreign control, provided for the withdrawal of all British forces to the Canal Zone. It also had social and political consequences of which the most profound — though that was quite unforeseen at the time — was the expansion of the Egyptian army and the recruitment of a new kind of officer for the purpose. The reduction — in certain cases the total remission — of fees for attending the Military Academy enabled young men from lower-class backgrounds, provided they had graduated from secondary school, to enter an institution which had hitherto been more or less the exclusive preserve of a pampered élite.

Inspired by a mixture of motives — the desire for material security and social prestige as well as patriotic fervour — hundreds of youths flocked to enrol at the Academy. Among them was Anwar Sadat. It was 'the highest hope [he] had'. His reasons, he would have us believe, were entirely patriotic. It was one of the endless ironies of his life, he recounts, that 'the British helped me to join the Military Academy when the reasons why I wanted to join in the first place was to kick them out of Egypt'.[17]

At the Academy, Sadat sought to deepen his knowledge of Egyptian history. He was still an admirer of Mustafa Kamil, the fiery, turn-of-the-century orator, but he felt that he had been wrong not to advocate force against the British. Sadat's questions went further, however. Were the British the only culprits? What about the royal family, a family of non-Egyptians? What about Khedive Tawfiq, great-grandson of Muhammad Ali, who had allowed the British army to parade in Abidin Square, Cairo, thereby legitimizing the British occupation of 1882? Was not the regime responsible for all that had happened and was continuing to happen? Had not the court which sentenced Zahran at Denshawi been composed entirely of Egyptians — judge, prosecution and defence lawyers alike?

These questions still troubled him when he passed out from the Academy in 1938. However, 'with that graduation, the energy that had been pent up for years in my subconscience was released . . . my feeling of inner strength was still there, naturally, but, as an officer in the armed forces, I now felt possessed of material strength as well'. Of all his heroes, he records, Zahran was still closest to his heart. 'I believed that nothing but physical force could deliver Egypt alike from the British and the corrupt government of the day. Why wait, then? We should immediately set up an organization, I thought, within the armed forces, which would carry out the revolution I had dreamed of. That was the road to deliverance. There was no alternative to it.'[18]

The Nasser complex

The foregoing is based on Sadat's own account of his childhood and early youth, the only one available. Persuasive or otherwise, we have set it down essentially as he tells it. It was upon his graduation· from the Military Academy that Sadat experienced an event which, for once perhaps, he could truly describe as destiny-shaping. This was his first encounter with Gamal Abdul Nasser, the giant in whose shadow he was to live until, in 1970, chance finally brought the hero's role within his own grasp. From now on there are two, entirely contradictory accounts of his career. Both are his own.

Nasser, too, had been born in 1918. His actual birthplace was Egypt's second capital, Alexandria, but he, too, was basically a *fellah*, with a village, Beni Morr in Upper Egypt, that was as much his own as Mit Abul Kom was Sadat's. Like the schoolboy Sadat, he became deeply involved, emotionally and practically, in the political turbulence of the times. He took part in student demonstrations; he was struck by a policeman's baton in one, in another a British bullet scarred his forehead for life. He was obsessed by the idea of national regeneration and the expulsion of the hated foreigner. He had his pantheon of heroes, too, which did not, of course, exclude Hitler who, for so many Egyptians, had the double merit of defying the British and embodying a new, exciting, above all successful ideal of leadership. And, like Sadat, he had his adolescent dreams. 'Where is the man who can rebuild the country so that the weak and humiliated Egyptian can stand up again and live free and independent?' Gamal asked in a letter to his closest friend in September 1939. 'Where is dignity? Where is nationalism? Where is the so-called activity of our youth? . . . They say the Egyptian is a coward, that he is afraid of the slightest sound. He needs a leader to lead him in the struggle for his country. . . . We have said several times we are going to wake the nation from its sleep. But, alas, so far nothing has been carried out.'[19]

Manqabad garrison in Upper Egypt was the scene of the historic encounter between the two men. Sadat has written of his first posting there. Military life in this remote outpost was hard enough, he recalls, without the stupid and despotic commander who made it almost intolerable. Fortunately, however, the Manqabad nights brought us real relief. In an atmosphere of brotherhood and friendship we forgot the miseries of our day, the physical and moral sufferings, and even the bitterness of exile on a distant mountain. We did not understand why a youth of manly bearing—straight as a sword—and quiet sensitivity used to keep us company.... He lived with us and like us, but he seemed thoughtful and sad, grave and reserved. Hardly had we started to tell a joke than Gamal Abdul Nasser interrupted us to take us back to more serious matters. He was marked by the early loss of his mother, a grief he always bore, and which taught him very young the meaning of human suffering, tempering his soul in the stern acceptance of destiny. His heart overflowed with sympathy for all those in misfortune.... His moral rectitude, his generosity and breadth of vision drew us to him. The enthusiasm which animated him, his self-assurance, his commanding presence exerted an irresistible influence over all those who approached him. He imbued us with his ... faith in Egypt's destiny. He was the living source at which we refreshed our exalted spirits. He soon became the pole of attraction for a host of ardent followers who did not then imagine that their leader would inaugurate a new era. He was singled out by fate....

What did he tell us as we listened to him gathered round a camp fire on the mountain of al-Sharif? In essence, he told us: 'We are fighting imperialism, monarchy and feudalism, because we are opposed to injustice, oppression and slavery. Every patriot desires to establish a democracy that is strong and free of all tutelage. This aim will be achieved by any means, by force of arms or otherwise. Of its nature, society requires justice and equity for all. It points us the way: it shall be through Revolution.'

In a word, it was round the camp fire at Manqabad that the seeds of the 1952 Revolution were sown, and Nasser was the uncontested architect and strategist of all that followed. In Manqabad they took a solemn vow and, thus bound, 'we no longer belonged to ourselves, we were but soldiers mobilized in the service of a just cause: that of the liberating Revolution.'[20]

That, in *Révolte sur le Nil* (published in 1957), was the first description of the Manqabad encounter that Sadat gave us. But what Sadat set down for posterity at one stage of his career is not merely at variance with, but is often diametrically opposed to, what he set down at another. By contrast, this is how he describes the encounter in the last book he wrote, *In Search of Identity*, the autobiography which appeared in 1978. Here Nasser is 'a serious-minded youth, who did not share his fellows' interest in jesting, nor would he allow anyone to be frivolous with him as this, he felt, would be an affront to his dignity. Most of my colleagues therefore kept their distance and even refrained from talking to him for fear of being misunderstood. He listened to our conversations with interest but rarely opened his mouth. I immediately realized how serious he was and wanted to know him better. However, he had obviously erected an almost insuperable barrier between himself and other people. He kept to himself so conspicuously, in fact, that our relationship at the time never went beyond mutual respect, and even that was still from a distance.'[21]

If it was Nasser's haughtiness which kept him apart from his colleagues, Sadat himself was 'particularly distinguished' from them by one thing only: his pursuit of culture, in which he was 'very interested'. While others frittered away their free afternoons at the cinema or in search of 'other entertainments', he would sit at a café smoking a hookah and happily reading books he had ordered from Cairo.[22] Sadat, not Nasser, was the commanding personality to whom the others instinctively looked up. 'Meetings took place in my room in the officers' mess. It happened to be a senior officer's room, practically a small apartment. . . . We met there every evening, drank tea and talked. Without giving away my purpose I worked hard during our long conversations to open my colleagues' eyes to the realities of the situation and the position of the British in particular.' The discussions went on 'night after night', so much so that his room came to be known as 'the National Assembly'. His colleagues 'mostly lacked any political consciousness'. The impression gained is that, other than as a taciturn observer, Nasser played no part at all in these late-night seminars.[23]

It was in Manqabad, Sadat recounts, that he began to act upon his revolutionary ideals. At the time he was in the cavalry, permanently posted to the provinces. He had to be in Cairo, at the heart of things. So, in 1939, he got himself transferred to the signals, which enabled him to move to Maadi, 10 miles south of the capital.

There, I began my contacts immediately and on a very large scale – covering most army corps. . . . Contacts were originally confined to fellow officers in the same corps, mostly my coevals, but, encouraged by Hitler's successive threats to the British in 1939–41, I widened the circle gradually. Many senior and junior officers were approached and actually responded to our call, namely, that we should seize the opportunity and carry out an armed revolution against the British presence in Egypt.

Thus it was, concluded Sadat, that the original Free Officers Organization, founded by himself, came into being.[24]

The reason why, in *Révolte sur le Nil*, Sadat reproduces the orthodox and basically credible story of the 'Manqabad vow', and embellishes it much to Nasser's personal advantage is simple enough. In 1957 Nasser's prestige was at its height; he was the idol of the Arabs everywhere, a giant of the emerging Third World. At home his rule was personal and authoritarian. In time, most of the original Free Officers, after disagreeing with him, were pushed aside or withdrew of their own accord. Only two, Sadat and Hussein Shafi, remained faithful to the end. And from no one did loyalty to the leader bring forth such gratuitous adulation, such systematic ingratiation, as from Sadat.

The reason why, twenty years later, in *In Search of Identity*, he glorifies himself at Nasser's expense is likewise simple. This is the posthumous revenge of the servant who becomes master. Doubtless all leaders are governed in what they do both by their appraisal of objective reality and by the needs, often hidden, of their own peculiar psyches. It is only the relative weight of each that varies. In Sadat it was the needs, the not-so-hidden needs, of a very peculiar psyche which predominated to an unusual degree. The Manqabad encounter, and his contradictory accounts of it, are the first evidence that he was a man of complexes, and that the chief among them was his 'Nasser complex'. Naturally, Version Two of his career is now the authorized one. It is impossible to attribute the contradictions between it and Version One to lapses of memory, negligence, a cavalier attitude towards facts, or even a rather extreme, but not yet abnormal, measure of that equivocation and hypocrisy which are the occupational vices of politicians. They are more serious than that. His rewriting of history is so flagrant, so self-incriminating that history will not find it hard to judge him. He would appear to have been intuitively aware of that. Presumably that is why, inside Egypt at least, he sought to preserve the sanctity of the authorized version by prohibiting all unofficial histories of the 1952 Revolution. In 1975 he set up a special committee, headed by Vice President Husni Mubarak, to write an official one, and this committee alone was to be granted access to the relevant documents.

Taking on the British army

For the next stage of Sadat's career, spanning the Second World War, we drew on both Versions One and Two. Frequently divergent in substance and — self-deprecation supplanted by self-aggrandizement — in tone as well, there is, however, no outright falsification of one by the other, for in this period of Sadat's life Nasser played no part. Other accounts do, in some measure, corroborate Sadat's own. But, in any case, less interesting than the events themselves is the light which they — or rather the manner in which he relates them — shed on the mind and methods of the man himself. He turns them into a kind of picaresque farce, and the violent impetuosity, the hare-brained scheming of the second lieutenant of signals prefigure the surprises which, as President of Egypt, he was later to spring upon an astonished world.

General Aziz Masri now takes Nasser's place as the shaper of Sadat's destiny. At the time General Masri was a legendary figure. As an officer in the Ottoman army he had played a key role in the Young Turk movement before disillusionment had led him to join other Arab officers in conspiring against it. Sentenced to death, but released after an international outcry, he returned to his native Egypt as a national hero. He participated in the Arab Revolt, broke with its leaders, and returned once again to Egypt where his service in so many causes — but above all that of Arab emancipation — his intrepid adventures and his openly advertised pro-German, anti-British sentiments fascinated young officers of Sadat's generation.

As it happens, Manqabad was also the place where Sadat first met General Masri, who was visiting it in his capacity as Inspector General of the Armed Forces. For Sadat it was hero-worship at first sight. His exultation was understandable. It is understandable, too, that, in contrast with Nasser, Masri should emerge from Version Two with his reputation as pure and unsullied as in Version One. For the general was already in his sixties. He posed no threat to Sadat's self-esteem. He was a father-figure whom a young, ambitious, would-be revolutionary could look up to for inspiration and advice in a student-master relationship free from rivalry and competition.

It was the war, and the lightning victories of Sadat's boyhood hero Hitler, which brought him and General Masri together again. Under General Rommel, the Germans were blazing a trail across North

Africa; by April 1941 they were on Egyptian soil and approaching the Suez Canal from two directions. In this extremity, the British had decided to man Egypt's western defences on their own, and they ordered the Egyptian army not merely to withdraw, but to hand over its arms as well. Sadat was stationed in Marsa Matruh, on the Mediterranean coast, not far from the Libyan frontier, at the time.

I was livid with rage [he recalls], it was a military humiliation. . . . I contacted all my fellow officers and we concurred on disobeying the order. . . . If the British insisted on their demand they would have to fight for it. . . . The army command acquiesced and fresh orders were issued so that we withdrew with our weapons intact. It was at that time, in the summer of 1941, that I actually laid down the first plan for a revolution. It was agreed that all units withdrawing from Marsa Matruh would assemble at a definite time near Mena House Hotel, at the end of the Alexandria–Cairo motorway, regroup, and march into Cairo to topple the British and take over. The British were so weak at the time that my colleagues and I felt confident enough to embark on the adventure without fully considering the consequences. True, there was a definite plan and I had all details ready; neither the Moslem Brotherhood nor any other organization had any part to play in it; but was this enough? What happened, however, was that I led my unit from Marsa Matruh and, in one stride, we were at al-'Ajami, just outside Alexandria, where we spent the night. I felt very happy. The next day would see me at the Mena House Hotel, with the other units. We would study the plan, make assignments, and choose a suitable time for marching into Cairo to carry out our long-dreamed-of revolution.

However, Sadat blithely continues,

none of that happened. No units were near to Mena House when I got there; we washed our vehicles and sat down, my soldiers and I, to wait for them. We waited in vain. They must have gone ahead, I thought, having waited too long. So I ordered my unit to proceed to our camp in Maadi. Thus the first plan I laid down for a revolution came to grief. It might have been a blessing, for if we had tried and failed, the authorities would have been doubly vigilant, the army would have been closely watched, and the revolution of July 23 1952 would never have taken place.[25]

That is Version Two. If it sounds like a figment of his later, self-aggrandizing imagination, his more modest, cloak-and-dagger exploits of the time are not—though, as he and others relate them, they invariably seem to end up as much the same Chaplinesque farce.

It was on behalf of the ageing but irrepressible General Masri, now dimissed from the army as a Nazi sympathizer, that Sadat carried out his first major assignment. By May 1941, the British were in danger of losing control of Iraq and its oilfields. Rashid Ali Kailani, aided by Germany, had declared war on their meagre forces in the country. General Masri wanted to join them and the Germans were ready to help get him there. Sadat's task was to furnish the general with transport to a point on the Cairo–Fayyum road where a German plane would pick him up and fly him to Beirut. In Version One, the car simply broke down and it was 'impossible to repair'.[26] In Version Two Sadat was not there at all, for, having fallen under suspicion, he had been transferred from Maadi to Marsa Matruh.[27] However, Masri's other collaborators later managed to seize a military aircraft. Unfortunately, hardly had they taken off than they crash-landed; Hussein Sabri, the co-pilot, had turned the oil pump off instead of turning it on. According to Version One they hit a tree; according to Version Two it was a telegraph pole. Whichever it was, both pilots and fugitive emerged unscathed. They were imprisoned on charges of conspiring against the security of the state and released in 1942 after pledging to take no further part in subversive activities.

In Version Two Sadat describes how he, too, was arrested near Marsa Matruh and taken to Cairo for questioning, from which he emerges as fearless in the face of the hated occupier, loyal to his friends and cunning in his own defence. Asked whether he had any link with General Masri, he replied: 'Indeed I have. The Intelligence asked me to break that link but I didn't listen as I saw no crime or offence in maintaining it.' As to whether Masri had sought his help in getting away, Sadat was evasive. His contacts with Masri were 'based on love and loyalty. I have been impressed by his character since he visited us in Manqabad.' He had had no advance information about the escape. 'How could I . . . when I've been 340 miles away from Cairo?'[28]

Sadat was not deterred. A year later he attempted an altogether more ambitious enterprise—'to recruit an entire army' to fight on the side of the Germans who had now reached El Alamein, a mere 65 miles from Alexandria. General Rommel was to be informed that, in return for German recognition of Egypt's complete independence, Sadat and his comrades were ready to ensure that not one British soldier would leave Cairo. 'These were the terms of the treaty dictated by me and flown to El Alamein on board the aircraft piloted by Ahmad Saudi Hussein. I was twenty-two then, and the treaty was endorsed by my colleagues (with the exception of Abdul Nasser, who was away in the Sudan). To ensure its successful implementation and to give teeth to our resistance, I went to the glass market and bought 10,000 bottles—the sort we used to make Molotov cocktails.' Aerial photographs were taken. 'The film and the draft treaty were put into a bag and given to Saudi to fly to Rommel in Alamein.' Naturally, Sadat goes on, the aircraft was British-made, a Gladiator, 'so, although Saudi gave a signal of friendship, the Germans shot it down and Ahmad Saudi was killed'. That was that. By now the reader will not be surprised to learn that, although the episode did take place, the role which Sadat attributes to himself is to be found only in Version Two.[29]

Now it is back to the cloak-and-dagger exploits of Version One. One evening in the summer of 1942, Sadat relates in *Révolte sur le Nil*, there were three light taps on the door of his fellow-officer Hassan Izzat. 'There stood two emissaries of Marshal Rommel, Hans Appler and Sandy. . . . My comrade hastened to bring them to me.' They sought Sadat's expertise as a wireless operator. As it turned out, however, they were less interested in espionage than in living it up on a houseboat rented from Hikmat Fahmy, a celebrated belly dancer. Sadat's own role appears to have been confined to making off with the powerful, brand-new transmitter which he had promised to repair for them. His doubts about Appler and Sandy's credentials soon grew into certainty. He was shocked to hear that 'the National Bank had changed into good Egyptian currency more than forty thousand pounds-worth of forged sterling banknotes, that the transaction had been done through the good offices of a Jew who, naturally, pocketed one third of the sum as a commission'. Visiting the houseboat he found himself, to his disgust, in a place 'straight out of the Thousand and One Nights, where everything invited indolence, voluptuousness and pleasure of the senses. In this dissolute atmosphere the young Nazis had forgotten the delicate mission with which they had been entrusted.' On his second visit, he found them 'dead drunk in the company of two Jewish women'. But by now Sadat could not extricate himself and when the two were caught he was soon grabbed in his turn.[30]

Sadat, tried by a mixed British-Egyptian court, again confounded his interrogators. For the full account of what, in retrospect, he portrays as the climax of his early struggle we turn again to Version Two. At one time it looked as though he was going to be shot at dawn, but, with the tide of battle moving their way,

> the British began to cool down a bit and their attitude to our case began to change. So, one day in Ramadan, an hour before sunset, the Chief of Staff of the Cairo military zone summoned me to inform me that in accordance with a supreme royal decree I would be relieved of my duties. I stripped off my rank. Muhammad Ibrahim Imam, chief of the Police Political Department, approached me and said: 'You must come with me to the Cairo Governorate Headquarters; certain formalities must be attended to.' I realized that they were about to arrest me. I asked: 'Where exactly are we going? I want my orderly to know so that he can bring me my breakfast.' 'To the Aliens' Jail,' he said laconically.
>
> As we walked together, the image of Zahran rose before my eyes almost visibly all the way to the Aliens' Jail. I saw him advancing towards death with his head held high, happy at what he had done. At last I had achieved what Zahran had done before me. Overcome by this feeling, I realized, as never before, that Zahran was *not* defeated. He was executed, but his will was not. Was I not an extension of that same will, which had possessed me from early childhood? The will to challenge, the will to triumph?
>
> We reached the jail. As I walked up the staircase to my room, I was overwhelmed by a strange joy—the joy of acknowledging a vast inner strength which I alone recognized. I had won, just as Zahran had won, although he was hanged and I was stripped of my rank and arrested.[31]

Upon ascending to his cell, like Zahran to his scaffold, Sadat found, in this British-administered institution, a bed, blanket, chair, small table, cigarettes, newspapers, books and a life which 'was not on the whole too bad'. Still, it had been a shock at first.

> I strode up and down my room in sheer bewilderment . . . for hours on end. At length, I sat down on the floor and leaned back against the bed . . . perhaps because in that position I felt closer to nature or simply because I was used to sitting on the ground in our village. The village . . . suddenly, I was thinking of the village! True, it was only a thought, but it gave me immeasurable strength.

My village was there in the heart of the Nile Delta and I should naturally go back to it. Why worry, then, or wonder about my destiny? A man's village is his peace of mind. . . . I realized that to be a simple peasant was enough to make me the happiest man on earth. . . . It is still so, in effect. Whatever the time and circumstances, the feeling that I am a peasant gives me a rare self-sufficiency. Indeed, the land is always there. I can go back to it at any time; I can work it myself, with my own hands, and that would be enough — more than enough. I control my fate; my will is mine alone; I am my own master.[32]

From the Aliens' Jail Sadat was moved, in December 1942, to a detention centre near Miniah, about 240 miles south of Cairo. This turned out to be a 'huge sumptuous palace, standing in isolation on the banks of the Ibrahimiyah Canal, surrounded by areas of dry land and backing on to a small village not very different from Mit Abul Kom'.[33] A year later, he was moved again, this time to a detention centre at Zaytoun, north of Cairo, where, among other things, he and his prison-mates bred rabbits. 'We initially bought two or three pairs and in three months' time our rabbits had multiplied to fill up the only spacious hall in the house.'[34]

Security was evidently lax. For in 1944 Sadat and five prison-mates cut a hole in the roof, and one night they climbed out and down into the street, where, by pre-arrangement, an Oldsmobile was waiting. After 2 miles they had a puncture. One of them, Hassan Izzat, proposed going to a garage to get it fixed. But Sadat refused. 'You carry on and do what you want; you'll be the runaway detainees, as decided. Muhsin and I have something different in mind.' Muhsin Fadil and Sadat spent the rest of the night at the house of a Frenchwoman, a friend of Fadil's, 'a great lady, in fact, who represented the spirit of the French people at their best — a noble, freedom-loving people, just like the Egyptians . . .'

'In the morning a breakfast table was laid, complete with Arabic newspapers — it was perfect. We had breakfast, thanked her, then went out and hailed a taxi to the royal Abidin Palace.' They sauntered into this august residence, signed their names in the Royal Ceremonies Book and then 'stated that we were detainees at Zaytoun, that we had come expressly to tell the king that the government should not submit to the British authorities; that it was completely unacceptable that we should be treated so badly; that the two of us would, of our own free will, return at once to the detention centre'.

They entered this statement in the Ceremonies Book, to the consternation of the official in charge. The Master of Ceremonies was hastily summoned. He recognized Sadat at once, having been governor of Miniah when he was detained there, and warned them that 'our decision was sheer lunacy and that it would simply lead from one crisis to another . . . we took a taxi and returned to Zaytoun. The gates opened wide, so we drove right in and reported back.' Instead of being punished for their escapade, the jail-breakers found that their conditions improved considerably, and they had a relatively quiet time until October 1944. Then, with a change of government, all political detainees were released except for Sadat and his group, who went on hunger strike in protest. His colleagues gave up, he alone holding out until he was moved to the Qasr al-Ayni hospital. There his former prison-mate, Hassan Izzat, visited him and arranged for a second and permanent escape.

Sadat was on the run until the end of the war and the lifting of martial law. He seems, by his own account, to have had a much rougher time than he did in prison. He was out of work. He had to walk from his home in Kubri al-Qubbah to al-Atabah every day, 'which was more than twelve miles [actually it is about one mile], simply because I could not afford the tramway fare of 6 millimes'. Nevertheless, he continues,

I have always been a perfectionist, and that applies to the way I dressed as well. At the time I had a jacket which I loved . . . and which I had worn only a few times before my detention. I decided to sell it to a second-hand shop in town. I took it and went to the shop, but a few yards from it I got cold feet and stopped dead. I was terrified the shopkeeper would think I had stolen the jacket, as it was unlikely a man in rags would be in possession of such a smart garment. I changed my mind and returned home on foot, carrying my jacket. I knew, to be sure, that the shopkeeper would ask no questions. Indeed, I was certain that he would pay reasonably well for it and that, however little, his price would help me out in such terrible straits; but I simply could not have my image tarnished in the eyes of a perfect stranger, whatever the cost.

Well [he concludes], what about my image in my own eye? Did it live up to my expectations? I was a free man once again, it is true, but did I feel like a prisoner who has just been released? Obviously not; Egypt was still shackled and the people were as far from controlling their own fate as ever. So the minute I regained my freedom, I started to form a secret organization, feeling that personal liberty could hardly be real until my entire homeland had been liberated.[35]

Assassin

Once again, it is open conflict between Versions One and Two. For in the seven-year period between the end of the Second World War and the 1952 Revolution, Nasser comes back into Sadat's life. But this time, in the way it treats the central issues, Version Two is nearer the truth. In this account Sadat uninhibitedly portrays himself as the advocate and practitioner of the terrorism and political violence which he had disavowed in Version One.

It was an era of extremism. The decay of the monarchy under a dissolute King Farouk, Britain's accelerating retreat from empire, the creation of Israel, upheavals in the Arab world and the economic aftermath of the war — all this made of Egypt a hotbed of intrigue and conspiracy, of fanatical idealism and thinly disguised skulduggery. Of the semi-clandestine organizations which challenged the throne and the established political parties the most formidable was the Moslem Brotherhood, religious fundamentalists led since 1929 by Hassan al-Banna, whose influence spread through much of the Arab world. The Young Egypt Society sought to adapt the doctrines of fascism to a specifically Egyptian and Islamic environment. There were revolutionary Marxists of various hues. And there were the young army officers who cultivated ties with all political movements, but identified themselves with none of them.

Everyone was tempted by the politics of violence. But one man who soon tried to resist the temptation was the young Colonel Nasser. He underwent the change of heart which he subsequently recorded in *The Philosophy of the Revolution.* 'I confess — and may the Public Prosecutor not take me severely to task for making such a confession — that political assassinations struck my then [in the 1930s] inflamed mind as the inevitable positive action to be taken, if we were to save the future of the Homeland.' But 'gradually the idea of political assassinations . . . began to die out.' He did take part in one attempt. The target was a particularly dangerous enemy of the Free Officers Organization. But afterwards he spent a miserable night praying for the life of the person he had tried to kill and was overjoyed to learn from the morning's newspapers that his attempt had failed.[36]

In Version One Sadat acknowledges the restraining influence which Nasser exerted on his own rash impulses. Nothing more excited his penchant for the spectacular gesture, the swift retaliation than the colonial arrogance of the British. In 1945 the newly installed Prime Minister, Nokrashi Pasha, went to the British embassy to present his country's latest demands. The ambassador, Lord Killearn, would do no more than speak to him for a few minutes at the foot of the stairs, and then all but dismissed him. Sadat was not alone in his outrage; but, in him, the latent Zahran also cried out for instant revenge. He wanted 'immediate reprisals against the British'—nothing less than to blow up the British embassy with everybody inside. 'Gamal listened attentively, examined the plan in its smallest details. Then he tossed his head and said "no".'[37]

Nasser was not always on hand to hold him back. The murder of Amin Osman, a former Minister of Finance, on 6 January 1946 was one of those political assassinations which the subsequent career of the assassin has endowed with a much greater place in history than it would otherwise have deserved. In Version One Sadat indignantly repudiates any role in the killing. The culprits had vowed to make no confession, come what may. But under torture one of them, Hussein Tewfik, did so—not out of cowardice, but to protect a woman from dishonour. He denounced the terrorist group, gave away its meeting place and all the names he knew. 'I was more than a little surprised to learn that my name had been mentioned, although I had never been mixed up with the group, directly or indirectly. Nevertheless, I was arrested and detained for thirty-one months, which were the most atrocious of my life. But when my innocence was finally recognized, I was released purely and simply.'[38] This miscarriage of justice sets him off on a general denunciation of terrorism. He disapproved of all these assassinations, he writes, not because he felt any sympathy for the victims, who were of little consequence, but 'because such senseless acts were contrary to our principles and we did not wish to align ourselves with a group made up of disreputable elements and fanatics more concerned with self-glorification than anything else. . . . We never considered the technique of terror as a necessity, even a temporary one, in the conquest of power.' It was, in fact, the Moslem Brotherhood, Sadat asserts, who killed Osman, and many others too.[39] Abdul Munim Abdul Raouf—he writes of a former comrade—had 'devoted himself body and soul to the Moslem Brotherhood, who, forgetting the original aim of their association, gradually indulged in politics: their movement came to be dominated and perverted by a mystique of violence. . . . Who would have suspected, at that time, that this idealist would take part in a campaign of terror and assassination and debase himself to the point of being implicated in an attempt, on 28 October 1954, against the life of President Gamal Abdul Nasser?'[40]

Sadat at first seemed a shade bashful about changing his story to the one eventually given us in Version Two. Thus in a 1974 television interview he recalled that he 'was accused of plotting for the assassination of some politician called Amin Osman here'. Asked if he really had, he laughed: 'Well, er, to a certain extent I trained those students and those young men . . . that was my main accusation—that I trained them to use hand grenades and pistols . . . and so I trained them. Yes, I trained them.'[41]

Three years later, writing *In Search of Identity*, he had overcome these inhibitions. What made it all the more startling—all the more indicative of his irresistible desire for self-dramatization—was that these memoirs address themselves essentially to a Western audience, which, he knew, was liable to be particularly shocked by his revelations. Yet, not merely did he admit the Osman killing, he boasted about it. Osman's offence had been to liken the relationship between Egypt and Great Britain to a Catholic marriage.

That declaration was tantamount to a self-imposed death sentence. On January 6 1946, the sentence was carried out. Amin Osman had returned from Britain a couple of days earlier, had called on the British High Commissioner in the afternoon, and in the evening went to the [Arab] League Headquarters. According to plan, Hussein Tewfik was waiting for him at the door of the building. As Osman was about to take the elevator, Tewfik fired his pistol at him. Tewfik, in calling him, applied the rule that forbade the shooting of a man in the back.

There was a blackout in Cairo at the time [Sadat goes on], and Tewfik could have got away easily. As it happened, an Egyptian air force officer called Mursi who was passing by witnessed the entire incident and alerted everybody. People started to give chase and actually cornered Hussein. He had two hand grenades I had given him but not to use except in an emergency and away from people. He hurled one of them behind the wall of Sarduq al-Dayn, and the explosion did the trick. His chasers fled with no casualties at all, and he returned quietly to his home in Heliopolis. I was sitting all the while at a nearby café. When I heard the explosion, I rushed to the scene to make sure no one was hurt. Then, reassured, I took the train and went home to Kubri al-Qubbah.[42]

Thanks to the air force officer the police were able to arrest Hussein Tewfik within hours. He was not able to establish an alibi. Nor was Sadat, and it is with some bitterness that he goes into his friend's behaviour under interrogation. No longer is he the gallant gentleman who only confessed under torture to protect a woman's honour. 'He would not talk at all on his first day in custody,' Sadat relates, but, after he had held out for a second day, 'the clever attorney asked the press to hint that it was a *crime passionnel*. Knowing that Hussein was a paranoid case, the attorney set the trap and Hussein immediately fell into it. To defend his reputation, Hussein Tewfik made a full confession. . . . I realized that Tewfik had made a clean breast of everything. He had omitted nothing down to the minutest detail, almost like a tape recorder.'[43] As a result, a few days later Sadat found himself back in the Aliens' Jail.

Not only does Sadat claim complicity in the Osman murder, but also in an unsuccessful attempt on the life of Nahas Pasha, the former *Wafd* leader, now become Prime Minister, whom the hero-worshipping schoolboy used to watch on his way to the National Assembly. In Version One the attempt had been passed off as little more than a prank which 'caused more laughter than tears'. One of his men, a lieutenant in the Coastguards, had hurled a shoe at Nahas on his way to Friday prayers. The shoe missed the Prime Minister and struck the man beside him, the Minister of Religious Affairs, instead.[44] But in Version Two Sadat observes that 'Nothing is more painful for young men than to be disillusioned in a leader who was once their idol.' On 4 February 1942 the British had forced Nahas, virtually at gunpoint, to accept the premiership. This, for Sadat, was enough to turn 'a peerless symbol of patriotism, self-sacrifice and devotion' into a traitor. 'We therefore decided to get rid of him.' It was the Pasha's custom to make a speech every year on the Prophet's birthday at a club in central Cairo.

Several members of our organization and I lay in wait for him as his car left Garden City and joined the stream of traffic in Qasr al-Ayni Street. . . . I had trained our team in the use of hand grenades. Hussein Tewfik was picked as the one to do it, and he did hurl the grenade at the right time. However, as the driver of el-Nahas's car was forced to speed up a little to avoid running into a tram in Qasr al-Ayni Street, the grenade exploded six seconds too late and missed the car altogether. The splinters hit a bus carrying ATS girls of the British armed forces. . . . We withdrew quietly. We took a tram back to Ismailia Square which was only a few minutes' walk from the scene of the incident. We went to the Café Astra, our favourite meeting place. It was at the Astra that we decided to get rid of Amin Pasha. . . .[45]

It seems, however, that Sadat's career as a terrorist was more extensive than even he, in Version Two, is prepared to admit. Improbable though it sounds, he appears to have participated in other attempts to kill Nahas which took place while he was a prisoner on trial for the murder of Amin Osman.

It was not until two years after their arrest that Sadat, Hussein Tewfik and their accomplices came to court. The trial lasted from January to August 1948. Sadat was released without conviction after the principal defendant, Hussein Tewfik, escaped. It was halfway through the proceedings that two attempts on Nahas's life took place. On 5 April a bomb was hurled at his car. Then, on 25 April, a car packed with dynamite exploded outside his villa in Garden City in the early hours of the morning; it wrecked the house and damaged that of his neighbour, the deputy leader of the *Wafd*, Fuad Serageddin. The blast was heard all over the city.

According to histories of the 1952 Revolution and the memoirs of some of its participants, it was the Iron Guard that tried to kill Nahas. The Iron Guard, says Muhammad Naguib, the first figurehead President of the Republic, was formed 'to keep an eye on patriotic officers'.[46] It was a direct, clandestine arm of the Palace, specializing in assassinations, that operated independently of the army and the Royal Guard. Its *éminence grise* was Dr Yusif Rashad, naval officer, physician and adjutant to King Farouk. The attempt on Nahas was among its first operations.[47]

Sadat does not conceal his connection with Dr Yusif Rashad. He was 'a good friend', and at the same time 'one of the best weapons in [the] arsenal' of the Free Officers. Through him Sadat both obtained information about the king's activities and intentions and 'spun a few yarns designed to mislead the king'.[48]

In his four-volume *Story of the 23 July Revolution*, Ahmad Hamroush, a Free Officer himself, records that

71

no sooner had it been formed than the Iron Guard began its terrorist operations. . . . On 5 April 1948 Abdul Raouf Nureddin, in the company of Anwar Sadat, opened fire on Mustafa Nahas from a Royal Palace car. It was supplied by Captain Abdullah Sadiq of the Palace Fire Brigade and driven by Fahmi Abdul Maguid. Abdul Raouf missed, in spite of the close range. Then, on 25 April, Mustafa Kamal Sidqi and Abdul Raouf Nureddin proceeded to blow up Nahas's house by means of a car packed with high explosives.[49]

While Sadat contended that Nahas deserved to die as a traitor, Hamroush was of the opinion that it was the elder statesman's 'firm stand on the national issue' which earned him the Iron Guard's attention, along with his refusal to countenance a *rapprochement* between the Palace and the *Wafd* party without the holding of fresh elections. 'Thus', comments Hamroush, 'the terrorism to which some officers, together with a number of intellectuals, resorted after the Nazi defeat in order to kill occupying soldiers—thus did this terrorism end up as an instrument in the hands of the Palace to get rid of its own enemies and the enemies of imperialism at the same time.'[50]

That Sadat was in prison at the time did not necessarily rule out his terrorist activities—for whichever side he was practising them. Security, in those dying days of the monarchy, was more nonchalant than ever. For example, Hussein Tewfik, the chief defendant in the Osman case, enjoyed a degree of freedom not usually granted to a man on trial for murder. The chauffeur of his father's car told the court that escorting officers used to allow him to take the prisoner on drives round the outskirts of Cairo after visits to the doctor. It was after one such visit that he 'made a dash for it'.[51] As for Sadat himself, he recalls that 'we were allowed to go out from time to time' and he took advantage of this to make frequent visits to an army dentist friend of his at the military hospital, at least an hour's drive from the Aliens' Jail. 'I enjoyed the taxi drive very much. . . . True, a police officer always escorted me, but it never really mattered. I asked the dentist not to touch the bad molar so that I could come to see him more frequently. My guard always watched the dentist at work but could never guess that while he apparently dealt with my teeth, the molar itself was never touched. . . . Sometimes, I called on my father . . . and had tea with him.'[52] Not much doubt about the opportunities for unauthorized extramural activities there. But if, as

Ḥamroush and others insist, Sadat was a member of the Iron Guard or—in the words of General Naguib—one of 'a number of officers released [from prison] as a bribe', such activities were not unauthorized at all, and Sadat was a hired assassin of King Farouk himself.[53]

Of heart and health, clothes and careers

In Version Two, Sadat devotes a whole chapter, 'The Liberation of Self-Cell 54', to the sufferings of his second incarceration, the physical discomfort, loneliness, soul-searching—and the eventual triumph of the spirit. In the light of his regular outings, and 'tea with his father', it is hard to believe that life in Cairo Central Prison, whither he had been transferred from the Aliens' Jail, was quite the nightmare he describes it as. His physical sufferings were at any rate soon alleviated by the generosity of Hassan al-Banna, Supreme Guide of the Moslem Brotherhood, for whom, in Version Two— unlike the first—Sadat acknowledged an 'unbounded' admiration. He was able to furnish his cell with a proper bed, table and chair, to buy extra food—and Eno's Fruit Salts: 'I haven't been able to do without them for a very long time now, almost thirty years.'[54]

It was in Cell 54, where he 'could only be his own companion', that Sadat experienced what he calls his 'self-confrontation'. But the thing that seems to have troubled him most was his marriage—not because his wife and three children were deprived of husband, father, breadwinner for the second time, but because he was contemplating divorce.

Sadat had married very young. By the age of twenty-four, when he went to prison for the first time, he had fathered three daughters. It had been an arranged marriage contracted with one of his relatives 'in the conventional manner common in the countryside . . . part of, if not the crowning of, the process of growing up'. 'Contradictions inherent in the marriage' emerged when Sadat joined the Military Academy. He began to understand that he and his wife had nothing in common. But he could not leave her. 'In fact, I never thought of it as I was governed by certain values I could never violate.'[55] Erosion of those values had begun much earlier, however, when he was still a cadet. He had visited a distant relative near Cairo, one of whose daughters was acquiring a French education at the *Lycée*. The thought occurred to him that 'she would make a different kind of wife', but was immediately revolting. He 'rose in rebellion' against himself, angry and disgusted. Just because he had enrolled in the

73

Military Academy, should he abandon his wife? Where were his sense of loyalty, his values? He felt ashamed.

Yet the problem continued to bother him. It was a class problem. The simple village boy, now with a foot on the first rung of a ladder to higher things, felt that he was 'destined to engage in public life, even as an army officer . . . and public life meant mixing with all kinds and "levels" '. In the solitude of Cell 54, the problem loomed large. In fact it became 'pressing to an unprecedented degree—even harassing. . . . I was aware of the veins in my temples, throbbing madly when I went to bed at night and again when I woke up in the morning. . . .' He was convinced that his 'very being depended on that particular situation'.[56] He instructed his wife to stop visiting him in prison. And when, nine months later, he was released, he told her it was impossible for them to go on living together and he made arrangements for a divorce.

Although he seems to have decided that no wife could have a role in the hectic life he led, this did not deter him, a few months later, from taking a second one. For in Cell 54 he had also realized that what caused him most suffering was the lack of a 'love relationship'. 'For a man's life to be complete, he must have a female partner to whom he is bound in mutual love.'[57] Shortly after his release his friend and collaborator of earlier, conspiratorial days, Hassan Izzat, whisked him off to Suez to meet his family. There he encountered Jihan Safwat Raouf for the first time. At fifteen, she was exactly half Sadat's age, deeply patriotic, fascinated by politics, and, having followed press accounts of the Amin Osman murder trial, she was already in love with this peasant-patriot-revolutionary. Sadat asked for her hand in December 1949 and they were married five months later.

Actually, his first preoccupation upon leaving prison had been his health. He went to Helwan, a fashionable watering place which numbered Winston Churchill among its recent, illustrious patrons, to 'cure [his] ailing stomach'. He then went shopping for new clothes. He had two suits made to measure, bought himself some shirts and a 'new type of socks [sockets they were called] which seemed to have been first introduced into "fashionable Cairo" while [he] was still in jail'.[58]

Next Sadat went into partnership with Hassan Izzat, who was running what he mysteriously describes as 'a kind of trading concern via Suez with the Saudis'. Business was slack and Izzat thought that it would pick up if he had 'the hero of the Amin Osman case, the talk of the media, on his side'.[59] It worked. But Sadat soon fell out with his friends who, he alleges, cheated him of two-thirds of his share of the profits. So, with sixty sovereigns in his pocket—'a fortune'—he went back to Helwan to resume his mineral water cure. But the money went quickly to pay for the 'good living' he enjoyed.

He then tried his hand at journalism. But his spell at the Dar el Hilal Publishing House was brief, for Hassan Izzat reappeared on the scene to tempt him away from writing into what, this time, promised to be big business indeed. Together they signed a contract to bring drinking water to fifty-two villages in the Sharqiya province. Such was Sadat's ingenuity that the work was completed in six months instead of a year. The two partners made a profit of £6,000. They landed another contract, this time to bring water to villages in the Miniah area, on which Sadat estimated that they 'might have cleared no less than £30,000 net profit'.[60] Whether he felt such windfall gains were strictly in line with his 'village ethics' he does not explain. In any case, nothing came of it, because this 'friend who loved me, hid nothing from me and looked upon me as his conscience'[61] swindled him again. Hassan Izzat accused him of helping himself to £2,000; this was 'a stark lie', Sadat told him, and 'with no more than £1·20 in my pocket I said goodbye'.[62]

During this period of trial and error Sadat toyed with the career for which such a restless variety of pursuits did perhaps indicate that he was best equipped. Certainly, of all the whims of the young revolutionary this one most accurately foreshadowed the aptitudes of the mature statesman whom the world came to know. In 1948 the following advertisement appeared in the Cairo quarterly *al-Fusuul*: 'I am a dark youth, 1·69 metres tall, 31 years old. I go in for comic acting, and I am ready to play any role in the theatre or cinema. Anwar Sadat.' (The authors were unable to establish the precise date of this quotation, but are satisfied of its authenticity. One of the difficulties facing the researcher is the removal from public archives of documents relating to this period of Sadat's career.)

But most significant of all, perhaps, is what, according to his own account, he did not think or do during his time in Cell 54 and after. One cannot but note a curious lack of interest or involvement in the momentous political and military developments of the period. It is true that when the first Arab–Israeli war broke out on 15 May 1948 Sadat was still in prison and, according to his memoirs, the war much affected him. 'God knows what I suffered at the time! It was agonizing to witness the Israeli raids on Cairo, violating the sanctity of Ramadan, our holy month, but I was helpless and could do nothing about it.'[63] Yet he could have done something two months later. While he was taking the waters at Helwan, refurbishing his wardrobe, sorting out his matrimonial problems, seeking 'financial stability' through lucrative business deals—while he was doing all this, most of his fellow officers, not excluding his fellow-assassin, were fighting, and some were dying, for Palestine. Long before 15 May an undeclared war had already been raging between the native Palestinians and the Jewish settlers who strove to drive them out. Egyptian officers had applied for and been given permission to join civilian volunteers, many of them from the Moslem Brotherhood, fighting on the Palestinians' side. Gamal Abdul Nasser and several of his comrades who later formed the Free Officers Organization were among the first in the field. It was the battlefields of Palestine, and their shocking exposure of Arab corruption and incompetence, which ripened Nasser's conviction that 'the real battlefield was in Egypt' (see p. 40). In some measure, too, it was patriotism which motivated Hussein Tewfik's escape from prison. In a letter to journalist Ihsan Abdul Koddous, published in Cairo newspapers, he wrote: 'by the time you receive this message I shall be on my way to Palestine, to liberate the Holy Land from the Zionist gangsters.'[64]

One cannot help wondering why Sadat did not feel it was his 'destiny' to rush, like Tewfik, to the Palestinian front instead of to the tailor. It was not until 1950 that, disenchanted with business and his acting talents unrecognized, he decided to try his luck again with the army. That presented no difficulty. He went to see his 'good friend', Dr Yusif Rashad, the head of the Iron Guard. 'I felt that was the only way I could accomplish the mission—the vocation—that, to me, was everything.'[65] Rashad proved most helpful. Within a few days the king's doctor and adjutant had arranged for Sadat to meet the Minister of War, Muhammad Heidar Pasha, who promptly instructed that 'this boy . . . is to be reinstated immediately as from today'.[66] A military decree was issued and Sadat returned to his first profession with the same captain's rank that he had had when he left it. Colonel Gamal Abdul Nasser and his closest friend and collaborator Abdul Hakim Amer, were, he said, the first to welcome him back.

Missing the revolutionary bus

It would seem, however, that Nasser never really trusted him. 'Gamal is at the helm', Sadat concedes in Version One, and only he and Amer knew the exact names and number of those belonging to the Free Officers Organization (Sadat, probably exaggerating, puts it at about 1,000).[67] It appears that the nearer Nasser got to staging his *coup d'état*, the more cautious he became in the choice of his closest confidants, with a purging, or pushing to the periphery, of all those who had secondary links and loyalties he did not trust. He persuaded his comrades that only he could maintain contacts, on a purely expedient basis, with groupings outside the army. According to one authority, Sadat, with his Moslem Brotherhood and, more suspect still, his Palace connections, no longer figured among the top ten conspirators.[68]

The coup came much sooner than originally envisaged. The events of 26 January 1952, the notorious Black Saturday, persuaded the Free Officers to advance their timetable for seizing power. In Ismailia, the previous day, some seventy Egyptian policemen had died when British troops stormed their beleaguered garrison with tanks and artillery, and the next day the outraged mob descended on the heart of Cairo, burning and sacking the Shepheards Hotel, the Turf Club, cafés, bars, cinemas and other symbols of foreign rule and native opulence. Egypt was clearly ripe for revolution. As Sadat wrote:

26 January was an orgiastic display of collective exaltation, a reckless, unrestrained sedition, of despair and hunger. . . . As the capital was plunged in anarchy, the king was holding a banquet in Abidin Palace, the Prime Minister, if you please, was at his manicurist and the Minister of the Interior was busy taking possession of a building he had just acquired. These facts shed a rather crude light on the morality of the highest authorities of the state. History offers no example of such degeneracy.[69]

Sadat pointed out that in the five years that followed the Second World War prices had risen fourfold, more than twice the increase in wages. Without a proper system of direct taxation, the state was incapable of halting an inflation which bore most heavily on the poor. 'This deficiency was one of the final errors of the regime.'[70]

So the day was not far removed when, at last, Sadat would play his part in the making of history. Till then his career as hero and revolutionary had been a series of unfortunate fiascos. Now, with zero hour at hand, he was assigned the secondary, but eminently public, task which befitted an officer of the Signals Corps. He was chosen to read the prepared statement over Cairo Radio that proclaimed the dawn of a new era. But through ineptitude, as the more charitable would have it, or through precautionary guile, he all but blundered yet again. Summoned to the critical rendezvous on the eve of the coup, he went to the cinema instead. In Version One he tells the story in the matter-of-fact tone of one who does not deem it necessary to explain such extraordinary insouciance. He was in el-Arish when he was instructed to join Nasser in Cairo immediately. It was 21 July and the coup would take place between 22 July and 5 August.

On the morning of 22 July I was sitting in the train for Cairo. It was 4.30 in the afternoon when I got to Cairo station, and I decided to spend the evening with my children [presumably of his first wife] in one of the open-air, summer-time cinemas near to my house. I reckoned I would go the next morning to meet Gamal Abdul Nasser and get my orders for carrying out the plan. As usual, the cinema showed three films. I sat with my children in the cinema through all three. During this time Gamal had come to my house in his famous little Austin. But he didn't find me and the *bawab* [doorkeeper] did not know which cinema we had gone to. Gamal came back a second time an hour later, and when he did not find me left a note with the *bawab* saying: 'The plan will be implemented tonight; rendezvous at Abdul Hakim Amer's at 11 o'clock.' On that night Gamal had been in his car to every quarter of Cairo like Mercury himself to issue orders to his comrades. . . . No sooner had the *bawab* given me the note than I found myself bounding up the stairs to my room, leaving my astonished children with the *bawab*. . . . I put on my uniform, got into my little car and sped off. . . . But I did not find anyone at Abdul Hakim Amer's. . . . Where should I go? . . . I was confused. . . . I decided I should go to the army headquarters, for, if the operation was under way, our forces must have reached it. I sped through the streets of Cairo as fast as my little car would go. At Qishlaq Abasiah an officer stopped my car. When he saw my rank he spoke to me in a firm and decisive tone, although he was only a lieutenant. But he was a Free Officer. . . . I went my way and reached Qishlaq al-Sawari. But the road was blocked there. I now knew that the operation really had begun, particularly when I heard hundreds of shots fired from the direction of the High Command. I wanted to pass through the cordon which our forces had set up. But the officer prevented me. He was very strict with me, because I didn't know the password. My situation was dreadful. Without a password, a junior officer would not let me through the cordon, except over his dead body! So what was I to do then?! How could I convince him that I was a Free Officer; how could I get him to let me throw myself into battle with our forces? I saw many silhouettes in the distance. They were our forces overthrowing the regime. And I was behind the cordon and a junior officer was holding me back, starting to get tough with me. Hundreds of thoughts flashed through my mind. Have any of my comrades been hit? What is Gamal doing now? Where is Abdul Hakim? Where were they all and what were they doing? I went back to my car and tried to cross Qubbah bridge. . . . But there the way was blocked too, but the cordon officer knew me. . . . I approached the cordon, my nerves relaxed, a little hope blossomed in my breast, I was going to get through and take part in the operation! But no sooner had I drawn near than I heard the voice of my friend the lieutenant forbidding me to advance. He came up to me and saw my face. But the expression on his own face did not augur well. Although he knew me he did not know that I was a Free Officer and he arrested me immediately. My heart filled with dismay and my head nearly exploded. I tried, but without success, to make him understand that the friendship which bound us should be enough in the battle of life and death. But he did not trust me, because I did not know the password. I did not know what to do and the sound of shooting close at hand only increased my alarm! But, suddenly, hope filled my breast again. . . . I heard a distant voice that resembled that of Abdul Hakim Amer. I felt salvation was nigh. . . . Lorries carrying soldiers and officers were passing in front of me. It was our forces starting to overthrow the regime! I found myself shouting at the top of my voice: 'Abdul Hakim, Abdul Hakim, this is Anwar!' And the shadowy figure of Abdul Hakim came close and only then did my friend the officer let me free.[71]

Amer was in command of the detachment laying siege to the army headquarters. He was always the quiet type, Sadat wrote later, and when the hour of battle struck, whether in Palestine or on this fateful night, his nerves were like tempered steel. This 'legendary hero', his task accomplished with almost clockwork precision, drafted the statement which Sadat broadcast to the people at seven o'clock on the morning of 23 July.

On 26 July Sadat was dispatched to Alexandria, where the king was spending the summer, with the text of an ultimatum calling on him to abdicate and leave the country that same day. Sadat handed the text to General Muhammad Naguib, the Free Officers' figurehead leader, who handed it to the newly appointed Prime Minister, Ali Maher, who in turn presented it to the king. At six o'clock that afternoon, as Farouk sailed for exile in the royal yacht *Mahroussa*, Sadat stood aboard the destroyer which fired a 21-gun salute.

> A reign was over. One Egypt said farewell to another. Farouk got the retribution he deserved. He was brought down by his own depravities before he was by his people. . . . He left a people in distress, with curses on its lips, an Egypt debased, exhausted, on the brink of perdition. . . . The monarchy had crumbled under the weight of its misdeeds. . . . The laws of nature cannot be violated with impunity. Events have their own implacable logic; nothing can impede them. In Egypt they culminated in the day of 26 July.[72]

Uncle Gamal

From the moment he read his proclamation on the morning of 23 July until, on 28 September 1970, he again went on the air to announce the death of the 'immortal leader', Sadat was a faithful son of the Revolution. In the first decade of the new era, he held a variety of posts which brought more limelight than real authority. By inclination he was the most voluble of the Free Officers, and in his official capacities, beginning with the editorship of the regime's newly created mouthpiece, the newspaper *al-Gumhuriyah (The Republic)*, he had ample opportunity to indulge this propensity. In his role as public relations man for the new order—for that, at most, is what he was—he distinguished himself less by the cogency of his arguments on its behalf than by their extravagance. His newspaper articles, his speeches and the full-length books were all rehearsals of Version One, with a vengeance. They were Sadat the actor who hid his real self in the self-deprecating, almost comical part he assumed as a foil to Nasser the hero, the ultra-loyalist who could only advance his own interests through another's favour, the humble servant who more than earned his master's scornful nickname of *Bikbashi Sah* ('Major Yes Yes'). ' "If he would occasionally vary his way of expressing agreement", Nasser quipped, "instead of forever saying *Sah* [quite right], that would be easier on my nerves." '[73]

There were, it is true, differences of opinion between the two men. In fact, the king had hardly sailed for exile before his successors were at loggerheads with one another over the nature of the regime that should replace him. Should it be a 'dictatorship' or a 'democracy'? That, according to Sadat, was the fundamental issue which set Nasser apart from his colleagues at the very first meeting of the newly formed Revolutionary Command Council. Nasser was alone in his insistence on democracy; the other seven were for dictatorship, and none, by his own admission, more ardently than Sadat himself. 'Each one of us took the floor', he recalled in a speech nineteen years later, 'and then he, God bless him, spoke last. . . . We all favoured dictatorship; we said there was absolutely no way to eradicate corruption and injustice in this country except through dictatorship. . . . The seven of us spoke as with one voice: dictatorship, and from tomorrow there should be a purge to cleanse the country with scaffolds in the public squares.'[74] It had been an almost bloodless coup. The more the pity, in Sadat's opinion, that there had been no 'massacres against the Palace, the feudalists, imperialism, the agents of foreign states, the *pashas* and the usurers [*samasir*]', that 'the streets and every inch of the country had not flowed with the blood of the revolution's enemies so that, having annihilated them by force of arms, its leaders could achieve its popular purposes.'[75] Twice they took a vote; twice it was one for democracy and seven for dictatorship. Nasser, who had only just been elected chairman of the Council, announced that he was resigning. 'Gathering up his papers he wished God's success on his comrades but warned them: "You must know that the road which begins in blood inevitably ends in blood and leads to the destruction of the country. . . . The parties at least showed some fear of the king. . . . So their dictatorship had its limits to some extent. But what about ours?" Now the king has gone, he said, "there would be no obstacle before us and we would be able to do whatever we liked." '[76]

In relating this episode, Sadat was not merely demonstrating that democracy was superior to dictatorship, he was demonstrating it on the unassailable ground that Nasser had said it was. Disagreement merely dramatized the inevitability of agreement. The disciples naturally erred, but happily the master was always there to set them right. Nineteen years later Sadat recalled their dispute and reconciliation as if it were being re-enacted before his eyes.

We never imagined that Gamal would leave us and go. . . . Dead silence prevailed for some time. Then we decided to start the discussion anew and for two hours we went round in a vicious circle. Why? Because he was the dynamo, the inspiring and moving power. . . . Suddenly, we ended the discussion and said that it was impossible that Gamal should leave us. . . . Thus, we returned to our true nature. . . . Gamal was our brother, our friend, our loved one. What was the solution, then, some asked? The solution, we said, was to ask Gamal to come back and take over the leadership at any price. At 3 a.m. two of us went to him and brought him from his house to sit at the head of the RCC table. Then we resumed our work as if nothing had happened. . . . I am relating this story in order to say that Gamal was not an ordinary person among us. . . . No, Gamal had a special position. Until then we had not understood the full extent of his abilities. In this battle, however, he returned . . . to his place among us at the head of the RCC. We felt we had achieved a great victory. This was not because Gamal had come back, but because we had conquered our own selves. One can imagine now what path the country would have followed if we had adopted the dictatorial way.[77]

In fact, they did adopt the dictatorial way, though without the bloodletting which—let us assume for polemical effect—Sadat himself had recommended. They did scrap the constitution and dissolve the political parties. This was necessary, Sadat explained, because, though the Free Officers were not communists like Mao Tse-Tung, they were bent on changing Egypt as radically as the Great Helmsman was changing China. 'The Egyptian masses must be masters of their own sacred right. No longer should the peasants be inveigled into electing as their representative the landowner who plundered their daily bread; no longer should the wretched of the earth, led by hirelings and imposters, demonstrate with shouts of "Thief, thief, but we want him all the same." ' Nasser and his companions were not 'rulers, they [were] revolutionaries, and the difference between rulers and revolutionaries is great.' So when they proffered their hand to the parties they 'asked them to revolutionize themselves as the Free Officers had done'. But the parties would have none of it.

And how, in any case, could that be expected of them, 'the *beys* and *pashas*, the feudalists, the reactionaries, the capitalists and the usurers' who 'voted to spend a million and a half pounds on repairing and embellishing the yacht on which the king was pleased to make his cruises while millions went without their loaf of bread', whose only ambition was to exploit the constitution, elections, civil liberties and the 'so-called free press' to 'return to the seats from which the revolution had removed them'?[78]

Dictatorship versus democracy was to remain a contentious issue, but, until Nasser died, the stand which Sadat took towards it was determined by one consideration only: his master, right or wrong. It did not matter what the system was, or claimed to be, so long as Nasser remained the uncontested head of it. Dictatorship with Nasser was incomparably superior to democracy without him.

This consideration underlay all Sadat did and said. He went, characteristically, to extremes. In the early years of the new order, as Nasser swept from triumph to intoxicating triumph, some praised and glorified him; but Sadat well-nigh deified him. 'Gamal, O Lord, is your magnificent creation, your conquering genius, your true servant, your reliant one, your inspired one, the bearer to his people and his nation of the message of righteousness, dignity and peace.' It was with this incantation, thrice-intoned, that Sadat closed his book *My Son, This Is Your Uncle Gamal.*[79] Elsewhere, in 192 pages of uninterrupted adulation, we learn that the object of it was, after all, sprung from human loins. 'Egypt, my son, is ruled by your uncle Gamal Abdul Nasser, who is an Arab Egyptian. He belongs to the Arab tribe of Beni Morr; he comes, he and his forefathers, of the soil of Egypt, and in his veins courses the hot blood of the Nile of Egypt. Gamal Abdul Nasser, whose name I gave you, my son, is my friend, my chief, whom I have loved and respected since we were junior officers in 1938.'[80] The 'Manqabad vow' of twenty years before had been richly rewarded. Ever since then, friendship had been 'the basic principle which your Uncle Gamal [had taken] as his slogan, because it conformed with his nature, and was the source of his ardour and creative power.' He was 'his own most severe and exacting critic, while, with others, he was the most forgiving and charitable of men'. He was 'always calm and knew what he wanted'. He was a deeply thoughtful man, and once he had resolved upon a course of action 'no power on earth could divert him from it'.[81]

There was, in short, no virtue in which Sadat did not find him super-abundantly endowed; it would be superfluous to enumerate them. Though mortal—if only just—Nasser was none the less the instrument of God's will. 'Your Uncle Gamal, my son, has fought a fierce fight, and is still fighting it, not just for Egypt, but for all humanity and the good, the right and the just that God ordained for it.'[82] 'And through him the Lord made us victorious upon many a field.'[83]

After consolidating his Revolution in the teeth of 'the pedlars of politics' at home, Nasser went on to score his famous foreign victories, each of which furnishes Sadat with the occasion for further rapturous commentary. In April and May 1955 Nasser emerged as the hero of the Bandung Conference, that great gathering in which the newly independent nations of Afro—Asia came together to debate their place in the world. 'Your Uncle Gamal, my son, managed to triumph in the battle of morals, and peoples numbering one billion five hundred million souls stood behind him, while his enemies, who sought to bring the world back to the law of the jungle, screamed in his face.'[84]

Bandung was followed in August by the famous Czech arms deal, which broke the West's monopoly in this field and deprived it of a key instrument of pressure on the most powerful Arab country. Egypt was able to procure, 'of its own free will', all the weapons it needed. There could be no such plain dealing with the United States. The price for American arms was the standard 'mutual security pact' whose blessings were already enjoyed by more than forty countries.

> They told us that by signing it we would not have to pay one millime. The Egyptian army would be flooded with free arms. The offer was wrapped up, American-style, in tinsel and enticing propaganda. On the surface it was amazingly innocent, but its real nature revealed itself to us line after line. . . . The Egyptian army would come under the supervision of an American military mission responsible for training, coordination, advice and assistance in the formulation of plans. . . . It was nothing but a new form of colonialism, harsher and more damaging than what we had suffered under Britain.[85]

Egypt had no choice but to turn to the East. It had become 'a matter of life and death. . . . Either we submitted to America and Britain and made peace with Israel on its terms and it was all over with Palestine and a million refugees, or we deprived ourselves of arms, Israel attacked and invaded us and the refugees would number 24 million from the Nile to the Euphrates.'[86]

Other forms of subjugation, too, Nasser resisted with all his might. For 'the people's prosperity' American capital would have been welcome. So inquiries were made. But

> ... the reply came from Washington in the form of a standard agreement just like the mutual security pact, all tinsel and enticement. . . . Twenty-three countries had signed it. . . . And now, after poverty and destitution, these countries are wallowing in a paradise of plenty. Just sign, so that you become the twenty-fourth. . . . But we soon discovered that in this agreement America exposed its true face. . . . The capital would enter the country, an innocent commercial operation, in the name of Mr So and So. Mr So and So loses no time in getting out and the innocent commercial capital becomes the property of American government and American policy, protected by the Sixth Fleet. . . . We rejected the agreement because, in essence, it was the worst form of imperialism the world had ever known. . . .[87]

The next great triumph was the nationalization of the Suez Canal Company, a brazen stroke of defiance which, for Sadat, was 'more splendid, more immortal' than the Czech arms deal because it was 'the end of one history and the beginning of another'.[88] It was Nasser's reply to the American and British withdrawal of financial assistance to build the Aswan High Dam. The dam was to be the pride of the Revolution, vital for Egypt's development, but the policy of the Western powers was 'to starve and impoverish the people of Egypt'. That, in turn, was part of a conspiracy to remove Nasser, who was deterring Arab states from joining Turkey, Iran and Pakistan in a Western-sponsored regional alliance. In 1955 Iraq did join, and the so-called Baghdad Pact was born. Nasser's implacable hostility prevented others such as King Hussein of Jordan from following suit. For an Egypt which had just thrown off the imperial yoke, wrote Sadat, the Baghdad Pact was intolerable; besides, it ignored the fact that the 'real enemy is Israel, which lies in the heart of the Arab world'.[89] 'But those who conceived this alliance made of Russia the only danger to the area. . . . It is obvious, of course, that, in addition to serving the aims of America it also—in the first instance—serves Israel; for the Arabs' attention is diverted to Russia—the imaginary foe—which lies thousands of miles from the region.'[90]

The real villain was Secretary of State John Foster Dulles. What else could one expect of a 'gambler and adventurer' from Texas, 'the home of cowboys who live off gambling and adventurism'?[91] The withdrawal of financial aid was announced with such 'extraordinary impudence that it was like telling the Egyptian people to get rid of Gamal Abdul Nasser and then America would open its coffers for building the High Dam, and undertake scores of other projects to boot.'[92] Dulles also wanted to 'prove to the world that Russia was not serious in its offer to finance the High Dam, and that there is no God but Dulles, possessor of dollars and a unique genius, king of gambling and adventure'.[93] But it did not work, and the 'three great conspirators flew into a rage'. On 29 October 1956, Israel invaded Sinai 'in the most vile, mean and despicable conspiracy the world has ever known'. Britain and France delivered their ultimatum calling on both sides to withdraw from the banks of the Canal. But Nasser confounded them by ordering his army to withdraw from Sinai; 'this decision, my son, will remain for ever as one of the great deeds which, in fulfilment of God's wishes, Gamal accomplished for our glory and honour.' At the same time, the Soviet Union, brandishing nuclear missiles, served its 'famous ultimatum' on Britain and France.

In this account, Sadat did pay fleeting tribute to President Eisenhower, who took a 'stand deserving thanks and esteem' while Dulles 'the adventurer' was undergoing an operation in hospital. But no sooner had the Secretary of State risen from his sickbed than he tried to 'achieve without war the goals that Britain and France had failed to achieve with their armies'.[94] He called his plot the Eisenhower Doctrine, and its object was to 'isolate' Egypt, which was held to be an accessory of 'international communism'.[95]

American policy in 1957 was just what it was in 1952, only worse, brazen where in the past it had affected a certain modesty. I believe, my son, that there are a number of reasons for this. First, the God of America is deaf, dumb and blind, for it is the Dollar. . . . Another is the domination of world Zionism over everything in America. That is no accident, for the God of Zionism is the same as the God of America. . . . It is the Dollar. America's goal, like Zionism's, is world domination. The American conscience is subservient to the Zionist conscience, which knows no justice, values or rights. Justice, for America and Zionism, is every crime that America commits, and all the world's virtue, if it brings America and Zionism no gain or profit, is but vice. For Israel is America's foster-child, its handiwork, the flesh of its flesh. . . . No matter, to America, that this state arose on plundered land, usurped rights, corpses, skulls and massacres which make humanity blush with shame.[96]

In the event, Dulles fared no better than Eden. He did not 'isolate' Nasser; on the contrary, he furnished Arabism—in the person of Nasser—with the champion it needed; he gave the hero his defiant role. 'Glory and national dignity', recorded Sadat, 'were restored to an ancient people . . . to a region inhabited by a nation the colonialists called "Arabs" with disdain and disgust. . . . Overnight the word "Arab" acquired a deep and awe-inspiring significance which gave the nation and its friends pride and struck fear into the mighty, the pirates, the imperialists.'[97] Egypt and Syria became the United Arab Republic in the first inspiring step towards fulfilment of a long-cherished dream.

It was the apogee of Nasserism. Although this great movement of Arab history owed its success to the man who gave it its name, it was sustained and fortified by 'the hand of honour' proferred at every battle waged along its triumphant way. 'Do you know this hand?' inquires Sadat of his infant son. 'It is the hand of the friendly Soviet people. Blessed, O Lord, be this clean and sincere hand; blessed, O Lord, be this noble friendship, and the Soviet people's love for Gamal. . . .'[98]

A letter to Hitler

If, in the shadow of the Giant, Sadat had any independence of mind, any controversial opinions of his own, it was only in the unguarded moment, in a context falling outside his relationship with Nasser, the new regime or his place in it that he exhibited them. And, being a man of such assiduous, self-effacing sycophancy, that did not happen very often.

Sometimes, however, the price of fame is the searching light it casts on earlier obscurity, the stain which some perhaps forgotten imprudence, discovered and diligently disseminated by those who wish to harm him, leaves upon the great man's name. Zionist propagandists are forever on the look-out for what, in the court of Western public opinion, can be presented as evidence of anti-Semitic prejudice. An imprudence which, from the moment he became President, they did not allow Sadat to forget, was indeed trivial, but undeniably significant for the insight it furnishes into the quality of his mind. Given the abhorrence in which Hitler is held by civilized societies, for the propagandists, dissenting views from the Arab world inevitably provide the most telling proof of the thoroughly *un*civilized instincts that inspire its relentless desire to 'destroy' the Jewish state. Sadat was no longer the naïve, hero-worshipping schoolboy when he wrote his celebrated letter to the dead Hitler, he was a mature man of thirty-five, and—a member of the ruling Revolutionary Command Council—he was hardly obscure either.

In September 1953 a news agency reported that, according to one of his former associates, Hitler was still alive; he had escaped, incognito, to Brazil. The Cairo weekly *al-Mussawar* took the opportunity to ask a number of public figures what, supposing the news were true, they would say in a letter to the resurrected Führer. Of the seven asked, five were uncomplimentary; the well-known journalist Ihsan Abdul Koddous advised him 'to go back to his hiding-place, for there is no room in the free world for a dictator; do you remember the millions you killed, do you remember the gas chambers?' But it seems that the most prominent of the seven had shed none of his adolescent enthusiasm:

I congratulate you with all my heart [Sadat exulted], because, though you appear to have been defeated, you were the real victor, you were able to sow dissension between Churchill, the 'old man', and his allies on the one hand and their ally, the devil, on the other. Germany is victorious because it became necessary for the world balance [of power] that Germany be created anew, whatever East and West might think. There will be no peace until Germany is restored to what it was, and this is what West and East will bring about in spite of themselves. . . . So much for the present and the future. As for the past, I think you made some mistakes, such as opening too many fronts or Ribbentrop's shortsightedness in the face of Britain's 'old-man' diplomacy. But you are forgiven on account of your faith in your country and people. That you have become immortal in Germany is reason enough for pride. And we should not be surprised to see you again in Germany, or a new Hitler in your place. Anwar Sadat.[99]

A lamb among wolves

'Where did I stand in all this? How much part did I take in all these events and how did I view them?'[100] Answering that question in Version Two, Sadat furnishes the now familiar corrective. Ostensibly, he did play a part—and even in activities that were obnoxious to him. In 1962, for example, Nasser appointed him Secretary General of a 200-member Constituent Assembly. Its outward purpose was to draft a 'national charter', its real one to 'keep the people busy trying to understand [the charter] and fathom its ideological implications'. In other words, it was just a 'trick' creating the impression that Nasser took an interest in the problems of the ordinary man and wished to solve them.[101] Though Sadat might appear to have lent himself to such tricks, in spirit, in his real self he had long since set himself apart.

As we have seen, Sadat has barely crossed the threshold of *In Search of Identity* when, repudiating his account of the 'Manqabad vow' given in Version One, he claims that it was he who, way back in 1939, set up the Free Officers Organization and goes on to imply that, taking advantage of his imprisonment in 1942, Nasser usurped his leadership role.[102] For it was while he was in gaol that Sadat's friend Abdul Mun'im Abdul Raouf—the same Abdul Raouf who, according to Version One, sold out to the Moslem Brothers and their mystique of violence—contacted Nasser upon his return from the Sudan 'with a view to recruiting him in the Free Officers Organization on account of his outstanding record'. 'This was a rule that I had laid down, that only officers of outstanding performance in the armed forces should join our organization. . . . Nasser immediately accepted. It wasn't difficult for him afterwards to remove Abdul Raouf and take over command of the organization.'[103]

If, having taken Sadat's rightful place, Nasser subsequently re-admitted him to the inner circle of the Free Officers, it was not on account of those two virtues, friendship and loyalty, which so impressed the author of *Révolte sur le Nil* and *My Son, This Is Your Uncle Gamal*. He now reveals that Nasser was virtually incapable of either. He wonders why, in 1951, Nasser decided to bring him into the Free Officers Constituent Council. His 'decision . . . may appear to indicate a sense of loyalty on his part for, although I originally created the Free Officers Organization, I stayed away from it for eight years.' 'However,' he goes on, 'Nasser was not the kind of man to be motivated by such loyalty to others. . . . It wasn't easy for Nasser to have anybody for his friend, in the full sense of the term, because of his tendency to be wary, suspicious, extremely bitter and highly strung.'[104] So why *did* Nasser bring him into the Council? 'Out of his sharpness of mind. . . . He gathered I was a man of principles and lofty values. It wasn't difficult for Nasser to realize . . . that my inclusion in the Constituent Council would make me permanently loyal thereafter to the man who thus appeared to be loyal to me.'[105]

Nasser was no democrat either. He surrounded himself with yes-men, who 'took no action beyond the implementation of orders', men whose only interest was 'magnifying Nasser's self-image in his own eyes and so maintaining their own posts and power'.[106] It now appears that the first great controversy—'dictatorship' versus 'democracy'—was really a power struggle the like of which Sadat, feeling himself 'far above their petty conflicts', would have hardly imagined possible had he not witnessed it with his own eyes. When Nasser pressed the case for democracy, Sadat at first wondered whether he had gone mad. For even in Version Two, where he is addressing a presumably admiring West, he concedes that he was 'perhaps the most ardent in defending dictatorship, stemming from my eagerness to serve Egypt's interests—for what may be achieved "democratically" in a year can be accomplished "dictatorially" in a day. It never occurred to me at the time that the whole exercise was a trial of strength, that Nasser simply wanted to prove to everybody at the beginning of his term of office as Chairman of the Council that he could impose a decision.' Nasser got his way by bluster and browbeating. Upon the seven-to-one vote against democracy, 'he stood up and shouted: "I cannot accept this decision . . . I hereby resign all my posts." He went home. At dawn, informed that the seven had relented, he came back. He had won, by our consent and *authorization*.' (Sadat's italics.)[107]

Yet if there is one central charge that Sadat was resolute in pressing against Nasser's regime, it is precisely the dictatorship which he did install. This was the poison which spread through the whole body politic. It is without explanation or embarrassment that Sadat makes his own swift transition from advocacy to execration of dictatorship. Suddenly, democracy is a blessing where once it was an abomination. Suddenly we learn that 'one-man rule is fraught with dangers', and 'because no one man can really know everything, some of his assistants will concentrate power in their hands and, so to speak, run amok — creating power blocs, just as had happened in Nasser's case.' What the Revolution did, through dictatorship, was to build a

mountain of hatred — the spirit of hatred which emanated in every direction and at every level. . . . Instances were rife of men working for the regime who spied on their own kind just like the Fascist regimes. Can anyone sink lower than that? . . . The gravest injustice done to the Egyptian people was the 'cultivation of fear', that is, rather than trying to build up the inner man we did all we could to make him feel frightened. . . . People thus turned into dummies. They became puppets in the hands of the rulers, who did what they liked with them. . . . Nothing irritated Nasser more than a discussion of democracy and a reference to his dictatorial rule.

The yearning for freedom was 'something that he never understood to the day of his death'.[108]

If, even in Version Two, Sadat discerned an occasional redeeming feature in Nasser, he found none in those men of roughly equivalent status to his own who formed the President's immediate entourage. Gone were the halcyon days of pure and youthful comradeship, the spirit of Manqabad, when he, Sadat, was tutoring, guiding and organizing his disciples for the great enterprise that lay ahead. All that had vanished by the time he was re-united with them in the early 1950s. Now they were just 'the pack'; the Revolutionary Command Council was riven by hatred, jealousy, egoism, lust for power; its members sought to divide the country into 'spheres of influence', for their own benefit and that of their friends, relatives and hangers-on. Marshal Amer, Nasser's closest companion, was the worst offender, the most outrageous in his patronage. Sadat did his best 'to merge into the "pack", subordinating [his] individual entity to that of the team', but it was to no avail. 'Why', he asked, 'did they attack and ridicule me, as though I was an outsider who wanted to usurp their rights or a stranger who spoke a different language?' It particularly shocked him that Nasser, not trusting him either, joined in these attacks. On one occasion, he recalls, Nasser grew 'livid with rage . . . and burst into an attack as though I was against him rather than being on his side. His words were strangely bitter and the vituperation poured forth in all directions, almost if a volcano had erupted in his chest.'[109] At first, he could not understand why he came in for such abuse. Only later did he realize that since Anwar Sadat, the 'hero' of the Amin Osman case, was the only revolutionary leader known to the public, the others were jealous of his 'long history of struggle'.[110]

As for the 'colossal achievements' of Nasser's early years, even they had a facile, fortuitous character which, however splendid they seemed at the time, owed little to the profound transformation of an existing social order which is the purpose of revolutions. Easy enough to see that in retrospect, but Sadat saw it at the time. Of the exploit which, above all others, was to turn Nasser into one of the historic figures of the twentieth century—the nationalization of the Suez Canal—Sadat recounts that, after listening to him harangue an adoring populace, he took him aside and told him: 'Listen, Gamal . . . if you had consulted me, I would have told you to be more careful. This step means war, and we're not ready for it. The weapons we have, we've only just received from the Soviet Union.' Suez, in fact, taught Sadat that 'it was always futile to depend on the Soviet Union'. For the famous ultimatum to Britain and France 'was nothing in effect but an exercise in muscle-flexing and an attempt to appear as though the Soviet Union had saved the situation. This was not, of course, the case. It was Eisenhower who did so. Both Britain and France obeyed his orders and withdrew their forces by 23 December. Israel followed suit.' Nasser, unlike Sadat himself, failed to learn the obvious lesson that 'Israel's strategy is based on creating a rift between the United States and Egypt.' Indeed, he did exactly the opposite. He attributed the Anglo–French fiasco to the spurious Soviet warning. 'This was absurd, because it was the US attitude . . . that turned our defeat into victory.' Nasser was deluded by the 'fable which came to be associated with his name both in Egypt and the Arab world—that he was a hero who had defeated the armies of two great empires, the British and the French. . . . He could never see that he had in fact been militarily defeated.'[111]

Of course, according to this telling of the tale, all the other triumphs which followed Suez—the thwarting of the Eisenhower Doctrine, the Syrian–Egyptian union, the advent of socialism—were as much a sham as it was. Needless to say, as we have seen, what Version Two omits to mention is that not only did Sadat extol these victories as they happened—insofar as he had an executive role he participated in achieving them.

A picnic on the Red Sea

The one enterprise which was really to debilitate the Egyptian Revolution—not merely in itself but, more seriously perhaps, in its ultimate, unforeseeable side-effects—was the military intervention in the Yemen. And if there was any one enterprise in which Nasser did grant Sadat an influential, executive role it was this one.

In recent times the land once known as Arabia Felix only deserved that title if stability secured at the price of medieval theocracy and implacable opposition to almost all forms of progress could be said to confer it. Revolution in the Yemen was therefore long overdue and when, upon the death of the wily old despot, Imam Ahmad, it finally came in September 1962, Nasser was naturally among the first to welcome it. And when it became clear, as it quickly did, that the republicans were going to have a hard time imposing their new order, Nasser, the pan-Arab champion smarting from setbacks elsewhere, naturally had an interest in lending them a helping hand. But few Egyptians knew anything about that wild, exotic land, and when Nasser dispatched Sadat on a fact-finding mission he did so less because his emissary had any special qualifications for the task than because he boasted one of those fortuitous, family relationships which tend to play such a disproportionate and damaging role in Arab politics: one Abdul Rahman Beidani was married to the sister of his wife Jihan. It was through Beidani and Sadat that Nasser had foreknowledge of, and probably an active part in, the military *putsch* in Yemen led by Brigadier Abdullah Sallal.

Born in Cairo of an Egyptian mother and an Uzbek father, Beidani was only a 'Yemeni' through his stepfather. He was a latecomer to the ranks of the republican opposition and, judging by his earlier career, his motives for joining it were strictly opportunistic. Until he quarrelled with him, he had been Imam Ahmad's business agent in West Germany. It says little for Nasser's judgement that, on the strength of the Beidani connection, he should have appointed Sadat as his special adviser on Yemeni affairs. But he did, and together with Field Marshal Amer, the Egyptian commander in chief, Sadat became the most regular high-level visitor to the country. It was he who, in November 1962, signed a mutual defence pact with the infant republic. Beidani was installed as its first Prime Minister, with the other pro-Egyptian loyalist, Brigadier Sallal, as President. It must have been Sadat and Amer together—though in Version Two Sadat claims that it was just himself—who persuaded Nasser to back the republicans to the hilt.[112] Sadat told the National Assembly that it would be 'a picnic on the Red Sea'.[113] Pitted against the Egyptians and their republican allies were the royalists, led by Imam

Ahmad's heir, Muhammad al-Badr, whose backers were Saudi Arabia, Jordan and Western-supported conservative regimes of the Arab world. During five years of civil war, the Yemen was to be the arena for a wider ideological conflict. For Sadat, unrepentant even in Version Two, the war was a good opportunity to train the Egyptian army in new techniques. Furthermore, since King Saud had financed the break-up of the Syrian–Egyptian union, and led a propaganda campaign against Egypt, the war was also a good opportunity 'to teach [him] a lesson'. The Egyptian intervention 'precipitated his removal from power and the take-over of King Faisal—a remarkable gain not only for Saudi Arabia, but for the entire Arab world'.[114]

Opportunity though it was, Sadat none the less concluded that 'the Yemen war was a military failure for Egypt', for it 'had a regular army fighting an enemy well versed in guerrilla warfare'. Nasser clearly had the deepest misgivings from the outset. The Yemen furnished a springboard for his regional ambitions, but it had all the makings of a dangerous trap as well. When the republicans staged their coup, he planned to lend them moral and symbolic support, or, at most, a few arms, aircraft, and advisers. He understood the strain which a deepening military commitment would impose on his ambitious programmes of industrialization and development at home. He also understood that conflict with Saudi Arabia would antagonize the United States; and that he did not want because, though it preferred unreservedly pro-Western regimes, the United States still looked upon Nasser as an anti-communist influence in the Middle East and plied him with financial and other assistance in competition with the rival superpower.[115]

Although, on Sadat and Amer's advice, Nasser lost little time in sending troops to the Yemen—there were 15,000 to 20,000 of them within two or three months—he was simultaneously looking for a diplomatic settlement. In December the United States recognized the Yemeni Republic. It did so against the wishes of its most important Arab ally, Saudi Arabia, and Britain, which saw in its old enemy, Nasser, a threat to its colonial rule in South Arabia (now South Yemen).

But the American disengagement plan foundered and, after another on-the-spot investigation by Sadat and Amer, more troops were dispatched to the support of the embattled republicans. All the while, however, Nasser was persevering in his diplomatic efforts and, in March 1963, assisted by the United States, he reached another disengagement agreement with the Saudis. In June the United Nations Security Council agreed to send observers to supervise its implementation. But in the end nothing came of it and a year later the observers were withdrawn. A dismal cycle set in. Nasser would take some fresh diplomatic initiative, always involving greater concessions than before, only to revert, when it failed, to the ever more costly military alternative. Twice he reached agreement with his great Arab adversary, King Faisal, Saud's successor. In September 1964 the deal was struck discreetly in the corridors of a plenary Arab summit conference; in August 1965 it required a spectacular rendezvous, exclusively devoted to the Yemen, on Faisal's home ground in the Red Sea port of Jeddah. Twice the agreement came unstuck when those on the ground attempted to apply the broad principles which their respective champions had agreed upon at the summit. And so, by 1966, Nasser had committed 70,000 troops to a war which has been aptly described as Egypt's Vietnam; he had gone so far in antagonizing the people whose cause he had espoused, that, detaining the authentic republican leadership in Cairo, he governed through unrepresentative puppets. Not only had he forfeited America's good will, he was staking his prestige on a dangerous power struggle against most of the American-supported regimes in the region.

In Version Two, Sadat has no doubt who was to blame. It was Field Marshal Amer. For he, 'as usual', had taken 'the wrong actions throughout', and turned the Yemen war into an opportunity for personal gain and the expansion of his influence. Sadat produces no evidence for these charges, though there was certainly some truth in them. For it was common knowledge that Amer treated the army as his private preserve and that, all-too-affable, easy-going commander that he was, he presided over a system of nepotism and patronage which was inimical to military discipline and efficiency. The Yemen war accelerated a process that was already well advanced. Some aspects of the fighting—open skies for the air force and police-type duties for the army—deepened the complacency of the high command. There were extraordinary field promotions for officers who lacked the necessary training and qualifications. Most pernicious of all, however, were the social consequences of corruption in high places; fortunes were made from a rampant black market in the luxury goods which officers sent home customs-free at government expense. Special treatment for Yemen veterans, in housing and other services, became a national scandal.[116]

If Amer was to blame for all this, why, one might ask, did Sadat not tell Nasser so at the time? He certainly knew what was going on, for, in the first stages of the war at least, he and Amer worked in virtual harness as Nasser's chief executives in the Yemen. Actually, there appears to have been little doubt in Nasser's mind as to which of his henchmen was the main culprit. Amer was chiefly responsible for military affairs, but Sadat proved no less inept on the political side which was his particular domain. In a jocular aside at the Jeddah summit, Nasser is reported to have told King Faisal: 'The man who got us into this whole mess is sitting right there beside you.' He pointed to Sadat. 'Settle your scores with him.' 'Anwar is to blame,' he had told the king at their previous meeting, 'he led me to believe that we could finish off Imam Badr's hordes in less than two weeks.'[117]

It all seems to have sprung from the Beidani connection. Sadat's half-Egyptian relative misled everyone about the real state of affairs in a country he could barely call his own.[118] He did not last long as Prime Minister. By February 1963 he was back in his Cairo exile. A few months after that he turned up in Aden, apparently on business, and from that British colonial outpost castigated the republican rulers as 'sectarian fanatics'. In reply, they called him an 'impostor' and 'imperialist hireling' whose disreputable past had been exposed by documents found in the 'palaces of deposed tyrants'. Sadat, in due course dismissed as Nasser's special adviser on the Yemen, also receded into the background from which chance had projected him.

The future President's assessment, many years later, of the higher political benefits of Egyptian intervention had little to commend it. Certainly the replacement of the dissolute, decrepit Saud by the stern, sagacious Faisal was a gain for Saudi Arabia and the Arabs, but it can hardly be said that the Yemeni war was the cause of it, for it was coming sooner or later anyway. Nor can it be said to have helped Nasser in the Yemen either. Quite the reverse. Weak and vacillating, Saud had considered acquiescing in the *fait accompli* and recognizing the new-born republic from the outset. That was also a course favoured by some younger, liberal princes, and a month after the coup four of them—led by Saud's half-brother Talal—defected to Egypt, where they declared their allegiance to Nasser and the pan-Arab Revolution. But upon his accession, Faisal produced a stiffening of the Saudi resolve and, sometimes in defiance of American advice, he held unswervingly to the original aim he had

more; he wanted a thoroughgoing reform of the whole system whose weakness the defeat had so disastrously exposed. That, at least, was the project which he laid before the Higher Executive Committee of the Arab Socialist Union (ASU), Nasser's one-party political monolith, at its first meeting since the war. After Amer's disgrace, the Committee's membership had been reduced to six. To his five colleagues Nasser proposed a 'new system', an open one with a real opposition party which would do away with the present 'dictatorship of a group of individuals'. It is not clear whether he really meant it, or whether he thought it was practicable, but what is clear is that while all five opposed his proposal, none did so with such vehemence as Sadat. With the enemy on the Suez Canal, he argued, not to mention 'the black picture left by the deviant behaviour of Abdul Hakim Amer', there could be no question of an 'opening', of the formation of a second political party, for 'it would only be an opening for the dogs yapping after power! . . . The new party would resort to demagogy. Its leader would raise slogans like: let's hand over Yemen to the enemy. . . . In such circumstances, tearing the country apart with an opposition would be intolerable, for our people are good and loyal and have confidence in this man'—and, in high excitement, he pointed to Nasser—'and all of us are confident that Abdul Nasser is the leader who will bring us safely to shore.'[123]

Nasser withdrew his forces from the Yemen before the end of the year. But the republic did not fall to its enemies. It rid itself of its pro-Egyptian puppets and, in the last, decisive encounter of the civil war it held off a seventy-day royalist siege of the capital, Sana'a. The Yemeni settlement was part of a larger bargain which, from a position of weakness, Nasser struck with King Faisal and the conservative, oil-rich Arab regimes; he called off his pan-Arab 'revolutionary' offensive in return for regular subsidies to Egypt and other 'front-line' states. At the same time, paradoxically, he came to rely more and more heavily on the Soviet Union, which re-equipped and re-trained his shattered armed forces and eventually, supplying pilots, missile crews and some 20,000 'experts' of one kind or another, took a direct part in the defence of the Delta. Dr Kissinger, President Nixon's National Security Adviser, reacted menacingly. The Eastern Mediterranean was in danger of becoming 'a Soviet lake', he told journalists in a background briefing; the Russians' military presence should be 'expelled'.[124] As for the 'system', it remained essentially unchanged.

One reason why Nasser had tried to change it was because he

doubted whether he had more than ten years to live.[125] He was a sick man. In the event he only had three years. The shock of the defeat, and the struggle to overcome it, undoubtedly hastened his end. During that period Sadat was in the news from time to time on assignments involving more show than substance. The most original —and certainly the most interesting in the light of his subsequent career—was his virtuoso performance as the head of the Egyptian delegation to the Islamic Summit Conference in Rabat in September 1969. In the course of what Cairo Radio called a 'violent argument' with the Shah of Iran, a pillar of the pro-American, traditionalist camp, Sadat confounded his opponent with quotations from the Persian poets. 'And no sooner had Mr Sadat finished than the hall rang with applause; the Shah and all the members of his delegation were obliged to join in this thunderous ovation, so as to overcome the embarrassment in which the Shah had plunged them.'[126]

On 21 December 1969 another summit conference—an Arab one —convened in Rabat. The day before, Sadat was in the news again, though no one paid much attention at the time. He was appointed Vice President, a post which had been suppressed since early 1968. To what, other than his total loyalty, Sadat owed this sudden elevation is far from clear. But it was almost certainly a tactical move of the moment rather than the anointing of an heir-apparent. A news agency speculated that Sadat would take over much of the administrative burden of government, allowing Nasser to concentrate on 'top political and military policy matters'.[127] In retrospect Sadat, not surprisingly, attached far profounder significance to the appointment than anyone did at the time.

One of the events of that period [he writes in *In Search of Identity*] had far-reaching effects. One day—on December 19, to be precise—in a good mood and a moment of inspiration, Nasser turned to me and said: 'I am leaving for Morocco, Anwar, in two days' time, to attend the Arab Summit Conference. As you can see, intrigues are being perpetually hatched against me. It is quite likely that they will "get" me in one of these, and I don't want the country to be at a loss after me—I don't want to leave behind a vacuum. I have therefore decided to appoint a Vice President. You will be sworn in before I leave.' I was aware that Soviet agents had started their intrigues when one Soviet physician [Shazurov] visited Egypt, saw Nasser, and no doubt intimated to certain people that the heart attack Nasser had had was serious and that

he hadn't long to live. I thought over what Nasser had said care-
fully, then answered: 'Gamal, is this your considered opinion?
Gamal! I don't want to be Vice President. I shall carry on, and
work side by side with you. If I must have a title, "Presidential
Adviser" will be quite adequate!' 'Oh, no!' he said. 'You must
call tomorrow to be sworn in.' The next day I called on him,
accompanied by Hussein al-Shafei, to take him to the airport as
we always did. At home, and in the presence of al-Shafei, he asked
me to be sworn in. I agreed. When we were at the airport to see him
off, Nasser announced the news to everybody.[128]

Sadat's new eminence brought him few extra duties but even these
he mismanaged, in Nasser's eyes. Indeed, after more than thirty
years of devoted service, he fell into serious disfavour. He made two
mistakes.

The first was political. On 20 June 1970 Egypt received the text of
the peace plan put forward by Secretary of State William Rogers.
It was the first such independent American initiative since the June
1967 war. Shortly afterwards Nasser went to Moscow for medical
treatment, and for consultations in the light of which he would
decide whether to accept or reject the initiative. He decided to accept
it, knowing full well that, after three years of steadily growing tension
along Israel's frontiers, the 'war of attrition' across the Suez Canal,
and the spectacular rise of the Palestinian resistance movement, to
do so would generate controversy and consternation throughout the
Arab world, all the greater for the three-month ceasefire which the
Americans had wrung from him. Nasser's official reason was in line
with standard dogma that every chance of achieving a peaceful
solution should be explored, however slight it might be. His real one,
according to various accounts, was to give his soldiers a breathing
space in which to prepare for the military solution. A plan for cross-
ing the Suez Canal — code-named Granite I — was on the drawing-
board. In his opinion, the Rogers initiative had no more than a
one-half per cent chance of success. But it was vital to build up
Egypt's anti-aircraft defences, complete the emergency training of
Egyptian missile crews and then — in violation of the ceasefire terms —
to push forward the missile 'wall' as close as possible to the Canal. To
persist in the war of attrition while Israel enjoyed complete aerial
supremacy was to bleed to death.[129] But while Nasser was away
Sadat called a meeting of the ASU Higher Executive Committee
and recommended that the Rogers initiative be rejected. Presumably,

he had wrongly guessed his master's mind. Nasser's Arab adversaries acclaimed Sadat as a patriotic opponent of his 'sell-out'.

Sadat's other mistake was personal. Not content with the Nile-side villa they already possessed, Sadat and his wife Jihan hankered after the splendid residence adjoining it. It belonged to a General Ibrahim Mogi. During Nasser's eighteen-day absence Sadat offered him a price for it which he rejected. So Sadat served him with a 'requisition' order. Upon his return Nasser promptly cancelled the order and sent Sadat on 'extended leave'. (One authority maintains, however, that the villa scandal was a frame-up.[130]) The affair was the talk of the town, and people in the know were saying that it had sealed Sadat's fate as Vice President. Nasser had decided to 'accept his resignation'.

Nasser's last two months were among the most hectic of his life. He had to contend with the negotiations set in train by the Rogers initiative, the race to set up the missile sites, the Black September civil war in Jordan and, finally, the terrible strain of the emergency Arab summit conference in Cairo. It is perhaps not surprising that, if he thought about the replacement of his Vice President at all, he decided that such a minor problem could wait till these far graver ones, tearing the Arab world asunder, were brought under control.

But at six o'clock in the afternoon of 28 September 1970 Sadat was asked to go to Nasser's home 'for a very important reason'.

I changed quickly and went to Manshiat al-Bakri. I was immediately shown into Nasser's bedroom. He was lying in bed surrounded by doctors. They told me he had died an hour before. I lifted the bed-cover to see his face—it looked very much alive, as though he were simply fast asleep. I put my cheek against his but did not feel the chill of death. I turned to the doctors and said: 'It's not true. . . . What you're saying is wrong. . . . It can't be right!' They said they had done everything possible, and even used an electric cardiac restorer, to no avail. 'But try again. . . . Surely you can try again,' I said, at which they burst into tears. It was explained to me that they had been working very hard for two hours, but the will of God could not be reversed. I ordered that the body be taken to the al-Qubbah Palace. . . . Nasser's death was a tragedy that shook the Arab world.[131]

When, in the midst of Nasser's amazing, tumultuous funeral, Sadat 'suddenly collapsed',[132] perhaps it was something more than the nervous excitement of the occasion which caused his breakdown. For he was free, at last, to emulate Zahran, the *fellah*-hero of his youth, free to dismantle and bury the idol who, for eighteen years, he had so assiduously helped to build up.

3

No Voice Louder than the Battle

Sadat renews the ceasefire

No sooner had Sadat, in his capacity as Vice President, announced Nasser's death than another announcement followed: as Vice President, he would step into his shoes. There were grave doubts whether that was what Nasser would have wanted, and rumours that, before he died, he had tried to intimate that it was not. But in the absence of a clear last will and testament the casual promotion of a year before took on a momentous posthumous significance, conferring upon Sadat that precious air of legitimacy which competing 'centres of power', as rival factions were known, were all too ready to acknowledge. All that the disciples had to guide them was a provisional constitution, and that was punctiliously observed.

A joint meeting of the Cabinet and the Higher Executive Committee of the ASU had appointed him provisional President until the installing of a permanent one. A week later the Higher Executive Committee nominated him for the post. The nomination was unanimously approved by parliament. On 15 October the people gave their verdict in a plebiscite in which, according to the official count, 7,187,653 out of the 8,420,768 registered electors cast a vote—6,432,587 of them in favour of Sadat and 711,252 against. In his acceptance speech the new President expressed his pride in the result, not because such a handsome majority—90·04 per cent—had said yes but because as many as 9·96 per cent had said no. These, he humbly conceded, were not objecting to the July Revolution, they were expressing 'their reservations with regard to the presidential candidate himself'. 'I do not regard this as a rejection', he said, 'but as

104

a deferred judgment.'[1] The official count was probably honest enough. It was the last time during Sadat's presidency, notable for the frequency of its referendums and popular consultations of various kinds, that he was to score a democratic triumph of anything less than 99·9 per cent.

In reality, the people were not voting for Sadat. They were voting for continuity, or, as the slogan had it, 'for completing the path' his predecessor had begun, and at the end of which lay the undefined, but 'inevitable' victory. They had little choice. When a great man dies, and no obvious *primus inter pares* can be found to take his place, continuity is the watchword to which all cling. By way of compromise they are likely to select a new leader who is as weak and malleable as his predecessor was strong and masterful. The most suitable candidate might even be the one who, by the criterion of intrinsic merit, is the least suitable, the one who, until his sudden elevation, not only lacked a mind or a will of his own, but, to keep in favour, outdid everyone else in the extravagance of his servility. Such a one was Anwar Sadat.

Not, of course, that he was emerging from total obscurity. On the contrary, he was very well known to the Egyptian people though generally not, as we have seen, in any role that had brought him real responsibility. It would have been more flattering for Sadat if he really had come out of the shadows for, in spite of all his exposure, this symbol of continuity was indeed so unprepossessing that, though they voted for him, the people could not hide their disbelief in his leadership, and expressed it, characteristically, in a spate of humorous anecdotes. Shortly after Nasser's death—went one—a Cairo taxi driver took his country cousin on his first tour of the city. Stopping at a café in a populous quarter the cousin saw a big picture of the 'immortal leader' shaking hands with his successor. 'Ah,' he sighed, 'our beloved Nasser, our beloved Abu Khalid. God rest his soul. But who is that with him?' Not himself recognizing Sadat, but eager to demonstrate his sophistication, the taxi driver replied, with assurance, 'Oh, that's the owner of the café.'[2]

At first Sadat appeared either to be genuinely stunned—as well he might be—at his fortuitous pitchforking into such exalted office, or to be acting out that modest, unassuming role which would reassure those whose support, at this stage, he could not do without. It was probably a mixture of both. 'You have invested me', he told the people, 'with an honour which, God knows, has never crossed my mind throughout my life; nor have I striven for it.' He pledged to uphold the 'sublime ideal' which Nasser had bequeathed.[3] His first appointment was to name Ali Sabri as one of his two vice presidents.

In the wake of the 1967 defeat and the disgrace of the army, Sabri had been entrusted with the task of reconstructing the ASU, turning it, within Egypt's one-party system, into the main power base of the regime, the instrument through which the people were consulted and their support mobilized. At least, that is what he was supposed to have done; in fact he had made of it an empire, and a powerful one, in his own image. Nasserism was an amorphous doctrine, as diverse in those who professed it as it had been haphazard in its genesis. But under Ali Sabri and his henchmen the ASU embodied that interpretation of the doctrine, broadly speaking left-wing, radical, pro-Soviet, which had been gaining ground in Nasser's last years. 'Deepening the Revolution' was their principal slogan. Their 'right-wing' opponents could claim, with equal textual authority, that the counter-slogan, 'the open society', represented the true spirit of Nasserism. But they were in the wilderness. On Nasser's death, three Free Officers submitted a memorandum calling for the establishment of a collective rule to include all those companions of the 'immortal leader' who, like themselves, had left high office over the years. The rejoinder they earned, duly published in *al-Ahram*, must have been the one they expected: those whom Nasser had put aside must remain aside. It was Nasser, said *al-Ahram*, who had 'given Sadat his vote'.[4]

The elevation of Ali Sabri was reassurance that Sadat intended to preserve the institutions exactly as he found them; for the time being he was not prepared to say what he personally thought Nasserism should or should not be. Besides, the ASU, through its Central Committee, had already said it for him. It had said that the ASU, together with the National Assembly, was not only the sole expression of the popular will; it should now have a 'greater responsibility' than before. Preserving the institutions naturally meant preserving the policies and, chief among these—as the Central Committee also hastened to inform Sadat—was 'the struggle to liberate Arab land'. 'The battle', it said, 'has priority over everything else . . . everything should be sacrificed for the sake of victory.'

President Sadat's first major decision with regard to the 'battle' concerned the ceasefire which was due to expire on 7 November. He decided to renew it for a further three months. The murmurs of disapproval which greeted his decision were stilled by the militant words which accompanied it. 'Only in one case', Sadat assured the armed forces on 30 November, would it be renewed again, 'only if there is a definite timetable for Israeli withdrawal.'[5] Two months passed and he was still making that point as insistently as ever. At a rally in the Delta town of Tanta he pledged that 'there will be no compromise and that unless a timetable is drawn up for Israeli withdrawal we shall not renew the ceasefire.' 'Are you *really* fed up,' he asked his audience, 'are you *really* tired of fighting?'[6] The crowd roared back: 'We shall fight, we shall fight, Sadat. Lead us to liberation.'

Two days later the United Nations mediator, Gunnar Jarring, was in Israel. But in the joint statement he managed to elicit there was no hint of such a timetable, only the traditional, obstructionist formulation that withdrawal, insofar as there was one, should be to 'secure and agree borders . . . specified in the peace treaty'. As the critical day, 5 February 1971, approached, a resumption of hostilities seemed almost inevitable. In response to Anglo-American representations, the Egyptian Foreign Minister, Muhammad Riad, announced that hostilities would be staved off only if Jarring made material progress. On 3 February *al-Ahram* reported that 'according to all the indications, Jarring's mission had yielded no results'. Cairo Radio added, for good measure, that the United States was 'pushing the situation to the point of no return as far as the chances for Middle East peace and an inevitable Arab–American showdown are concerned'.

On 4 February President Sadat addressed the National Assembly. He built up suspense with a review of events since the 1967 war. He lavished praise on the Soviet Union, Egypt's partner in the relationship which was 'a model and example of international brotherhood and unity of forces struggling against imperialism, terrorism and aggression'. Turning to the rival superpower, he asked: 'What does the United States want?' He had put this question to President Nixon himself in a written message, but had not had a reply. The American attitude was the same as ever—'total support for Israel'. Finally, he came to the issue which everyone had been waiting for—the ceasefire. 'We cannot,' he insisted, 'we have no right to, allow the ceasefire to be applied indefinitely while Ambassador Jarring's efforts make no progress. . . . Otherwise the ceasefire lines will become a *fait accompli*, political lines similar to the 1949 armistice lines. . . . This we cannot allow under any circumstances.' In Israel's behaviour he could discern no sign of willingness to apply UN Security Council resolutions. 'On the contrary. . . .'

Millions of Egyptians braced themselves for the expected announcement: the ceasefire was now at an end.

But [Sadat went on], many countries and members of the Security Council whose understanding of our position and sympathy with our struggle we trust . . . have urgently pleaded with us to control ourselves. . . . So, while adhering to our first and inevitable duty to liberate our territory occupied during the 1967 aggression . . . we accept the appeal of the United Nations Secretary General . . . and we shall refrain from opening fire for a period we cannot prolong beyond thirty days and which will expire on 7 March.

At the same time, he disclosed, Egypt was ready to embark on a bold new initiative to break the deadlock. It was ready to start work immediately on re-opening the Suez Canal to international shipping provided that, during this month, Israel undertook a partial withdrawal from the east bank of the waterway, this being the first stage of a timetable leading to the full implementation of Security Council Resolution 242.

He was making this offer, Sadat said, after 'thorough, sincere and responsible discussions' with his colleagues.[7] In reality, however, it had been his own brainchild; he had informed the others of it only minutes before he was due to speak. They were very angry, or at least Ali Sabri and his ASU associates were. They accused Sadat of wanting to 'sell out to America'. He certainly was anxious to demonstrate a good will which, if his public pronouncements were to be believed, the United States hardly deserved. He appeared to share the opinion of Muhammad Heikal, editor of *al-Ahram*, who, with all the authority that his intimacy with Nasser lent him, had been arguing in the columns of his newspaper that while Egypt could not but place its chief reliance on the Soviet Union, it had nothing to lose by trying to 'neutralize' the United States, by attempting through diplomatic persuasion to wean it away from its overwhelming, irrational commitment to Israel. Sadat asked Heikal to assure the Americans, privately, that the initiative was entirely his own and owed nothing to the Russians.[8]

Since the 'immortal leader' himself, by introducing the ceasefire in the first place, had made a gesture to the United States which ran wholly counter to his public posture, it was rather disingenuous of Sadat's critics to condemn him for renewing it once again for essentially the same reason; all the more so since the Americans in general knew little about Sadat—his past record of anti-American tirades can hardly have been very familiar to them. He could reasonably hope, therefore, for a more sympathetic response than his predecessor was ever likely to have got. The real reason for the anger of the Ali Sabri 'power centre' was precisely because Sadat had not consulted them. He was no longer the weakling they had installed. He was growing with the job; he was becoming a power centre himself and a formidable one—though it would be hard to say in what measure he owed this stature to his own aptitudes or to that special mystique which, since Pharaonic times, the ruler of Egypt has always enjoyed.

Still, had Egyptians known about the conflict at the top, many among them would have sided with Ali Sabri. The renewal of the ceasefire—or 'the withholding of fire', as Sadat in an attempt to make it more palatable now called it—came as an anti-climax after all the impassioned speeches about the virtual inevitability of breaking it.

Sadat got short shrift from the Americans. A message from President Nixon which reached him only four days before the end of the new extension told him that if he thought the setting of such early deadlines constituted a form of pressure on the United States he was mistaken.[9] As for Israel, its attitude was hardening, not softening. Golda Meir called Sadat's offer 'an insult to our intelligence'. None the less, when his month was up on 7 March, Sadat claimed, in another speech, that a diplomatic result of 'great importance' had now been achieved—'the complete isolation of Israel from the world community and world opinion'. Even the big powers, no matter what their position on the Middle East crisis, had found the Israeli response to his proposal negative, and not at all in the interests of world peace. But the people were growing impatient and, of more immediate import to Sadat, the Ali Sabri group was now on the warpath—against him as well as the Israelis. They had been invoking Nasser again, submitting that in August 1970 he had given orders to prepare for crossing the Suez Canal with the aim of seizing the Sinai passes. At a joint meeting of the War Council and the ASU Executive Committee they argued that the army was now ready to launch Operation Granite, as it had been called. It was to oppose them that Sadat, unwilling to take the plunge, came up with yet another formula of surpassing ingenuity. He formally repudiated the ceasefire, but hastened to add that this did not mean that 'diplomatic activity will stop and that the guns alone will speak'. Egypt would choose the time of the battle.[10]

The guns did not speak, but with this ceasefire that was not a ceasefire tension rose to new, almost unbearable heights. The next day, 9 March, civilians were evacuated from the Canal Zone and a partial black-out was declared in Cairo. President Sadat conferred with army commanders and invested provincial governors with special powers. He presided over a meeting of the Committee for Preparing the Country for War. Journalists were briefed by the Information Minister on the 'role of the press in the battle' and 'mobilizing the masses for sacrifice'. Every day *al-Ahram* devoted several pages to various aspects of the war effort. 'Waiting for the Order' was the title of one such dispatch from the front; it portrayed an entire army ready for every eventuality—from those manning the most sophisticated electronic devices to those who would cross the Canal. The front-line troops were receiving their orders to withhold fire on a strictly daily basis. A dispatch from New York, published in *al-Ahram*, reported that the general feeling at United Nations headquarters was that the quiet along the Canal could last another two weeks at most.

This whole campaign to prepare the country for war was of course designed to avoid it by forcing the issue on the diplomatic front. Egyptian alarums did now seem to be having some effect in those quarters where Sadat desperately hoped that they would. The Americans were worried. Intelligence sources reported that the Soviet Union was supplying new hardware to Egypt on a massive scale. Senator Henry Jackson said on television that there had been a 'long and continuous airlift involving Russia's latest commercial transport, carrying obviously military transport on an urgent basis'. Secretary of State William Rogers warned that 'if the situation is not worked out in the reasonable future, a very dangerous situation would develop and possibly lead to World War III.' The Administration, while denying any intention of putting pressure on Israel, did not conceal its belief that it should show more flexibility. 'Our policy', said Rogers, 'is that the 1967 border should be the border separating Egypt from Israel . . . on condition that satisfactory arrangements can be made for the demilitarization of Sinai . . . and concerning Sharm al Shaikh.' While Egypt would have no truck with the demilitarization of Sinai, officials saw in this the first public expression of the Administration's private assurance that Security Council Resolution 242 meant complete Israeli withdrawal from Sinai.

Israel was now very much on the defensive. American newspapers began to speak of the 'coming American–Israeli crisis'. Then, towards the end of April—the month which, according to Sadat, would decide between peace and war—Rogers disclosed that he was embarking on a Middle East tour. This was indeed something. Not since 1953 had an American Secretary of State—in the person of John Foster Dulles—set foot on Arab soil. There was a slight toning down of the belligerent rhetoric. In his May Day speech President Sadat threw out a challenge. 'The country which gives Israel everything from a loaf of bread to Phantom bombers claims that it cannot pressure Israel. Isn't it ridiculous? In spite of everything we prefer to believe [what America says] and give it another, and perhaps the last chance to make an effort for peace.'[11] Heikal was now writing that May was likely to be the decisive month, 'the month of defining stands, the stage in which all parties reach the end of the road'.[12]

On 4 May Rogers arrived in Cairo. He was obviously a nice man. He said and did all the right things. He evoked five thousand years of Egyptian civilization, and hoped that, while he did not have time to visit the ancient monuments, he could help to build a monument of peace. He visited President Nasser's tomb and paid a courtesy call on his widow. He also publicly stressed those features of the hoped-for peace which his hosts wanted to hear. Yet the Egyptians remained convinced that all this personal affability would count for little against the fundamental intractability of the problems he had come to solve. *Al-Ahram* wrote that the gulf between Egypt and Israel remained 'enormous'. 'It is difficult to imagine Israel accepting Egypt's terms, impossible to imagine Egypt accepting Israel's.'[13]

The Egyptian newspaper was, of course, right. In Jerusalem on 6 May Rogers ran into a brick wall. He returned to Washington voicing a cautious optimism which was shared by neither Arabs nor Israelis. On 10 May Egyptian Foreign Minister Muhammad Riad concluded that there had been 'no progress'. Two days later President Sadat rated the chances of peace at 'not more than one per cent'. American pressure had, as always, succumbed to the counter-pressure which, through their extraordinary hold over American domestic politics, Israel and the Zionist lobby could mobilize against it. Surely this was the end of the road. Surely there had to be an explosion.

There was, but it did not come from across the Canal.

Correcting the Revolution

It was a political explosion on the home front. Nasserist continuity had become untenable. Beneath those disputes over the ceasefire lay a

111

much deeper rift. Who was to rule Egypt? Anwar Sadat and the 'state' or Ali Sabri and the 'party'? As the conflict intensified, Ali Sabri and his supporters openly asserted their right to convert their ASU power base into the base of the whole regime. That is what Nasser had intended, they said, as the ASU alone was empowered to interpret the 'immortal leader's' teachings. The 'state' should therefore be subordinate to the 'party'.

The ASU, not so much in its own official, constitutional capacity, but through those inroads—whether legal and above-board or, more often, family-based, clandestine and conspiratorial—which it had made into the 'state', was already very strong. Through Shaarawi Gumaa, the Minister of the Interior, and Sami Sharaf, the former head of Nasser's bureau and now Minister of Presidential Affairs, it dominated the all-pervasive security apparatus. The Minister of War, Muhammad Fawzi, was their man. So was the Minister of Information, with the whole propaganda machine—radio, television and much of the press—at his command. Ali Sabri was no communist; indeed, as a former Prime Minister he had lost no sleep over the imprisonment—and sometimes the torture, even to death—of hundreds of attested communists. But he enjoyed the Russians' support. For they saw him and the organization he controlled as the instrument of 'revolutionary transformation' through which they could preserve and deepen their stake in the country. For years Soviet theoreticians, echoed more tactfully by their Egyptian counterparts, had been discussing the lines on which the ASU should develop. In general, what they wanted to see was a dedicated core of militants emerging from the ranks of this amorphous monolith, many millions strong, to fashion a highly disciplined 'vanguard party' that should promote 'scientific socialism' and the 'dictatorship of the proletariat'.

Naturally, Sadat would have none of this, and naturally, too, he was as adept at invoking Nasser's own words in support of his case as his opponents were in support of theirs. 'I remember what Gamal said. He said: "I am responsible before God, before the people, before my conscience and myself, I am responsible for everything that happens." That is what Gamal said.' Who could doubt the meaning of such a text? As President, his successor was the true, the elected representative of all Egyptians. There was a covenant, Sadat said, between him and his people. He was the embodiment of national unity.[14]

On paper, at least, Ali Sabri was stronger than Sadat, but in the final analysis he was no less a creation of the late President than Sadat was; the Nasserist credentials of each were as good or as bad as the other's. Ali Sabri had once been as arbitrarily set down from his post as ASU Secretary General as Sadat had been raised up to his as Vice President. Intrinsic merit had little to do with the matter.

It was not the ceasefire, but a dispute over another Nasserist legacy, which brought the struggle to a head. In October 1969, with the 'Tripoli Charter', Nasser had agreed to bring Egypt into eventual union with Libya and the Sudan. A year later Sudan was no longer interested, but Syria took its place and on 17 April 1971 it was announced that President Sadat, President Assad and Colonel Gadafi had agreed to form a Federation of Arab Republics. Ali Sabri and his men strenuously objected. The Syrian regime, they said, was not to be trusted. As for the Libyans, not only were they 'a bunch of boy scouts', their leader was 'mad'.[15] In reality they opposed the union for the same reason that Sadat favoured it. It meant that Egypt would have to develop new ruling institutions, and that would furnish Sadat with the opportunity to cut the ASU down to what he considered to be its proper constitutional size.

According to his own subsequent account, Sadat had long known that the crunch was coming and, though always calm and master of himself, he slept with a pistol at his bedside. For one thing, he wanted to win friends, lay his plans. For another, always according to his own and other admiring accounts, he was inaugurating a whole new style of leadership. God knows, he had never sought the Presidency, but now that he had it, he felt he 'wielded a tremendous *real* power, which he had to use in doing good'. This was his 'forte' and he 'proceeded from the ideals [he] had always adopted, inspired by [his] love of Egypt and [his] desire to make the country a happy one'. He knew the kind of people Nasser had surrounded himself with—people who never 'paid any regard to the interest of Egypt and wanted nothing but to remain in power, seeking their own interests and motivated by hatred and jealousy . . .'[16] He had continuously told Nasser about that, especially after the 1967 defeat. He had pressed for a complete 'rebuilding', for a 'state of institutions', for a 'distribution of roles', for a 'responsible Prime Minister', and so on. Moreover, Nasser had agreed with him: 'The country is run by a gang,' he used to say.[17] But though Sadat never ceased to press such advice on his chief, he went no further than that when Nasser failed to heed it. It simply was not his nature. He could not, without real power, bring himself to enter the sordid mêlée. He preferred to remain a 'spectator' for, according to a flattering study, *Sadat, the Pioneer of the Intellectual Revolution,*

113

by Nabil Raghil, he was Socratic by disposition, much given to the contemplation of the human condition.[18]

However, given real power, he was now determined to challenge many existing conditions and ethical codes in existence at the time. The Socratic disposition gave way to another, always latent in him— the conviction which, according to Raghib, he shared with the great twelfth-century Sufi mystic, Muhyeddin Ibn Arabi, that the true believer combines piety with action, that 'he confronts the realities and happenings of life, struggles for right and its victory'.[19] It was incumbent upon him to get rid of 'the gang' but, owing to the high principles that were to inform his new-style leadership, he could only do so after exhausting all the resources of love, which was 'the basic element of [his] constitution'.[20] He would give the 'power centres' every chance to mend their ways. Thus, on 16 October 1970, the very first day of his presidency, Sami Sharaf had come to him with a heap of papers. Sadat recalls the episode in his memoirs.

'What is this?' I asked. 'The text of tapped telephone conversations between certain people being watched.' 'Sorry,' I said, 'I don't like to read such rubbish. If it contains any information regarding state security I'll look at it and give you a decision. If, however, this is a record—which I assume it is—of telephone conversations between ordinary citizens I'll have nothing to do with it. And, anyway, who gave you the right to have the telephones of these people tapped? Take this file away.' I swept it off my desk. He collected the papers and went away, but not before I had ordered all telephone tapping to be stopped. In future no tapping would be done except through a court order. My order was carried out instantly.[21]

Evidently, however, the order was not carried out—and Sadat knew it. As the plot thickened, he coolly awaited the material evidence he needed to confront the plotters. It was a time when 'his behaviour became a mystery even to his family . . . and he went into his bedroom, placing his pistol by his bedside. And every night his lady wife made sure that the bedroom was properly locked.'[22]

His elaborate scruples notwithstanding, it was really Sadat who struck the first blow. 'My timing, as the struggle against them intensified, was accurate. Zero Hour was May Day 1971.'[23] On that occasion he made a speech replete with the usual reference to the coming 'battle', sharp criticism of the United States and fulsome praise of the Soviet Union. The sting was in the tail. Almost as an

114

afterthought, he threw in a warning about those who seek for themselves a position from which to impose their will on the people. . . . The people—together with Gamal Abdul Nasser—have toppled all centres of power. . . .'[24]

The warning went almost unnoticed by the assembled multitudes, lost in transports of wild applause, but not by the Vice President, sitting on the platform beside him, to whom it was addressed. The next day Ali Sabri was 'relieved' of all his responsibilities. The event drew far more attention in the West than it did in the Egyptian press, which devoted one line to it. For the timing—four days before the arrival of Secretary of State Rogers—could hardly have been more significant. It was not until after Rogers had left and all the hopes vested in his mission had been disappointed, that Sadat completed what Zero Hour had begun. He still needed his 'material evidence'. It came in ironically appropriate form. That pathological obsession with the tapping of telephones, even one another's, was 'the gang's' undoing—that and the patriotic vigilance of an obscure police officer.

It was two o'clock in the morning of 10 May when Major Taha Zaki of the Ministry of Interior presented himself at Sadat's Nile-side residence and, to a protesting secretary, insisted on waking up the sleeping President. The motives for this highly irregular demand were the purest: he could not bear to see his country 'torn by a power struggle while enemy armies still occupied its soil'.[25] He came bearing tapes and when, after much difficulty, the presidential household managed to produce a machine to fit them, Sadat sat listening till four in the morning. They included a conversation between two of the principal members of 'the gang' and revealed that Sadat had already escaped an attempt on his life. This is the cloak-and-dagger tale as Sadat and his faithful propagandist, Moussa Sabri, editor of *al-Akhbar* tell it, but a more reliable authority, Muhammad Heikal, also relates a similar version.[26]

Four days later, assured that he could count on the army against War Minister Muhammad Fawzi, Sadat dealt the *coup de grâce*. He dismissed Interior Minister Shaarawi Gumaa. A galaxy of ministers and high officials, all members of 'the gang', promptly resigned in protest. This, they apparently believed, was their trump card; without ministers responsible for the armed forces, intelligence and information, and without most of the leading lights of the ASU, Sadat would face a kind of constitutional collapse. But their hopes—if such they really had—were quickly dashed. Sadat accepted all their resignations on the spot. It was the party which collapsed, not the

115

state. The ASU was exposed as the time-serving bureaucratic machine, without popular roots, which it had always been, and the so-called 'secret organization' within its ranks turned out to be very much less than the highly motivated shock troops of 'revolutionary transformation' which Ali Sabri, and the Russians, fondly hoped they were. Within hours all Sadat's adversaries were under arrest or behind bars. Just in case they, or their followers, were thinking of some desperate comeback, Sadat had to strike a less forgiving posture than, in the light of his self-portrait, he would perhaps have liked. If they did try anything, he exclaimed, 'I shall cut them in pieces.'[27]

It was Sadat the gambler, with his eyes on the main chance, who had pulled it off. He now proceeded to make the most of his triumph. He put on display the theatrical talents he had sought to employ twenty-two years before. Now the whole of Egypt was his stage, and in self-confident, ebullient mood he performed his part to perfection. The substance of what he told his people may not have been very convincing, but after all the turgid, cliché-ridden ideological fare to which they were accustomed, it was at least entertaining. He broached the dreadful secrets of the conspiracy, divulging nothing very specific, but creating the illusion of taking the people into his confidence.

His office at home had been tapped. This had actually happened, he added with the grave emphasis that such a shocking revelation seemed to deserve, in the house of the President of the Republic.

> People had been warning me. . . . But I told them, nonsense, no one would dare do such a thing. As I told you, all my life I have had to be sure of something before I judge . . . but I regret to say that yesterday . . . in my study, in my house, in the house of the President of the Republic, we found a device—and it occurred to me [he went on with no less depth of feeling] that scores of thousands of telephones are being tapped.[28]

From now on such practices would cease. He had given orders and would himself personally see to the destruction of the infamous archives which 'the gang' had compiled over the years. Sure enough, a few days later, Sadat presided over a ceremonial bonfire of telephone transcripts and secret dossiers in the courtyard of the Ministry of the Interior. 'Everyone had talked to Nasser on the telephone,' marvelled columnist Moussa Sabri, years later. 'If Sadat had wanted he could have raised a hundred "Watergates", not just one . . . But he ordered that all those tapes be burned.'[29]

More revelations followed. The press had a field day. When the Minister of the Interior had seen things going wrong, he had ordered the destruction of all incriminating documents relating to his 'secret organization'. They were so plentiful as to fill a minibus and—at a remote spot 9 miles from Cairo—they took a full three hours to burn. Most astonishing of all—recorded on tapes which apparently did not go up in Sadat's bonfire—was the conversation which three conspirators, General Muhammad Fawzi, Shaarawi Gumaa and Sami Sharaf, had had with their late master. Through a medium at Ain Shams University, they had sought guidance from the spirit of the 'immortal leader'. General Fawzi asked whether his 'timing for starting the battle was right or not'. In other words, commented Muhammad Heikal, the destiny of Egypt was being decided by men who had grown so accustomed to taking orders from Nasser when he was alive that they sought to go on doing so after he was dead. And they were so determined not to miss a word of this advice from beyond the grave that they recorded every séance on tape.[30]

Sadat called it the 15 May Corrective Movement. He asked the National Assembly (now to be renamed the People's Assembly) to draft a permanent constitution. The existing constitution was a long-lived provisional one. It was now that Sadat, recalling his *fellah* origins, took to stressing what he called the 'ethics of the Egyptian village'. It was in the village, he maintained, that 'citizens take pleasure in doing their duty for its own sake without expecting praise or reward'. The family was all-important. The wise ruler was he who played 'the role of vigilant *paterfamilias* for the good of all members of the family without exception'.[31] In drafting the constitution, Sadat said, the Assembly should look to the village in order to make of Egypt 'one big family' with 'science and faith' as its motto. He dissolved the ASU, which was to be reconstructed through free elections from base to summit. He himself would not stand again for the Presidency at the end of his six-year term, and other holders of public office should follow the same practice.

It was, at this stage, no more than a corrective *movement*. Sadat made that clear in a second televised fireside chat. This time there was a message in the melodrama. Not only had the power centre bugged the President's office, they had defiled the memory of the 'immortal leader' by breaking into his safe to get at his private papers. This instalment of the story began with Huda, the daughter of President Nasser, telephoning Sadat, much to his astonishment, at 10.30 on the evening after the night of the tapes and insisting on seeing him immediately. She told him that her father always used to keep a notebook at his bedside and he had the habit, whenever he woke up in the night, of confiding to it any ideas which passed through his mind. Some of these notebooks, along with official state papers, were in Nasser's personal safe when he died. After the forty days of official mourning his children had insisted on opening the safe and disposing of the contents—for that had been their father's wish—but Sadat had been loath to do it. How could he—he who, even now, could hardly bear to walk down Caliph Mamoun Street, where Nasser used to live? So he had told Huda and her eldest brother, Khalid, to do it themselves, keeping the private papers and handing over the official ones to him. What they came to tell him that night was that someone had broken into the safe. They knew, because the papers were disarranged, and their father had always been a very meticulous man. The villain of the piece, Sadat made clear, was none other than Sami Sharaf—and this was later confirmed in *al-Ahram*, which reported that the fingerprint expert was so overcome that he had tears in his eyes as he went about his work.[32]

And what did Nasser confide to his notebooks in the middle of the night? Here was the nub. Among other things, apparently, he recorded his belief that the most recent ASU elections, in which the Ali Sabri group had emerged victorious, were not the free ones they should have been. And this confirmed what Nasser had once told Sadat himself—that there had been 'deviations' which, once the 'battle' was over, should be corrected.

It was de-Nasserization in Nasser's name. 'The people of 15 May'—those who came out into the streets to acclaim the corrective movement—and 'the people of 10 and 11 June' were one and the same, the now jubilant but then distraught masses who, in the hour of black defeat in 1967, had swept a resigning Nasser back into office. Sadat, in other words, had finally established himself as the true heir of his 'immortal' predecessor. Although he was beginning a frontal assault on the institutions that Nasser had built, it was still too early for him to set about demolishing the ideals and policies which he embodied, let alone the sacrosanct personage himself. But from now on, whenever the Egyptian press or radio spoke about 'the leader' there was no doubt whom they meant. The era of Anwar Sadat had truly begun.

In fact, however, he was at least implicitly challenging even the ideals and policies too. It was an authentic Egyptian heritage to which he was appealing, and though he was doing it in Nasser's name, it was a heritage which, in practice, Nasser had violated. At this early stage it was of course far from sure that Sadat was really going to restore all that was best in the pre-revolutionary tradition, but at least he seemed to deserve the benefit of the doubt.

There were those, his semi-official idolators, who had no such doubts from the outset. For them this was already the full-scale corrective *revolution* which he himself subsequently claimed it to be. The first to call it such, Moussa Sabri, set the tone for a new cult of personality of which he has remained a prominent and extravagant practitioner. 'I knew a father', Sadat had said in the second of his post-conspiracy speeches, 'whose daughter died for lack of 1½ piastres [about two pence or ten cents].' Sabri took up the story a few days later. It concerned a young officer whose daughter suffered from anaemia. The doctor prescribed nothing more than a plentiful diet of sugar, but the poor father, after a day's labour, could raise no more than one piastre. An *oka* (2½ lbs) of sugar cost 2½ piastres. In despair the father had to make do with barley sugar instead, and, being covered with flies, it caused his daughter to die of gastro-enteritis. 'This father', revealed Sabri, 'was none other than Lieutenant Anwar Sadat, cashiered from the army for patriotic reasons', the same Anwar Sadat by whose hand 'the forces of darkness are [now] being scattered, the spectre of fear dispelled.' And in *al-Gumuriyah*, until the week before a leading mouthpiece of the fallen power centre, one Ahmed Abdul Hamid, an actor, made public confession of an error now happily corrected. 'I, my leader, who said no in the presidential referendum, did so because I held the clique which you have eliminated responsible for the misfortune of Egypt. Now that it is eliminated, I can say yes, because, on 15 May, the miracle occurred.'[33]

For the great mass of ordinary Egyptians, 'freedom and democracy' were no doubt devoutly to be desired, but their daily bread was more so, and where that was concerned they had long since stopped believing in miracles. Besides, they had little idea what all the fuss was about. All they knew for sure was that there had been a *dawsha* (a row) behind the scenes, and Sadat had got the better of it. The masses, Egyptians say, are like that stock figure in city life, the *bawab* (the doorkeeper). He sits in the entranceway of middle-class residential Cairo. He sees smart people going in and out. He hears voices raised in argument, and sometimes the *dawsha* turns into a fight. Somebody comes out and announces that such and such has happened. Somebody else comes out and announces something else.

Others come and go. But no one asks the *bawab* whether he has an opinion on the matter. He shrugs and goes on with the opening and shutting of doors.

The Russians in

With the downfall of the Ali Sabri power centre the Soviet Union had suffered the severest setback in its long and patient drive for supremacy in the Middle East. So, at least, Western commentators were saying at the time, and Sadat was to confirm later that they were right. Ali Sabri had been nothing less than 'the chief Soviet agent in Egypt'; he and his four henchmen—Soviet agents all—had commanded a five-to-three majority in the ASU Higher Executive Committee. With his corrective movement, therefore, Sadat had destroyed the 'Soviet power bloc' in Egypt.[34]

At the time, however, he and the entire state-controlled Cairo press poured scorn on such Western 'fantasies'. 'Can anyone imagine', asked the left-wing editor of *Rose al-Yussef*, a survivor of the purge, 'that this old and colossal pyramid of good relations will melt like ice in the sun?'[35] And indeed, no sooner had Sadat finished off its 'agents' than he moved to repair relations with the Soviet Union itself. In fact, on the face of it, he took Egypt further into the Russian embrace than it had ever gone before. He appeared to forsake those hallowed ideals of independence and non-alignment for which the July Revolution stood. It had always expressed itself, this prickly national pride, in a rejection of all foreign pacts and alliances. While, in earlier days, that meant opposing Western powers which sought to impose them, it was now the Soviet Union, once a valuable counterweight to Western ambitions, which seemed to be pushing for its own, no less insidious, form of domination.

At first the Kremlin reacted to the setback with an ominous silence, accompanied by the holding of much-publicized 'military manoeuvres in the south of the Soviet Union'. But then, apparently, the Russians concluded that, for all their massive stake in the country, they could not treat Egypt as they would an East European vassal-state. They sought to limit the damage, to forestall more of it. Hardly had the dust of conflict settled than President Podgorny and a high-powered delegation descended on Cairo, bearing a treaty of friendship and cooperation all ready for Sadat's signature. He complied. There was more in it for him than there was for the Russians. In the joint communiqué the Soviet Union 'expressed its deep satisfaction at the will of the Egyptian leaders and people to keep to the progressive, anti-imperialist path charted by the late President Nasser'. But this was a satisfaction which it could not really feel. If, at little cost, Sadat had merely lent his name to the ideological jargon beloved of the Kremlin, he, as the inconstant partner, had secured something much more substantial in return. Not only had he put the Soviet Union firmly in its place, he was rewarded for doing so. The Russians entered into a more binding commitment, involving their whole international prestige, to achieve a peace settlement on Arab terms—or, failing that, to furnish the means for prosecuting the military alternative.

In years to come, Sadat was to disclose—and it was doubtless true—that it was the Russians who insisted on the treaty. He had acquiesced in it, 'perhaps mainly to allay the fears of the Soviet leaders . . . for suspicion is second nature to Russians, whether under the Czars or communism'.[36] But at the time he claimed that the insistence had come from his side. Sadat was also later to disclose what, after only a few months as President, he already thought about the Russian promises to deliver desperately needed arms supplies and their alleged failure to do so, or the outrageous conditions they tried to impose. Only six weeks before it had made him 'livid with rage'. On a secret visit to Moscow he had hurled the latest insulting offer back in the faces of the assembled Soviet leadership. 'Nobody', he said, 'is allowed to take a decision on Egyptian affairs except the people of Egypt itself—represented by me, the President of Egypt! I don't want the aircraft.'[37] Yet for the present he continued to praise the Soviet Union in language which, even to those ignorant of his real feelings, was on the extravagant side. He had insisted on the treaty, he said, 'because science and technology in their latest forms are only to be found in the Soviet Union and the United States. One of them is a true and sincere friend who supported us in our darkest hour. The other declares that it will maintain the balance of power in Israel's favour. Consequently, I do not hesitate to ask the friend to give me the science and technology to confront this major challenge.' The Soviet Union was unstinting in its support for peoples struggling for liberation. It gave economic aid without strings. All this, Sadat said, was 'a reality, not rhetoric'. And it was consummated in the treaty by which Egypt 'set the highest store'. The relationship was 'one of principle and not a provisional one, a permanent relationship, not a transitional one. We have stood together, and we always shall, in the camp of world revolution opposed to imperialism.'[38]

There was confusion in the West. Some who had excitedly discerned the makings of a Western comeback in Egypt were wondering—like the *New York Times*—whether Egypt was 'on the way to becoming another Soviet satellite'. As for the Israelis, they appeared to have little doubt about it. For Prime Minister Golda Meir, 'the Soviet Union has gained control of Egyptian policy', and, given their earlier anxieties over Sadat's courtship of the United States, the Israelis did not disguise their satisfaction at an apparent reversal which, in their opinion, made them an indispensable ally of the 'free world' in the struggle against communism.

The Year of Decision

With his personal authority consolidated, with his major arms supplier mollified and pledging support, and with the prospect of internal reforms that would end the dark, repressive side of Nasserism, Sadat now appeared to be strongly placed to confront, once again, the overriding challenge from which there could be no escape. He returned with a vengeance to the famous slogan: 'No voice louder than the battle'. On 5 June, anniversary of the 1967 war, he proclaimed his Year of Decision. He pledged that 'the battle will end, one way or another, in 1971'.[39] On the nineteenth anniversary of the July Revolution he said it again with greater force: 'We shall not allow 1971 to pass without deciding the issue, whether through peace or war—even if it means sacrificing one million lives.'[40] It was the same old formula—threatening war with the weapons the Russians were going to provide in the hope that, through the American diplomatic initiatives his threats would inspire, he would never have to wage it. Without the Ali Sabri group breathing down his neck, he was no longer obliged to put his deadlines on a monthly, weekly and, finally, almost daily basis. He had a full six months' respite.

None the less, the country was restless. It soon became clear that Sadat's idea of 'freedom and democracy' was not very different from his predecessor's. He would not expose his newly won mastery to any unnecessary risks. In the reconstructed ASU, Sadat warned, there was to be no room for reactionaries, opponents of socialism and Nasser's line, waverers, corrupters and other undesirables. In September the Ali Sabri power centre went on trial for high treason; but it was not before an ordinary court which, in the spirit of Sadat's reforms, it should have been, but before a special 'revolutionary' court, secret and hand-picked. When strikes—a symptom of the deteriorating economic situation—broke out at the Helwan Iron and Steel Works, pride of Nasser's industrialization programme, and other factories, there was no word of it in the 'free press'. When the newspapers finally did speak, it was to say that 'a small minority' had used force to bring their colleagues out on strike, and that Sadat would suppress any future strikes with 'all possible severity'. And the local trade union and ASU branches, 'freely' elected only a month before, underwent a root-and-branch purge. During the summer violent events in the Arab world had their ramifications in Egypt. In concert with Colonel Gadafi of Libya, Sadat helped re-install President Numairi of the Sudan after a communist-led coup had brought him down. Sadat took strong exception to a statement by the General Union of Egyptian Workers deploring the 'bloody events in fraternal Sudan', the executions and anti-communist witch hunt. There was also unease as King Hussein of Jordan and his formidable Prime Minister, Wasfi al-Tal, completed what Black September 1970 had begun. When the king's bedouin troops, in a final ruthless push, drove the Palestinians out of their last strongholds in the north of the country, Sadat could not have done much to stop them. But he barely tried.

It was the demoralization of 'no war, no peace' that was corroding everything, and Sadat sought to divert attention from troubles on the home front. Hard on the heels of the labour unrest and the Sudanese and Jordanian upheavals came the referendum on the Egyptian–Syrian–Libyan federation. This, he said, would be the 'cornerstone of the battle'. He won an overwhelming paper victory—a 99·98 per cent vote in favour—but the people were much more interested in the outcome of the Year of Decision which, with no sign of a diplomatic breakthrough, now had only four months to go. Did Sadat really intend to go to war this time? It began to look more and more like it when, on 11 October, he arrived in Moscow at the head of a high-powered delegation. While President Podgorny stressed the desirability of a peaceful settlement, Sadat was militant. 'Force and force alone', he told a Kremlin banquet, 'can be used to liquidate aggression on our land.' The Egyptian people were faced with 'the most severe challenge—the Zionist-imperialist aggression'. Recalling that it was the 'immortal leader' who had initiated the Soviet–Egyptian relationship, he assured his hosts of his 'love of the Soviet Union, its people and its party'.[41]

And then, on 20 November, as the press was counting the days till the end of the year, Sadat told the armed forces that 'the hour of battle has come'. Perhaps this was God's wish. For eight months he had been trying, through the Americans, to exploit the less than 1 per cent hope that 'our forces might cross the Canal without an assault'. But the hope was now dead. 'Our decision is to fight.' 'While you await the order to cross,' he told his army, 'I ask you to press on with your hard, intensive training, for the Crossing is a one-way road. Next time, with God's help, we shall meet in Sinai.'[42]

The government once more 'mobilized' for war. The black-out was re-imposed, the 'battle committees' reactivated. And this time there was a new touch; Sadat went into his 'bunker'; he donned military uniform and moved to the armed forces headquarters. There was an escalation of the rhetoric too; to get the Israelis out of Sinai, officials were saying, Egypt was ready to sacrifice *three million* lives. The rising tension got a fortuitous boost. The Black September terrorist organization made its debut with the assassination of the Jordanian Prime Minister, Wasfi al-Tal, on the steps of Cairo's Sheraton Hotel. Restive students pronounced their own verdict of 'not guilty' on the four Palestinians who had thus done their patriotic duty, and called on Sadat to do the same by resuming the fighting across the Canal. Already Sadat's much-vaunted 'sovereignty of the law' had been abused in one direction by bringing the Ali Sabri group to trial before a secret revolutionary court; now it was abused in another by granting the four Palestinian killers bail and eventually free passage out of Egypt. It was a mere pandering to the public mood.

And so, indeed, was the whole mobilization itself. What was this black-out when lights blazed in all ministeries and public buildings; this rallying cry of 'everything for the battle', when Cairo's prosperous bourgeoisie was living it up as though they were already celebrating victory; these endless TV and radio directives on how to behave during air raids, when the Cairo municipality was busy replacing air-raid shelters with parking lots for the Mercedes and Peugeots that were being imported in such profusion? Besides, could any mobilization be taken seriously that came after five years of enemy occupation, after eighteen months of repeated assertions that the chances for a peaceful settlement were less than 1 per cent, and in the eleventh month of the Year of Decision?

And so the Year of Decision petered out in precisely the ignominious way that the cynics had forecast, with highly sophisti-cated official definitions of what that most over-used word in the Arab political vocabulary—*decisive*—actually meant. Among many others, Sadat's definition was:

Our strategic position as regards the necessity of deciding the issue in 1971 remains what it was. The final decision has been made in the sense of harnassing all resources for the battle of liberation. It is now in effect. There can be no going back. . . . Some may ask when we shall join the battle. . . . But the timing of the battle cannot be a matter of public discussion, since it depends on delicate internal, Arab and international factors. Our position must be: no war slogans, only war behaviour.[43]

And, of course, there was the usual crop of satirical jokes, along the general lines that Sadat, rather than extend the ceasefire, had issued a decree extending 1971 instead.

But it was all getting beyond a joke as Sadat found out when, in an attempt to justify his *in*decision, he regaled his people with another of those intimate 'fireside chats' which had served him well enough in the wake of the Corrective Movement. He treated his 'children'—as he often called his audience—to the kind of story which only children could be expected to believe.

. . . On Sunday, 9 July 1967, only one month after our battle with the enemy [Sadat began in the manner of the teller of fairy-tales], when an Israeli armoured brigade moved towards Kantara West [on the Israeli-occupied side of the Canal] . . . our command reached a decision which it then laid before President Gamal Abdul Nasser, God's peace be upon him. . . . Military principles dictated immediate action. President Gamal Abdul Nasser approved this decision, as a result of which our bombers and fighters went up. Our bombers and fighters stayed in the air for two hours while fog filled the whole area. . . . President Gamal was informed about twelve o'clock that our pilots could not see their targets, because there was fog everywhere. . . . At one o'clock President Gamal rescinded the decision . . . for he was—as I previously said—a military as well as a political genius.

Fog over Sinai at noon in the height of summer seemed a highly unlikely circumstance. However, having captured his children's attention with this hitherto unrecorded episode in the life of the 'immortal leader' the story-teller proceeded to draw a parallel between Nasser's stroke of genius and his own. For, in December 1971, in the final month of the Year of Decision, Sadat had found himself in precisely the same position. The armed forces had been poised to receive his order to start the battle. 'But then the fog appeared. . . .' Not, this time, a literal, a meteorological fog, but a war between two friendly countries, India and Pakistan . . . which developed into a conflict between the two big powers. . . . Just as Gamal took his decision at one o'clock on Sunday, 9 July 1967 [again Sadat stressed the parallel between his predecessor's and his own action] so I issued my decision to General Sadiq and instructed him to wait. It was imperative to revise our calculations.

The usual tributes to the Soviet Union made, he went on to accuse the United States of manoeuvring throughout 1971 to try to negotiate separate solutions between Israel and each of its neighbours in turn. The United States had taken his own initiative, he said, and 'somehow twisted it and turned it into a partial agreement with Egypt . . . not even a comprehensive agreement with Egypt. . . . They moved towards a partial settlement . . . and as time moved on, they coveted more. It became a partial settlement of the partial settlement with Egypt.'[44] Later Sadat was to claim that he did not expect his children to believe his fairy-tale.

I knew . . . that as a result of having previously declared that 1971 would be the Year of Decision, I would now have to face a campaign of denigration. And so it turned out. Perhaps in the hope that Jewish public opinion might forgive him his standing by me at one famous time in the past when Golda Meir had rebuked him publicly, US Secretary of State William Rogers made a speech . . . in which he said that 1971 had come and gone and no decisive action had been taken by Sadat. He went on to say that the United States would supply Israel with more weapons, military equipment and everything else she needed. . . . It was all part of the ferocious psychological campaign being waged against us, exactly as I had expected.

Sadat conceded that he 'didn't really give' the Egyptian people 'all the facts', that, on the contrary, he 'defended the Soviet Union in every public statement and speech [he] made'. Mercifully, however, the Egyptian people did not believe what he was saying: they had 'as always enough political discrimination to realize that the Soviet Union was to blame for it all'.[45]

Some of his children certainly did not believe it. The 'fog' speech may have lulled, confused, or even convinced the naïve. But for the country's ardent youth, the students and the political activists, it was as a red rag to a bull. Did Sadat take them for fools? Did he think they did not know what was going on behind the scenes, that if anyone was creating all the fog, it was Sadat himself? Cairo University students staged a sit-in at the Gamal Abdul Nasser hall. They adorned its walls with mocking posters. One, an imaginary newspaper headline, read: 'War Delayed; America Delivers More Fog' (a jibe that played on the close resemblance between the Arabic words for fog and tank). Another poster asked: ' "What did you do in the war, Daddy?" "Nothing, I got caught in the fog." ' The students set up their own 'congress' and they submitted to the President questions and proposals in which they expressed not only their unhappiness with both superpowers but with Sadat's manner of dealing with them.

If Sadat was not getting the Soviet weapons he needed, then why didn't he come out openly and say so? Yet when they applied the same faculty of 'political discrimination' to the anathemas he reserved for the other superpower, the students found them even more insincere. After their latest arms supplies to Israel, Sadat had gone so far as to say that the Americans were 'in a state of war with the Arabs'.[46] Yet he was courting them behind his people's back—they knew that from the interviews he gave to American newspapers. It was not simply the things which Sadat saw fit to tell the rest of the world which exasperated the students—that he was eager to send the Russians home, that he had already agreed to so-called 'proximity talks', that he was even ready for direct negotiations if Israel committed itself to withdrawal—it was the fact that he withheld them from his own public. For these and many other concessions were carefully excised from the versions of his interviews published in the Cairo press. It was typical, they said, of Sadat's 'double talk'.

For that summed up what the students wanted—straight talk in place of evasion and subterfuge. The policies themselves were naturally important, but first of all they wanted to know what these policies were. And of that they had no idea; they were being ruled from day to day, from gimmick to gimmick, from promise to false promise. There was no better illustration of this, they said, than the assertion in Sadat's 'fog' speech that he was now going to 'bring the home front in line with the military front'. That was the great new task which he urged upon his countrymen. In other words, the students concluded, the latest mobilization, and all the earlier ones, must have been a sham. Even as he had announced his decision to fight, even as he had gone into his bunker, he knew that the home front was not ready. Here he was publicly admitting it himself.

All this was infuriating enough, but truly intolerable was the fact that news of their agitation was rigidly screened from the public at large. The self-proclaimed Higher Committee of the National Student Movement reckoned to speak for some 60,000 under-graduates of Cairo University alone, not to mention half-a-dozen other seats of higher learning, and to a large extent it undoubtedly did; yet moderately framed though it was, not a word of their petition reached the pages of the Cairo press. Like the striking steel workers the year before, the students had now got the measure of Sadat's new freedoms. The last straw came when, first by a ruse and then by force, the authorities tried to end a protest that was still confined to the university campus; the students responded by taking it into the heart of Cairo itself. They swarmed across the Nile bridges into Liberation Square. There they gathered round the plinth that awaited—and still awaits—Nasser's statue, they harangued the populace, and sallied forth from time to time to do stone-throwing battle against the police armed with shields, batons and tear gas grenades.

After the demonstrators had eventually been dispersed and hundreds of them arrested Sadat delivered his verdict on the affair. The Higher Committee of the National Student Movement was the 'Committee of National Treason'. It represented a small clique, a 'deviationist minority'. The 'student base' was sound. All that was needed was to 'eradicate this disease from its midst'. Behind the riots Sadat discerned an incongruous variety of motives. At first he said they had links with Ali Sabri's fallen power centre. Then he implied that the Palestinians, who had 20,000 students in Cairo, were behind it. But that did not prevent him from likening the movement to the French student revolt in 1968 which, according to him, had been inspired by the Americans and Zionists. He said that he acquitted his 'children, the students, of any relations with Israel'. They would be released. He added, however, that 'during this our war, they did what they did and Israel quoted what they said and printed it in leaflets.'[47]

The student demonstrations were undoubtedly an authentic expression of Egyptian patriotism, spontaneous, largely classless, directed neither by right nor left. The students spoke of 'sweet Egypt' and 'beloved Egypt'. Their heroes were men like Ahmad Orabi and Saad Zaghloul, leaders of the nationalist struggle against the British and champions of a long and honourable tradition in which Sadat certainly deemed himself to stand. In Egypt's modern history, students had played a leading role in triggering movements of opinion that eventually proved irresistible and if, this time, other elements of the population had failed to join in, there would surely come a time when they did. There was an end-of-an-epoch feeling in the air. Now, instead of 'Can Sadat survive?' the doubters were asking 'How long can he survive?' And that old question, 'Is it going to be war or peace?' was giving way to another, 'Which will come first, the war or the coup?' Sadat surely had to do something.

The Russians out

Apparently all that Sadat could come up with was more of the same: more rhetoric, more hyperbole. In the middle of the student agitation he resorted to that old stand-by: a government face-lift. Dr Mahmud Fawzy, the septuagenarian sage, was replaced as Prime Minister by Dr Aziz Sidqi. And why form this new team only a few days after the old one had presented its programme to the People's Assembly? Because this was the government of 'total confrontation and continuous action', and Aziz Sidqi, a dynamic young technocrat of fifty-one, was capable of working twenty-four hours a day. Obviously he was just the man Sadat needed to accomplish the urgent task of 'putting the home front on a level with the war front'. The change to a war economy, Sidqi said, would entail a 'just distribution of the burdens of the battle among all categories of the population'. Investment would henceforth be concentrated on the war effort. There would be new restrictions on the import and sale of luxury goods. Austerity measures would include a ban on the purchase of new cars for government departments and public companies, whose furniture entitlements would also be severely curtailed.

But clearly Sadat realized he would have to come up with *something*, and it looked more and more as if the Soviet Union was going to have to furnish it. No sooner had the new Cabinet been installed than Sadat, acknowledging for the first time that there had after all been 'misunderstandings' with the Russians, paid yet another visit to Moscow, three-and-a-half months after his last one. He was going there, he said, to fix a new Zero Hour for the battle which had not been cancelled, but merely deferred by that untimely 'fog' on the Indian sub-continent. He was, his people understood, going there to secure the offensive weapons required to match the new Phantoms and Skyhawks which had 'doubled the number of raids Israel can mount against Egypt'.[48] In Moscow—according to his own, much later account—Sadat asked the reason for the delay in sending the weapons which the Soviet leaders had promised me. Brezhnev said he was personally to blame. It was due, he said, to the necessary paperwork, the inevitable red tape, and similar things. 'I am not convinced of that,' I said, 'and if this is repeated I will have to act — a decision will have to be taken.' I was beside myself with rage. I reiterated what I had told them on my previous visit, particularly that we didn't want Soviet soldiers to fight our battle for us and that we sought no confrontation between them and the United States. The meeting ended with them reading out a list of the weapons which they promised would be shipped 'forthwith'. They were not the essential weapons I wanted but they were better than nothing.[49]

At the time, however, the visit yielded no public indications that the Soviet Union had overcome its misgivings about Egypt's ability to wage a war or its reluctance to furnish the offensive weapons — apparently such items as Scud ground-to-ground missiles, MiG-23 interceptors, and supersonic TU-22 bombers — for the purpose. None the less, according to the state-controlled *al-Ahram*, the visit had been a 'huge success', a 'turning point in the course of the Middle East conflict'. The Soviet Union appeared to be restored to full favour; Soviet–Egyptian friendship, enthused the left-wing weekly *Rose al-Yussef*, was 'immortal' and 'whatever the false steps, they cannot change its essence'. *Al-Ahram* cautioned, however, that the results were 'not for publication — at least for the time being'.[50]

In spite of the 'huge success', there was no more talk of Zero Hour. Instead, a few days after Sadat's return from Moscow, Dr Gunnar Jarring, the long-suffering UN mediator, was back in the Egyptian capital for the first time in two years. It was true, Sadat said by way of justification, that Israel would never withdraw 'until its blood is shed in Sinai'. But there was a difference between continuing political activity and a political settlement. 'A political settlement means envisaging a settlement without battle. That is impossible. But the battle includes political action.' And he added a new and, subsequently famous, slogan — '*Sabr wa Samt*' ('patience and silence') — to the already bewildering and contradictory repertoire.[51]

If renewed diplomacy and 'patience and silence' sounded a little out of tune with all the fiery speeches that had gone before, Sadat made up for it when opportunity offered. On 5 April he announced that Egypt was breaking off relations with Jordan. The Palestinian National Council, the audience he was addressing at a meeting in Cairo, erupted in wild applause. Nothing less than a diplomatic break would suffice to express Egypt's displeasure at King Hussein's newly proclaimed plan for the establishment of a United Arab Kingdom which, incorporating a semi-autonomous Palestine state on the West Bank, was 'aimed at emptying the Palestinian cause of its content'.[52]

A few days later, the Prophet's birthday furnished another opportunity. What the Israelis and the Americans seemed to forget, said Sadat, was that Egypt was true to Muhammad's divine message. Jerusalem was the property of the Moslem nation and

> . . . we shall recover this, God willing, from those about whom our Book says: 'abasement and humiliation have been pitched upon them' . . . They talk about direct negotiations. They were neighbours of Muhammad, peace be upon him, in Medinah . . . and he negotiated and concluded a treaty with them, but in the end they proved to be a mean, vile and treacherous people. The most splendid thing our Prophet did was to evict them from the entire Arabian Peninsula. They are a vile and treacherous people. They are a conspiratorial people who have been raised in perfidy.

Sadat promised that on the next anniversary Egypt would celebrate 'not only the liberation of our land but also the defeat of Israeli conceit and arrogance, so that they may once again return to the condition decreed in our Holy Book: "abasement and submission have been pitched upon them".'[53]

Yet if anything appeared to stand in the way of such promises and their fulfilment it was precisely the Soviet Union on which Sadat was counting. That at least was what more and more Egyptians were saying. And what they said Sadat could no longer ignore. Such thinking found its most influential expression in a petition which ten leading personalities, including three Free Officers, Kamaluddin Hussein, Zakariah Muhyieddin and Abdul Latif Boghdadi, submitted to the President. The petition was not published – at least not until Sadat deemed it expedient – and thereby gained more notoriety than if it had been.

'The policy of alliance with the devil', the petition said, 'is not objectionable until it becomes favourable to the devil.' Not everyone in Egypt regarded the Soviet Union as the devil, and on one point the petitioners had no doubt: it would be 'sheer insanity for Egypt to abandon the friendship of one of the two superpowers.' But there was this growing feeling among many Egyptians that the Russians were getting more out of the Egyptians than they were getting out of the Russians. It stemmed in part from awareness of their own inadequacy, from the need to find some explanation for their failure, after five years, to make any dent in the Israeli occupation of Sinai. It was in the army, naturally enough, that such feeling was strongest. Ironically, but not surprisingly, the more the Russians helped, the more unpopular they became. The sheer size of their presence—some 20,000 'advisers' or 'experts'—was enough to guarantee friction; the task they had to perform even more so. What was militarily sensible—that Russians should give orders to Egyptians—was psychologically damaging. It would have been so, even if the advisers had been models of tact, but they were not; and while the Soviet ideologues back home dwelt rather insultingly on the need for a thoroughgoing reconstruction of a decadent 'bourgeois' army, the Red Army personnel in the field sometimes went about their task in a rough and boorish way that hurt Egyptian pride.

As the relationship soured, the War Minister, General Ahmad Sadiq, won prestige as the man who stood up to the Russians. He ordered the repatriation of a general who had likened Egypt to an 'unfaithful mistress'. Military opinion communicated itself to the public at large—and especially to those quarters which, through prejudice or self-interest, were predisposed to share it. There was the old plutocracy which the revolution had by no means completely destroyed, the *nouveaux riches* whom it had helped to spawn; the political right and the bourgeoisie in general. There were the pious masses who deemed Soviet communism a 'godless' creed; and there was that far from insignificant class of opinion-moulders, the taxi drivers, waiters, chambermaids, *concierges* and *bawabs*, who spread it abroad that these Russians were not only a dour, uncongenial lot, they never even gave a man a decent tip, unlike the Western *sahibs* of old. It might have been ungrateful, but it was none the less real.

Nor was it all prejudice and self-interest; beneath lay a healthy patriotic concern. 'The relationship between the Soviet Union and Egypt', the petition went on, 'must return to the natural framework of relationships between a newly independent country, which is anxious to protect its independence, and a great power whose strategy—by virtue of its ideology and interests—embodies the desire to expand its influence.' Sadat had recently had quite a hard time persuading the People's Assembly that he had not granted the Russians sovereign bases in the full, objectionable sense of the word; he had only granted them 'facilities', as Nasser had before him, to provide them with water, supplies, relaxation and repairs. That may have been true, though it would appear that, at Cairo West airport for example, Sadat yielded more sovereignty than Nasser ever had.[54]

But even if true, it was a distinction that many found hard to swallow. Furthermore, even if the Soviet Union did not interfere directly in Egypt's internal affairs, it had sensibilities of its own which Sadat took care not to offend. In a panel discussion organized by *al-Ahram*, two high officials had said, in substance, that the Soviet Union continued to give its attention to Vietnam at the expense of the Middle East. For that, Sadat saw fit to send his future Foreign Minister, Ismail Fahmi, and his future press spokesman, Tahsin Bashir, on 'open leave'.

From his memoirs we know that what the Egyptians felt towards the Russians, a general resentment, amounted in Sadat to an almost pathological hatred. And by the spring of 1972 it must have been reaching new heights. For on 25 April he paid his fourth visit to Moscow since he became President. This time it came a mere ten weeks after the previous one. Publicly at least, he kept his feelings well under control. He declared himself 'very happy' with the outcome and in the joint communiqué—which acknowledged the right of the Arabs, if need be, to recover their territories by other than peaceful means—Kremlinologists detected a slightly less grudging Soviet commitment to the Egyptian war effort. That interpretation was lent greater plausibility a few weeks later when Marshal Gretchko, the Soviet Defence Minister, arrived in Egypt. All of a sudden the Cairo press, normally so miserly with military 'secrets', ran riot with them. 'President Sadat and Marshal Gretchko Visit Air Force Base'; 'Aircraft Whose Speed Exceeds 3,000 Kilometres per Hour Take Part in Spectacular Display'; 'President Sadat and Marshal Gretchko Praise Egyptian Combat Skill and Mastery of Modern Equipment'; 'Our Pilots Photograph Israeli Military Bases as Far Afield as Sharm Al-Sheikh'. So, in perfect unison, ran all the banner headlines. In other words, everything that was being said about the Russians' unwillingness to supply the most sophisticated offensive weapons was so much malicious rumour.

Or was it? Colonel Gadafi of Libya had the temerity to dismiss the whole exercise as a charade. That he was right to do so seems confirmed by what Sadat later confided in his memoirs. 'Gretchko had a statement prepared which, he said, had to be issued by us, acknowledging receipt of long-range bombers, which was untrue.'[55] At the time, accomplice in the charade, he pinned yet more decorations on the Soviet Marshal's much-bemedalled chest. And in his speech commemorating the first anniversary of the Corrective Movement, Sadat waxed indignant about the Free Officers' petition. He could not understand this bias against the Soviet Union at a time when the United States' 'hostility towards us has become more and more obvious throughout 1971, and especially since the beginning of 1972. . . . Isn't the Soviet Union our only friend who has never ceased to help us?' Certainly there were misunderstandings, but they were between friends. To talk of a 'deteriorating of relations with the Soviet Union is to play into the enemy's hands. Some imagine that they can fish in troubled waters, but I tell them: all those who play such games will pay the price.'[56]

When the inevitable happened, when Sadat, the gambler, took another of his decisions—the one he had hinted at in his visits to the Kremlin—he went far beyond what any of these 'fishers in troubled waters' had recommended. In the same impetuous spirit with which he had broken the Ali Sabri power centre a year before, he threw out all his Soviet experts. But this time he was taking on not just the 'Soviet agents' inside Egypt—whom the Russians could disavow—he was taking on the Soviet Union itself; and it was not just the culmination of an internal power struggle, it was a decision that bore vitally on the highest interests of the nation. Sadat—so he says—left his advisers gasping. When, on 8 July, he informed the Soviet ambassador of his decision, the only other person present was Hafiz Ismail, his Adviser for National Security Affairs. It was the first that he had heard of it, and 'his jaw dropped and remained hanging down for the rest of the interview'.[57] Even the Minister of War, General Sadiq, the Russians' *bête noire*, tried to counsel Sadat against such an extreme step.

Recalling the decision and its antecedents, Muhammad Heikal, an intimate of Sadat, as he had been of Nasser, says that 'after studying all the documents and talking to all the people most closely involved' he still cannot make up his mind what exactly precipitated it. It seems that what Sadat saw as the Soviet Union's evasions and delay over the supply of arms, and the troubles it was causing him in the army, brought matters to a head. Both sides in the Middle East conflict have always deemed their patrons' readiness or otherwise to supply them with arms as the most sensitive barometer of how they stand in their eyes. The Israelis are positively neurotic about it. By this criterion, many Egyptians felt there could hardly be a more telling contrast between the largesse of the Americans and the meanness of the Soviets. The final affront came in May when, as a contribution to international *détente*, the two superpowers decided on the necessity for 'military relaxation' in the Middle East. For Sadat, not only did this mean that the Soviet Union set more store by winning the goodwill of the rival superpower than it did by preserving that of its Egyptian ally, it meant that the Soviet Union was content to perpetuate the intolerable situation of 'no peace, no war', if it did not actually welcome it as a means of maintaining its influence over an ally which it manifestly did not trust. For at least Sadat did once concede that the Russians 'never trusted me. They said I was pro-American and convinced Ali Sabri that I was selling Egypt out to the Americans.'[58]

It was profoundly humiliating for the Russians. They had been given two days to get all their men and equipment out. After springing the surprise on them, Sadat offered the Soviet leadership the opportunity of a face-saving formula. He dispatched Prime Minister Sidqi to Moscow to propose, among other things, the issue of a joint communiqué to the effect that the Russian advisers were going home on the completion of their mission. But Brezhnev, recalled to Moscow from his Black Sea retreat, apparently refused. 'You asked for the experts. If you want them to leave, that is your decision, and we will comply with it. But we are never going to be the party to a cover-up story and will not take the responsibility before history of suggesting that they are being withdrawn at our request.'[59]

That version of events was not very wide of the mark. In early 1970, as Israeli Phantoms roamed the Egyptian heartland at will, President Nasser had all but begged the Russians to assume direct responsibility for his defences and, responding on a massive scale, the Russians had all but turned the Delta into a forward area of the Warsaw Pact. Sadat was subsequently to erect the expulsion of the Russians into one of the heroic, dragon-slaying myths of his rule, but, as with many such myths, he had himself, at one time or another, inadvertently undermined his own pretentions. Six months before the expulsion he confided to a Western journalist: 'The Russians themselves, I must be fair, don't want their soldiers to stay here in Egypt. Every time I try to prolong their stay I must use all my efforts to convince them.'[60] And the Russians left very quietly;

though humiliated they were not unhappy, it seems, to lay down an onerous and potentially dangerous burden. Sadat let them keep some of their port 'facilities'; he expressed the desire 'to safeguard Soviet–Egyptian friendship' and proposed a meeting 'within the framework of the Treaty of Friendship and Cooperation'. They left almost too quietly for Sadat—for he was still to need them and he knew it.

It was almost the reverse of the *something* he had hoped for—but it won him more instant prestige than if he had got all the offensive weapons he wanted. Those who had always chafed against socialism and the Soviet connection that seemed to underpin it were naturally delighted. The masses were jubilant too. The reasoned criticism of the Soviet Union of the better-informed became, with them, an unthinking revulsion that held the Russians to be the root of all evil. The exultant, thankless 'the Russians are leaving' now on everyone's lips, contrasted almost indecently with the grateful relief of 'the Russians are coming' which had followed the 1967 defeat. Then the populace had prayed for an airlift of Soviet arms. Now they blessed Allah for the airlift that was ferrying their 'friend and ally' out. 'If Sadat were to hold a referendum,' one Western observer drily remarked, 'he would probably record his country's first spontaneous 90 per cent approval.'[61] The masses did not stop to think about the consequences of Sadat's decision. All they knew was that he had done something bold and defiant. Through him Egypt had humbled a country much more powerful than itself, and the response which that engendered was not just patriotism, it was—though of course they did not know it—spurious emotional compensation for their own crushed and miserable condition.

Among the intelligentsia, there were those, on the left, who considered that Sadat was lurching into the imperialist camp. There were others who considered—though he was still invoking Nasser at every opportunity—that he was now deviating from the path which the 'immortal leader' had charted. And there were those who pragmatically argued that whether or not the Egyptians liked the Russians, they were saddled with them, that they alone commanded the military and diplomatic weight to counter that which the Americans deployed on Israel's behalf. It was folly to humiliate them. 'In trying to change strategies like changing shirts', said one Beirut newspaper, 'the Arabs find themselves completely naked, worse, alone'.

In the West there was gratification—and astonishment. Gratification that, following the downfall of Ali Sabri a year before, the Soviet Union had received another body blow in its drive for supremacy in the Middle East. Astonishment that, in delivering the blow, Sadat should have thrown away the one great bargaining counter which, in his search for a peaceful settlement, this Soviet presence represented. The obvious *quid pro quo* for American pressure to get the Israelis out of Sinai was a diminution of the Soviet presence. Sadat knew that very well. In a famous indiscretion, Dr Kissinger had once said that it was America's aim to 'expel' the Russians from Egypt (see p. 99). The Saudis were no less keen on that than the Americans. As we have seen, Sadat has been shown to have had a long-standing, rather mysterious friendship with the business tycoon Kemal Adham, King Faisal's brother-in-law and intelligence chief. But if, through this connection, the Saudis were already strongly placed to exert influence on him, the influence was greatly reinforced by the key role in Arab and international affairs which a number of factors—the formidable personality of King Faisal, the decline of Arab 'revolution' and above all the geological accident of immense subterranean wealth—had conferred upon an intrinsically weak, backward and underpopulated country.

According to Heikal, Kemal Adham paid a secret visit to Cairo two months after Sadat became President.

He talked about the Russian presence in Egypt, saying how much it alarmed the Americans and pointing out that this was important at a time when the Saudis were trying to get the Americans more actively interested in the Middle East problem. President Sadat's answer was that Egypt depended on the Soviet Union for so much, whereas the Americans were providing Israel with everything it asked for, to the extent that during the war of attrition they had been able to bomb Egypt for seventeen hours consecutively. . . . But he added that if the first phase of Israeli withdrawal were completed he could promise that he would get the Russians out. Kemal Adham asked if he could pass this on to the Americans and the President said he could. But the President's remarks were leaked by Senator Jackson, presumably with the intention of helping Israel by creating bad blood between Egypt and the Soviet Union.[62]

When he came to Cairo in May 1971, Secretary of State William Rogers had suggested that President Nixon might be more forthcoming if President Sadat were to reduce the Soviet presence. In spring the following year, Prince Sultan, the Saudi Defence Minister, visited Washington, where the hint of a *quid pro quo* was repeated; he stopped in Cairo on his way home and told Sadat. Sultan was in Cairo the day that Sadat sprang his bombshell on the Soviet ambassador.

Western astonishment was nowhere greater than in the American administration; there they were in a better position than anyone else to appreciate just how desperately Sadat, for all his diatribes against the United States, was looking to it for his ultimate salvation. Dr Kissinger was flabbergasted. 'Why has Sadat done us this favour?' he asked his aides. 'Why didn't he get in touch with me? Why didn't he demand all kinds of concessions first?'[63] Gratification, astonishment — and an almost universal belief that peace in the Middle East was now an altogether more realistic possibility than it had been. A few of the more far-sighted pundits and editorial-writers did concede that, without Russia's restraining hand, Sadat might now feel tempted to go to war; but they were inclined to rule the possibility out because without Russia's military support, war now seemed a more desperate gamble than ever. Most commentators, however, hardly entertained the possibility at all. For the *New York Times* the expulsion 'dramatically improved' the prospects for peace. In the American capital, a *Washington Post* reporter concluded that the expulsion 'graphically demonstrates Egypt's realization that it has no military option for solving the Middle East crisis'. Military commentators conjured up pictures of Egyptian technicians struggling in vain to maintain all that highly sensitive electronic gear — exposed to the sand, heat, condensation, insects and bacteria of the Delta — which the departing Russians had left in their incompetent, half-trained hands.

Sadat knew better. The expulsion, he wrote later,

> lay within the strategy I had laid down; no war could be fought while Soviet experts worked in Egypt. The Soviet Union, the West and Israel misinterpreted my decision to expel the military experts and reached an erroneous conclusion which in fact served my strategy, as I had expected — that it was an indication that I had finally decided not to fight my own battle. That interpretation made me happy; it was precisely what I wanted them to think.[64]

Of course, it was easy for him to say, with hindsight, that all his apparent gambles were really mature decisions, carefully planned strokes in an inexorably unfolding grand design. He was even to say it retrospectively of such an early and clearly improvised decision as his February 1971 offer to re-open the Suez Canal. On the other hand, it is hard to imagine that, with the Russians still massively entrenched in his country, Sadat would ever have planned and executed his Crossing. Whether he knew it or not, he had laid the foundation for his master-stroke, his greatest gamble of all.

Fish, milk and tamarind

The elation at home was short-lived. Sadat had 'liberated' Egypt from the Russians, but he still had to liberate it from the Israelis. If that had been temporarily overlooked, people quickly awoke from their forgetfulness. In a five-hour speech commemorating the twentieth anniversary of the Revolution, Sadat launched into a long and lyrical account of its achievements and renewed his pledge to complete the task which Nasser had begun. Recalling his predecessor's celebrated formula — 'what was taken by force can only be restored by force' — he set his face firmly against any 'national or international bargaining' over Arab territories. There could be no question of direct negotiations with the enemy. Such negotiations, in the nature of things unequal, would not be real negotiations, but would lead to capitulation. Evidently the Americans had been urging this course upon him. But he did not 'want to hear this talk'. The Americans did nothing but 'lie and cheat and deceive'. 'All the gold of Washington', Sadat swore, 'will never make us give up our principles.' Faced with one superpower which helped the enemy 'with everything it possesses, with everything in its power, with mad enthusiasm', and with another which, though still a 'friend', had proved wanting, Egypt had only one resource left. That was 'self-reliance' — its own and, it was to be hoped, that of the Arabs in general. 'If necessary, Egyptian and Arab nationalism will remain alone on the battlefield, but it will never surrender.'[65]

It was a defiant speech, almost Churchillian in tone, and some of those who had applauded the Russians' expulsion as a sign that 'realism' was gaining ground in the Arab camp, and urged more of it, were piqued to find their opinions and advice so summarily spurned. 'It would appear', wrote the *New York Times*, 'that the Egyptians are determined to bring down new catastrophes upon themselves and the whole Middle East. . . . President Sadat and Egyptian missile crews have already undermined hope that . . . the expulsion . . . might mean a turn towards rationality and peace in the Middle East.' His threats now rang 'more futile and foolish than ever'.

The Churchillian touch had not been unrehearsed. For it was in Churchill and wartime Britain that Sadat and his officials now found a reservoir of justifications. Thus Egypt might have lost a battle, but it had not lost the war. The 1967 war, the so-called 'Setback', had only been Egypt's Dunkirk. The crucial difference, however, which the regime could hardly point out, though others might, was that, unlike Britain, Egypt simply was not fighting. Sadat could hardly expect the plaudits of the *New York Times* as a great wartime leader but he was not getting them from his own people either. Realizing that, he felt constrained in this self-same speech to propose the kind of measures which a Churchill would never have dreamed of introducing. He called upon the People's Assembly to promulgate a law for the 'protection of national unity'. It loyally complied. 'National unity', said Assembly president Hafiz Badawi, 'is our most powerful weapon against the enemy. It was always the weapon with which we faced our enemies in battle. National unity is not our invention—it comes to us from the Koran and the Holy Books.' By now some Egyptians were wondering whether Sadat, in order to make up for the offensive weapons he said he had failed to get from the Russians, was planning to send them into battle armed with national unity instead. 'Of course,' Badawi went on, 'no one imagines that in passing this law the People's Assembly is putting any restrictions on freedom. It is protecting and guaranteeing freedoms. But freedoms without controls are chaos.'

It was 'no voice louder than the battle' erected into law—and draconian law at that. The mere spreading of rumours now became a criminal offence, the penalty for which varied according to the gravity of the rumours. Anyone who put them about 'without sufficient thought for the consequences'—that is, presumably, by accident—would be liable to an unspecified term of imprisonment. Anyone who 'deliberately propagates false or biased news, statements or rumours prejudicial to national unity' would be liable to imprisonment plus a fine of between £E100 and £E500. If these took a 'sensational form directed towards the army' the penalty became an unspecified period of forced labour—likewise for rumours spread in connivance with a foreign power. As for the most mischievous form of rumour-mongering—that perpetrated in connivance with a 'hostile power'—it was to be punishable by nothing less than hard labour for life.[66]

The new law inspired more of the very transgressions it was supposed to prevent. And political jokes—the regime was now trying to put a stop to them too—flourished as rarely before. Ridicule could not be stemmed by ridiculous legislation. It was all becoming a bad case of 'fish, milk and tamarind'—which is how Egyptians describe a situation of indescribable confusion. The flood of contradictory postures, policies and pronouncements which had issued from Sadat's two-year presidency was like an endless dish of fish, milk and tamarind, which the people could surely not be expected to digest much more of. Or, to borrow Egyptian idiom again, the country seemed to be governed by a troupe of *galla-galla* men, illusionists, who could not produce the great feat of magic that was billed as the climax of their act. Time was running out. The audience was jeering impatiently as trick followed inferior trick, with the patter to match: purging the power centres, correcting the Revolution; the 'sovereignty of the law'; 'science and faith'; 'the ethics of the Egyptian village'; the Year of Decision; Total Confrontation and Zero Hour; mobilization and battle committees; throwing out the Russians and surreptitious approaches to the Americans; 'patience and silence' and 'everything for the battle'; and now 'the protection of national unity'. Everything, in fact, except the battle itself, and lifting the intolerable burden of 'no peace, no war'. Surely Sadat and his *galla-galla* men would soon be howled off the stage altogether.

Those two worlds—the *galla-galla* world of Sadat's own creation and the real world his people inhabited—were separated by a gulf that was inexorably widening. Make-believe was apparently locked in ceaseless, losing conflict with reality. Propaganda had always been a key component of Nasserism and in that respect, for all Sadat's claims to the contrary, there had been no change at all. Dr Abdul Kader Hatem, re-installed as Deputy Premier and Minister of Information and Culture, presided once again over the empire he had built for his late master. He had his headquarters in the thirty-eight-storey Nile-side monster that dominates Cairo. From transmitters in Alexandria, Cairo Radio broadcast to five continents in thirty-four languages. The Egyptian press was an autonomous, but closely guarded province of Dr Hatem's empire. Through his propaganda chief Sadat tried to foist *his* world on his people. But it was a labour of Sysiphus. When the people protested, when reality

141

encroached on illusion, his first instinct was to appease and cajole the encroachers with another trick or two, and his second was to repress and intimidate them, with the instruments he had inherited from Nasser and the new ones, such as his national unity law, which he had constructed for himself.

There was demoralization everywhere. 'No peace, no war' was like a cancer eating away at the structure of society. 'Where will the black smoke rise next?' asked a Cairo newspaper, speculating not about the next Israeli raid, but about the extraordinary spate of fires, in the capital and elsewhere, that had been destroying public utilities, factories, trams, trains and historic buildings. At first they were officially attributed to negligence, a common enough disease in Egypt. But investigation soon revealed graver causes. It turned out, for example, that twenty brand-new trams had been set alight by a venal official who had ordered second-grade models from abroad, charged the National Transport Board for the top-grade and pocketed the difference himself. A railway official had burned down a station to conceal his profits on the sale of tickets. A fire at the famous Mehalla al-Kobra cotton weaving complex, originally attributed to an electrical short-circuit, was in reality an attempt to disguise the theft of a large quantity of cotton fibre. Corruption, endemic in Egypt, was obviously getting worse, and few doubted that the higher up the hierarchy you went, the worse it became. Those who were found out were the mere scapegoats for the real culprits above them. Even so, this arsonism was a new and highly disturbing phenomenon. Students and intellectuals who had been victimized, even imprisoned, for denouncing negligence and corruption were now threatening to take the law into their hands and return 'fire for fire'.

For many the 'black smoke' rose from some deep and dark recess of the national psyche. Obviously, and prosaically, corruption was part of it, but also at work, they felt, was some irrational destructive instinct from within the people themselves, some primitive social protest born of the overwhelming frustration in which all of Egypt lived. It seemed poignantly appropriate that not just trams and trains, but the country's national heritage—first the country's famous Cairo Opera House, then the Gohari Palace of Muhammad Ali—were going up in flames. 'At least', ran the caption of an *al-Ahram* cartoon, 'whatever the Egyptians do in 1972, they can scarcely burn down the Pyramids'.

The cancer struck unerringly at society's weakest points. Sectarian strife between Moslems and Christians has been rare in Egypt in modern times. Egypt's Copts belong to the oldest Christian rite. In 1972 there were officially about three million of them but the Copts themselves reckoned that they numbered up to some seven million. With perhaps legitimate, but no doubt irritating pride, they are apt to consider themselves the most authentic of Egypt's inhabitants, a symbol of continuity, pre-dating Islam, that goes back to the Pharaohs. Under Nasser's revolution they had suffered pervasive, if unofficial, discrimination which had left them underrepresented in the upper reaches of the administration, the public sector and the armed forces.

On 5 November 1972 a Coptic church at Khanka, 20 miles south of Cairo, was partially destroyed by Molotov cocktails. Virtually the entire Coptic priesthood of Cairo immediately converged on the town for a protest prayer. Moslem bigots greeted them with shouts of 'God is Great', and Pope Shenoudeh III, the dynamic young leader of the Coptic community, embarked on a dawn-to-dusk fast until the authorities settled the affair to his satisfaction. It was idle to look for the specific cause behind this outbreak of sectarian violence. It was the deeper ones that mattered. They lay in the general exasperation which prompted some within the Moslem majority to seek solace in a rigorous, fundamentalist interpretation of their faith. The more bigoted roused their co-religionists against the Coptic minority, charging them with disloyalty to the country or of plotting to 'take it over'. The Copts, already resentful of the disabilities under which their community suffered, permitted their own bigots to react in ways that tended to justify the suspicions against them.

Typically, President Sadat and Dr Hatem's propaganda machine detected a scheming foreign hand in it all. With his own eyes —Sadat said in his speech commemorating the twentieth anniversary of the Revolution—he had seen leaflets that were harmful to Moslems. 'They came from abroad, from the United States in fact.' He had also seen leaflets harmful to the Copts, 'and they, too, came from the United States'. He turned a resolutely blind eye to the real causes within; for to acknowledge those would have been to acknowledge the real nature of the disease, and his own failure to check its spread.

And there came trouble within the army itself. On 12 October a captain led a convoy of three armoured vehicles to the square outside the Hussein Mosque, an important place of worship in populous

143

central Cairo. There he harangued the congregation, more numerous than usual during Ramadan, calling for 'immediate war' against Israel, regardless of the consequences. The army wanted to fight, he said, not to eat sand. The Cairo press, briefly mentioning the affair, described the officer as 'mentally deranged'.[67] Doubtless he was. There were many stories of soldiers going crazy or committing suicide out of the sheer boredom and despair of life at the front. The affair must have unsettled the regime, because Dr Hatem delivered a strong protest to the British ambassador about the BBC's coverage of this and other incidents. At the end of October, Sadat dismissed his War Minister, General Ahmad Sadiq, as a 'defeatist'—he later explained—who had 'lied' to him about his country's preparedness for war and caused him to lose many nights of sleep.[68] Apparently Sadiq simply did not believe, as a soldier, that Egypt could start a war now or in the near future.[69]

Stories quickly leaked out of an attempted coup which would have replaced Sadat with his disgraced but popular War Minister. Scores of officers were said to have been arrested. The government at first denied the rumours as a campaign by Zionist-inspired news media 'hostile to Egypt'. Then it partially confirmed them, by officially admitting that some air force officers had been arrested for interrogation. Changing tack again, it proceeded to declare war on those who were disseminating any version of events at variance with its own. The 'Voice of the Arabs' attacked the BBC—much listened to by Arabs who had lost faith in their own radio stations—as a 'factory of lies'. It reported that 'political quarters' in the Egyptian capital were contemplating a 'total boycott' of the BBC and the enforcement of severe penalties against any Arab working for it. Many letters and cables, the radio station reported, had been received from Arab writers, entertainers, and just ordinary listeners, demanding such retaliation 'unless the BBC stopped within a short time serving as a Zionist tool'. In his memoirs, Chief of Staff Saad Shazly was later to confirm that there had been a plot. The plotters, led by a dismissed, dissident general had planned to arrest the President and 'everyone who mattered' at the forthcoming wedding of Shazly's daughter on 9 November.[70]

Trouble in the army was an ominous portent for Sadat. The army, whose support he had secured through General Sadiq in his showdown with Ali Sabri and the ASU, was the mainstay of his power. Now another institution which had gained a little weight since the Corrective Movement was growing more assertive too. True, the

People's Assembly was in no sense a real threat. But in November it was suddenly infused with an unwonted critical spirit. Partly, no doubt, it had been inspired, for tactical reasons, from the top. None the less, never before had an official institution so closely reflected the feelings of the ordinary people in apparent defiance of authority as when the Chamber rejected a policy statement by Prime Minister Aziz Sidqi in which he claimed that his government had now prepared the country 'for all eventualities' in the struggle with Israel. 'If this is true', protested one deputy, 'what are we waiting for? Why doesn't the battle begin?' The Assembly also took Dr Sidqi to task for gratuitously offending the Soviet Union—for 'diverting the battle from the direction of striking at the enemy to the direction of destroying the alliance with a friend'. In other words, the government of Total Confrontation and Continuous Action had failed to do what it had pledged to do when it took office during January's student riots: to put the home front on a level with the war front.

Inevitably that was how students saw matters too. There was no manipulating them. Appeasement had not worked for long. There had been material sops (such as freedom to travel abroad during the summer vacation) and political ones (such as the right to publish student newspapers that enjoyed significantly greater freedom than the national press). It was the 'resignation' of General Sadiq which had set the students off this time. The right took the lead with a rash of wall posters with a distinctly religious flavour to them: 'God forgive you, Sadat', 'We cannot liberate Jerusalem with atheist arms.' A mere three months after the expulsion of 20,000 Soviet experts, Sadat, in his dire need of weapons, had been trying to mend his fences with Moscow and extremists on the right strongly objected to what they regarded as renewed subservience to the Soviet Union. The various currents soon coalesced, as before, in a common stream of angry protest which deliberately challenged Sadat on his own ground. The calls for *real* democracy as well as for *real* mobilization meant that Sadat's liberalization was no more serious, in the students' eyes, than his preparations for war. They set up 'committees for the defence of democracy' while their wall posters protested that 'the Jews are on my soil, and the police at my door'.

The students were merely the spearhead of a much broader movement of opinion. Others, too, were trying to breach Dr Hatem's propaganda empire. In September 500 writers and artists had signed a protest declaring that 'Egypt's culture is dying a slow, painful death under a stranglehold of innumerable restrictions: censorship, religious, social and political bigotry, graft and corruption.' It had been 'reduced to a commodity subject primarily to considerations of profit and loss'. The censor was only tolerant of 'frivolous sensuality, reactionary thought and drivel'.

There were, of course, some forms of self-expression beyond the censor's reach. Irrepressible humorists, highly gregarious, long subject to alien and oppressive rule, the Egyptians easily carried their culture underground. Poetry, for example, copied, cyclostyled, set to music and sung, made a remarkable vehicle for uncensored news. Widely diffused within the country, and percolating outside it, it reassured the people that their world, with all its physical and emotional pains, was indeed the real one, not that of Sadat and his *galla-galla* men. Leading exponents of the genre were the inseparable pair, Ahmad Nagm and Sheikh Imam. Nagm, a slightly built man with the air of a tired schoolboy, composed the ballads. Sheikh Imam, blind since birth, set them to music and, accompanying himself on the *oud* (lute), sang them at student rallies, private political get-togethers and semi-clandestine gatherings of one kind or another. Patriotic and satirical, vivid and witty, the ballads made eloquent commentary on the events of the time, and the pretentions and pomposities of those who shaped them. Inevitably Nagm and Imam had something to say about the 'battle', and inevitably, too, the ballad remained a top favourite until the battle actually came. For solo voice (the Authority) and chorus (the People), it mocked the most famous and most jaded of the regime's ever-growing repertoire of inspirational slogans.

Authority:
>No voice louder than the Battle,
>Beautiful songs and melodies for the Battle,
>Every effort and every arm for the Battle,
>And committees for the Battle,
>Greetings, my boy, for the Battle
>Greetings, for the lady Battle,
>Greetings, O *Bey*, for the Battle
>And also for the owner of the house of the Battle,
>Of paramount importance, this Battle,
>We must mobilize the people for the Battle,
>One million men for the Battle.

People:
> We baked black bread, the colour of the Battle,
> And we ate black bread, the colour of the Battle,
> The people starved for the sake of the Battle,
> But where *is* the Battle?

Authority:
> Silence, boy, and dance for the Battle.

People:
> Silence O *Bey*, where *is* the Battle?

All:
> No voice louder than the Battle.

Sadat had not set any kind of deadline for the end of 1972. But it was an embarrassing landmark all the same, for it meant that not only had he failed to make good his original Year of Decision, he had let another full year pass without one. Nothing daunted, on 28 December he expressed his satisfaction with those who, Dr Hatem notwithstanding, were attempting to point this out. He also welcomed 'the discussions of the youth in the universities, their congresses and opinions'. They would be allowed to continue without fear. The future belonged to the country's youth, so 'how can we keep them away from its problems?' And he coined a new slogan: 'Freedom can only be guaranteed by more freedom.' But then he reverted to an old one. 'The time has come to raise no voice louder than the battle', he warned, 'when only the call for liberation must be heard. . . . Egypt's enemies are exploiting these democratic trends.'[71]

The next day the security forces pounced. About 100 student leaders, lawyers, writers and journalists were arrested. Among them was Ahmad Nagm. Students at Cairo University immediately went on the rampage. It was a repeat of the events of January 1972 but on an altogether more menacing scale. The universities were closed down. Altogether about 2,000 students were arrested and about 100 of their hard-core activists held for prosecution. This time the students won much wider public sympathy than before—they and their mothers. For women started staging demonstrations of their own. They were cleverer than the ever-vigilant secret police. On the *Id el-Adha*, the Feast of the Sacrifice, the mothers surreptitiously assembled in the famed Ezbekieh Gardens, where, upon a signal, they whipped out banners and placards and shouted: 'You are sacrificing our sons for the Feast'; 'Our sons for Sinai and not for Egyptian gaols.' That the students spoke for many more than themselves, even some of Sadat's supporters now acknowledged.

But Sadat would have none of it. For him it was another conspiracy. The 250,000-strong 'student base' was — as it had been the year before — 'completely sound'. It was the familiar 'small cliques' which had caused all the havoc. This time, he told the People's Assembly on 31 January 1973, the prime movers had been the 'adventurist left'. They had been plotting against the regime since the summer — a plot that was to have come to fruition on 1 January, with a seizure of power, first in the universities, and then in the country as a whole. In October the 'retrograde right', profiting from the chaos caused by the left as well as by Egypt's 'pause with a friend' (a euphemism for the expulsion of the Russians), had stepped in to promote its own nefarious ends. Sadat also spoke darkly of 'pashas who began to form shadow cabinets and prepare to take over power', of 'professional people who encourage deviation and mutiny' and of journalists who 'feed foreign correspondents with false news about Egypt'.

Thus, despite the soundness of the student base and the smallness of the deviationist clique, Sadat was, on his own admission, challenged from left and right, by the intelligentsia and by the privileged classes. He spoke as one besieged on all hands. 'For the first time in the history of our country', he solemnly declared, 'there has been deviation from the basic political line of the 1952 Revolution.' He called on the great mass of ordinary Egyptians, the 'active forces of the people' as the Nasserist formula had it, to stand firm against 'a right which holds that a privileged minority should run the country, and a left which wants to establish a dictatorship of the proletariat'.[72]

Authorized by the People's Assembly to 'take what measures he sees fit' in order to protect national unity, the alliance of the active forces of the people and the student base, Sadat proceeded to form a new body whose title spoke for itself.

He was waiving his own rules as he did so. The 'state of institutions' inaugurated by his Corrective Movement was supposed to enshrine the principle of the separation of powers — one man for one job. But the President of the Disciplinary Committee of the ASU — for such was the title of this new body — was also the Speaker of the People's Assembly: the same Hafiz Badawi who, in an earlier assignment, had presided over the secret trial of Ali Sabri and his fallen power centre.

Badawi was originally a country lawyer raised from obscurity after delivering a flowery and obsequious speech before President Nasser. He had memorized the Koran by the age of ten. 'Islam', 'traditional values', 'the ethics of the Egyptian village' were his trinity. He and other members of the Disciplinary Committee typified the resurgent rural bourgeoisie — ostentatiously devout, narrow-minded men who cloaked their poverty of intellect in florid oratory and sought to lord it over the peasantry. Such men were naturally thrust to the forefront in a regime that was not only moving to the right but was, in its decadence, now devoting itself less and less to the welfare of the people as a whole than to preserving the vested interests of the new order which it had brought into being. They also seemed to represent something in Sadat's own subconscious, that part of him which, beneath the liberalizing and enlightened exterior, had earlier brought him into close sympathy with the Moslem Brotherhood and the quasi-fascist political underworld; a streak of vindictiveness, bred of an inferiority complex, whose full dimensions only the later years of his presidency were to reveal.

The Disciplinary Committee issued lists of 'deviationists' who had strayed from their 'basic duties' as 'active' members of the ASU. They included writers, journalists, lawyers, engineers and doctors. Their principal offences appeared to have been the signing of a petition asking for the release of the students. They did not include Egypt's two most distinguished men of letters, Tawfiq al-Hakim and Naguib Mahfuz. None the less, Dr Hatem ordered radio and television to boycott their works, not even to mention their names. For in Sadat's opinion, 'if Israel had paid millions of pounds, it would not have been able to perform more than Egyptian pens . . . Beware that the Jews don't take part of your brain as they have taken part of your land.'[73]

For all Sadat's strictures against the 'retrograde right' it was the left that bore the brunt of the Disciplinary Committee's punitive wrath. But it was not so much their radicalism which caused offence, or any design to bring down the regime — for they had none — it was simply that they sought to exercise their critical faculties, and, in so far as that was possible in Dr Hatem's empire, to bring reality into the world of illusion.

Meanwhile, as their 'deviationist' elders were being held up to obloquy, the student leaders had formal charges brought against them. These read more like a commendation than an indictment.

149

They had written articles for university magazines condemning Zionism and imperialism, calling for 'people's war', and exhorting Christians and Moslems to rise above confessional animosities. One defendant was accused of having in his possession a book by a 'Zionist agent'—the agent in question being none other than Muhammad Darwish, a leading Palestinian poet, several times imprisoned by the Israelis, who, when choosing exile in 1969, was honoured as a hero in Egypt and rewarded with a highly paid position on *al-Ahram*. The magistrate expressed amazement at such charges, and ordered the students' release. The court order was, however, subject to the President's approval, and he vetoed it.

Sadat's 'freedom and democracy' was collapsing. Only by launching an inquisition could the *galla-galla* men hold the stage. But it was impossible, even by imprisoning them, to silence these purveyors of reality. Within three days of his incarceration in the thousand-year-old Citadel of Cairo, Nagm's own versified account of this 'conspiracy' to bring down the regime, *The True Story and the Legend*, was being recited up and down the Nile valley.

Time for a shock

On 26 March, President Sadat made himself Prime Minister with the task of preparing the country for 'the stage of total confrontation' with Israel. He had not wanted to do it, he said, because that might seem to be inconsistent with his 'state of institutions': 'it might be misunderstood, or, at least, conspirators might try to strip it of its aim.' However—in an apparent reference to the student riots and the tensions they had produced within the regime—he said that the 'state of institutions' was becoming the 'state of contradictions'; and that was intolerable during 'the stage of total confrontation'. He was determined, he assured a joint meeting of the ASU Central Committee and the People's Assembly, 'to unify responsibilities without encroaching upon the philosophy of the state of institutions'. He would co-operate loyally with both; therefore, at a time of 'unification of responsibilities, we shall have extended participation to the maximum'. Besides, he was only assuming his new role 'for a limited time and a specific assignment'.

It was Greek to the man-in-the-street, who only understood that Sadat was concentrating more powers into his own hands than his predecessor ever had; that in addition to President and Prime Minister, he was now Supreme Commander of the Armed Forces, president of the ASU Central Committee and—yet another newly acquired post—Military Governor. Furthermore, he was going to stand no nonsense from his critics. He asked parliament to enact a new law granting the Socialist Prosecutor—such was his title—new powers to 'protect society from deviationism'. Whatever the advantages of Sadat's new office, the disadvantages were clear. He had put himself in the front line. He had run out of scapegoats. Or, as he put it, 'I have decided to take my fate in my own hands.'[74]

The 'specific assignment' he had undertaken was his great gamble, the Crossing, and he all but publicly said so. At least he said about as much as any leader planning a war could say, short of announcing the date. It was the Americans who had driven him to it. In February he had sent Hafiz Ismail, his National Security Adviser, to Washington in yet another bid to interest the Americans in a peaceful settlement. It happened in the middle of the student riots. It caused something of a sensation in Cairo. His critics were stunned—almost to the point of grudging admiration—by the sheer brazenness of a leader who, while ceaselessly denouncing the United States as the incorrigible villain standing behind Israel, suddenly and without any discernible change of heart on the Americans' part, dispatched his own 'Henry Kissinger' to plead with President Nixon himself. With what reckless disdain the Nixon administration treated this last brave try, Sadat later related in an interview with Arnaud de Borchgrave of *Newsweek*.

If Hafiz Ismail [he said] had conducted these talks with Golda Meir, the results would have been less ridiculous. They have not and will not exert pressure on Israel. Quite the contrary. . . . And on the heels of Hafiz Ismail's mission, Washington released the details of the new Phantom deal and aid for the development of Israel's new home-made fighter bomber. Everything was discouraging. Complete failure and despair sum it up. There is only one conclusion—if we don't take our own case in our own hands, there will be no movement. . . . I'm not begging. There is no sense in turning the clock back. Everything I've done leads to pressure for more concessions. . . . Every door I have opened has been slammed in my face by Israel—with American blessings. . . . The situation is hopeless and—make no mistake—highly explosive. . . . The situation here will—mark my words—be much worse than Vietnam. . . . The time has come for a shock. . . . Diplomacy will continue as before, during and after the battle. . . . All West

Europeans are telling us the same thing. And what's more, they are right. Everyone has fallen asleep over the Middle East crisis. But they will soon wake up to the fact that the Americans have left us no other way out.

'In other words', de Borchgrave asked, 'one has to fight in order to be able to talk?' 'At the very least,' Sadat replied. 'As you say, times have changed. And everything is changing here, too — for the battle.'

'I can only conclude from what you say that you believe a resumption of hostilities is the only way out,' de Borchgrave pressed. 'You are quite right. Everything in this country is now being mobilized for the resumption of the battle — which is now inevitable.'[75]

Of course, Sadat *had* said such things before — time without number — but there was a quiet earnestness, a fatalistic serenity in his tone that set these remarks apart from the theatrical sabre-rattling that was his usual public style. It is remarkable, in retrospect, that no one really grasped the significance of what he was saying. Dr Kissinger dismissed it as bombast. Indeed, a 'bombastic clown' was all that Kissinger had ever considered Sadat to be.[76] It was an unflattering view of the Egyptian leader, but one for which Kissinger could be pardoned, shared as it was by many of Sadat's own countrymen. So little credence did anyone place in what Sadat, the 'donkey', said that even those who did notice the difference in tone could not really bring themselves to believe that it portended anything new.

Why should this not be yet another cry for American help? After all, it was being accompanied by yet another of those mobilizations that came round like the seasons. 'Battle committees' were once again in permanent conclave throughout the country. Hundreds of young men were supposedly volunteering for the newly formed 'popular resistance forces'. Air-raid shelters were being built, basements cleared. Mock air raids were staged; a partial black-out imposed. Sadat had gone into his 'operations room'. Surely, the sceptics said, a leader who is really planning to go to war does not shout his intention from the rooftops — especially the leader of a country which had learned, twice in a generation and in the most painful of ways, how useful it is to take the enemy by surprise. And if Sadat was, after all, up to something, few believed that it would be much more than a dramatic gesture, a commando raid across the Canal, or a massive raid into Sinai — something which, as he put it, would cause a 'shock'. But a full-scale 'war of liberation', an Israeli-*blitzkrieg* in reverse – that was beyond anyone's wildest imaginings.

With hindsight, other portents became recognizable as such. Since the dismissal of General Sadiq in October 1972, the Russians had been growing more forthcoming. In his *Newsweek* interview, Sadat told de Borchgrave that they were 'providing us now with everything that's possible for them to supply. And I am now quite satisfied.' He wasn't really: he was probably just saying so to impress the Americans. He wasn't getting all the offensive weapons he thought he needed, but it seemed that the Egyptian command was now resigned to this. 'The type of weapons does not matter,' wrote columnist Ihsan Abdul Koddous, a confidant of Sadat, 'what matters is that the weapons can be used for hitting the enemy and repelling enemy blows. In other words, I do not think that Egypt, as she imports these weapons from the Soviet Union these days, is faced by the problem of the type of weapons now that it has solved the problem of the steady flow of weapons.'[77] The dimensions of this flow were such that Sadat was later to confirm that he was being 'drowned' in new hardware. 'Between December 1972 and June 1973, we received more arms than in the whole of the two preceding years.'[78]

It was because Kissinger did regard Sadat as a 'bombastic clown', because his experts were apparently telling him that Israel could reduce Egypt to complete impotence in a matter of hours while the Western world secretly whistled in admiration – it was precisely because of such unflattering opinions that Sadat was able to take Kissinger, Israel, and all the others who shared them, so completely by surprise. The role of the world's buffoon was hardly one that Sadat relished. 'Remember,' said the admiring Moussa Sabri, after it was all over, 'remember, Arabs, how he suffered in silence.' None the less it was the role which, paradoxically, was to ensure him of his great triumph and enable him, after the Crossing, to assume the heroic and statesmanlike vocation to which he had always aspired.

Sadat had taken his decision; throughout the long, hot summer his own 'fate', and Egypt's too, lay with the generals to whom he had entrusted its execution. Methodically, and with infinite discretion, they prepared for Operation Badr. They did so against a background of miscellaneous happenings that tended to reduce even further any expectations that Sadat possessed either the will or the means to administer any 'shock', let alone turn the area into another Vietnam.

Egypt lent itself to yet more diplomatic haggling; but it was futile. The Security Council passed a unanimous resolution highly critical of Israel's general posture; but its effect was entirely vitiated by the abstention of the United States. Parting company even with its closest European allies, it described it as 'highly partisan and unbalanced'. There was another outbreak of Egyptian displeasure with the Soviet Union. The Nixon-Brezhnev summit of June 1973, and the superpowers' evident determination to consolidate *détente*, were construed as an indication—as one Cairo newspaper put it— that all Egypt could expect from the Russians was 'good wishes'. President Sadat was falling foul of his closest Arab partner, Colonel Gadafi. He no longer wanted that unity with Libya which—or rather his original enthusiasm for which—had precipitated the May 1971 showdown with the Ali Sabri power centre, and which, after a 99·98 per cent vote in favour of it, he had described as 'the cornerstone of the battle'. Or at least he did not want the kind of instant, total fusion which the impetuous young Colonel had seduced him into—or apparently thought he had.

In late August Sadat took off on a secret five-day tour of Saudi Arabia and other Arab countries. He found a disconsolate Gadafi waiting for him on his return to Cairo. He tried to placate him with a face-saving announcement which preserved at least the façade of unification, but there was no disguising the fact that relations between Sadat and the oil-rich conservative, pro-American states were now developing into the new cornerstone of his Arab strategy. In September he resumed diplomatic relations with Jordan; King Hussein, stoutly pro-American too, was thus re-admitted into the fold of Arab respectability without any atonement for the misdemeanour, the ruthless expulsion of the Palestinian guerrillas from his kingdom, which had placed him outside it. On 14 September the Israelis shot down—or so they credibly claimed—no fewer than thirteen Syrian fighter-planes for the loss of one of their own in a dogfight off the Syrian coast. If any proof was needed that, more than six years after the 1967 war, Israel still enjoyed almost complete mastery of the skies, this was surely it.

Yet things were not what they seemed. 'Moderate', conservative, pro-Western Saudi Arabia could furnish Sadat with the kind of support—through diplomacy, financial aid, the deployment of the 'oil weapon'—which he could never get from the radical, fire-breathing Gadafi. King Hussein—though he evidently did not even know it—was being courted for the important, if precautionary, military role he could play on the Eastern front. The loss of thirteen Syrian aircraft was a price worth paying for helping to keep Israeli pilots, now more overweeningly self-confident than ever, in ignorance of the secret weapon, the bristling forest of SAM missiles, that lay in wait for them when, on 6 October, they were to throw all they had into a desperate effort to stem the enemy advance into Sinai and Golan.

It was to commemorate the third anniversary of the death of President Nasser that Sadat made his last public appearance before the Crossing. He made it an occasion for clemency. He announced that all journalists expelled from the ASU as deviationists would be reinstated. 'It is not in my nature', he said, 'to harm a man in his work, his profession and his livelihood.' He also instructed the courts to discontinue their proceedings against those students due to face trial for their part in the New Year riots and demonstrations. Clearly, if he was going to win his great gamble he would be facing no more mutinies from students, journalists or anyone else; if he was going to lose it his fate was sealed anyway.

His anniversary encomium was also marked by an unusual sobriety of tone.

Perhaps you have noticed [he said] that there is one subject which I have not mentioned, the subject of the battle. I did this on purpose. We have had enough of words. I want to tell you just one thing. We know our goal and we are determined to reach it. There is no effort, no sacrifice that we shall not accept in order to do so. I won't promise anything or go into details. But I shall simply say that the liberation of our territory is the fundamental task before us. With God's help we shall carry it out, we shall succeed, we shall regain what is ours. That is the will of our people, the will of our nation. It is the will of God.[79]

His audience had not in fact noticed, or, if they had, they did not much care. They were sated with words. They did not heed them any more. But, eight days later, they were to recall the curious, quiet solemnity of this man who, in a few astonishing hours, had put on the stature of a modern Saladin.

4

'My Friend Henry'

The Israeli counter-crossing

It was on 16 October, ten days into the war, that Sadat savoured his moment of supreme triumph. In his address to the People's Assembly, the Hero of the Crossing pledged to fight on until all of Sinai was liberated—but, once that was accomplished, Egypt and the Arabs would make full and final peace with the State of Israel. He did not know that, even as he made this historic offer, his triumph was already in jeopardy. He did not know about the new and alarming development on the battlefield. At this stage, perhaps, his military commanders were at least as much to blame for what was happening there as he was. Or, in a deeper sense, one could say that the responsibility was not a personal one at all. It was inherent in that rigid, hierarchical spirit, inimical to individual initiative, which was still the bane of the Egyptian military machine. And that, in turn, was the reflection of a whole society whose excessive, immemorial respect for established authority the July Revolution had done little or nothing to change.

The brilliant planning and execution of the Crossing could not be gainsaid. This new-model Egyptian army had proved itself equal to Israel in a set-piece campaign where, with the advantage of surprise, every unit was able to adhere to the precise and particular task the master-plan had assigned it. But it was not its equal in a fast-changing war of movement, for here the *élan*, imagination and offensive daring of the front-line commanders, coupled with rapid communications and the sophisticated coordination of all the fighting arms, are the virtues that will ensure victory. If the Egyptian army did not achieve an overwhelming superiority in that first great thrust, it was always likely that it would gradually lose its ability to dictate the course of the struggle, and fall prey to the characteristic strengths of the enemy. That point had long since been passed on the northern front. There, in the first hours of the combined Arab onslaught, the Syrian advance had posed a much greater threat than the Crossing itself; in regaining the Golan Heights, the Syrians were poised to smash down into the Israeli heartlands. But the small band of Israeli defenders averted the threat; in a desperate contest in which neither side yielded much to the other in courage or fortitude, the lightning versatility of the few eventually prevailed against the ponderous resolution of the many. Within four days, the Israelis, fully mobilized, were driving the attackers back across the rock-strewn, basalt plateau until, penetrating deeper than they had ever done before, they were within 20 miles of Damascus itself.

A few hours after President Sadat spoke on 16 October, Israeli Premier Golda Meir addressed *her* parliament. There could be no doubt, she told the Knesset, that the Arabs were once again bent on the total destruction of the State of Israel. As for Sadat's ceasefire terms, and his call for the immediate evacuation of all the occupied territories, she rejected them outright. 'The time for a ceasefire will be when the enemy's strength is broken. I am certain that when we have brought our enemies to the verge of collapse, representatives of various states will not be slow in "volunteering" to try and save our assailants.' And, in a laconic but sensational intimation that the Israeli army was again on the way to achieving that aim, she announced that a task force was now 'in operation on the western bank of the Suez Canal'.

At one o'clock that morning General Ariel Sharon and 200 men had paddled across the Canal just north of the Great Bitter Lake. If the Egyptians were hyper-cautious and slow-moving, this was Israeli panache carried to extraordinary lengths. Israel's most headstrong commander was defying not only his superiors but the most elementary rules of warfare in pursuit of his *tour de force*. To cross into 'Africa', to strike the enemy where he least expected it, was certainly in keeping with the Israeli *blitzkrieg* tradition, but to achieve it Sharon had by all orthodox criteria taken almost suicidal risks.

He hoped by dawn on 16 October to have established a broad corridor down to the east bank of the Canal, a bridge across it, and at least a credible beachhead on its west bank. A whole division of tanks should then have begun pouring across the waterway. Instead, there was a highly exposed corridor, no bridge—and no prospect of one for at least twelve hours—and, for beachhead, the merest toehold. Furthermore, flatly disobeying orders, Sharon did not instruct his little force to dig in for a desperate holding operation against the expected Egyptian counter-offensive but split it up into raiding parties which were sent out in search of anything that was worth attacking.

The Egyptian War Minister, General Ahmed Ismail, had gone to the People's Assembly to hear President Sadat speak. On his return he learned of the 'infiltration of a small number of amphibian tanks'. It was possible to destroy them quickly, the message said, and a 'storm battalion' had been moved up to confront them. Later in the day a military communiqué admitted the counter-crossing. 'The enemy', it said, 'sneaked across the Bitter Lakes with seven tanks in an attempt to raid certain positions on the west bank of the Canal.' There was nothing to worry about, however, because 'our artillery destroyed three tanks and scattered the remainder, which our forces are pursuing.'[1]

Israel, however, persisted in claiming otherwise. According to its own communiqué, issued at six o'clock in the afternoon, an Israeli force had been operating west of the Canal behind Egyptian lines 'for the past twenty-four hours'. It had hit artillery and missile positions. The Egyptian people took the news of the Israeli penetration calmly, for they were still lulled by the gratifying knowledge that, in this war, their own communiqués had been proving more accurate than the enemy's. They waited confidently for the next one that would duly announce that the 'remainder' of the Israeli force had been dealt with. It was not until the next day, however, that their expectations were fulfilled. The military spokesman said that the force had now been wiped out. But the claim was again contradicted by his Israeli counterpart who said that the force was still operating on the West Bank, and was still attacking missile and artillery positions.

The truth was that Sharon's astonishing enterprise had been saved by the even more astonishing Egyptian response. When every possible allowance is made for the characteristic weaknesses of the Egyptian army and the characteristic strengths of the Israeli, it is still not enough to account for the calamity which now ensued. The decisive factor lay elsewhere, in the determination of President Sadat, after the glorious Crossing, to run 'his' war 'his' way in defiance of all military logic. That, at least, is the verdict of General Saad Shazly, the Egyptian Chief of Staff, and though it is a harsh one he supports it with cogency of argument, wealth of detail and professional authority in his personal testimony, *The Crossing of Suez*.[2]

The key to an understanding of Sadat's arbitrary interventions in the conduct of the war lay in his relationship with his War Minister, General Ahmed Ismail. Shazly does not hide his contempt for this 'weak man, alternating between submissiveness and bullying'. Twice dismissed by him, he 'hated Nasser'; he 'wholly identified with Sadat'. He shunned responsibility, preferring to receive orders rather than to give them. 'Another virtue in Sadat's eyes' was his deep unpopularity with the troops. 'But the unforgivable point is that Ismail was also a dying man . . . he had cancer. . . . I regret writing about Ismail as I do. But the truth must be told. Ismail was unfit for his job; and his weakness had terrible consequences for his country. The wickedness lies in the man who appointed and then manipulated Ismail, knowing as he did that Ismail was a dying man.'[3]

According to Shazly, the calamity the counter-crossing turned into was the result of a series of blunders, the first occurring two days before General Sharon paddled across the Canal. This was the decision to push the Egyptian offensive deeper into Sinai in a bid to seize the Mitla and Gidi passes. Such an offensive had never been part of Egypt's war aims; Shazly himself had 'passionately and continuously' opposed it on the grounds that Egypt simply did not have sufficient capability, particularly in the air. The decision was a 'political' one, and it was with heavy hearts that Shazly and his commanders put it into execution. 'Barring a miracle', he writes, 'the attack had no chance of success whatever.' It meant sending 400 tanks against 900 in well-prepared positions and in the same 'penny packet' fashion that had cost the Israelis themselves so dear in their initial response to the Crossing. So it was that in a few hours on the morning of 14 October, the Egyptians lost more tanks—250—than they had lost in the whole war till then. 'Even now', wrote Shazly six years later, 'I have no idea why the attack was mounted. It was, of course, President Sadat's decision. He has since claimed that he did it to relieve Israeli pressure on the Syrian front. That has to be nonsense. There has to be another explanation for Sadat's decision. Only he knows it.' That was 'the first catastrophic blunder . . . from which all other blunders followed'.

The next day, 15 October, 'a dot appeared on our air-defence screen in Centre Number Ten, moving swiftly north over the Canal zone and out over the Nile Delta. We knew what it was. We had seen it before . . . an SR-71A, the American reconnaissance counterpart of the MiG-25'. Within a few hours, it could be assumed, the Israelis would be in possession of the battlefield intelligence it had recorded—that the disastrous thrust into Sinai had left Egypt's strategic reserves on the west bank of the Canal more dangerously depleted than ever. Ordinary caution required the withdrawal of tanks from east to west to guard against an Israeli attempt, always foreseen, to cross the Canal and take the Egyptian bridgeheads from the rear. General Ismail turned down Shazly's 'urgent request' to put this into effect, arguing that withdrawal 'might panic our troops'. 'His unspoken reason was that he was to accompany the President to the People's Assembly next morning and wanted no suspicion of weakness to tarnish his triumph. So began Blunder Number Two. . . .' The Israeli penetration came to pass as Shazly had feared. Returning from the People's Assembly, Ismail summoned a conference to deal with it. He rejected Shazly's plan, which would have involved tank withdrawals from Sinai, and put forward a 'reckless' one of his own.

A few hours later the President . . . joined us in the Operations Room. Ismail explained tomorrow's plan. I regarded it as so wrongheaded and dangerous that I pressed my counterproposal to the President in the hope that he would overrule Ismail. Suddenly Sadat lost his temper. 'Why do you always propose withdrawing our troops from the east bank?' he shouted. 'You ought to be courtmartialled. If you persist in these proposals I will courtmartial you. I do not want another word.' I was deeply hurt. I tried to explain why such manoeuvres were forced on us by our weakness on the west bank, but Sadat was in such a temper he would not even listen.

By midnight the orders for Ismail's counter-attack had been given. But the Israeli bridgehead was expanding all the time, and for this crucial battle the Egyptians could only pit three armoured and one infantry brigade against six armoured and two infantry brigades. And 'our plan of attack was calculated to further worsen our chances'. By midday, 18 October, Israel had won the battle of Deversoir.

Their next step must be to pour across more armour, split it and thrust north and south simultaneously behind both our armies. Drastic action would be needed to stop this. But would the President and his Minister of War have the courage to take it? Already the regime was falling victim to its own lies. With cynical irresponsibility Ismail was announcing and our media were reporting that the enemy penetration still amounted to seven tanks hiding in the thickets around Deversoir. Our own armed forces were by now the principal victims of this nonsense. Convoys found themselves ambushed. Rear headquarters, guard units—most damagingly, SAM batteries—found themselves under sudden fire without the faintest idea what was going on.

At two o'clock that afternoon Sadat was back in the Operations Room. 'Ismail described the situation. At last the pair were driven to adopt my own plan to withdraw armour from the east bank. They proceeded to sabotage even this.' For they had decided to withdraw only a single armoured brigade. 'What good could that do now? . . .' It 'was not going to contain, let alone roll back, an enemy bridgehead now two divisions in strength.' Ordered to the front to 'raise morale', Shazly returned to headquarters in the afternoon of 19 October to advise Ismail that, the situation continuing to deteriorate,

we still had more troops on the east bank than we needed, but too few on the west bank to counter what was now a very real threat to encircle both our armies. I proposed we withdraw the four armoured brigades that were still on the east bank. Ismail refused. No unit would be withdrawn from Sinai. I went to confer with my assistants. I did not hide my conviction that unless we withdrew armour from the east to save the west, the outcome now looked grave. But what could we do? One of them suggested that I call the President and put the situation to him. I agreed. I went back to Ismail and told him that I and my senior staff wanted the President to come to Centre Ten to learn the situation for himself. Ismail was reluctant. It was a bit late, he said [it was about 22.00 hours]. I insisted that he call the President and only after getting a positive answer did I leave the room . . . *22.30 hours*. The President arrived, accompanied by the Minister for Presidential Affairs, Abdul Fatah Abdullah. They went directly to Ismail's office where they remained closeted for more than half an hour while the rest of us cooled our heels in the conference room off the Operations Room. *23.10 hours*. The trio emerged. The meeting began. In turn Sadat asked each commander except myself to make his report. I was not asked to speak. The reports were truthful, detailed, frank. As the last one finished, the President said simply: 'We will not withdraw a single soldier from the east to the west.' Still I made no comment. 'Say something,' Abdullah whispered. I ignored him. What was

161

there to say? Ismail should have told him my considered judgement that the withdrawal of four armoured brigades was our only hope; yet here was this man saying not a soldier must move. I had wanted the President to know the facts. Now he did. He could not claim that he had been kept in ignorance. The fate of the country was in his hands. In his memoirs, Sadat says I wanted to withdraw *all* our forces to the west bank, but that the other commanders at the meeting said: 'There was nothing to worry about.' Nonsense.

Even after the withdrawal of the four brigades the Egyptians would still have had 90,000 men in Sinai, with 500 tanks—not to mention other weaponry—to the enemy's 300. 'To suggest the withdrawal of all our troops from the east bank in such a situation would have been madness. To refuse to withdraw the four armoured brigades was a combination of madness, ignorance and treason. This was our fourth and fatal blunder.'[4]

It did not take long for the people, in Cairo and the country as a whole, to sense that something had gone badly wrong, and already, on 17 October, news was spreading by word of mouth that the situation at Deversoir was far more serious than the army command or the newspapers admitted. News has a way of filtering through the strictest censorship even, or perhaps especially, in wartime. In spite of the desert the front was at some points virtually adjacent to the densely populated rural heartlands. Wounded men, ambulance drivers, hospital staff gave away 'military secrets' unwittingly and these spread through the populace with amazing speed. Soon, rumour had it that the Israeli army had not only set up bridgeheads, it was moving on the capital itself. The effect was electric.

For the first time since the Suez war of 1956, the Egyptians were directly, almost physically, conscious of the enemy presence; it was right there, not just in the sandy wastes of Sinai, precious though they were, but in the villages and lush green, Nile-watered pastures of the Delta itself. When Britain, France and Israel had invaded the country, President Nasser had authorized the distribution of hundreds of thousands of rifles. He had driven incognito through the streets of Cairo, personally testing the mood of the people, and when they recognized him the crowds had shouted: 'We shall fight, we shall fight.' Men and youths had rushed to the Canal. But in 1956 there had been no 'war' in the real sense; nor had there been in 1967, only a knock-out blow that left the whole country numb and prostrate with shock. This time, the gamut of emotions—anguish, grief, joy, pride and hope—that any people feels when its fighting sons are being truly put to the test possessed the nation. 'Give us arms,' was the cry. Now something of a Battle of Britain spirit was gaining ground. Sadat, with his stirring address to the nation, had helped to stimulate it. No one would have blamed him if, like Churchill in 1940, he had admitted the full measure of the nation's peril.

Instead, he did his best still to hide it. Rather than put his trust in the army commanders and the people, in Egyptian and Arab 'self-reliance'—the phrase so often on his lips since the expulsion of the Soviet experts—he turned in desperation to the superpowers. In the first dizzy triumph of the Crossing, he had rejected all suggestion of a ceasefire; apparently the Russians had proposed one, arguing that Sadat had already achieved his privately stated aim of 'changing the balance of military and political power in the Arabs' favour' (according, for example, to the Soviet ambassador in Cairo, Vladimir Vinagradov).[5] Fearing that they would have to bear the full, initial brunt of Israel's counter-offensive, the Syrians, too, had been keen on a ceasefire, and even more so when those fears were realized. Now that it was Egypt's turn to suffer grave reverses, Sadat was all too eager for a ceasefire. The Russians were the first to learn the full scope of the disaster. They were so alarmed, in fact, that Prime Minister Alexei Kosygin had to make a last-minute cancellation of a scheduled meeting with the Danish Foreign Minister. The 'urgent mission' on which he had been called away was in reality a secret visit to Cairo, where, in the space of two days, he had five encounters with President Sadat. For all their dislike and mistrust of the Egyptian leader, the Russians could not tolerate another 1967. Their own prestige as a superpower was at stake: Egypt had fought with Soviet arms; the massive Soviet retraining effort had helped to forge this new military machine whose triumph was now in such grave danger of being swept entirely away. Humiliating though the expulsion of their experts had been for the Russians, it could now be seen, in retrospect, to have been mutually advantageous, in that neither they nor the Egyptians wanted the world to say that the decision to go to war had been a Soviet one, or that Russians were fighting on Egypt's behalf.

At first, it seems, President Sadat sought to mislead Kosygin about the true state of the battle. 'There had been a Stalingrad in Sinai and they would not admit it,' the Russians said.[6] When, on the morning of 18 October, Sadat finally confessed to him, the situation proved even worse than Kosygin had imagined. The Russians at first tried to secure American acceptance of a ceasefire which diluted Sadat's publicly proclaimed war aims: instead of total Israeli withdrawal to the 1967 frontiers, withdrawal to those frontiers with minor corrections; and instead of an immediate, a phased withdrawal. Dr Kissinger replied that while he had no objection in principle, now that the battle was swinging so decisively Israel's way, he had no chance of winning the acquiescence of America's protégé.

At three o'clock in the morning of 20 October, Sadat got in touch with the Soviet ambassador to ask for an immediate Soviet-sponsored ceasefire. By 21 October, he was ready to end the fighting on terms for which he might just as well not have fought at all. In the small hours of the morning of 22 October, the Security Council passed Resolution 338, calling on all parties to cease fire within twelve hours, in the positions they then occupied. They were invited, upon the cessation of hostilities, to begin 'the implementation of Security Council Resolution 242 in all its parts'. 'Negotiations between the parties concerned' would begin immediately 'under the appropriate auspices aimed at establishing a just and durable peace in the Middle East'. It was back to square one; for it had been precisely to break the intolerable impasse of 242—a resolution so vague that Israel, battening on to its territorial conquests, rejected all friendly Western, let alone Soviet or Arab, interpretations of it—that Egypt and Syria had waged the war they had so long and loudly threatened.

If the superpowers, half in concert, half in competition, had rescued Sadat *in extremis*, they had simultaneously deprived Israel of another of those total victories to which it had grown accustomed. But Resolution 338 had made no provision for policing the complex, uncertain ceasefire lines, and Israel, alleging (inventing, according to Shazly) Egyptian violations, lost no time in pressing home the encirclement of the Third Army to the east of the Canal. By nightfall on 23 October, it had closed the trap: the road to Suez, the beleaguered force's only supply line, was in Israeli hands; two divisions, 45,000 men with 250 tanks, were completely cut off.

The Russians were furious. They thought they had been double crossed, that, after agreeing to a ceasefire in Moscow, Dr Kissinger, returning to Washington via Tel Aviv, had encouraged the Israelis to believe that they could finish off the job they had begun. On 24 October, the Soviet ambassador to Washington handed Dr Kissinger a message from Soviet leader Leonid Brezhnev; in harsh, peremptory language, it threatened that if the United States was not prepared to join in the dispatch of forces to impose the ceasefire, the Soviet Union would act alone—a threat which the United States, aware that several

Soviet airborne divisions had been assembled on a 'ready-to-move' alert, was inclined to take very seriously. Consistently opposed to such joint intervention, it responded swiftly and vigorously; it ordered a grade-three nuclear alert, the first of its kind since President Kennedy had outfaced the Kremlin in the Cuban missile crisis of 1962. It had hardly gone into effect than the Soviet threat—real or imagined—was dissipated. With the help of two more Security Council resolutions, a United Nations emergency force arrived in the battle zone.

There was great disappointment at the ceasefire in the Arab world. Some countries, such as Iraq and Kuwait—which, though they had contributed troops, lay far from the battlefield—rejected it outright. President Assad of Syria accepted it two days after Sadat; but he did so with the utmost reluctance and, in an attempt to save face, he sought to impose the one condition he knew the enemy would never accept: 'the complete withdrawal of Israeli forces from occupied territory and a guarantee of the rights of the Palestinian people'. In a speech five days later he valiantly tried to explain the painful fact that the war had ended with the enemy in possession of more territory than when it had begun. The ceasefire, he said, had taken Syria completely by surprise. Its army had been conducting the kind of long struggle in which it was positively advantageous to lure the enemy into taking more territory, the better to achieve the final goal; unfortunately, the war had stopped just when Israel was in possession of that territory.

'There is no doubt', warned the leading Beirut daily *al-Nahar*, 'that if the ceasefire decision were put to a plebiscite in the Arab world it would be unanimously, or almost unanimously, rejected. There is a great gulf between the absolute confidence public opinion put in the political leadership as a result of the war and the universal—or almost—mistrust with which, perhaps unjustly, it greeted the ceasefire decision.'[7] The reaction stemmed from historical experience. The Arabs recalled the advantages—seizure of territory never again to be relinquished—which the Israelis had derived from the truces that punctuated the first Arab–Israeli war of 1948. There had been consternation at Nasser's acceptance of the ceasefire in 1967—even though his army had been completely destroyed—and again, in July 1970, when he had ended the war of attrition across the Suez Canal in return for a new American peace initiative. All the signs had been that Sadat took the popular view. Early in the war, one of his closest confidants, Ihsan Abdul Koddous, had disclosed that, in planning the

165

war, Egypt had taken into account the 'need to carry on for days, weeks, months and years. This means the fighting will continue until a situation is reached in which fighting is no longer necessary. This means we reject any discussion of a ceasefire before the reasons for opening fire are no longer there.'[8] A mere thirty-six hours before Egypt did accept the ceasefire, Koddous had warned of the dangers of doing so; Israel, he said, would use it to prepare for a strike destined to drive the Egyptians back across the Canal and revive the myth of its invincibility. And just a few hours before, in a bid to commit him more deeply to the fray, Sadat had assured King Hussein that the battle would go on for weeks yet.[9] In Syria, the Deputy Foreign Minister had insisted that, with their greater manpower, resources and strategic depth, the Arabs were much better placed for such a long war than the Israelis.

Many Egyptians shared the incomprehension and dismay. At the UN, Egypt's Foreign Minister, Dr Muhammad Zayyat, denounced it as a *diktat* which Egypt could not accept. He was dismissed from his post. And the dismay turned to anger upon Sadat's acceptance of a second ceasefire, and then a third, after the Israelis, in flagrant violation of the first two, had cut off the Third Army. Soldiers and civilians on the spot bridled under the restraints imposed upon them. A brigadier in the still-intact Second Army is reported to have threatened to mortar any of his own troops who disobeyed the ceasefire order. In the encircled city of Suez, the inhabitants spontaneously took up arms in defiance of the authorities. They were led by Sheikh Salama, *imam* of a small mosque; he shot an officer who had been ordered by the governor to hoist a white flag and, from his minaret, broadcast an appeal for resistance to the last man.

Sensing real danger, Sadat sought to appease discontent by ordering a mobilization of people's militias to join those already in action in the Canal Zone. Offices for the recruitment of volunteers were opened all over the country. In Cairo, young men hurried to join up; some of the more fashionable of them thought they had better have their Beatle-style locks shorn first. They were taken in lorries to training camps between Cairo and the Canal. A few days later they were back in Cairo, protesting that there had been no training camps, only assembly points where they sat around waiting and listening to 'empty talk'. Denied the right to fight, these young men—like the rest of Egypt—were reduced to asking agonized questions, to which, they knew, they would also be denied the answers. If Egypt was victorious (as the propagandists said it was), and if the Third Army was not surrounded (as they said it was not), and if the Israeli counter-crossing, though finally admitted, still amounted to no more than a 'pocket' (as they insisted it did), why on earth, then, didn't Sadat order his army to wipe this 'pocket' out?

Within a week of his triumphant appearance before the People's Assembly, the Hero of the Crossing was already beginning to totter on his pedestal. Many were those who fell back into the scepticism and the downright disbelief they had experienced upon hearing those first extraordinary communiqués in the early hours of the war. It was proving to be what they had suspected all along: not the real battle, which might have yielded a lasting, honourable settlement of the Arab–Israeli conflict, but a *mise en scène* for the *Pax Americana* which certainly would not.

Enter the Americans

If the generals were originally responsible for the Israeli bridgehead, Sadat was not merely responsible for the calamity into which it grew, he chose, ever after, to ignore its diplomatic consequences, to pretend, certainly before his people and perhaps even to himself, that it had never really happened. The October war was a great victory; that was a fundamental truth; from now on it would be heretical to suggest otherwise. It was as if he and his whole propaganda machine remembered only the glorious Crossing and quite forgot about the one the Israelis had mounted in reverse. If he deigned to mention it at all, he derided it as 'television war'. Indeed, he had foreseen it all along. On hearing about the Deversoir 'pocket' he had quickly taken control of the situation.

> I told Shazly: within an hour and a half you must be in Ismailia to accomplish the mission we agreed on, imposing a blockade round the Bitter Lake. The Jews must enter this area, but not beyond it, so that all the Israeli force is in my hands, prisoners all. The Deversoir operation was so much theatre. I had given specific instructions to the Higher Council of the Armed Forces five days before the battle that the army commanders should be completely cool, because the Israelis would resort to theatrics, to television operations. In order to sow confusion, they would land in some isolated spot, deep [behind our lines], on the Red Sea, for example, taking television and camera crews with them, so that they could broadcast that they have landed, captured and occupied. This kind of theatrical action

167

is carried out in swift, *blitzkrieg* style, for the purpose of producing psychological collapse. The Jews think the Arabs are hotheads. When the Deversoir operation took place, I knew from the beginning that this was the kind of operation it was. So I said to Shazly, 'You must get to Ismailia in an hour and a half and prevent the Israelis from going beyond the area we have assigned them. I don't want to talk in detail about what happened in the three days which followed . . .[10]

But later, in his memoirs, Sadat did furnish more detail, explaining that Shazly had failed to follow his instructions, thereby enabling the Israelis to expand their 'pocket'.

On October 19 al-Shazly came back a nervous wreck. He said we ought to withdraw our forces from the east bank of the Canal because, he claimed, a threat was now posed to our forces on the west bank. . . . I went to the command headquarters and studied the situation very carefully. . . . Having realized the true dimension of the situation, I convened a meeting of all commanders. . . . They were all (except al-Shazly) of my opinion—that there was nothing to worry about. Consequently I issued an order, which I believe was even more important than that of the fighting order of October 6, that there should be no withdrawal at all (not a soldier, not a rifle, nothing) from the east bank of the Canal to the west.[11]

Shazly had come back a 'nervous wreck' and during that night, Sadat claimed, he had secretly relieved him of his command. Later, he appointed him ambassador in London, 'because the man did cross, and penetrate the Bar Lev line. I shall always remember that foreign correspondents wrote during the battle that traffic was more orderly at the front than in Cairo. That was his doing.'[12]

It could still be said that, though the October war was far from being a victory, it represented a greater blow to Israel than it did to the Arabs—or rather, properly exploited, it should have done. In spite of the counter-crossing, it still marked a fundamental shift, at Israel's expense, in the balance of power in the Middle East. For the first time in the history of Zionism the Arabs had attempted to achieve a *fait accompli* by force of arms, and had partially succeeded. The setback was not just military; more important, it affected all those factors, psychological, ideological, diplomatic and economic, which make up the strength and vigour of a nation. It left deep and enduring doubts about the whole future of Zionism and the Jewish State. In three

weeks, according to the official count, the Israelis lost 2,523 men—
two-and-a-half times as many, proportionally speaking, as the
Americans lost in the ten years of the Vietnam war. Whereas the 1967
war had reinvigorated Israel's flagging economy, this time it nearly
broke it. 'We, our children, our grandchildren will have to pay for this
war,' lamented the Minister of Finance, and his forecast was followed
by a series of savage austerity measures, drastically reducing living
standards, which contrasted ominously with the soaring revenues of
the oil-rich Arabs. Israel's economic dependence on the United
States, now financing it to the tune of $2,500 million a year, was
complete. Its diplomatic isolation, again with America as its only real
friend, was frightening too. Contrary to Israeli expectations, the oil
weapon really had been made to work. The Arabs, the Secretary
General of the Arab League went so far as to suggest, were emerging
as a 'great power'. Certainly they were a great, and potentially
immense, new force on the world stage.

If the Israelis had read their situation wisely they would have
responded, in a truly conciliatory way, to the conciliatory mood
which, for the first time, had overtaken the Arabs. Arab public
opinion, led by the Palestinians themselves, was now ready for the
kind of settlement—a mini-state of Palestine in the West Bank and
Gaza—which already seemed to be in the making. For, feeling that
the underlying balance of power was now shifting in their favour, the
Arabs could afford to be more magnanimous. And—response of a
negative kind—such readiness arose, too, from apathy and fatigue;
the people were tired of a struggle which their governments had
conducted with such incompetence. But the Israelis squandered this
first, and possibly last, opportunity for a real, enduring peace.

Nor could any Arab leader with experience of their obstinacy,
obsession with physical security and ideological bigotry have seri-
ously expected otherwise. Sadat at one time certainly did not. He had
waged the October war in the conviction that wisdom had to be
forced upon the Israelis. Yet in the diplomacy that followed the war
he abandoned that conviction. Or at least he behaved as if he did. He
dissipated the Arabs' strength. Their strength lay in their unity. But
their unity was a very fragile thing. For they lacked the attributes of a
true 'great power'. They were not strong through their political and
social systems, their modernity and dynamism. It was at least as much
in spite, as because, of themselves that they had achieved what they
had in the October war. Their regimes were frequently tyrannical and
unloved; corruption was widespread; jealousy and suspicion lay just

beneath the surface. They had no institutional means of collective decision-making. Their potentialities were largely accidental; they lay in the size and strategic location of the territories they inhabit, and, more recently, in the wealth and bargaining power that oil bestowed—potentialities that required only a minimal community of purpose to convert them into an awesome force. It had been Sadat who, in the spontaneous *élan* of the war, had achieved that community of purpose. It was Sadat who now destroyed it.

Why did Sadat do it? Objective circumstances certainly made their contribution. But subjective factors, the needs of his own peculiar psyche, undoubtedly began to play an abnormally important part in shaping his actions. The Crossing had been his personal apotheosis. After that intoxicating triumph he could not make public confession of the sobering truth, he could not admit that his feat of arms had been anything less than the great victory it at first seemed to be. The admission would have been difficult for any man; but for Sadat, with his congenital sense of inadequacy and his compulsive desire for posthumous revenge on the 'immortal leader' who so cruelly made him feel it, it was all but impossible. As a result, Sadat's whole postwar diplomacy was founded, not merely on a false premise, but on a deliberate deceit.

He had pledged an end to the debilitating state of 'no war, no peace'. A victory of the dimensions he claimed should automatically, and quickly, have yielded the victor's spoils: a just and lasting peace as the Arabs, by a broad consensus, defined it. But since it was no such thing, he found himself throwing away the Arabs' assets one by one. The position of relative strength which, in spite of the counter-crossing, he had enjoyed on the morrow of the war, was reduced, as time passed, to one of abject weakness and desperation. He took the easy road, the only one his temperament allowed. The Israelis did have something to offer Egypt: they did not hold that Sinai, unlike the West Bank, was an inalienable, God-given part of the Jewish homeland; they did not consider it vital to their security as they did the Golan Heights. In order to recover Sinai for Egypt, Sadat embarked on a stealthy, go-it-alone diplomacy, the effect of which was to make it even harder for everyone else, Syrians, Jordanians and Palestinians, to recover *their* territories.

From the outset, it is true, Sadat swore to uphold his pan-Arab obligations. He was solemnly bound to a collective Arab strategy, the be-all and end-all of which was a 'comprehensive' settlement of the everlasting Palestine problem. The only alternative, he said, to 'Arab coordination was an Arab civil war that would put Israel's mind at ease and relieve it of the trouble of confrontation'.[13] Naturally, no one merited higher consideration than Syria, his wartime partner.

> I act in accordance with principles and values which I shall never forsake. I owe President Assad a debt of honour until the Day of Judgement; I shall never forget it. He is the one man who took the decision of 6 October with me. You all owe him a debt, every Egyptian and every Arab. . . . I repeat that it is impossible to forget Assad, the man and his people. We shall not forget him. We shall not sell him out. We shall not act against him in anything, even if he should act against us. We owe him a debt of patriotism. Syria and Hafiz Assad are one and the same. Without the opening of two fronts simultaneously, Israel would have dealt with each one of us separately, as is its habit.[14]

But Sadat protested too much. The Arab leaders distrusted him and none more so than President Assad. They feared, rightly, that his original aberration, the acceptance of the ceasefire, would inexorably lead to others. The short-lived, intoxicating triumphs (though none to compare with the Crossing) that lay along the road he had taken would be achieved at the Arabs' expense.

It was the Americans who coaxed him down this road. The war, the creditable military performance of the 'blood Arabs' and the economic disruption wrought by the 'oil Arabs' had come as a shock to a superpower predisposed to look at the Middle East through Zionist spectacles. It shattered complacency in high places. The Americans were now ready to exert themselves seriously in the cause of peace. And in the person of Henry Kissinger they had a Secretary of State uniquely equipped for the challenge. He had the almost unprecedented personal power and prestige to attempt bold new approaches; as a Jew, immune from the charge of 'anti-Semitism', he was well-placed to resist the all-powerful Zionist lobby; he had the intellectual grasp and the historic vision to master a conflict of rare complexity and emotional intensity. As a statesman and strategist, freshly honoured with a Nobel Peace Prize for his role in negotiating the peace agreement in Vietnam, he relished just the kind of situation which the Middle East now presented—he liked to strike while the iron was hot, he had enormous stamina and verve, and he hated failure.

Dr Kissinger quickly developed 'something which the United States had never really possessed before—an Arab policy'.[15] And

Anwar Sadat was to figure as the central pillar in that policy. After his first meeting with him, Kissinger decided that he was 'dealing not with a clown, but with a statesman',[16] and sought to persuade Sadat that it really was a new America he represented—an America prepared, without abandoning its special relationship with Israel, to take an altogether more sympathetic view of the Arab case; an America ready to put into practice the 'even-handedness' which a few bold spirits had previously dared to advocate but which the Administration, cowed by the Zionist lobby, had never more than dallied with. An America ready to meet the Arabs halfway: for the very idea of acknowledging Israel's existence as an independent state was, for the Arabs, by any true perspective, an act of historic magnanimity; the Americans implicitly acknowledged that when they accepted the idea that the least the Israelis should offer in return was their withdrawal from the occupied territories and the establishment therein of some new order that satisfied the legitimate rights of the Palestinian people.

Officially, perhaps even sincerely at first, America was wedded, like Sadat, to a 'comprehensive' Middle East settlement. Nothing was spelt out in advance. Dr Kissinger explained that he saw peace as a process, attainable by evolutionary stages. A series of partial or interim agreements would lead to the final one. The basic trade-off was 'security' for Israel against 'sovereignty' for the Arabs. The more security—firmer and firmer commitments to non-belligerence—the Arabs gave the Israelis, the more sovereignty (in the shape of territory) the Israelis would restore to them. Eventually, in return for full 'recognition'—exchange of ambassadors, open frontiers and all the features of normal relations between states—Israel would give up all occupied territories. It was called step-by-step diplomacy.

President Sadat was more than susceptible to Dr Kissinger's overtures. In the aftermath of the October war he finally decided on that reversal of alliances which had been foreshadowed by the May 1971 Corrective Movement and the expulsion of Soviet advisers a year later. It was a fundamental choice. For eighteen years, though officially non-aligned, Egypt's reliance on the Soviet Union had steadily grown, chiefly because, faced with a highly aggressive, heavily armed Israel and a West which seemed to appease its every whim, it had no choice but to seek arms where it could find them. Nasser had had no special affection for the Russians. Sadat had a good deal less. Nor—apart from the doctrinaire left—were the Egyptians fond of them. It was only to have been expected that, with independence, having thrown off European mastery, they should have turned to the Russians, but they had long since shed any illusions that they could get on better with the East than with the West.

The war should have enhanced the Russians' prestige. Yet many Egyptians were instinctively averse to praising them. Some even preferred to evoke supernatural aid. In his Friday sermon, the Rector of al-Azhar, the highest religious authority in the land, related that a member of his family had seen the Prophet Muhammad in a dream, fighting with the Egyptians in Sinai. This was a sure sign that God was on their side. When, in *al-Ahram*, a university professor warned against such irrational interpretations of Egypt's military success, since they insulted the skill and valour of its soldiers, outraged letters from the man-in-the-street called the professor a 'communist' who was trying to make out that Egypt owed everything to Soviet arms.

The West, duly purged of its colonial ambitions, had become for Egyptians a pole of attraction that the Soviet Union could never be. It was a natural swing of the pendulum; and the only thing that could interfere with it would be the West's, particularly America's, deep-rooted predilection for Israel. That, however, did not deter Sadat. Kissinger reminded him that if the Soviet Union could help the Arabs make war, only the United States, through its unique influence on Israel, had the means to achieve peace. Sadat was only too anxious to agree. Had not Nasser himself implicitly acknowledged the point when, three years before, calling off his Soviet-assisted war of attrition across the Canal, he had accepted Secretary of State Rogers' peace initiative?

Moreover, Sadat had much to offer the Americans in return. 'Egypt', his new Foreign Minister, Ismail Fahmi, told a banquet in Washington, 'is the gateway to the Arab world. If you win the friendship of Egypt, you win the friendship of the Arab world.' That might seem to be self-evident. But, in fact, it flew in the face of a prevailing American orthodoxy which the Zionists, profiting from the widespread ignorance about the Middle East, had been largely instrumental in shaping. Already, the orthodoxy had been severely dented by the October war. In one angry, unexpected blow, King Faisal made the point which he had vainly been trying to put across by gentler means: that far from being an asset to the West, Israel was a potentially dangerous liability.

The oil-boycott began to bite; fuel rationing, electricity black-outs and industrial cutbacks hit Europe and America. And President

Sadat, on whose behalf Faisal had acted, told America that all it had to do to end this nightmare, and prevent a worse one in the future, was to recognize where its real interests lay—and act accordingly. No Arab country was better placed to help it secure those interests than Egypt. For Egypt was the great power of the Arab world. Its population—some 37 million at the time—accounted for one-third of the Arab people; it was the seat of the Arab League, lynchpin of concerted Arab strategies; no one could make war without Egypt, and no one make peace. It had been the fountainhead of the post-independence Arab 'revolution'; it could now be the guarantor of stability and 'moderation'. Please Egypt, and America would please the Arabs. That did not require very much. America only had to enforce the kind of peace which, theoretically, it had itself come to regard as just and reasonable.

There is probably no people on earth more ready than the easy-going, good-natured Egyptians to let bygones be bygones. Given results, they would quickly forgive America all its past sins. But, characteristically, Sadat could not wait for results. He could not wait to disentangle himself from the old partner, a Soviet Union which he had long detested anyway, and fling himself into the arms of the new one. A mere twenty-four hours after the United States had demonstrated, with its worldwide nuclear alert, to what extraordinary lengths it was ready to go in support of its Israeli protégé, Ismail Fahmi, in Washington, was posing for pictures with Dr Kissinger's arm round his waist. Two days later, the pictures graced the front pages of Cairo's newspapers; readers were speechless with shock.

Only a few days after that Kissinger descended on Cairo and correspondents were calling it love at first sight between him and Sadat. Sadat quickly dubbed the Secretary of State 'my friend Henry'. By his own account he certainly lost no time in sizing up the man he was dealing with. 'We began our meeting with caution in what we had to say; but after an hour of discussion I was convinced that Kissinger was a man to be trusted; he spoke logically, his perspective was clear. . . .' Sadat was soon as lavish in his compliments as, before the war, he had been relentless in his censure. Kissinger was 'a strategist and a man of vision, imagination and, perhaps most important of all, trust'. He was the first American official to prove himself to the Arabs as 'a man of integrity—direct, frank and farsighted. I trust him completely.'[17]

The flatteries were not all one-way. Kissinger, flamboyant, effusive, a showman like Sadat himself, considered them to be an essential part of his diplomatic art. And if he did not know it already, he must have quickly divined it—his new friend was peculiarly susceptible to them. 'I hear', Sadat was asked by one of his devoutest admirers, 'that he told you in front of Ismail Fahmi that you were the first to beat him at strategy.' 'You don't have to publish that,' Sadat replied, 'I don't like to talk about what goes on in private meetings. . . .'[18] Sadat did fancy himself as a strategic thinker, and such a compliment from the master-strategist himself must have had the disarming effect doubtless intended.

With the coming of the Americans, Sadat found himself the object of the kind of attentions which gratified him most. He had a new, altogether grander stage on which to act. The man who had dismissed the Israeli counter-crossing as 'television war' accomplished in 'typical Goebbels style', was to become, in the Kissinger era, the supreme addict, and victim, of 'television diplomacy'. No American leader went anywhere without his airborne retinue of newsmen, recording every word and gesture, however unmemorable they might be. There was no greater yardstick of prestige than the ballyhoo to which, as America's great new friend and ally, Sadat, too, was now to be entitled. He was certainly to have a much better chance to display his qualities of urbanity, charm and elegance through association with the media-conscious leaders of the Western bourgeois democracies than with the dour *apparatchiks* of the Kremlin.

Sadat had already made up his mind, even as he met Kissinger for the first time, that he would work for a 'common strategy' with the United States.[19] It was still too early to say so in public, but the signs were already there, crying out for an explanation. He furnished a truly remarkable one.

There had been two reasons, he told the foreign press on 31 October, for accepting the ceasefire. The first was that the two superpowers had jointly guaranteed the 22 October ceasefire lines and the immediate implementation of Security Council Resolution 242. The correspondents were unconvinced, and Sadat knew it. Asked how soon the Israelis should relinquish the occupied territories, he replied: 'Immediately!' Pressed about his interpretation of 'immediate', he snapped back: 'Immediate!'

But there was an audible intake of breath from his audience when he gave his second reason. 'Our estimates—which proved correct according to a statement by the Israeli Minister of Defence—were that Israel would be able to fight for only fourteen days with the same strength and violence with which we fought them.' So, on the eleventh day of the war, 'only three days remained after which Israel would have been short of ammunition. There and then, the United States intervened and not only with ammunition. . . . We were also surprised to see modern American weapons which had not yet been used by the American army itself. The US opened its arsenal . . . the supply of TV-guided bombs was officially announced. . . . Nothing was hidden . . . the American arsenal was widely and abundantly opened. . . .'

In his memoirs, he enlarged on the American intervention. It was the United States, he said, which had urged the Israeli counter-crossing and, in furnishing hour-by-hour battlefield intelligence garnered by satellite, had made it possible. With the air bridge, the United States had had the effrontery to ferry tanks and sophisticated weaponry directly into occupied Egyptian territory itself; the giant transports landed at el-Arish, the capital of Sinai, 'immediately behind the front, quite openly, so as to turn Israel's defeat into victory'. There had come a point in the battle when 'I noticed that every time I destroyed a dozen tanks, more tanks were to be seen on the battlefield'. In the first part of the war, the Israelis had failed to knock out a single missile battery but now

two American rockets were fired at two Egyptian missile batteries and put them out of action completely. . . . I recalled what the United States had done on the German front during World War II, and then on the Japanese front. The US air raids on German military targets and German cities were so intensive that 1,000 aircraft took part in each raid, and taught the Germans a lesson never to be forgotten. The atomic bombs dropped on Hiroshima and Nagasaki taught the Japanese an equally unforgettable lesson.[20]

In his address to the People's Assembly—unmentioned in his memoirs—a fortnight before, Sadat had warned the United States that the 'flood of new tanks, new planes, new guns, missiles and electronic equipment pouring into Israel' did not frighten Egypt. His audience had gone wild. But now he told the foreign correspondents: 'Frankly, I am not going to fight America—I fought the Israelis for eleven days . . . but I am not ready to fight America. . . .' It was his next words that took his audience's breath away. In spite of everything, he said: 'I can say that America's stand with regard to the establishment of peace is a constructive one.'

He came up with a matching reason, no less ingenious, for turning against the Soviet Union; not immediately, however, for the Soviet Union had, after all, just backed him to the point of provoking an American nuclear alert. Later—when his anti-Soviet feelings were in full, public spate—Sadat made out that the backing had not been what it appeared to be at all. Quite the reverse. 'Everybody believed that the Soviet Union had backed us and established an airbridge to help us, but that wasn't the situation. I faced the United States and Israel; while the Soviet Union stood behind me, ready to stab me in the back if I lost 85 or 90 per cent of my arms, just as in 1967.' In spite of the Soviet refusal to supply the arms needed, Sadat explained that Egypt achieved 'the direct opposite of what the Soviet Union had expected. The Soviets wanted to prove to us that we were not capable of waging any kind of war because I had expelled their experts, and that Egypt should once again resort to reliance on the Soviet Union.' President Boumediène of Algeria, who had secretly visited Moscow in a bid to extract arms, cash in hand, from a begrudging Kremlin, supposedly reported back that 'while the Americans and the Israelis *are* eager to defeat President Sadat, the Soviet Union is a hundred times more eager to defeat him'.[21]

It was an astonishing switch of alliances. But perhaps Sadat was right. Perhaps the United States really would pursue a 'constructive' course. He had Dr Kissinger's word for it and, as he said, he trusted him completely. Even so, the United States had just laid on the most spectacular display of partisanship in the history of the Arab–Israeli conflict. That was proven fact. And no one said it more insistently than Sadat himself. Now he blithely stood all his pre-war arguments on their head. The offences which, on a lesser scale, had been the case for defying America now, because of their sheer magnitude, became the necessity for befriending it.

Shuttle diplomacy: the first Sinai Disengagement Agreement

At 1.30 in the morning of 27 October, just two days after the Israelis had with the utmost reluctance accepted a third and altogether more peremptory ceasefire call from the Security Council, an Egyptian officer made his way through a barbed wire cordon to the Israeli lines. Outside a large tent emblazoned with the Star of David, Major-General Adli al-Sharif was greeted by Major-General Aharon Yariv, the former head of Israeli intelligence, who told him: 'Two valiant armies have fought for three weeks. Now let's try to work out an honourable peace.' The bright starlight faintly illumined the impedimenta of men at war strewn about the sandy waste. A thin sliver of tarmac, the road from Cairo to Suez, cut through it. Here, at Kilometre 101, was the first landmark on a journey whose final destination was to astonish the world.

Although no American was present at Kilometre 101 to witness the encounter—which was supervised by the newly arrived UN emergency force—Dr Kissinger was very much there in spirit. Conducting the talks for Egypt was Shazly's replacement as Chief of Staff, General Abdul Ghani Gamassi, and as these proceeded the state propaganda machine put on a show of spirited self-confidence, all threats and bluster, in keeping with the October 'victory'. The men at the front had their fingers on the trigger, press and radio said, and if the Israelis did not withdraw to the ceasefire lines they had so flagrantly violated they would be driven out by force. Sadat said that he was 'restraining [his] military men with great difficulty because they want to liquidate this problem. . . . The Third Army is occupying positions on the East Bank and is as firm and solid as a rock. Part of the Third Army, in fact the major part, is on the West Bank behind the Israeli forces. . . . I could, of course . . . have hit and pushed forward and destroyed all the forces stationed between the two parts of the Third Army.' He had not done this because he was committed to the ceasefire; 'a completely new situation was just beginning. . . .'

At the same time, the Egyptian authorities left no doubt that the 'front-line' states were still counting on the 'supporting' states, the 'blood Arabs' on the 'oil Arabs'; the shooting war might have ceased, but it was vital that the economic one should continue. 'We cannot imagine', said *al-Ahram*, 'that the oil weapon will be abandoned now.'[22] And sure enough, not only did the Arab oil producers agree to stick to their original programme, which called for a 5 per cent cut in output every month until the complete withdrawal of Israeli troops had been achieved, they decided to cut it by a full 25 per cent. On his first visit to the Middle East, Dr Kissinger urged King Faisal at least to modify an embargo that was aimed principally against the US. The king assured him that it had caused him deep pain to impose it in the first place, that nothing would please him more than to lift it altogether, but America should first announce that Israel 'must withdraw and permit the Palestinians to return to their homes'.[23] This was in line with Faisal's publicly stated intention to maintain the embargo until all the Arab aims had been achieved—'no matter how long it takes'.[24]

If the Arabs, and many Egyptians, were alarmed at the ceasefire, their misgivings deepened after the meeting at Kilometre 101. They rightly suspected that Sadat's outward pugnacity was one thing, his actual conduct quite another. The Egyptian army did not have the upper hand at Suez, whatever Sadat may have stated to the contrary. General Shazly has summed up his claim in two words: 'total lies'.[25] The plight of the Third Army was desperate; Egypt had to submit to every 'humiliating condition'.

At Kilometre 101 the Israelis refused to return to the October ceasefire lines. The most they would allow was the establishment of a vital relief corridor for the passage of food, water and medicines to the beleaguered Third Army. They did so on Dr Kissinger's insistence; it was a service he rendered Sadat on the strictly pragmatic ground that only if the two adversaries were in conditions of approximate balance could he hope to achieve results—but not if one had crushed and humiliated the other. The corridor itself was a typical piece of Kissinger sophistry which enabled Sadat to pretend that it was controlled by the UN, not by the Israelis; the road from Kilometre 101 to Suez was punctuated by UN checkpoints, but the Israelis had the right to inspect everything that passed along it and in their search for concealed guns and ammunition they spread 'even blood plasma upon the sandy pavement, where we watched it bubble, like the blood of St Januarius at Naples, in the heat of the desert sun.'[26]

The relief corridor was the outcome of a much broader decision Kissinger had urged upon Sadat, whose acceptance of it had finally persuaded him that here was a man with whom he could really do business. It 'became the basis of their friendship and the foundation of future American policy'.[27] What Sadat had decided was to accept Kissinger's proposal that, instead of wasting time and credit in arbitrating the whereabouts of the violated ceasefire lines, he should try for 'something much bigger'. If Sadat would give him a few more weeks, Kissinger said, he would try to negotiate a 'disengagement' along the Suez Canal. He would get the Israelis out of 'Africa' altogether, then away from the Canal and deeper into Sinai.

All the while, of course, Sadat remained publicly committed to pan-Arabism. At an Arab summit conference in Algeria soon after the war he had pledged that, in return for a free hand in the conduct of his peace-making strategy, he would scrupulously respect the collective Arab interest and, in spite of the American-encouraged objections of an absent King Hussein, he had joined the other leaders in anointing the Palestine Liberation Organization the sole legitimate

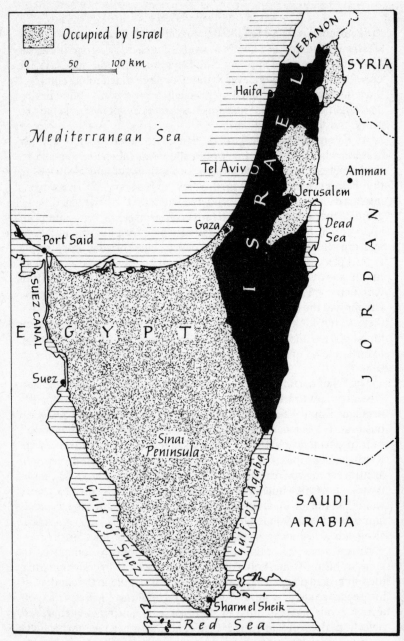

The Middle East at the close of the 1967 war

representative of the Palestinian people. But, in reality, he and Dr Kissinger were pushing the peace-making down a road which other Arab or Arab-supporting parties could not follow without a sinking feeling that they would have to drop out somewhere along the way.

All was prefigured at the Geneva Conference. Just before Christmas 1973 there assembled in the Palais des Nations a company that seemed peculiarly in keeping with this season of goodwill. For the first time in the history of the Middle East struggle, Arab and Israeli foreign ministers came together, beneath the same august roof, with the eyes of the world upon them. A goal of which the world had all but despaired, peace between Arab and Jew, seemed at last to be coming within grasp.

But Geneva was Dr Kissinger's show. Although the conference had been formally convened by Dr Kurt Waldheim, the UN Secretary General, that meant little. Israel disdained the UN and all its works for the same reason that the Arabs esteemed them. Israel is the child of the UN, the only one of its kind, but it has been a delinquent child, with a unique record of censure by the organization which gave it birth; countless UN resolutions are unassailable evidence of the strength of the Arab case. If the UN were to play an effective and impartial role in the peace-seeking forum, the moral balance would inevitably have tilted in the Arabs' favour. So, deferring to the Israelis, Kissinger ensured that its role was ceremonial only.

It is true that, together with the United States, the Soviet Union was co-chairman of the conference. For reasons of ideology and self-interest, the Russians had long cast themselves as the Arabs' champion against American 'imperialism', of which Israel was its aggressive, expansionist outpost in the Middle East. But on this occasion, for some reason, the Russians were remarkably complaisant; Foreign Minister Andrei Gromyko gave Kissinger his head. As for the rest of the international community, neither Britain and France, permanent members of the Security Council, nor the European community, whose pro-Zionist enthusiasms were never extravagant as America's, were represented at all.

There was no question of any but the 'front-line' Arab states attending: the 'supporting' states, even the oil-rich among them, were not invited to play the kind of direct role to which their spectacular new influence on the Arab and international stage seemed to entitle them. And among those front-line states—generally defined as Egypt, Jordan and Syria—only the first two showed up. Sensing that it was for form's sake only that Kissinger sought a Syrian presence at Geneva, President Assad stoutly refused to furnish it. King Hussein, loyal protégé of the West, did oblige but, as his representative Prime Minister Zeid Rifai, confided later, 'It was the most peculiar conference I ever attended, no terms of reference, no rules of procedure and no agenda.' The formation of a separate Egyptian–Israeli military committee on disengagement was sprung as a disagreeable surprise on this former Harvard student of Dr Kissinger's.[28] As for the true, the Palestinian heart of the Middle East conflict, although Dr Kissinger had promised Sadat to arrange for some kind of Palestinian representation at Geneva, his capitulation to the Israelis on this score had been swift and complete; there would be no Palestinians there, he promised, in any other form than 'safe' members of the Jordanian delegation.

This inaugural session of the Geneva Conference, which also turned out to be its last, was, then, no more than a 'comprehensive' cover for a 'bilateral' deal, what Edward Sheehan, the chronicler of Kissinger's diplomatic odyssey, called a 'public-relations drumroll for a mouse-sized marvel'.[29] The Israeli–Egyptian military committee did continue to meet in Geneva but, without the weight of Kissinger behind it, it was mere 'chattering'.[30]

Only when Kissinger re-entered the diplomatic fray on his third visit to the Middle East in as many months was the deadlock broken. The original conceptual framework for a disengagement agreement actually came from General Moshe Dayan; Sadat accepted it and, at his prompting, Kissinger began the first and easiest of his famous 'shuttles'. Four days of commuting aboard Air Force One, his elaborately equipped Boeing, between Jerusalem and Aswan, where Sadat was recovering from bronchitis, and the mission was complete. It was a method which narrowed the range of participants to the limit. In Israel, every decision required the approval of the cabinet, and eventually of the Knesset but, in spite of his much-vaunted 'state of institutions', there were no such constraints on Sadat. He met Kissinger alone. Nothing could be pleasanter, on a January day, than to savour the voluptuous warmth of Egypt's southernmost resort, but that can hardly have been much consolation to Dr Ismail Fahmi, his Foreign Minister, and other high advisers, who were reduced to sunning themselves on terraces overlooking the west bank of the Nile while, on the opposite shore, Sadat received his 'friend', straight from the biting chill of Jerusalem, in a pink sandstone villa behind its screen of mango trees and thick tropical foliage. It was the perfectly contrived stage for the emergence of 'Henry Superstar'. With the domestic scandals of Watergate inexorably closing in upon him, President Nixon badly needed a foreign-affairs triumph. On 17 January, he was able to announce the signing of the Sinai disengagement agreement, second landmark in Sadat's go-it-alone diplomacy and the first of those Oriental miracles which, with Sadat as their ever more obliging medium, Kissinger and his successors were able to perform before an admiring Western public.

The Israelis did not get all they wanted out of the agreement. They did not get the promise of non-belligerency on which they had initially insisted. But, in the light of his original war aims, Sadat got very much less. Where, now, was his insistence that he would never stop fighting until Israel had withdrawn from all the occupied territories? He *had* stopped fighting, and here he was settling for an Israeli pullback to a line roughly 15 miles east of the Canal—the merest fraction of Sinai. Hard though the Israelis naturally tried to make it seem like one, this was no real concession at all. Unless they were to use their African 'pocket' for a full-scale resumption of the war (and neither superpower would have stood for that) they had every reason to withdraw from it altogether and take up positions which—as General Dayan had suggested even before the war— would make better defensive sense than the 'impregnable' Bar Lev line itself.

This paltry pullback carried no promise of more to come. All that Sadat was getting was the assurance that the agreement 'constitutes a first step towards a just and durable peace. . . .' Furthermore, the withdrawal, such as it was, was to be reciprocated. Even as Kissinger was embarking on his 'shuttle', Sadat, his ministers and the state-controlled press had been saying that any 'thinning out' of Egyptian troops in Sinai was out of the question. Yet this is just what Sadat now agreed to, on an almost unbelievable scale.

For there were two elements to the agreement. The first was a direct, public agreement between Egypt and Israel. This was not, so the Egyptians insisted for the benefit of a suspicious Arab world, a *political* agreement, but a military one; and it was to make this elaborate point that, after all the peregrinations between Washington and Geneva, Jerusalem and Aswan, the Kissinger show returned once more—though without the superstar himself—to that bleak, improbable spot on the Cairo–Suez highway, Kilometre 101, for its signing by the Israeli and Egyptian Chiefs of Staff. This public document made vague mention of a new 'deployment' of forces, of 'limitations' of armaments; and the Cairo press, in tendentious definition of these seemingly innocuous concepts, sought to convey the impression that, insofar as there was any withdrawal, it was an Israeli one only. It was the secret letters, addressed by the United States to the governments of Israel and Egypt and promptly leaked by the Israelis, which contained the real defining of the terms between them. The principle of reciprocity in its own, newly liberated territory meant, for Egypt, a reduction in forces from 60,000 to 7,000 men on the east bank of the Canal, restrictions in the number and size of artillery pieces, and a zone, 30 miles wide, in which surface-to-air missiles were forbidden. It was a scandal, and Sadat knew it. Why else should he have begged for such a typical, if transparent, piece of Kissinger sophistry to disguise it? But even that was not the end of it. A mere four days before the agreement was concluded, Egypt, through its Foreign Minister, had roundly asserted that it would only open the Suez Canal to international shipping 'within the context of a final settlement'; yet, in a secret 'Memorandum of Understanding', Kissinger conveyed to the Israelis Egypt's promise to clear the Canal, rebuild its cities, and resume peacetime activities in the region.

Not unnaturally, the Arabs were unhappy with the agreement, and unhappiest of all was Egypt's wartime partner, Syria. Officially inspired leaks from Damascus intimated that Syria might break off diplomatic relations with Egypt in protest against what one official had reportedly denounced as 'a unique picture in the history of treachery against the people and army in Syria and the Arab nation'.[31] It was only with difficulty that Yasser Arafat, a born conciliator, explained away the angry outbursts of unrulier comrades. Of course they did not say so publicly, but Sadat's own highest officials were none too happy either. Foreign Minister Fahmi felt that Kissinger could have delivered more territory; General Gamassi considered the agreement militarily unsound, a great impediment to the resumption of war should future diplomacy come to nothing.[32] One famous Egyptian would not hold his tongue. In his weekly column Muhammad Heikal, the editor of *al-Ahram* and former confidant of Nasser, had been warning against the pitfalls of Kissinger's step-by-step diplomacy, which, he said, threatened to isolate Egypt completely, to undermine the Arabs' new-found strength and solidarity, as indispensable to Egypt as Egypt was to the Arabs, and to deprive Egypt of a Soviet counter-weight to the United States. In open defiance of Sadat, he said that he discerned no real change in American Middle East policy. His persistent criticism was all the more persuasive in that, in the days of Soviet pre-eminence, he had always pressed the case for a countervailing American involvement; his 'pro-American' opinions used to earn him the sometimes furious denunciations of the 'pro-Soviet' guardians of Nasserist orthodoxy. No one had done more than Heikal to help Sadat consolidate his authority in those first three precarious, pre-war years. And so, deposed from the editorship of the Arab world's most famous newspaper, fell the last great pillar of the Nasser era.

As Dr Kissinger left Aswan on 19 January, Sadat kissed him beneath the mango trees. 'You are not only my friend,' he said, 'you are my brother.'[33]

The Golan

Upon the urgings of President Sadat, Kissinger returned home via Damascus. There he found President Assad as angry as he had expected—but willing, none the less, to consider disengagement for himself. Kissinger braced himself for the next round of shuttle diplomacy.

Each one was necessarily more difficult than the last. The principal constraint on American diplomacy was the power of the Zionist lobby, and it was Kissinger's basic method to confine himself, in Israel's interest, to the periphery rather than the centre, to attempt minor breakthroughs rather than the fundamental ones which he deemed impossible. But if the scope for progress by such means was everywhere limited, it was even more so on the Golan than it was in Sinai, because the territory in question was much smaller, because the Israelis were obsessed by the military importance of retaining it, because they mistrusted the Syrians even more than the Egyptians, and because their negotiating strategy was to divide their enemies by offering more to one than to the others.

Long, arduous and exasperating Kissinger's Golan shuttle did indeed prove to be. He spent a full four weeks commuting between Jerusalem and Damascus, haggling over every gun emplacement and observation post. It represented a thoroughly disproportionate call on the time, energy and talents of the world's most powerful Foreign Minister. Yet, all things considered, he got off lightly. He owed that largely to President Sadat.

After the Sinai disengagement, Kissinger complained that, in the light of America's commendable exertions, the maintenance of the oil embargo could be interpreted as blackmail. Since, for most Arabs, whatever services, if any, he had rendered them did not begin to compensate for America's long record of devotion to Israel, his complaint appeared better calculated to encourage the maintenance of the embargo than its lifting. But Sadat thought otherwise. He who had pressed hardest for the use of the oil weapon in the first place was now the keenest to have it sheathed. In the run-up to the disengagement, even as his state-controlled press was telling the oil producers that Egypt expected them to keep the weapon in play, Sadat was making secret promises to his friend Henry.

In December Kissinger told President Nixon of Sadat's assurance that he would 'get the oil embargo lifted during the first half of January' and that he would 'call for its lifting in a statement which praised your personal role in bringing the parties to the negotiating table and making progress thereafter.' On 28 December Nixon addressed a letter to Sadat: 'I must tell you in complete candour', he wrote, 'that it is essential that the oil embargo and oil production restrictions against the United States be ended at once. It cannot await the outcome of the current talks on disengagement.' Sadat sent back a message through Shirley Temple Black, the American delegate to the United Nations, who had seen him privately: 'I will lift the embargo,' he told her, 'I will lift it for President Nixon.'[34] General Shazly attributed Sadat's eagerness to the calamity at Suez: 'The whole Arab world', he records in his memoirs, 'was now to pay the price for the encirclement of the Third Army.'[35]

No sooner had he got his disengagement—but before Assad had got his—Sadat made public his contention that the United States now really *had* done something for the Arabs, and that it deserved a commensurate reward. So the Arab oil producers, who had originally vowed to go on cutting and cutting again until the Israelis withdrew from all occupied territories, gradually eased their pressure. First they reduced the cutbacks, then they made a complete lifting of the embargo dependent on an Israeli commitment to withdraw rather than on withdrawal itself, and finally, on 18 March, they lifted it (except for four countries) without any condition at all.

It is true that, on a visit to Washington in February, the Saudi and Egyptian foreign ministers had sought a price of sorts—that Kissinger should do something for Syria—but it was anything but an exorbitant one. For Kissinger would have undertaken the Golan shuttle anyway; the situation there was too dangerous for him not to.[36]

The Syrian government presented disengagement in the Golan as a

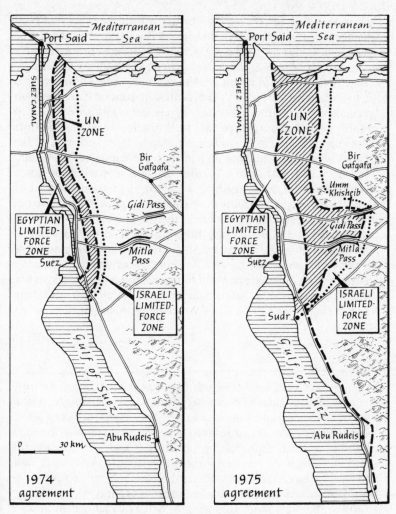

Sinai disengagement agreements of 1974 and 1975

victory won through the war of attrition which the army had been waging for a full eighty days. But it was clearly far from that. The agreement, signed on 31 May 1974, failed to incorporate the famous 'linkage'—the demand, constantly reiterated, that any disengagement should be tied to a firm Israeli commitment to withdraw from all the occupied territories. The nearest it came to that was an innocuous formulation that the agreement constituted 'a step towards a just and durable peace'. Territorially, the Israelis did little more than relinquish the additional ground they had won in the October war. True, they gave up Kuneitra, the 'capital' of the Golan, which they had held since 1967. But that was a mockery at which Assad, desperate for something to show, had to connive. For Kuneitra represented no more than a minuscule pocket. Moreover, in inviting the Syrians to repopulate it, the Israelis knew full well that they could not and would not. For not only had they dynamited almost every building in the place, they refused to let the Syrians clear the minefields which surrounded it. And, entrenching themselves on an overlooking hill that gave them complete military supremacy, they were so close to the city that the Star of David fluttered provocatively on its perimeter and busloads of American tourists gaped down its streets.

Sinai Two

In Cairo the Golan agreement was hailed as vindication of the trust which President Sadat had so wisely placed in Dr Kissinger. It was time to dramatize and sanctify the new friendship. So, only seven months after the American airlift to Israel, only two months after the cessation of Arab economic hostilities, and with the Israelis still firmly implanted in Jerusalem, the whole of the West Bank and almost all of Sinai and Golan, Richard Nixon became, in June 1974, the first American president to pay a state visit to Egypt—or, indeed, to any of the other Arab countries, as well as Israel, which he also took in. He stood to get more out of it than Sadat. He was more than ever desperate for a foreign triumph that would somehow divert attention from Watergate. Sadat was delighted to oblige, placing that national asset—the good-natured, gullible, easily mobilized Egyptian masses—at the disposal of his applause-hungry guest. It was an exotic show, and American televiewers were not to know that, to supplement those who had gathered spontaneously, peasants were brought in by the truckload from the countryside, workers were given time off with extra pay, and government offices were instructed to furnish 'suitably dressed' representatives who would add a touch of respectability to the pageant. 'Welcome Mr Nixon, We Trust Mr Nixon', the banners and the cheer-leaders proclaimed as the two statesmen stood upright in an open limousine, contemplated the Pyramids, or travelled through the lush rural squalor of the Delta in the ornate, brass-and-mahogany railway carriage to which, like other trappings of the monarchy, Sadat was becoming increasingly addicted.

The visit consecrated the end of Soviet supremacy in the Middle East. By this time Sadat was beginning to unburden himself in public of all the pent-up animosities towards the Russians which for so long—while he felt he still needed them—he had done his best to keep to himself. His strictures were punctuated by increasingly unconvincing protestations that he wanted nothing better than good relations with both superpowers, and even, later in the year, by moves towards a genuine reconciliation. But it was a temperamental inadequacy of Sadat's, as well as a justification of his own inconstancy, that he divided the world into true friends and sworn enemies, good men and bad—and in this division the Russians were now irredeemably cast with the latter.

The carnival in Cairo did not save Nixon from disgrace. His successor, Gerald Ford, owed no debt of gratitude to Sadat. But in any event the next disengagement should have been on the Jordanian front. That is what King Hussein expected. He had already put forward a proposal for an Israeli military withdrawal from the Jordan River of some 8 to 10 kilometres. The Israelis had countered with a proposal for a final settlement under which they would retain such large slices of territory, as well as a military presence along the river, that Hussein promptly rejected it for the insult it was. But Kissinger was sympathetic to his plea that unless he quickly regained the West Bank, which he persisted in regarding as an integral part of his kingdom, the PLO would pre-empt him.

At this time, the PLO's diplomatic successes were far outstripping its military ones. It was winning increasing recognition of its claim to speak for all the Palestinian people, wherever they might be. The only Arab ruler who still resolutely opposed it was King Hussein, who staked a rival claim of his own. It was a seemingly irreconcilable conflict that had grown out of the first Arab–Israeli war of 1948. The Hashemite Kingdom of Transjordan had absorbed the only substantial part of Palestine, the West Bank, which, thanks to the performance of the Arab Legion, had not fallen to the Zionists. The conflict came to a bloody climax in Black September 1970, when the king's bedouin troops broke the back of guerrilla power in Jordan. For the king to recognize the PLO's claim would in practice mean the relinquishing of all title to the fortuitously acquired, exclusively Palestinian half of his kingdom.

The Israelis were alarmèd by the PLO's diplomatic victories, and so were the Americans. That 'band of murderers', as the Israelis' called it, was bent on their 'destruction'; it had never renounced its original aim of 'total liberation', even if, in order to seduce a gullible Western public, it was now ready to settle for a mini-Palestine, co-existent with Israel, on the West Bank and in Gaza. It was obvious, the Israelis contended, that such a state would be no more than a platform from which to renew warfare against an Israel conveniently reduced to its earlier, more vulnerable dimensions.

So Kissinger sought Sadat's help to strengthen Hussein's hand. In a formal pronouncement, Sadat duly assured the king that, while the PLO represented the Palestinians outside his kingdom, he continued to represent the far more numerous ones inside it. This was intended to make clear to the Israelis that whatever West Bank territory they chose to disgorge would go to Hussein and not to Yasser Arafat. But in spite of their well-known preference for the Hashemite monarch over the 'terrorist' chief, they would not budge. And that suited Sadat's purposes, for he had his own secret reasons for wanting to see the PLO in the role to which the world has since grown accustomed, but the mere prospect of which at the time caused the Israelis and their supporters everywhere to wail and gnash their teeth. So Sadat did not try very hard to stave off the historic concession which his fellow heads of state urged upon King Hussein at the Rabat summit conference of October 1974. The king finally recognized the PLO as 'the sole legitimate representative of the Palestinian people', with the right to establish a 'national authority' over any 'liberated Palestinian territory', and thereby ceded juridically what, in 1967, he had lost physically.

Arafat called it a 'wedding feast' for the Palestinians. It was promptly followed by his celebrated address to the United Nations General Assembly. He came to the Assembly, he said, 'bearing an olive branch and a freedom fighter's gun. Do not let the olive branch fall from my hand.' But the more acclaim, the more 'recognition', Arafat won in the international diplomatic arena, the more it served Sadat's furtive go-it-alone, American-sponsored diplomatic purposes. For, by making disengagement on the Jordanian front more unlikely than ever, it focused attention on Sinai as the only possible way forward.[37]

The more the Arab world suspected his intentions, the more vehemently Sadat sought to reassure it. With Kissinger preparing for his next Sinai shuttle, he reverted to the bold, deadline-setting language, from before the October war, of 'no war, no peace'. In January 1975 he pledged that 'I shall accept nothing less than an Israeli move on three fronts (Sinai, Golan and the Jordan River)— and within three months. . . . If nothing is accomplished soon, and very soon, we shall go to Geneva, all of us, including the Palestinians, and explode the situation there. We ourselves will explode the situation at the time of our choosing.' By way of assurance to the Syrians, Sadat insisted that Egypt 'rejected and continues to reject the ending of the state of war unilaterally'. Moreover, if Israel attacked Syria, 'Egypt would move immediately to intervene'. 'I mean what I say, and America knows this.'

By now, however, the discerning Sadat-watcher had little difficulty in distinguishing between what he meant and what he did not. 'We believe that it would be tantamount to treason if we reject for any reason occupied territory which the enemy may return to us. . . .' This casually inserted, low-key rehearsal of his favourite—but, to other Arabs, entirely specious—argument for piecemeal disengagement meant far more than all the ringing protestations of his pan-Arab faith.[38]

As the price of another Sinai disengagement, the Israelis were demanding a pact of non-belligerency. Kissinger tried to impress upon them that this was more than Sadat could concede, that it could only come with formal, final peace, that he could not risk the resultant rupture with his brother Arabs. It was in Israel's own interest, he urged, to conclude a new agreement with Egypt which, even if it fell short of all it wanted, would push Sadat further down the road he had already chosen, fortifying him against all those forces, Palestinian, Arab, Soviet, which sought to divert him from it at Israel and America's expense. Kissinger's shuttle of March 1975 none the less foundered on the rocks of Israeli intransigence. If the Israelis could not have the non-belligerency pact they wanted, then the most they would do, in return for the less binding concept of 'non-recourse to force' which Sadat offered them, was to withdraw from only half the Gidi and Mitla passes. And that was something which Sadat simply could not sell to his army commanders, already deeply dissatisfied with the severe military constraints imposed by the first Sinai agreement.

Kissinger privately cursed and railed at the Israelis for their obtuseness, and President Ford publicly warned them that, unless they were more flexible, the United States would drastically reassess its policy in the Middle East—'including our policy towards Israel'. This was a clear threat to suspend economic and military aid; it could also have led, Ford hinted, to a public American definition of a final settlement, one that called for Israeli withdrawal, with minor frontier changes, from all the occupied territories. His warning constituted the severest rebuke America had administered to Israel since President Eisenhower had forced it out of Sinai in the wake of its 1956 invasion of Egypt. There was relief in the Arab world, and, to reassure the Syrians, Sadat agreed to the establishment of a high-level committee that would ensure 'the closest cooperation' between the two countries.

But the reassessment never came to pass. For one thing, the Israelis knew that, thanks largely to the military bounty which Kissinger, by way of encouraging them to negotiate at all, had heaped upon them, the Middle East balance of power had now tipped strongly in their favour. For another thing, the Zionist lobby proved once more what a formidable force it was. On 21 May 1975, seventy-six Senators wrote collectively to the President to endorse Israel's demand for defensible frontiers and massive economic and military assistance. Furthermore, Sadat himself, heartened by American exasperation, decided that Kissinger should have another go, and that another of those surprise, unscheduled concessions, offered for nothing in return, would help persuade him.

Originally, Sadat had insisted that the Suez Canal would stay closed until Israel's withdrawal from the whole of Sinai; then until the completion of a second-stage disengagement; now, after the failure of the March shuttle, he told his People's Assembly: 'Some expected me to react emotionally and keep the Suez Canal closed, but I shall do exactly the opposite.'[39] On 5 June, the eighth anniversary of the 1967 war, he formally re-opened the waterway 'for the good of our people and the world'. Resplendent in naval white, he sailed down it on board the destroyer *October* which was dwarfed, in the convoy that followed, by the American guided-missile cruiser, *Little Rock*, flagship of the Sixth Fleet.

So Kissinger did have another go and on 1 September 1975 Sinai Two was concluded. The Israelis knew that without grave risk to themselves they could hardly thwart him a second time. But knowing, too, how anxious he was to preserve Sadat's standing and his own, they were determined to exact a very high price.

They succeeded. True, they had to disgorge the Sinai passes, as well as the small Abu Rudeis oilfields on which Sadat had also insisted. But that was the indispensable minimum that Egypt would insist on in any agreement; and even then, to Sadat's bewilderment, Kissinger could not prise them entirely out of the Gidi pass, clinging as they did to certain footholds at its eastern extremity. Strictly limited in numbers and firepower, Egyptian forces advanced to what, since the previous disengagement agreement, had been the perimeter of the buffer zone. At Israel's insistence, Americans manned their own electronic listening posts in the new buffer zone, supplementing Israeli and Egyptian ones. In any case, as some Israeli generals privately conceded, the passes had little strategic value. And the most uninstructed layman could tell from a glance at the map that Israel still retained possession of a full nine-tenths of the Sinai Peninsula.

In return, the Israelis wrested from the Americans 'a moral, monetary and military cornucopia unattained by any other foreign power'.[40] The secret commitments to Israel were—as Kissinger's own aides admitted—'mind-boggling'.[41] The United States agreed to a contingency plan for meeting Israel's military needs in any emergency. It undertook to preserve and consolidate Israel's superiority by furnishing the most advanced and sophisticated weaponry, such as F-15 fighters, that its arsenals could offer. It would seek to 'prevent efforts by others to bring about consideration of proposals which it and Israel agree to be detrimental' to Israel's interests. It pledged neither to recognize nor negotiate with the PLO so long as that organization did not recognize Israel's right to exist or accept Security Council Resolutions 242 and 338. It would 'view with particular gravity threats to Israel's security or sovereignty by a world power'. It considered the disengagement agreement as valid in its own right, irrespective of 'any act or developments' (such as a war) between Israel and any other Arab state.

As for Sadat, he gave Israel the non-belligerency pact it sought in all but name. He also gave Kissinger a secret promise that if Syria attacked Israel he would keep Egypt out of it. There were secret promises, though far less convincing ones, in the opposite direction. Kissinger assured Sadat, in a written memorandum, that the United States would make a 'serious effort to bring about further neg-otiations between Syria and Israel'—a formulation so weak that, as

Sadat knew well, it amounted to exoneration in advance. He also promised that the United States would honestly strive to ensure Palestinian participation in a peace settlement. This last commitment was purely informal, however, and set against the precise, written counter-commitment to Israel it was all but worthless. As he had after Sinai One, Sadat assured Egyptian and Arab public opinion that there were absolutely no secret appendices to the agreement. Within two weeks, the *New York Times* and the *Washington Post* had leaked them all.

Arab civil war by proxy

Sinai Two, in fact, marked the end of the road for step-by-step diplomacy. President Sadat proclaimed that just as the first disengagement had been followed by a similar one on the Syrian front, so this would be followed by Golan Two. He told the People's Assembly that he had obtained an undertaking to that effect from President Ford and that 'the Palestinians will participate in a settlement'.[42] Egypt, claimed the Cairo weekly *Rose el-Youssef*, had insisted on this, and Israel had acquiesced. But President Assad promptly denied it. 'Nobody', he told a BBC interviewer, 'promised us that negotiations will begin.' Besides, he explained, 'what is important is not the start of negotiations, but the grounds from which they will begin, the course they will take, how they will be guided, and what they are expected to achieve.'

After the first Sinai disengagement, the Syrian regime had refrained as best it could from making public its anger in the expectation that its own disengagement would follow; but this time, in the virtual certainty that it would not, it threw away all such constraints. President Assad and his ruling Baath party issued a solemn indictment of what, according to Damascus Radio, could only be described as 'the agreement of treason'. In Syrian eyes, its effect was to 'freeze the Egyptian front at a time when the greater part of Sinai remains under the yoke of occupation' as well as to 'furnish Israel with better opportunities to concentrate its economic, political and military resources on the other confrontation fronts'. It ran counter to the resolutions of successive Arab summit conferences and their insistence on a pan-Arab, 'comprehensive' approach to a Middle East settlement. Furthermore, Sadat had completely ignored the Syrian–Egyptian 'coordination committee' which, under Saudi auspices, he and Assad had agreed to establish a mere five months previously, in the wake of Kissinger's last, abortive round of shuttle diplomacy.

Others—Palestinians, Iraqis, Algerians, Libyans and all the so-called 'radicals' of the Arab world—joined the chorus of condemnation. On the other hand, anxious to preserve its strategic relationship with Egypt, one key 'moderate', Saudi Arabia, endorsed Sinai Two as 'a step towards a final settlement'. Another 'moderate', King Hussein, still awaiting a disengagement on his own front, preserved a diplomatic silence.

It was seen, in the Arab world, as a case of history repeating itself. For in 1948, after the first Arab–Israeli war, the Egypt of King Farouk had been the first to conclude an armistice agreement with the victorious, new-born Jewish state. That—though quickly imitated by Israel's other three neighbours—was condemned as a defection from the common struggle. But in the end it turned out not to have been, because under the leadership of President Nasser Egypt was the only country to take part—and of course the main part—in all three wars that followed. There was no question but that Sadat, through his go-it-alone diplomacy, was appealing to that specifically Egyptian strain in his people's psyche which Nasser—and Sadat himself so long as it served his purposes—had subordinated to the heady new doctrine of pan-Arabism.

He was exploiting a feeling that the Egyptians had shouldered more than their fair share of the collective burden, that the maintenance of a vast army was a drain on the resources of a country whose poverty and overpopulation far exceeded those of any other in the Middle East, that the attempt to unify the Arab world under Egyptian leadership had brought little but jealousy, intrigue and ingratitude even from those—not least, of course, the Baathists—who had once urged it so strenuously upon them. The October war had added a new element; the explosion in the price of oil had heaped fantastic wealth on those Arabs, particularly the bedouins of the Gulf, who happened to possess it. If their vulgar enjoyment of fortunes they had gained through no exertions of their own was distasteful to the West, it was perhaps even more so to the Egyptians who, so poor themselves, felt that it was their own blood which had made the oil Arabs rich.

It was perhaps a legitimate sentiment, this nascent anti-Arabism, but, that said, it could hardly be denied that self-interest, quite as much as altruism, had caused Egypt to embrace Arabism in the first place, and that the overbearing manner in which it had embraced it was not the least of the reasons that had caused it to go sour; and now that Sadat was turning away from ideals which he himself had once so fervently espoused, he and his loyal propagandists did so with a demagogy, a disregard for an equally legitimate Arab grievance, which betrayed their uneasy consciences.

With this first, open split in Arab ranks since the October war, there was born a contradiction that was to grow more flagrant the further Sadat went down his chosen path—between a Sadat who continued to swear his undying, if aggrieved, loyalty to the Arabs and a Sadat who was only outdone by his press and radio in mocking and insulting them. Thus, on the one hand, Sadat would stand on the rostrum of the United Nations General Assembly and declare that 'Jerusalem, Nablus, Hebron, Mount Hermon and Gaza are no less dear to me than Egypt and Kantara or el-Arish'.[43] On the other hand, he instructed his semi-official mouthpieces to fulminate against the objects of his solicitude. 'What do our detractors want', demanded *Akhbar al-Yaum*, 'do they want the Egyptian people . . . to impoverish themselves even more, that the peasants and workers should be deprived of their most elementary needs, just so that those who throw stones at us can sit in their cafés, ply us with wise counsels and draw up our battle plans for us? Let those who wish to fight come to Sinai, bring their arms and their men with them. Egypt will welcome them'.[44]

Such ranting was not always so imprecisely aimed. It was permitted, in this exploiting of popular prejudice, to single out for special abuse those who led the Arab counter-offensive. That meant, above all, the rulers of Syria. In his first speech after the second disengagement agreement, Sadat expressed his 'pain' at their attitude. Behind it, he said, lay the Soviet Union and its 'flagrant incitement and attempts to divide the Arab nation'.[45] The theme was embroidered at length by the Egyptian press, one of whose leading pundits, Ihsan Abdul Koddous, said that it was all a result of 'Baathist bigotry exploited and activated by Soviet policy'. President Sadat, he explained, had always tried to overcome this bigotry through his personal relations with President Assad. Consequently, Syrian–Egyptian relations had continually alternated between periods when the personal relationship was dominant and periods—like the present one—when the Soviet-supported bigotry of the Baath party machine asserted itself.

All of a sudden, the Egyptian press discovered that the Palestinian leadership were so many marionettes too. The PLO's condemnation of the disengagement, said Moussa Sabri, editor of *al-Akhbar*, 'was an Arab pronouncement, but the ink with which it was written was Soviet'. All this noisy opposition, said *al-Ahram*, came from 'parrots' who did not understand what they were told to say.[46] The Moussa Sabris and their like went beyond mere abuse of the Palestinian leadership; they turned instead to innuendos, racist in tone, directed against the whole Palestinian people, who, parasites and wheeler-dealers, had sold their land to the Zionists.

The schism was deep, but not yet unbridgeable. Both Assad and Sadat wanted their share of *Pax Americana*. Assad was justifiably afraid that Sadat was depriving him of his rightful portion. Syria was not Egypt, and he could not of course aspire to be the leader of the Arab world. But if Sadat was bent on making Egypt America's gateway into the Arab world, Assad was determined that Syria should be at least the key which unlocked the gate. Ever since Sadat began to go his own way, Assad had resolved to build himself a power base from which, if necessary, to conduct a counter-strategy of his own. Setting out to increase the influence he commanded in the Arab world, and especially in the immediate, *greater*-Syrian environment composed of Jordan, Lebanon and Palestinians, to that end he had already entered into a form of 'unity' with King Hussein's Jordan. A few years before, that would have been deemed a most unnatural alliance; for Hussein was a miraculous survival from that 're-actionary' order which 'revolutionaries' like the Baathists had fought so hard to destroy.

Assad now sought to bring Lebanon and the Palestinian resistance firmly under his wing on the other flank. It was a process of self-aggrandizement that Sadat was determined to resist. At this stage, he did not wish irrevocably to divide or destroy his Arab adversaries. In Arabic commentaries on the conflict one word, *tahjim*, kept cropping up again and again. It means a 'cutting down to size' and it summed up almost everyone's purpose. Sadat wanted to bring his former wartime ally back into the peace-making. Although, as he had all too readily demonstrated, he was determined to put Egypt's interest first, he needed the Arab world, its wealth, its political and strategic weight, its pro-American connections, the better to promote Egypt's interest. Moreover, if he was selling Egypt as the gateway of the Arab world, he needed to show that he commanded its undivided allegiance, but if he could no longer do this by persuasion—by sticking to a truly pan-Arab, 'comprehensive' path—he had to try coercion instead.

It was in Lebanon that the schism took its most violent form, there that *tahjim* really came into its own. That small country's brutal and complex civil war was perceived in the Arab world, almost certainly correctly, as an inescapable concomitant of Kissinger's step-by-step diplomacy. After Black September, 1970, Yasser Arafat and his Palestinian guerrillas had moved in strength to Lebanon. The autonomous politico-military power base which they established there was an encroachment on their sovereignty which the Lebanese, or at least the traditionally dominant Maronite Christian minority, deeply resented. In 1975, the right-wing Maronite militias, the Phalangists and the Chamounists, took up arms against the guerrillas and their Moslem-leftist Lebanese allies in a war which, sporadic and small-scale at first, grew in scale and intensity after the second Sinai disengagement. Roger Morris, a former Kissinger aide, has recounted that while his master was working his diplomatic miracles the CIA was 'supporting covertly the fighting [in Lebanon] that inflicted an awful, temporarily crippling attrition on the PLO. . . . The Lebanese operation proceeded . . . while unknowing American diplomats . . . tried to arrange a ceasefire, and while congressional and executive oversight groups were consistently misled on the scope and purpose of our covert involvement in Lebanon'. The 'operation' was apparently carried out by 'a special, nearly autonomous Israeli section of the CIA' and it was not even sure whether Kissinger himself knew about this 'gruesome intervention' in Lebanon.[47]

President Sadat had no less interest than the Americans in shaping the course and eventual outcome of the war. This was the 'Arab civil war' which he himself had spoken of as 'the only alternative to Arab coordination', or at least, so long as it was confined to Lebanon, it was Arab civil war by proxy. Naturally, Sadat blamed the Syrians. It was the Baathist regime, he said, which, by fomenting the war, was turning Lebanon into a greater tragedy for the Arabs than Palestine in 1948.[48] Naturally, what the Syrians saw was precisely the opposite; the Sinai disengagement, their Foreign Minister said, had 'begun to yield its fruit in the streets of Beirut; it is part of a scheme to turn the struggle from one of Arabs versus Zionists to one of Arabs versus Arabs'.

The one rule for Sadat was to side with whoever was against Assad, and never mind what changing or infamous company he had to keep to do so. In the first half of the war, that meant that while Syria threw its weight, albeit cautiously, behind the Palestinians and their

Lebanese allies, Sadat favoured the right-wing Christians. But Syria won this first stage of the contest. It looked as though the war was over. The settlement reached between the various protagonists was essentially Syria's work, and it had achieved it through the application of just enough military pressure to establish a new political equilibrium of which it would henceforth be the guardian. Assad had thus added a few more blocks to the edifice of his *greater-*Syria.

Sadat was unhappy about his adversary's success. Far from being over, he told the Beirut weekly *al-Hawadith*, the 'tragedy is only just beginning; I don't advise anyone to put on clothes that are too big for him, because in the end he will fail and his misfortunes will increase.'[49] Sadat was right, and obviously had a hand in ensuring that he was. After four weeks of uneasy calm, the war did break out again, and this time it took an altogether graver turn.

In this second half, President Assad rounded on his former allies. For all of a sudden, the Palestinian resistance movement, getting the upper hand in Lebanon, were about to achieve a destiny-shaping freedom of action that would undermine his *greater-*Syrian designs. His was an almost unthinkable volte-face. Syria, the so-called 'beating heart of Arabism', had always been militant for Palestine; so to turn against the Palestinian guerrillas, however imperfect an embodiment of the supreme Arab cause they might be, was the worst heresy a Syrian ruler could commit. The Syrian army lent itself to the Christian militia's siege and conquest of the refugee camp of Tal al-Zaatar, climactic atrocity of a war already rich in gratuitous barbarism.

Of course, this slaughter of Arab by Arab, with hardly a finger raised in earnest to stop it, was an Arab disgrace. It was a symptom of the moral and political degeneracy into which most Arab regimes, especially, perhaps, those which still called themselves 'revolution-ary', had fallen. Ultimately, it was the policies of Sadat, more than those of any other Arab leader, which had provoked the carnage in Lebanon, but he was now able to portray President Assad as the main villain of the piece. It was not, after all, *his* army which was killing Palestinian men, women and children in their camps; not *his* army which was doing Israel's handiwork more effectively than Israeli could ever do itself. It was just what he needed; as the Syrian Baathists, original sponsors of 'popular liberation war', denounced Arafat and his men as anarchists and saboteurs, the Egyptian press gleefully reproduced the cries of genocide which they, in reply, heaped on their former benefactors. Having cursed the Palestinians in the aftermath of the second Sinai disengagement, Sadat now put himself forward as their only reliable friend and protector, dispatching arms and an Egyptian-based contingent of the Palestinian Liberation Army to Lebanon.

Arafat had at all costs to preserve what was left of his politico-military power base, and as the Syrian army lunged forward in the final battle of the war, he threw in some of his best troops against them. But it was not really they who halted the Syrian advance. An Arab world which could or would not move to prevent the appalling tragedy of Tal al-Zaatar, where only lives were at stake, now bestirred itself for things of greater moment: balances of power, spheres of influence and the prestige of regimes. Syria was breaking all the rules of *realpolitik*, arrogating to itself, by brute force, a regional preponderance which its Arab 'sister-states' could not tolerate. So now, when Arafat made his anguished appeal for an end to 'this massacre of our people', the kings and presidents heeded him. It was time, they decided, to stop this Arab civil war by proxy before it became an Arab civil war pure and simple. It was time for Saudi Arabia, guardian of Arab solidarity, to bring the wartime allies together again.

Sadat and Assad were reconciled at a meeting on 18 October 1976 in the desert capital of Riyadh. The two leaders struck a bargain that was consecrated a week later at a full-scale Arab summit in Cairo. Sadat acknowledged that Syria had a special place in Lebanon. The troops who had entered the country as aggressors and occupiers were now magically transformed into 'peace-keepers'. Egypt and Syria set up a Unified Political Command. According to the Egyptian Foreign Minister, Ismail Fahmi, this was 'an historic step on the way to unity . . . in the broadest and most comprehensive sense'. According to his Syrian counterpart, Abdul Halim Khaddam, it would 'surpass all previous unity formulas between the two countries'. It was the institutional guarantee Assad needed to keep his mercurial partner from renewed backsliding into go-it-alone diplomacy. Together they embarked on a great new 'peace offensive'. 'We are headed for Geneva and a final settlement,' Sadat said at the New Year; Geneva would be 'the final battle in the Arab–Israeli conflict'.[50]

President Assad had made his point. If, as the newly elected President Carter was saying, there could be no settlement without the Palestinians, Assad, more than anyone, now had the power to withhold or play that trump card, to incite the Palestinians against any peace which Syria could not accept, or to sacrifice them for any peace which it could. But if, in achieving this, he had 'cut the Palestinians down to size', he had been cut down to size in his turn. He had paid a heavy price in blood, in moral and political credit, and, as the burdens and frustrations of Lebanese 'peace-keeping' were soon to show, he had over-reached himself. Above all, having gone to such lengths in opposing the Sinai disengagement, he had now acquiesced in it.

In fact, Arabs everywhere had been diminished. For the Lebanese civil war was the most virulent outbreak of a malady that affected them all. It was therefore a thoroughly decadent order over which Sadat re-established Egypt's leadership. Moreover, that leadership itself was no longer rooted, as once it had been, in Egypt's manifest qualifications for the role, still less of the man who ruled it. It was a leadership in which, *faute de mieux*, the Arabs grudgingly acquiesced. But no sooner had Sadat re-established it than it was challenged, not by the Arabs, but by the hungry, downtrodden masses of Egypt itself.

5

An Uprising of Thieves

'Infitah'

That Sadat — as he was fond of saying — 'knew his people' in October 1973 there can be no doubt. A fundamental impulse, patriotism, had spurred the glorious Crossing. But Sadat had other, not unworthy, motives too. He wanted an economic 'crossing' as well.

As he subsequently told an audience of student leaders at Alexandria University:

> I shall not hide from you, my sons, that before the decision to go to war we had reached a very difficult economic situation. Without economic resistance there could be no military resistance. Our economic situation, six days before the battle, was so critical that I called a meeting of the National Security Council and told them we had reached zero. The army cost £E100 million a month, and all our tax receipts in one year were £E200 million, just two months' expense for the armed forces. There was nothing left for us but to enter the battle, whatever happened. We were in a situation such that if nothing had changed before 1974, we would have been hard put to it to provide a loaf of bread. After 5 October we received $500 million which saved our economy and gave us new life.[1]

It was, perhaps, rather crudely put, this notion of converting the blood of Egypt's 'martyrs' into petrodollars. And it shocked some of his listeners into the unedifying calculation that their fallen heroes were worth rather less than 100 dollars a head.

None the less, the underlying logic of it could hardly be gainsaid. War — a war for peace — was as necessary for Egypt's economic revival as it was for its dignity and self-respect. The accumulating billions of the 'oil sheikhs'—after a quadrupling of prices which the war itself had done much to precipitate—were simply the most dramatic of the new opportunities which presented themselves. Any Egyptian ruler, not just Sadat, would have had a right, indeed a duty, to exploit them on his people's behalf.

Since 1948, but especially since the shattering defeat of 1967, an already poor and backward country had lavished a crippling proportion of its national resources on a military machine which served the Arab as well as the Egyptian cause. And even without such a burden, drastic economic reforms were necessary for their own sake. For things had gone badly wrong with one of the proudest achievements of Nasserism, the 'socialist transformation' of the early 1960s which, bringing key areas of economic activity under state control, was supposed to have combined rapid development and industrialization with a new deal for the masses. 'Arab socialism'—as it was called—was a rather improvised affair; a kind of benevolent *étatisme* under which the assets of the 'exploiting classes', foreign and domestic, could be forcibly diverted into productive investment, with the newly created public sector as the driving force behind it. It got off to a tolerable start, but as a result of three main factors— the war effort, a soaring foreign debt aggravated by the closure of the Suez Canal and the loss of the Sinai oilfields, and structural defects within system itself—it failed to sustain its original promise.

The state-run industries, trapped in a vicious circle, proved notoriously inefficient. They produced overpriced goods of inferior quality for which there were no export markets outside the Soviet bloc—and therefore no hard currency, so badly needed for the renewal of obsolete plant. Favoured though industry was, the contribution which it made to the national income did not rise as a proportion of the whole. A creaking, labyrinthine bureaucracy, enmeshed in red tape, tripled in size. Worst of all, perhaps, was the rise of what, long before Nasser died, political theorists such as Muhammad Hussein were calling the 'new class'. It was they who administered 'Arab socialism'. But if it had been in a spirit of idealism—though that is questionable—that Nasser had entrusted them with the task, they did little to emulate that spirit. Indeed, all too often, they exhibited a venality, sloth and nepotism that brought 'Arab socialism' into disrepute and sapped the moral standards of Egyptian society as a whole. Corruption took many forms, but perhaps the most characteristic and offensive was the forging of clandestine alliances between the public and private sectors, with unscrupulous bureaucrats diverting to entrepreneurial accomplices commodities destined, at their artificially low prices, to ease the lot of the masses. By 1973 decline had become inexorable decay, and while Nasser and all he stood for were still technically sacrosanct, socialism was one more hallowed orthodoxy that was coming under bolder and bolder assault.

There could, of course, be no panaceas for socio-economic plagues of the kind that Egypt was suffering but, characteristically, Sadat made out that there could. If it is arguable that Nasser's acceptance of Secretary of State Rogers' peace initiative shortly before he died foreshadowed the go-it-alone, step-by-step diplomacy which was to bring his successor such opprobrium in the Arab world, a similar case can be made for saying that he would eventually have been pushed into economic policies of the kind Sadat was now adopting. Had Nasser lived, for how much longer could he have valiantly resisted the conclusion, on which Sadat was now acting, that war and development had become incompatible? Even now, Sadat did not provocatively and systematically repudiate Nasserism — indeed, when necessary, he laid claim to the legitimacy which it bestowed — but his economic new order, as he presented it, was a second 'revolution', as truly his own as the one it was to supersede had been Nasser's. He called it *Infitah*, the Opening. Just as the Crossing had brought victory on the battlefield, so this second crossing, *his* achievement too, would bring victory on the home front in the shape of prosperity for all.

President Sadat laid the October Working Paper, his blueprint for post-war economic recovery, before the People's Assembly on 4 April 1974. The first task in the 'new stage in the life of this ancient people', Sadat declared, was 'economic development at rates that exceed all we have achieved up till now'. There was to be 'an open-door economic policy at home and abroad that provides guarantees for funds invested in development'. The Arab oil producers were only too willing to invest their surplus funds in Egypt and other Arab countries, for they were 'motivated by noble, patriotic feelings and sound economic attitudes. . . . We welcome and encourage this trend, partly because we are in need of such investments and because we believe they will find a safe and stable climate here. . . . Therefore', he went on, 'we shall provide the Arab investors with all legislative guarantees and we shall offer them the absorptive capacity of the Egyptian economy in conditions of political and social stability and steadily growing economic development.' There was no room for misgivings, 'for fear complexes about our future security', because Egypt enjoyed 'the free national will to shape the future of the country'. The Opening would embrace the entire world, both East and West, 'because we are fully aware that wide-ranging international economic relations constitute the material basis for the freedom of political action'.

Infitah would bring with it technological know-how, rapid industrialization, the promotion of exports and the raising of standards. Free-trade zones should be set up that would attract new industries, absorb labour, create employment, generate entrepôt activities. Tourism should be promoted, but this meant more than 'merely building hotels': it called for the overall development of the 'civilizational environment'. Reconstruction of the Canal Zone would be extended 'to the heart of Sinai', which had to be transformed into an industrial, agricultural and tourist area, with free-trade zones as well as university faculties. All this, Sadat stressed, required change and development in the philosophy of planning. The best way to attract the investor was to present him well-studied, interrelated projects. This could be achieved by 'centralization of planning and decentralization of implementation'. The October Working Paper, Sadat concluded, heralded 'a glorious stage of construction and prosperity, of work and progress' in which every Egyptian must participate. Only thus 'can we be true to the spirit of the glorious Ramadan [October] War, and to the blood of our war dead'.

Infitah won the overwhelming support of the People's Assembly. That was to be expected, for the Assembly was dominated by Sadat loyalists and the resurgent right. Essentially, the right argued that Nasser's socialism had failed; the whole concept had been ill-conceived from the outset; it was time for Egypt to return to free enterprise and the Western capitalist fold.

There was, all the same, much opposition to *Infitah*—though it was denied an effective opportunity to express itself—which came not only from Nasserists, leftists or vested interests of one kind or another, but from those within the intelligentsia and enlightened bourgeoisie who feared that, beneficial though it might be in some ways, it would be very damaging in others. If 'correction' was Sadat's intention, such critics as these had no quarrel with him for, like the right, they were well aware that the Revolution had failed to live up to its original promise. In general, however, they argued that the

205

poor performance of the public sector stemmed less from the principles which governed it than from the manner in which they had been applied. Socialism, administered by fake socialists, had never had a fair chance; what was needed was the reform, not the uprooting, of the system. Provided that the state retained a planning and directional role in the economy through control over its strategic areas, there would be no objection to encouraging foreign investment and reviving the private sector. But they feared that much more than mere 'correction' would ultimately be involved; that, at worst, Egypt would fall once again under that foreign yoke which the 1952 Revolution had finally thrown off.

In the event, with the exception of agriculture, Sadat did not formally tamper with 'the gains of the Revolution'. The public sector remained intact. Indeed, he and the chief executives of *Infitah* frequently defended it. He dispensed with few, if any, of the benefits — free education, guaranteed employment for graduates, rent controls, profit-sharing for workers, social security payments and, above all, subsidies on basic commodities — of the welfare system. So, while all the rhetoric of the second Crossing made it sound bold, new and exciting, the defensive justifications that followed tended to stress how little was really changing. It was *not* an attempt to do away with the existing economic order but, by exploiting new international political and economic realities, to revitalize it.

There were no formal enactments destined to transform Egypt from a 'socialist' into a 'capitalist' society. At most there was to be a grafting of the one upon the other. The key instrument was Law Number 43 of June 1974 which, it was hoped, would encourage Western and Arab participation in the great recovery, notably through joint ventures assuring the Egyptian partner a minimum 51 per cent stake. One of the architects of *Infitah* reduced it all to a succinct mathematical equation: 'Arab capital plus Western technology plus Egypt's labour, markets and population explosion equals economic growth.'[2]

Resignation and plenty

It is said that when God appointed companions for all his created things, Resignation, for the Egyptians, went hand in hand with Plenty. That no doubt accounts for the patience and forbearance with which they wait upon the fulfilment of God's, and their own rulers', inscrutable purposes. When Sadat proclaimed his *Infitah*, the people were quietly persuaded that the miracle had already begun. They were impervious to the opposition's doubts and forebodings, and if, already, it was taking surprising forms which they had not been led to expect, all would surely right itself in the fullness of time. There were, after all, many hopeful signs.

All really hinged on creating a climate of stability in Egypt and the region as a whole, and that, in turn, could only flow from peace, or the serious prospect of it, between Arab and Jew. To many, at least, the first fruits of Dr Kissinger's shuttle diplomacy—the first Sinai disengagement agreement of January 1974 followed by the Golan four months later—seemed to augur well for a final settlement. The more progress Kissinger made, the more extravagant the propagandists became in their assurances about the foreign funds that would follow in the wake of peace. What more reassuring, what more solid proof of bounty to come, than the interest of one of the giants of American capitalism—a Rockefeller himself? As Kissinger was completing the first of his disengagement agreements, David Rockefeller, Chairman of Chase Manhattan Bank, was making a highly publicized tour of several Arab countries. He told CBS News about the image that Egypt was trying to project, and clearly it pleased him. 'I think', he said, 'that Egypt has come to realize that socialism and extreme Arab nationalism . . . have not helped the lot of the 37 million people they have in Egypt. And if President Sadat wants to help them, he has got to look to private enterprise and assistance.' Rockefeller had even consulted Israel's leaders on what was best for Egypt and 'they agreed with us. . . . They felt that the position of President Sadat vis-à-vis his own country is a constructive one, and they feel there's a better chance of ending the war if help is given to him to build his own country in a sound economic way.'[3]

After Kissinger and Rockefeller there descended on Cairo a host of Western statesmen, politicians, diplomats, fact-finders, men of religion and men of good will. Suddenly, they were all aware of Egypt's existence. Suddenly, they were anxious to promote 'peace in the Middle East', and more particularly between Israel and the most powerful Arab country. There came more bankers; businessmen and representatives; advisers, experts and consultants with their Samsonite cases and their bulging portfolios and prospectuses. They were going to instruct the Egyptian government how to run its economy on sensible Western lines; they were going to help repair or replace the country's groaning, overburdened infrastructure; they were going to teach the *fellaheen* of the Delta how to 'maximize' their grain output, and bring Harvard Business School methods to dark, insanitary Cairo shopfloors.

The most exalted of the visitors was President Nixon himself. For all the stage-management behind it, the welcome he received was so impressive, and the joint communiqué to which he and his host put their name promised an economic partnership so far-reaching, that Cairo newspapers could hardly refrain from proclaiming that salvation was at hand. The United States, the communiqué said, 'supports the ventures of American enterprises'. Those 'under consideration' covered 'petrochemicals, transportation, food and agricultural machinery, land development, power, tourism, banking and a host of other sectors'. The estimated value of projects under serious consideration exceeded two billion dollars. 'American technology and capital combined with Egypt's absorptive capacity, skilled manpower and productive investment opportunities can contribute effectively to the strengthening and development of the Egyptian economy.' The Shah of Iran, the great adversary of Nasser's day, had committed $700 million in aid and investment. There were contracts, too, with West Germany for $500 million, with Japan for $100 million and, in spite of the strained relations with the Soviet Union, the Eastern bloc was still chipping in, Romania with contracts for $100 million and Bulgaria $60 million.

And suddenly there were the tourists too. They crossed the Atlantic to behold the marvels of the Pharaohs, medieval bazaars, and the timeless, picturesque poverty of palm-fringed, mud-hut villages: the memorials of a civilization that was seven thousand years old, as Sadat and his media never tired of repeating. Famous hotels that had stood half-empty for years, Shepheards and Semiramis, and their brasher modern rivals, the Hilton, Sheraton and Meridien, were now filled to overflowing.

Nor were the Arab 'brothers' to be outdone. Perhaps they were not yet contributing as much as they might, but Sadat expressed his confidence that, just as they had rescued his economy from 'zero' upon the outbreak of the October war, so they would rally to the challenge of his ambitious new five-year plan. Meanwhile, here they were, the public was told, paying tribute to Egyptian valour. Some did, indeed, visit the battlefields and stood awed on the ruins of the 'impregnable' Bar Lev line. But after the monarchs, the sultans and the sheikhs had performed the official rites and pilgrimages, had laid foundation stones and handed over cheques for 'popular' housing projects in the war-devastated Canal Zone, their subjects lingered on to enjoy the profaner pursuits which Cairo and Alexandria had to offer. Throughout the long years of the cold war between 'revolutionaries' and 'reactionaries', between Nasser and the traditionalist regimes he had tried to sweep away, the oil-rich Gulf had been sundered from the fleshpots of Egypt. With the dangers of war and socialism seemingly exorcised for ever, they were now most pleasurably and profitably joined together again. The stark white *dishdashas* stood out against the dust-drab streets—and the inexhaustible funds drawn from their voluminous folds were showered upon furnished apartments, nightspots and marriageable daughters.

So, as the Israelis retreated into Sinai, these new invaders seemed to usher in the second Crossing which would turn 'ancient' Egypt, poor but proud, enfeebled but victorious, into a modern nation worthy of its magnificent past. By the end of 1974, accounts showed that $4·4 billion had been garnered in bilateral credits. For Sadat, it seemed, economic recovery was already an accomplished fact.

I sincerely and truthfully say [he told the Alexandria University students within ten months of the war] that our situation after 6 October is no less than an economic miracle which has never occurred in a country that has gone through a war of attrition and military confrontations. . . . We have managed to give each individual the main necessities of life in food, clothing, public services. . . . We can today raise our heads high and say that no country with such limited resources could achieve what we have achieved in the way of military victory, social justice, maintenance of the standard of living, increasing the rate of development, and securing a job for every graduate. . . . This is at a time when other countries stumble and deteriorate as a result of the rise in the price of major commodities . . .[4]

The people wondered at this. That a miracle was in the making they yearned to believe, but to be told that it had already occurred was something else. That there was already plenty—for a few—they could see; that it would make its way down to them they still had reason to hope, but it had not done so yet. On the contrary, they were experiencing greater want than ever. But Resignation was, after all, their appointed lot; they might murmur, but they did not yet revolt against adversity. As they waited in ever-lengthening queues for the ever-scarcer necessities of life, their betters, the politicians, economists and potential investors, began to seek an explanation for the enormous gulf between what Sadat and his supporters *said* was happening and what really was. Nothing is ever simple; none the less, the answer, at bottom, was simple enough. If, under Nasser, the fault lay less with socialism than with the 'socialists' who administered it, so now it lay more with the men of *Infitah* than with *Infitah* itself. What should have been a fruit of the best in socialism (its concern for the general good) and the best in capitalism (its dynamism) looked very much, instead, like an alliance of all that was worst in both. Since the Pharaohs, Egyptians have been imbued with respect for authority, but they only had to turn their gaze upward, to the very summit, for the supreme indictment of *Infitah*.

The Royal Family

If Nasser's socialism had not been very successful, at least it could not be held against him that his personal example was at variance with his political philosophy. For the eighteen years he was in power he and his family continued to live in the modest villa at Manshiet el-Bakri, on the road to Heliopolis, which he had acquired as a young officer. He was a hard worker. He rose early and retired late. He read a great deal, seldom took a holiday and remained in Cairo throughout the summer. His tastes were simple. His elder daughter, Huda, recalls having to beg her father to order a new suit when the collar of the one he had been wearing 'for ages' had become visibly frayed. When finally he agreed, his secretary discovered that his tailor had been dead for two years. According to his friend and confidant Muhammad Heikal, 'his family life was irreproachable . . . and where money was concerned, he received, in the form of donations, millions of pounds. He used them for Egypt's benefit and, on his death, there were £E2½ million in his public account, but only £E610 in his private account'.[5] Nasser's wife, Tahia, was a typical middle-class Moslem wife and mother. Well-bred, educated, somewhat shy, she was discreet in her dress and dignified in bearing. Although she helped her husband in his political activities before the Revolution, she was content to remain in the background after it. Her public appearances were low-key; soberly attired, often in plain black, she arrived and departed without fuss or fanfare.

It is sometimes difficult to tell fact from fiction in Egypt. Some at least of what was said about Sadat and his wife is doubtless untrue.

The authors therefore prefer to confine themselves to the known, the public and the obvious.

Nasser had no need to proclaim himself a *fellah*, a 'man of the people'. For the people always felt that he really was one of them. But the more Sadat did so, the more he seemed a *khawarga*—a foreigner—in their eyes. Nasser may have loved the substance of power, but Sadat quickly showed that he adored its trappings too. It was after the two Crossings—the military and the economic—that he indulged these propensities to the full. From then on, his presidency had little to distinguish it from the vulgarities of the monarchy he had helped to overthrow. The people called him King Sadat, or Farouk the Second, after the last, obese, pleasure-loving scion of the Muhammad Ali dynasty; or 'the Khedive', after the brilliant but extravagant Ismail, who had reduced Egypt to bankruptcy and European tutelage a century before. Sadat must surely have known what the people were saying, but he seemed to grow more regal, not less, more remote and ostentatious. The known, the public and the obvious—to cite six manifestations of it—were Sadat's obsessive elegance, his elaborate retinue, his numerous *pieds-à-terre*, his means of conveyance from one to the other, his indolence and his love of publicity.

In 1977, the year of Egypt's worst economic crisis, Sadat earned a compliment of sorts. The Italian Chamber of Haute Couture dubbed him one of the world's ten best dressed men. Certainly few heads of state lavished such attention on their own person as he did, from cuff links to the polished English cane which was one of his special affectations. Whether he was formal and dark-suited, casual and open-necked, there was always something of the mannequin, the fashion magazine, about his all-too-perfect appearance. Rarely did he wear the same outfit twice, and his vast assortment of 'costumes', by Balmain or Cardin, bore the most prestigious names. It was after the October 'victory', in his capacity as Supreme Commander of the Armed Forces, that Sadat crossed the sartorial borderline between an excessive, if perhaps harmless, passion for ceremonial display into a self-aggrandizing narcissism. His dress uniforms were foreign creations too. Sadat, all sashes, sequins, fancy breeches and riding boots, was presumably unaware that he looked the part for a title role in a vaudeville, but he can hardly have been quite as artless in his choice of honour guards, the latest of which, *feldgrau*, jackboots, goosestep and all, was surely modelled on Hitler's *Wehrmacht*. It was scarcely Egyptian, all this finery, but with the ritual pilgrimages to Mit Abul Kom he made up for it; there he donned his simple, made-in-Paris *gallabiyah*.

An Egyptian version of George Washington's log cabin was part of the cult which Sadat and his admirers fostered. The 'greatest joy' of a much-travelled leader was to return to his birthplace. He repaired there for such intimate occasions as his birthday, on Christmas Day, to savour 'hours of infinite purity and repose . . . sitting alone and communing with [himself] . . . contemplating [his] life and the people around [him]'. There he returned 'to his boyhood, to the good earth from which he came. There he feels at home. He is the owner of a little house that he has built for himself in Mit Abul Kom; his salary went on that and buying the land on which it stands.'[6]

The Egyptian press sustained this myth of the simple *fellah* in defiance of everything that knocked it down. For Sadat was no less extravagant in his choice of places to live and work in than he was in his couturiers. Hardly had he become President than he enlarged his smart, Nile-side villa in Giza by taking over the adjoining Muhammad Khalil Museum, which had been given to the nation by a wealthy collector. And he soon displayed that predilection for all things monarchic which was to come to fruition in his post-Crossing period. Abidin Palace—a sort of Buckingham Palace in the teeming heart of Cairo—used to be the official residence of King Farouk. It was a vast repository of all the sensuous *bric-à-brac* of Levantine decadence. It reeks, in Egyptian memory, of royal self-indulgence. After the Revolution it became a museum and the garden behind it was thrown open to the public. On coming to power, Sadat had it done up as his office, and all of a sudden, without explanation, a great wall went up around it which shut out the public again. Within ten years Sadat had acquired at least ten residences. He liked to winter in Aswan, nestling by the First Cataract of the Nile, and to summer in Alexandria. Much of the time in between he spent in Ismailia, which became his favourite resort after the October war.

To some, at least, of these establishments—such as the vast, green Barrages estate north of Cairo—he was entitled as head of state. But, for Sadat, the distinction between public and private seems to have been a superfluous one. Every now and then those who followed the doings of their president learned that he had gone into retreat at yet another of the 'resthouses'—as the press usually described them—which had apparently been put at his disposal. In Cairo he had one next to the Pyramids, conveniently located for a leader who so often had to pose for foreign photographers before those mighty symbols of Egyptian civilization. But he occasionally descended on others in far-flung corners of the land, at Burg al-Arab or Marsa Matruh on the Mediterranean, or Hurghada on the Red Sea.

Naturally, Sadat could not get about on such a scale without aeroplanes. He would take to the air even for the shortest of distances. He had his private helicopter — originally a gift from President Nixon, but when Congress rejected the allocation for it Egypt was left to pick up the bill. It was used for journeys even from his Nile-side Giza residence to Abidin Palace, five minutes' distance by car — presidential motorcades were no longer seen in the streets of Cairo except to receive honoured guests or to stage a 'triumphal' return from some 'historic' mission or other. A special landing strip for a helicopter or a small aircraft was constructed at Mit Abul Kom.

For longer journeys, he used the presidential Boeing 707, 'Egypt One'. Joseph Kraft, an American columnist inspired to much reverence by Sadat's statesmanship, described the atmosphere aboard as 'that of a royal court'.

> Sadat and his handsome wife, Jihan, occupied a comfortable forward cabin with berths and sitting room. Behind them, in what amounted to steerage of a Boeing 707, there was jumbled together a mixed bag of ministers, attendants, secretaries and security personnel. Only one of those in the cheap seats would move easily into the Presidential quarters: Othman Ahmad Othman, a millionaire contractor and buddy of the President, sometimes known as Sadat's Bebe Rebozo. . . . Several of the ministers tucked themselves away in the corner seats where they could be almost certain not to attract the attention of the President.[7]

If all this was far removed from the life of the *fellah*, so, too, was the leisurely tempo of his daily routine. Indeed, it is little short of amazing that a ruler beset by so many problems could actually devote so little of his time to affairs of state. Unlike the *fellah* who rises with the sun, Sadat would awake at nine o'clock when his valet entered his bedroom to open the shutters and switch on a tape-recording of the Koran — 'so the first thing Sadat hears on waking is the word of God.' After he had said his prayers, the tape-recorder moved to his favourite Arabic singers while he washed and shaved; he would then return to his bed to read the newspapers. He breakfasted on papaya and honey; something of a hypochondriac, he took care to nurse his delicate stomach. He would then dress 'and begin his work as President of the Republic'. That would last three or four hours, during which he received visitors and read reports and dispatches—though he disliked this latter chore and preferred to have them delivered orally. In the early afternoon he would take off alone on his keep-fit walk—extended to an hour and a half when he reached the age of sixty. To indulge this hallowed ritual he spent as much time as possible at the Barrages, 'because he loves green and hates desert'. This would be followed by a massage, a hot bath and a nap. He would then conduct more state business for a couple of hours. After a light supper, donning pyjamas, he would watch the two films, preferably Westerns, which unfailingly rounded off his day.

Such insights into Sadat's private life are not hard to come by. He himself used to parade them. It seems to have been an extension of his 'foreign complex', as his critics called it—that determination to show the West how Westernized and 'with it' he was. Relaxed, puffing at his pipe, exuding charm and sweet reasonableness, he did indeed go down well with the Americans, whom he took good care to flatter extravagantly. He was tireless in answering interviewers' questions, reminiscing about his past, discoursing at length on world affairs, and airing his dreams, hopes and ambitions for the future. But the Sadat he projected in this marathon, one-man show had little to do with the realities of the country he governed; it left his audience in the dark about the Egyptian people, *their* dreams, hopes and ambitions. It went down much less well at home when, for example, *Akhbar al-Yaum* devoted entire pages to a day in the leisurely life of the President, reverently recording such fascinating spectacles as Sadat washing his face, Sadat cleaning his teeth, Sadat shaving 'with his own hand', to accompanying captions such as 'Cleanliness is next to Godliness.'[8]

If Sadat assumed royal airs, then Jihan was his fitting queen. His second wife was sixteen years younger than him, and a good-looking woman who exerted a powerful influence over her husband. Before the October war she seldom made a public appearance. The wives of Moslem rulers seldom do. But after the *Infitah* and the courting of America, she was metamorphosed, as if by the touch of a magic wand. She was given the title of 'first lady' and her picture began to appear in the newspapers almost as regularly as her husband's, dressed as if for a garden party to visit the front, military hospitals, and rehabilitation centres for the disabled. Suddenly she assumed an interest—not apparent before—in the emancipation of women. And the Faith and Hope charitable organization was publicized around the world as her own brainchild. Yet everyone knew that it had actually been established and financed in the 1960s by Um Kalthoum, the great Egyptian singer, the Nightingale of the Nile, who was the true first lady of the entire Arab world until her death in 1974.

Jihan was almost as prodigal as her husband in granting interviews to foreign journals. The women's pages of leading Western newspapers, fashion magazines, and even America's *Playgirl*, solicited her views on subjects of feminine interest — including life with Anwar Sadat. To *Playgirl* she confided in True Romance style: 'Yes, yes. I love him so much.' No, Sadat never said he loved *her*. All the same, 'Sometimes I speak, saying such love things to him, "I love you, Anwar. Do you love me the same?"' Yes, she *had* changed him; she had 'made him sleep with stockings'. For she herself could not sleep without them. 'Wool ones, you know.' Sadat had never done this before, she elaborated; 'he took it from me . . . and now he can't sleep without them.' She had never mixed with ordinary people before 1967, she admitted. 'Well, I'm not from a rich family, but I was a little bit far, to be honest, from the very low people.' Her father was a cook and her mother a maid at the British Embassy. It was when she had started working with the wounded soldiers after the 1967 war that 'for the first time in my life I was involved with this kind of people'. She claimed that because, in the beginning, the 'people here were not used to a woman working', students and young people had considered her 'showy' and 'very fanatic people who are narrow-minded' talked about her as a 'forward woman'.[9]

The eight-page interview was interspersed with nude male pin-ups, advertisements for sex aids, 'cleavage building lifts' and the like. Even to the most broad-minded, sophisticated and uninhibited of her compatriots, this did seem 'forward'. Others applied to it a word much on Sadat's lips when he was condemning any deviation from the 'ethics of the Egyptian village'. It was *'aib*, 'shame', that the wife of the Egyptian President, a devout Moslem, should talk like that to any, let alone a pornographic, magazine.

The new royal family did it all on a presidential salary of $12,000 a year.[10]

The 'fat cats'

It was President Sadat, then, who set the moral example of *Infitah*.

He was the supreme embodiment of an ethos that impregnated the whole establishment. The 'new class' preferred Sadat to his predecessor. For although they owed their position to Nasser, they had feared him as a colossus who could put a brake on their excesses. Sadat, by contrast, was not merely weak. He was essentially one of them. He exuded self-indulgence, vanity and frivolity. Why should they be more fastidious than he? They had mastered the system, or the deft abuse of it, and now they were determined to exploit it to the full.

Sadat set the example not merely in his own person, but in those he admitted to the inner sanctum of power and influence. The most exalted of them was Othman Ahmad Othman, the man whom columnist Joseph Kraft, well versed in the sleazy Washington of Richard Nixon, called 'Sadat's Bebe Rebozo'; but if the Egyptians had a nickname for him, it was 'Sadat's Adnan Kashoggi', after the billionaire Saudi businessman and arms dealer. He stood at the apex of a pyramid, but the relationships he epitomized reproduced themselves all the way down to its base. He was the supreme beneficiary of that fusion of two orders — the old, decadent socialism and the resurgent capitalism — that was the essence of *Infitah*. It was back in the 1940s that Othman had founded the company which eventually grew into the largest contracting empire in the Middle East. He was a passionate advocate of old-fashioned, nineteenth-century free enterprise. 'If we do not hold to the complete freedom of the individual in a competitive context', he said, 'then we cannot bring about any progress.'[11] Ironically it was under socialism — which, along with Nasser and the Russians, ranked as one of his *bêtes noires* — that he first broke into the big time.[12] For it was Nasser who called on him to help complete the Aswan High Dam. The anathemas he heaped on socialism — or at least the version of it practised in Egypt — lacked conviction, as did those of other, lesser men of his kind. For if Nasser's original assault on the private sector, with land reforms, nationalizations, sequestrations and severe limitations on personal incomes, had dealt a heavy blow to the old bourgeoisie, it none the less created new entrepreneurial opportunities, seized by elements of both the old as well as the new bourgeoisie. It has been calculated that even during the first five-year plan, from 1960 to 1965, a full 40 per cent of investment funds found their way, through sub-contracting, into private hands.[13]

But it was only under Sadat that a fundamental ambivalence, fraudulence even, came flagrantly into its own. Othman Ahmad Othman was perfectly poised to take advantage of *Infitah*. For here, on the one hand, he was installed as Minister of Housing and Reconstruction with special powers, in his official capacity, to mastermind the post-war economic recovery. And there, on the other hand, was the same Othman Ahmad Othman, chairman of a gigantic construction company that employed 50,000 people. The familiar sign, Arab Contractors Company, stood high and proud over building sites the length and breadth of the land. The Cement King—as he was also known—seemed to have a stake in almost everything: housing projects and hotels, roads and bridges, factories and power stations. And now, after the *Infitah*, he became the Egyptian partner in a number of multinational enterprises, ranging from chicken farms and tourist complexes to the manufacture of soft drinks. To this bridging of two worlds his intimacy with Sadat furnished the central span. It was a dynastic alliance of which the arranged marriage of his son to the President's daughter, Huda, was no more than the final sacrament.

If Sadat's relationship with Othman Ahmad Othman, the self-made man, illustrated the basic, economic drive of the 'new class', that with another intimate, Sayyid Marei, illustrated a subsidiary drive that was as much social as economic—the cultivation of the old bourgeoisie which, though politically reduced by the Revolution, retained desirable qualities of breeding and sophistication. Marei was a polished scion of the landed gentry and a businessman to boot who, adapting himself to the new realities, had served as Minister of Agriculture under Nasser, but, like Othman, came truly into his own under Sadat as Speaker of the People's Assembly, and, a more important yardstick of the real power behind-the-scenes, as father-in-law to another of Sadat's daughters.

Lower down the pyramid, beneath the Othmans and the Mareis, there was a stratum, still very narrow, of exceedingly wealthy men, largely 'new class', whom the mildly left-wing weekly *Rose al-Youssef* dubbed the 'fat cats'. By and large, it was that same symbiotic relationship between the public and private sectors epitomized by Othman Ahmad Othman on which the 'fat cats' thrived.

Accordingly to one estimate, there were some 180 millionaires in Egypt at the outset of *Infitah*, and at least 2,000 families, comprising 33,000 individuals, with an average income of £E33,000 a year.[14] The satirical poet Ahmad Nagm lampooned the 'fat cats' in memorable lines:

Sitting in large fast cars . . .
Thick pasty necks
Fat bellies
Gleaming skin
Obtuse minds
Soaring incomes and
Swelling paunches . . .

Of lower middle-class, frequently rural, origins, they developed *nouveau riche* instincts in a society where, with perhaps 10 per cent of the population still accounting for 60 per cent of consumer spending, such instincts were strong. They set the style for the 'new class' in general, whose members, having joined the 10 per cent, had to keep up with the Ahmads and the Abdullahs. Characteristically, they had to have villas in Garden City or Heliopolis and a seaside place in Alexandria. They had to have Chivers Regal scotch behind their private bars and furnish their homes with a Levantine version of Louis Quinze. They had to drive sleek new Mercedes 200 SL-E's. They had to frequent former British clubs and marry their daughters at Shepheards Hotel or the Nile Hilton with a troupe of belly dancers in attendance.

The 'new class' were the luckiest or most unscrupulous ones. Beneath them was the ever-growing army of those (still a minority of the population) who, as a result of the Revolution, could, broadly speaking, be said to constitute the bourgeoisie. They were the beneficiaries and, in a sense, the victims of Nasser's imperfect, but laudable, attempt to give everyone an equal chance in life. For while they had acquired bourgeois aspirations they were largely denied the means to fulfil them. At the heart of this failure lay free education for all, particularly at the university level, and what had become its necessary corollary—guaranteed employment for graduates. For the Revolution had proved unable to generate the growth in national wealth which would have furnished truly productive employment of a kind to match their educational qualifications, dubious in reality though these might often be. It was an imbalance which the population explosion greatly exacerbated. Having created this 'Nasserist generation', the only way the state could begin to satisfy its minimum expectations was to absorb it into the bureaucracy, and it was this, rather than objective need, which accounted for the bureaucracy's phenomenal and superfluous growth.

Within this bourgeoisie, the gulf between those, the 'fat cats', who had really made it and those at the base of the pyramid was far greater, in straight material terms, than it was between the latter and the masses, urban and rural, from whose ranks the Revolution had raised them. But it was natural that, having taken this first, crucial step up the ladder of social mobility, they should seek to take more. Had Sadat's Egypt been one in which merit and honest exertion earned its just reward or—to borrow his own idiom—had it really been inspired by 'the ethics of the Egyptian village', that would have been no more than healthy, constructive ambition. But, in reality, it was no such Egypt and, in the moral climate of *Infitah*, those best placed to 'get on' were those whose consciences permitted them to subvert, for their own selfish ends, the system that had raised them to what they already were. For every 'fat cat' there were a thousand who wanted to become 'fat cats' too.

The disparities within it may have been enormous, but, taken in aggregate, this bourgeoisie pressed for, and secured—even without abuses—a far higher consumption of the nation's substance than its contribution to it deserved. The vastly swollen bureaucracy, citadel of the 'new class', treated itself to a growth in real income which, though low in absolute terms, greatly outstripped its growth in output. If, after the pioneering reforms of the 1950s and 1960s, President Nasser, searching for new sources of investment revenue, had hesitated to extract it from the bourgeoisie, old and new, his successor was even more reluctant. For the bourgeoisie, and especially its affluent few, had become his main political constituency, the power base which, even had he wanted to, he felt least able to antagonize.

Sadat, the Othmans, the 'fat cats' and the 'new class' in general represented a tiny minority but, through the wealth they avariciously hoarded or grossly squandered, through the false values they inculcated in a bourgeoisie which tried to catch up with them, through the bitterness they sowed in the hearts of the impoverished multitudes who had no chance of doing so—through all that the damage they did was incalculable. And nothing was to demonstrate it like *Infitah* in action.

'A little water and a little shit'

The pyramids, the Sphinx! For 5,000 years nobody's done anything to that sand. I mean, God is God. But man is man and can't you make it bigger, better? Create an oasis? Build a golf course? . . . I mean, to take a little water and a little shit and make an oasis

219

of green where there's only been sand for 5,000 years, to create a golf course where every plane from Europe on its way to the Middle East or Africa has to pass over and look down on that green symbol of life, where you can see Arnold Palmer play golf with pyramids as a backdrop—wouldn't that turn you on? I mean [Peter Munk pauses a moment for a disconcerting reflection], doesn't everybody think like that?[15]

Sadat did. For it was he who invited Munk to mastermind the Pyramids Oasis Project, rather than the high-flying international financier who pressed it on him. It would dwarf an earlier such scheme, proposed by his Ministry of Tourism, for a 'Disneyland' in the shadow of one of the seven wonders of the world. As its *pièce de résistance*, the Disneyland was to have had a 'plastic' pyramid housing a museum and other diversions for the instruction or entertainment of 'package tourists' making their pilgrimage to the original ones. That scheme, expected to cost a mere $50 million, had died amid a chorus of complaint from both Egyptians and foreigners, protesting at what one furious correspondent of the *Egyptian Gazette* called the 'Honolulu-ization' of Egypt. The world of high finance was rather astonished to learn that Sadat had summoned Munk, the one-time Canadian bankrupt, to be a partner of his 'in one of the most grandiose development flings since the Pharaohs first mobilized entire populations to raise their monuments of stone . . . to be the first man to be given carte blanche to trifle with the Pyramids since Napoleon had one of their points blown off 150 years ago [sic] for mysterious reasons of his own'.[16] Another partner was billionaire Saudi arms dealer, Adnan Kashoggi. Munk had risen to fame in Canada as the founder of Clairtone, purveyor of stereos, which was hailed in the early 1960s as the model Canadian corporation. After Clairtone collapsed, Munk rebuilt his fortune—'on paper at least, but then they were always largely on paper'—with the creation of a South Sea island resort conjured out of a Fijian bog and the take-over of the giant South Pacific hotel chain. Naturally, a millionaire's playground on the historic, almost sacred site that Sadat was offering had to have a golf course, and naturally, too, it had to be in the shape of the *ankh*, the ancient symbol of life. But that was just a detail in the 10,000-acre, $400 million residential-resort extravaganza complete with convention hotels, palm-fringed boulevards and $100,000 villas fit for film stars and oil sheikhs which was destined, in Munk's words, to become 'the new jet-set watering-hole, a kind of Palm Springs on the Nile'.

Sadat was carried away by the scheme; photographs appeared of him and Othman Ahmad Othman down on their knees poring over architectural designs. But this one, too, ran into a storm of protest led by Esmat Fuad, a professor at Cairo University. In a series of articles in *al-Ahram*, and later in a book, she campaigned in defence of Egypt's cultural heritage, dignity and sovereignty. She furnished details of every aspect of the deal, the initial price of the land, the astronomical profits to be made on its eventual resale as residential plots, and the danger the whole enterprise posed to the priceless antiquities in all 'that sand'.[17] Sadat defended the Pyramids Oasis Project before the People's Assembly but eventually retreated. In 1978, without warning, he abruptly announced the cancellation of the project. However, different versions of it have been cropping up ever since. For it was in perfect accord with the outlook of Egypt's ruling class in the age of *Infitah*; the exemplary marriage, in their eyes, of Western technology, Arab capital and Egyptian labour.

Boom in the cities

Though nothing came of Sadat's own contribution to it, property development was one economic activity which really did take off. With *Infitah*, a full half, or more, of private sector investment went into construction, some £E21 million in 1973 rising to more than £E60 million in 1974.[18] At the same time, about 65 per cent of all foreign capital invested in Egypt proper (excluding the Free Zones) found its way into this safe haven. There had always been a housing problem but, with *Infitah*, the problem turned almost overnight into a permanent crisis.

The boom wrought physical havoc in the heart of Cairo. Before the amazed eyes of its inhabitants, the city was changing at incredible speed. Familiar, sometimes well-loved landmarks disappeared in the twinkling of an eye. The day of the prefabricated high-rise had dawned. Gigantic cranes wheeled above freshly cleared building sites. Operated by foreign technicians, often supplemented by imported Korean labour, these awe-inspiring robots performed, in a matter of hours, tasks of hoisting and assembling which would have taken 'cheap' Egyptian labour weeks or months. 'Luxury' hotels, 'luxury' blocks of flats, 'luxury' offices and business centres sprang up along the banks of the Nile. They devoured the remaining gardens and greenery of more gracious days, they reduced to insignificance the city's ancient domes and minarets; luminous signs replaced the slaughtered trees. There had to be access to these high places of business, tourism and entertainment. So the car became king; but, far from disciplining the traffic, the elevated pedestrian crossings, the complex tracerworks of over- and underpasses, the tunnels and bridges, seemed to make it worse.

Cairo's creaking infrastructure, already monstrously overloaded, simply could not take the strain. The capital was said to have an 'absorptive capacity' of two-and-a-half million people. It now had a population of seven million. They depended on public services which had seen no expansion or modernization for decades. The sewage system—where it existed—began to flood not merely streets, but entire districts. Power cuts multiplied as the Westerners, oil-rich Arabs and local 'fat cats' installed the thousands of air-conditioners without which they could barely envisage life. Repairs could not keep pace with remorseless and accelerating decay. Armies of labourers—immigrants from the countryside, vagrants and down-and-outs—were mustered to tear up the streets and gash them with trenches in which foreign 'experts' could diagnose the causes of the breakdowns. Pedestrians—who still, of course, vastly outnumbered the vehicles—required good reflexes and steady nerves to get about the city. In the past they could deftly negotiate obstacles one at a time. But one day in 1976 a donkey, hauling its cart and driver, stepped into some water. It was instantly catapulted into the air, landing, frizzled and stiff, on its back. The driver only escaped death because he had been hurled 30 feet clear of the lethal pool. Exposed cables had electrified overflowing sewage. Now, with *Infitah*, the hazards were apt to come two or three a time in combined assault. Cairo had acquired the highest accident—and pollution—rate in the world.

The presence of so many foreigners—wealthy Arabs and Westerners on large salaries and expenses who could pay for housing what they paid in Kuwait or New York—infected the *rentiers* and real estate men with a speculative madness. It was only the foreigners and Egypt's own 'fat cats' who could now afford to buy or rent the kind of accommodation once within the range of the average upper- or middle-class family. The law governing furnished, as opposed to unfurnished, apartments already favoured the landlord. The unscrupulous ones took full advantage of it. As soon as they learned that foreigners were prepared to pay two or three times more in rent than they were already charging (and that was high enough) they confronted their tenants with the choice of matching these sums or getting out. Proprietors who before *Infitah* had leased unfurnished accommodation, on payment of reasonable 'key money' and at controlled rents, were seized with a frenzied desire to get rid of tenacious tenants whose eviction the law forbade. They harassed and hounded their victims; bribed, blackmailed and brutalized them, and even, occasionally, murdered them. Families who went away on holidays came back to find their homes in the possession of someone else. Mafia-type thugs burst into apartments, ordering the occupants to leave, and, if they refused, beat them up until they did.

It was often landlords who, in their greed, contributed to a type of disaster which, even more than colliding trains and capsizing boats, became a commonplace consequence of congestion and decay. In 1975 the People's Assembly estimated that Cairo needed a minimum of 62,000 new housing units a year. Of these, 20,000 were to replace buildings deemed to be in danger of collapse: 127,000 existing 'dwellings' were considered unsound. Sixty people died when such a building collapsed like a pack of cards. The landlord had put three extra storeys on to a two-storey, mud-brick structure, and then squeezed thirty-five families into its twenty-five rooms. Another speculator — though hardly his unfortunate family — could perhaps be said to have got his just deserts when the building he had recently completed crumbled over their heads. He had just put eleven storeys on a foundation designed to support four, and used adulterated cement into the bargain. Yet, although the authorities concerned knew that the building was unsound, they had taken no legal action against the speculator. It was a typical 'new class' alliance between corrupt officials and their entrepreneurial accomplices.[19]

Before *Infitah*, the contrast between a salubrious suburb such as Garden City with, say, 10,000 inhabitants per square kilometre, and a malodorous slum such as Bulak, with anything up to 160,000, had been shocking. It was even more so after it. For the 'popular' quarters of Cairo were growing more populous yet. The *fellaheen* were settling there at a rate of about 500 a day. At 4 per cent a year, its population was growing nearly twice as fast as the natural increase in the nation as a whole. For the city still had more to offer than the countryside.

The rape of the land

Infitah brought no relief for the peasantry from which Sadat was proud to have sprung. The peasant's plight in one of the world's oldest peasant-based societies had always been worse, though less publicized, than the urban workers'. Unemployment was higher in the countryside than in the towns, the minimum wage lower. The long-suffering *fellaheen* were now assailed from several directions at once—the building boom, the unleashing of market forces, and the encroachments of the state through its deliberate policy of 'de-Nasserization'.

Urbanization had long been making inroads into Egypt's precious 'black soil', built up over millions of years by the silt deposits of the Nile. Between 1963 and 1973, some 200,000 *feddans* (one *feddan* equals 1·058 acres) had been lost to buildings, roads and military installations. But after 1973 the process accelerated at a frightening pace in spite of all the 'strict' laws to contain it. By the late 1970s it was calculated that all the gains of the Aswan High Dam, some 900,000 *feddans*, or about one-eighth of the country's entire cultivated surface, had been wiped out. Urban sprawl had all but devoured the green belt which surrounded Cairo until the middle 1960s. It was eating away at the slender rim of vegetation which framed the Nile on its long desert journey to the Delta. At its most conscienceless it flaunted itself along Night Club Row on the road from Giza to the Pyramids which, a few years before, had been bounded by lush pastures. Awaiting the consummation of Disneyland or a plastic pyramid, it was meantime being lined with cabarets and dance-halls of vulgar design, jerry-built 'villas' and the inevitable, incipient slumland.

But *Infitah* not only reduced the total area of cultivation; it also reduced the peasant's share of it. The first great reforms of Nasser's Revolution had been agricultural—the abolition of the gigantic private estates whose owners were the chief supporters of the monarchy—and their redistribution, in two-*feddan* plots, among landless peasants. But although the state, through co-operatives and supply and marketing systems, acquired a strong influence over it, agriculture remained entirely in private hands and, accounting for one-third of the national income, constituted the largest single sector of the economy. The reforms did no more than slow down the worsening plight of the peasants. By the outset of *Infitah* more of

224

them were landless, both in absolute and proportional terms, than at the Revolution. Yet, with *Infitah*, discrimination against the peasantry was to become deliberate policy.

The impetus for discrimination came from a ruling class which was heavily influenced by the rural bourgeoisie, both new and old, and the ability to carry it through came from the fact that the peasantry lacked the political weight which the urban workers, when provoked beyond endurance, could throw into the scales.

In June 1975, the People's Assembly passed amendments to the Agrarian Reform Law, proposed by Muhammad Abu Wafia, brother-in-law of Mrs Sadat, which withdrew from the peasant many of the benefits conferred on him by the Revolution. They were eventually to lead to a doubling of the rent which he paid to the landowner. A later amendment doubled the maximum family land-holding from 100 to 200 *feddans*. Then, under yet another one, the sale of land by auction, outlawed by the Agrarian Reform Law, came back again. Instead of going to the peasant on a priority basis and on easy, thirty-year terms of payment, redistributed, reclaimed or improved land could now be sold off to the highest bidder. Opening at £E800 a *feddan*, the prices sometimes rose to £E7,000, the kind of sum which the *fellah* did not earn in a lifetime's toil. Many of the buyers were city-dwellers with residential, tourist or industrial projects in view. Government officials admitted that, while this was illegal, there were unfortunately ways of circumventing the law.[20] 'New class' alliances saw to that. But many buyers belonged to a growing breed of commercial farmers who used modern techniques to achieve high yields. Their lust for profit was great. Like most cultivators, they were obliged to deliver to the state a per-*feddan* quota of basic crops, such as cotton, wheat and rice, at a generally low price set by the government. But the quotas were determined by average yields. So the more efficient the farmer, or the more skilfully he juggled his crop rotations, the greater the surplus he could sell on the free market at several times the government price. With the new urban affluence—narrowly based though it was—sufficient to sustain demand, meat, poultry and dairy products did particularly well. Fruit and vegetables often did even better, with summer-time favourites—watermelons, seedless grapes, oranges, guavas—yielding the highest returns. Even the famous *laimoun baladi*—the delicious Egyptian lime which used to be all but given away—was now fetching the pre-*Infitah* price of oranges.

Naturally, like the commercial farmers, the peasants tried to switch from staples to the more profitable lines. It led them into a form of passive resistance. They would refuse to grow 'government crops'; they preferred to pay fines for violations of the prescribed rotation, and the rapid increase in the numbers imposed—from 43,000 in 1973 to more than 200,000 in 1975—illustrated the advantages of doing so. The government made half-hearted attempts to bring down the price of summer fruits, but, in the first case of the kind ever recorded in Egypt, growers were dumping their grape crops into the sea or feeding them to cattle rather than putting them on the market at the regulated prices.

Yet the *fellaheen* hardly grew fat on tactics such as these. In fact, they were by now deserting their land—sometimes selling it off at the auctions—as never before, tearing themselves from their immemorial roots in order to seek a better livelihood in the cities, or, in oil-rich Arab countries, to make other people's deserts bloom.

Merchants and middlemen

Commerce, in all its forms, was the third main area in which *Infitah* unleashed the acquisitive instincts of the private sector. After the October war the pent-up consumerism of the bourgeoisie, new and old, could no longer be repressed. That, and the influx of foreigners, created a demand for luxuries which merchants of the private sector made haste to meet. They filled their shops, showrooms and proliferating new 'boutiques'—of course there had to be a 'Boutique of the Crossing'—with everything from electrical appliances to French mustard, from cosmetics to instant coffee. Twice as much was being spent on private cars—coming in at some 2,000 a month—as on replenishing the country's stock of dreadful, dilapidated municipal buses. The consumer boom combined with the soaring international price of wheat to push up Egypt's import bill from £E632·3 million in 1973 to £E1,780 million a mere two years later.

In its well-founded exposés of private sector abuses, the weekly *Rose el-Youssef* concluded that all of Cairo's wholesale trade in fresh produce was in the hands of about 700 merchants, some of whom were making £E1,500 a day. The same picture repeated itself, it found, in the marketing of other products, be it fresh fish, paper, scrap metal or manually operated calculators.[21]

Nowhere, in fact, was the rapacity of the 'new class' more apparent than it was in trade, domestic or foreign. It was the traders who, *par excellence*, symbolized the marriage of decadent socialism

226

with unproductive capitalism, they who spawned a new breed of middlemen, fixers and brokers all hustling for fees and commissions, they who excelled in the science of *kusa*, or squash, the etymologically obscure vernacular word for corruption.

The traders thrived on the special circumstances produced by a combination of scarcity and affluence. Very rarely were quite ordinary commodities plentiful enough to meet demand, and practices long in the making were perfected and institutionalized in the rampant *laissez-aller* of *Infitah*. Public officials engaged in the distribution, at fixed or 'indicative' prices, of such items as flour, tea, sugar, soap, rice or cooking fat were now more than ever tempted to siphon off a portion of them to their accomplices in the private sector. The same was true of building materials, spare parts, fertilizers, pesticides and the like. In the countryside there was a trade in human beings. There, brokers exploited under-employed *fellaheen* by hiring them for less than the minimum wage, supplying them to private cultivators and entrepreneurs at a higher price, and pocketing the difference. The state itself, securing cheap labour for such projects as land reclamation, was one of the brokers' chief customers.[22]

Thus the whole pricing system, not just that for land and rents, was subverted. But it might be some quite small item, some sudden drastic distortion, that caused the most indignation. Once it was the dramatic increase in the price of shoes. In September 1974 workers demonstrated against the whole cost, shoes included, of equipping a child for the new school year. *Al-Ahram*'s famous cartoonist, Salah Jahin, depicted a schoolboy in front of a bookstore where he wants to buy his notebooks. An enormous merchant, looking down at him, is saying: 'If you want to buy paper, you'll have to go next door to the shoeshop—the owner bought all my paper to make shoes.'[23]

As the volume of goods diverted to the black market rose, so did profits. Characteristically, they in turn would be smuggled abroad to buy hard currency with which to import, legally or illegally, the luxury products which were sold, at such a tremendous mark-up, to the local bourgeoisie. Or they might go on the acquisition of urban real estate, and the construction, with black market materials, of luxury housing for Westerners, Arabs or the traders' own 'fat cat' confrères. A third course of action was to buy up the agricultural land which, with little investment, now yielded such high returns for commercial farmers. So it was that, under the auspices of *Infitah*, everything tended to interlock for the enrichment of the already rich, the lucky and the unscrupulous — to the detriment of almost everyone else.

The failure of industry

There was to be no economic miracle. The people were increasingly persuaded of that. Plenty would not be coming down to them. Or, in the language of the economist, *Infitah* meant, at best, growth without development.

With agricultural output now stretched to the limit, and yet falling further and further short of the people's needs, Egypt's whole future depended on industry. That was generally perceived as a fundamental truth; in 1974, for example, a leading planner argued that Egypt could only earn the money to import its food requirements if it increased its industrial exports thirty-fold by the year 2000.[24]

It is true that even under Nasser, since 1965, Egypt had been without an overall development plan, and as a result there was no identifiable public strategy to which the private sector was supposed to adhere. An ambitious eighteen-month 'interim plan' begun in 1974 had had to be shelved, and the planners seemed to have the greatest difficulty in preparing a realistic five-year plan to succeed it.

Although the private sector, agriculture included, generated more than half the national income in the first years of *Infitah*, it was still contributing only about 10 per cent of annual investment, and that went overwhelmingly into the kind of unproductive, low-risk, quick-profit fields that we have noted. It was much the same with foreign capital, which, especially from private Arab sources, went mainly into real estate.

As for industry — the production of goods — foreign investors were not really interested, or, if they were, they were quickly discouraged. Many an American, European or Japanese manufacturer sent a representative to take a look at the possibilities, but very few went any further than that. It was hardly the would-be investor's fault. The Arab 'brethren' acknowledged their fraternal debt to Egypt. Their money was more than available. In fact it was piling up for use. The problem lay in Egypt's ability to absorb it. Of the $4·4 billion theoretically pledged by the end of 1974, only a fraction had actually been released; for most were credits tied up to specific projects. The more than $2 billion proclaimed, during the triumphant Nixon visit, to be on their way had dwindled within a year to almost nothing. It was first of all the bureaucracy which deterred the investor. This proved even more languid, incompetent, obstructionist and venal than anyone had anticipated. 'Creative inefficiency', one foreign development specialist dubbed it: 'You can give Sadat all the power he wants and it'll still be like trying to push string—there is simply no follow-through.' The United States Agency for International Development (AID) found itself taking over the government's own functions; it drew up projects itself in order to forestall Congress's automatic withdrawal of the unspent portion of any allocation. Another deterrent was ports, telephones and communications in general. Nor was the general condition of the Egyptian economy at all encouraging for foreign investors since, apart from the few who were ready to pay high prices for foreign goods anyway, the domestic consumers were as poor as they were populous.

If the foreign investor was ready to invest, Egypt—the public or the private sector—was unable to make the necessary matching contribution. Under the 'interim plan', though scrapped anyway, Egypt was only to have contributed £E400 million out of a total of £E1,100 million. Whatever the source, whether public or private, the £E400 million in itself would have represented a very low rate of local saving, and therefore would already have been inflationary in effect, but since it was destined to come almost exclusively from the banks, being in practice a printing of money, it was actually even more so. The domestic financing was proportionally half of that achieved in Nasser's five-year plan. It illustrated the distortions, political, economic and social, of *Infitah* in action. Here was Egypt clamouring for funds which, being unable to spend them on productive investment, it diverted to meet its immediate balance-of-payment difficulties.

With a national debt which stood at £E1,250 million in 1973 (excluding the military debt of some £E2,000 million to the Soviet Union) and was being augmented by an annual deficit of £E249·8 million the same year, £E670 million in 1974 and £E1,386 million in 1975, the country was borrowing to repay earlier borrowings at crippling interest rates of 18 or 19 per cent. Ceaselessly lobbying to reschedule its debt repayments, the one obligation which, according to the *Financial Times*, it was punctilious about meeting was the $16 million a month which went on the purchase of Australian wheat. That vital consignment did not leave Melbourne until the shipment cost was paid.[25]

It was not just compassion that dictated such promptitude. True, wheat purchases accounted for half the country's import bill. Thanks in part to the workings of *Infitah*, Egypt was growing less of this traditional crop despite its ever-mounting need for more of it; and its price on world markets was soaring. True, too, the government sold it at home for much less than it bought it. By 1975 the state was subsidizing basic commodities to the tune of £E652 million a year. That was one-and-a-half times what it spent on the public sector wage bill, one-and-a-half times the anticipated domestic contribution to the 'interim plan'. The government had no choice but to pay on the nail for its Australian wheat; it was afraid, the *Financial Times* reported, that non-delivery would 'bring rioters into the streets and threaten the regime'.

The imports and subsidies were not improving the lot of the masses, merely ensuring that it grew worse less quickly. They could not offset the pernicious consequences of *Infitah*. The government claimed otherwise. Individual consumption, it once said, had risen by 30 per cent over a certain period. But what actually happened, the critics replied, was that the few were spending far more while the spending power of the many had actually declined. At one point, even the Minister of Economy was forecasting an inflation rate of 40 per cent.[26] Foodstuffs such as fruits and vegetables were often quite beyond the means of the masses. Bearing outrageous price tags, they could be seen going to waste in a country where, thanks to malnutrition, infant mortality was officially estimated at 116 per 1,000, but reached 200 or more in certain areas.

Yet the money was there. It was concentrated in the hands of the 'new class', of the parasites who, via the mechanisms of *Infitah*, thrived on the backs of the poor, of the upper reaches of a bourgeoisie which, in aggregate, absorbed such a disproportionate and growing share of the nation's wealth. Nobody really knew *how* much was there. The ostentation of the 'new class' only furnished a highly visible and offensive, but not very scientific measure of it. There were now said to be more millionaires in Egypt than before the Revolution. For the critics of *Infitah*, that was a bitter reproach, for its supporters it seemed almost a boast. Just how many millionaires was controversial; sometimes it was 500, sometimes 5,000. But to concede the fact, whatever the precise figure, was to concede that the system, by its own criterion, was a travesty of itself. For on personal incomes of more than £E10,000 a year tax was supposed to be confiscatory. Yet total revenue from income tax (excluding that deducted at source) was the princely sum of about £E3 million a year. There was little doubt, in fact, that corruption and class divisions were as great as they had been under the monarchy, and getting worse.

At the end of the Second World War, one Makram Obeid had published his *Black Book* attacking Nahas Pasha, the leader of the *Wafd* party, for corruption, or at least the toleration of it within his government. The book split the party and shook the whole political establishment. It was neither a doctrinaire leftist nor a diehard reactionary, but a middle-of-the-road critic of all extremes, who, upon re-reading Obeid's celebrated work, wrote that from a contemporary standpoint the whole scandal seemed a storm in a teacup, the affair of a few thousand pounds. Egypt would be lucky, he implied, to have scandals on so limited a scale today, and luckier still to have as much public indignation about their exposure.[27]

The regime knew *where* the money was all right, but it would not or could not get at it. So it would have to try and find it where it was not. And that would be dangerous. For there was a limit to what resignation, in the face of such insolent plenty, could endure.

Biting the bullet

On 1 January 1975, a mere five months after Sadat had said that a miracle had already occurred, workers took to the streets of central Cairo to assure him that, from their point of view, it had not. Not that Sadat or many of the capital's better-fed citizens were around to witness demonstrations which had begun early in the morning, and certainly not those of them who had chosen to bring in the New Year, at up to £E75 a head, at the nearby Meridien, a brand-new, Nile-side luxury hotel. Not many can have heard them shouting, for the first time, one of the aptest of their rhyming taunts: '*Ya Batl al-Ubuur, Feen al-Futuur*', 'O Hero of the Crossing, Where is our Breakfast?' It may have been Sadat and his generals who planned the Crossing, but it was the ordinary Egyptians who actually made it. And they had no breakfast, or, at least, they had a minimum wage which, at £E12 a month, was less than one-twelfth the 'cover' price for a New Year reveller and his wife at the Meridien.

These were the first major demonstrations since 1967 in which Israel, and the liberation of Sinai, did not figure. They were a warning signal: economics had now replaced politics as the primary pre-occupation of the common man—and the principal threat to the established order.

They were not the first of their kind. Only their scale and location made them very hard to hide. In fact, hardly had the euphoria of the October war died away than social agitation began. In 1974 there had been about 400 minor strikes and work stoppages. Very few of these events actually reached the pages of the 'free press', but the public had a general idea of what was going on from rumour, and from official leaks, allusions and indiscretions. But perhaps the most effective medium was the troubadours who captured the people's sufferings in song and verse. The famous pair, the blind singer Sheikh Imam and his songwriter, Ahmad Nagm, whose main theme, before 1973, had been the shame of defeat and occupation, now fastened on the imbecilities of *Infitah*. 'Wake up, workers of Egypt, your house has been invaded by the middleman, and he does not drink from polluted water.'

The New Year riots were quickly followed by another, more ominous upheaval. On 19 March, 33,000 workers went on strike at Mehalla al-Kobra, the country's largest spinning and weaving mills, demanding higher wages and improved working and living conditions. On the third day, 4,500 men of the Central Security Forces were sent in to end the strike while military aircraft flew over the town, breaking the sound barrier and shattering windows. Believing their mill had been bombed, the enraged populace took to the streets, armed with sticks, iron bars and stones, and stormed police stations and public buildings. They broke into the mill bosses' homes, dragging the contents of rifled cupboards and refrigerators into the streets, where they put all the imported luxuries, the cases of whisky and liquor, the frozen chickens and turkeys, on display under signs reading: 'This is how those thieves live while we go hungry.'

Such protests were essentially economic in origin—but took on a political character when students, the intelligentsia and opposition groupings lent their support to the strikers by demanding 'freedom and democracy' of a more authentic kind than that which Sadat, in his surreptitious campaign of de-Nasserization, had seen fit to bestow. The opposition, often semi-clandestine, subscribed to various credos. The name of Nasser—or rather of a certain, almost mystical ideal which he had come to embody—was more and more invoked. For the Nasserists, these largely spontaneous eruptions showed how dangerously Sadat was straying from that ideal. For

Marxists of various hues they pointed to the coming class struggle. And they were full of portent, too, for an opposition quarter which, long quiescent, was now better organized, and certainly more violent, than its secular, left-wing rivals. Islamic fundamentalism, which was yet to reveal itself elsewhere in the Middle East as the potent force it could be, was gaining momentum in Egypt. For the Moslem Brotherhood and like-minded politico-religious sects the eruptions were the intuitive gropings of the oppressed towards the new order, divinely inspired, which they planned to install. Though it was no longer dominant, the 'national' issue—Palestine, war and peace, *Pax Americana* and Dr Kissinger's 'shuttle' diplomacy—remained inextricably intertwined with the social and economic ones.

The authorities understood the New Year signal. On the one hand, they blamed the demonstrations on 'communists, Jews, spies and *agents provocateurs*'. At least 2,000 people were arrested. Some were charged—though never convicted—with plotting to overthrow the regime. On the other hand, the authorities acknowledged, in effect, that a genuine grievance lay behind them. After an emergency ten-hour meeting, the Cabinet announced 'drastic measures to meet the people's needs', the provision of basic foodstuffs in particular.

With his magic formula—'Peace plus *Infitah* equals Prosperity'—manifestly faltering, Sadat's impulse was to furnish more peace. More than anything else, it was the state of the economy that pushed him further and faster down Dr Kissinger's road than he had probably originally intended. He had sworn never to re-open the Suez Canal until the Israelis had withdrawn deeper into Sinai; he proceeded, in June 1975, to do so. In September he accepted the second Sinai Disengagement agreement, even though in essence it differed little from the one he had rejected in March. Such concessions, he hoped, would build business confidence, and the hard-currency earnings from shipping and the small Sinai oilfields would ease Egypt's chronic balance-of-payments crisis. But more peace produced little but more promises—and face-lifts, gimmicks and evasions.

A face-lift—after the Mehalla al-Kobra riots—was another change of government. Sadat replaced Prime Minister Abdul Aziz Higazi, an economist, with Mamduh Salem, his Interior Minister and a no-nonsense policeman. It was only one of Salem's urgent tasks 'to restore order and stability on the home front'. A second was to 'free *Infitah* from the complications of bureaucracy'. And a third was assigned to him in the kind of language that Sadat had so often deplored in the mouths of his critics. Some Egyptians—he admonished them in his father-of-the-nation style—imagined that the new conditions were a good opportunity to profit at the expense of everyone else. They were amassing fortunes in 'parasitic operations'. Such speculation, smuggling and 'illicit dealings in foodstuffs' would have to stop. 'If we cannot combat corruption', he said, 'we shall see class differences widen rather than narrow . . . and if we cannot control the wave of high prices, we will find that life has become too tough for the active forces of the people. . . .'[28]

Taking Sadat at his word, the new Prime Minister set up a special parliamentary committee to investigate complaints of corruption. It should not have been necessary if the old law, popularly known as 'Where did you get it from,' had ever been enforced. Tales of corruption were legion. Some got a perfunctory mention in the 'free press'. Astronomical figures were bandied about. Revenue officials were said to have pocketed no less than £E63 million in land taxes; £E50 million had been made on the sale of potatoes at exorbitant prices; the national film industry had unaccountably incurred losses of £E6 million. One ingenious abuse went unchecked, despite efforts to end it. Because of congestion in the port of Alexandria, as many as eighty ships at a time might be queuing up to unload. Yet when an American company proposed to speed up the process by introducing landing-craft techniques already employed on famine relief cargoes to Bangladesh—a step which would have helped ease food shortages and bring down inflation—harbour officials turned them down flat: they did not wish to forgo the 'commissions' they made on demurrage charges.[29]

The most important case to come before the parliamentary committee concerned the outgoing Prime Minister Abdul Aziz Higazi. With his connivance, it was alleged, Egypt had paid 30 per cent more for 1,000 Iranian buses than Sudan had paid for a similar consignment. But the committee lost its investigative zeal as soon as it realized into what exalted quarters it might lead. Higazi was cleared after stating that Sadat's own Secretary for Foreign Contracts, Ashraf Marwan, had negotiated the bus deal. Sadat himself pronounced Higazi's administration to have been an honest, if incompetent one. So the committee went into early retirement, and the law of 'Where did you get it from?' was relegated once again to the statute books.

The economic situation continued to deteriorate, and Sadat himself, while continuing to promise eventual plenty, conceded that it would have to be deferred. By early 1976 he was forecasting that Egypt would now need 'five more years of sweat and toil to improve [its] economy'.[30]He and Mamduh Salem, his new Prime Minister, were often accurate enough in their basic diagnoses. It was only the poor who paid their taxes, Sadat kept saying. Egypt suffered from too little production and too much consumption, said Salem. The problem was the cure. At the beginning of 1976 Salem attempted to save £E100 million by such expedients as cutting back on official receptions and public relations, imposing higher taxes on gambling casinos and increasing the price of petrol and alcoholic beverages. That was another gimmick, and evasion of the tough political decision—the redirection of the economy—which alone could stop the rot.

So, too, in essence, was Sadat's everlasting search for foreign funds. Although they were already flowing in on an unprecedented scale, they were never enough owing to the way the economy was managed. 'My problem is cash money', Sadat had told the Lebanese weekly *al-Hawadith* in early 1975; 'if you ask me now a direct question, "what do you require?", I would answer "cash money." ' The Arabs and Iranians were not lagging in their contribution to development projects. But he simply had to have 'cash money' for 'everything in our country has been drained dry'.[31] The problem still haunted him at the beginning of 1976. Egypt needed an 'economic transfusion' of $4,000 million in Arab aid over the next two years.[32] The word in international banking circles was that Egypt was once again falling behind in short-term debt repayment.

In late February President Sadat took off on one of his whistle-stop, fund-raising tours of the Gulf. The principal benefactors, Saudi Arabia and Kuwait, agreed on emergency aid and, more important, on the establishment of an Arab fund to support the Egyptian economy: the Gulf Organization for the Development of Egypt (GODE) as it came to be known. In March the ministers of finance concerned met in Riyadh to work out the details. The Cairo press reported that the fund would be capitalized at $10 billion; it would finance new investments and offer easy loans to meet Egypt's debt repayments. But, in April, the finance ministers of Saudi Arabia, Kuwait, the United Arab Emirates and Qatar disclosed that it was to be capitalized at only £E2 billion over a period of five years. Sadat and his financial advisers expressed their surprise and disappointment. It was all the more embarrassing for Sadat in that only days before his Gulf tour he had extolled Saudi Arabia for its generosity.

But he was still circumspection itself. He hoped that his Arab 'brethren' would not be 'annoyed' by his statement; he remained grateful for their assistance; he had not forgotten that first $500 million in the immediate aftermath of the October war; none the less, what had been required was not 2 billion but 12 billion dollars.[33]

It was as easy as it was popular to criticize the Arabs. There was doubtless much to criticize them for. They could and should have done more to narrow the shocking gulf between their wealth and Egypt's poverty. The Arab brothers were no longer the unstinting philanthropists they seemed to be at the outset of *Infitah*. The vast majority of Egyptians who did not benefit from their largesse concluded that they were paying through the nose for guests who snapped up land and property with barely a thought for the price, dumped Egyptian girls as soon as they married them, and generally behaved with a vulgarity and arrogance which rivalled that of Egypt's own new rich. The prejudice was mutual. For the Arabs were also having second thoughts about their 'noble Egyptian brothers'. They realized that they were looked upon as milch cows, taken for a ride at every turn, given second-rate service at exorbitant cost, neither loved, liked nor even respected.

So where *was* Sadat to find the cash? He was being pushed inexorably towards a recognition of the obvious: that he must find it at home—or at least enough of it, in proportion to the foreign contribution, to forestall disastrous deficit financing. And to do that he had to put his whole economic house in order. He was not lacking advice on how to proceed. The Soviet Union was still Egypt's principal trading partner, the Eastern Bloc the only serious market for Egyptian manufactured goods. But as the differences between the former allies deepened, Egypt found itself moving economically, as well as politically, into the West's sphere of influence, and therefore under growing pressure to conform to the West's conventional economic wisdom. The pressure was exerted directly by the United States or, indirectly, by those emanations of Western trading and foreign policy, the International Monetary Fund (IMF) and the World Bank. Naturally, the oil-rich Arabs tended to fall in with Western purposes. By the spring of 1976 the pressures had produced a turning point in Egypt's modern history, little remarked and less debated at the time, but one which John Waterbury, in his survey of the Egyptian economy, called as momentous for the country as any development since the overthrow of King Farouk, and 'fairly momentous' for the United States, in that Sadat now depended on it for his survival, economically as well as politically.[34]

What the United States, mainly through the IMF, urged upon Sadat was a 'stabilization' plan entailing a cutback in subsidies, the paring of public sector inefficiencies, the setting of a 'realistic' exchange rate to promote exports and attract foreign capital, the control of credit and consumption, and a retrenchment in investment outlays. 'Biting the bullet', Western financiers liked to call it. Proposals of the kind had been made before. First Nasser, then Sadat, had rejected them. The social consequences, coupled with the implicit subordination of Egypt to the West's economic purposes, appeared too high a price to pay. It would have meant a substantial dismantling of the socialist and welfare systems which had become an integral part of Nasserism. Both men deferred the tough political choice—opting instead for both development *and* a continued level of consumption which, added to the burdens of war, made true development impossible.

Now, however, Sadat could delay no longer. The pressures were mounting on all sides. There was no longer any doubt that Egypt accepted the general thrust of Western economic orthodoxy. Sadat began to talk of 'belt-tightening' and an austerity programme to be applied to the public sector. The Minister of Economy, Dr Zaki Shafei, stated unambiguously that 'we have full understanding with the IMF and the World Bank'. A World Bank team had helped prepare the long-awaited five-year plan. 'All that we need is three years of self-discipline. If we increase wages without increasing available goods, prices will continue to rise. What good is it to give a cost of living allowance of 20 per cent one day, only to have prices rise by 20 per cent the next?'[35]

Sadat still balked at specific measures. By the summer of 1976, as he was reproaching his Arab brothers for their miserliness, he was still holding out against a cut in subsidies and a floating exchange rate. As a result both the West—be it the IMF or even the private American banks—and the Gulf states (separately or through GODE) were as unforthcoming as ever with the 'cash money'. By now, a whopping £E1·25 billion deficit was being forecast for the second half of the year. As a Western banker put it: 'They need this money by the end of the year. They don't have it and they don't know where they are going to get it.'[36] An Egyptian banker did not disagree: 'Every twenty-four hours we spend two million pounds repaying accumulated loans and the interest on them, for every three million we spend on importing the basic needs of our people and factories.'[37]

Indeed, according to Dr Abdul Munim Kaissouni, the Deputy Premier for Financial and Economic Affairs, the situation was even worse than he had imagined. For he had found, upon taking office in November 1976, that there were 'secrets' he had not been told.[38] The task which faced this Western-orientated economist was therefore all the more invidious. He it was who had to prepare an austerity package swingeing enough to convince the international financial community that Egypt was absolutely determined to mend its housekeeping ways; he who, on 17 January 1977, told the Egyptian masses, via parliament, where the money would come from. It would come from them.

Dr Kaissouni's subsidy cuts

£E7,050 Million Budget Before People's Assembly

Kaissouni Hits Out at Low Output, Population Explosion, Maladministration, Payments Deficit, Investment Failure

£E277 Million Subsidy Cut. Taxes up on Imports, Petrol and Alcohol

Merely to glance at the newspaper headlines, that morning of 18 January 1977, was to wonder whether the government had gone mad. And to study the details of Kaissouni's statement to the People's Assembly the night before was to confirm the impression. It was, in effect, another of President Sadat's gambles, the most daring and draconian attempt at economic reform since he had come to power. What these measures would do, in cold arithmetical terms, was directly or indirectly to raise the cost of living by £E500 million. At the heart of them was a decision to cut in half the £E553 million which the government would otherwise have spent that year on the subsidizing of basic commodities. The prices of certain unsubsidized commodities were also to be raised, and higher customs duties levied on certain imports.

The most basic commodity of all was bread, taking the lion's share of the subsidies. Not for nothing is Egypt the only Arab country where bread is called *aish* (life). Subsidies had held the price of *aish baladi*—the round, flat, unleavened loaf—down to one piastre since the early 1960s. The other staple of the Egyptian diet is *foul*, or beans, the main source of protein for most people, substituting for the rare luxury of meat. The rest of the subsidies went on other foodstuffs, such as lentils, rice, maize, sugar, sesame and imported meat, or on household and personal goods, such as bottled gas, clothing, toilet soaps and animal fats, or on miscellaneous items such as pesticides and public transport fares. Some items were more heavily subsidized than others. Some were available without restriction at their subsidized prices; others were rationed and, in excess of a family's monthly entitlement, only available on the free market. There were also variations according to the grade of a particular commodity.

Without these subsidies, or with a drastic reduction in them, millions of Egyptians would cross the precarious line between subsistence and something approaching starvation. In January 1977 the *per capita* income stood at about £E100 a year (£E = approximately 65 pence at unofficial exchange rates). The official minimum wage was £E12 a month. It is true that Dr Kaissouni declared a 10 per cent increase in the wages of public sector employees, but this was no more than a transparent attempt to sugar the pill. For what he was giving out by this means, £E67 million, was far exceeded by the £E277 million—to mention only the subsidy cuts—he was taking away.

Now the price of bread was to double at a stroke. So at least the ordinary people feared, and even if their fears were exaggerated—for technically bread was spared—they were legitimate, because it was with characteristic obfuscation that officials and the oracles of the 'free press' had interpreted Dr Kaissouni's measures to a bewildered public. In general, of course, they sought to minimize the painful nature of this drastic economic medicine. But the headlines alone were enough; no soothing gloss could disguise their brutal underlying message.

For months, rumours had been circulating to the effect that something of the kind really was being planned. But few Egyptians had been able to bring themselves to believe the rumours, or to read the signs contained in the draft budget for 1977. In December, after a five-day debate in the People's Assembly, the 'opposition' parties, those minuscule adornments of Sadat's carefully managed parliamentary system, had rejected the budget. Speaking for the moderate right, Mustafa Hilmi Murad, leader of the Social Democrats, had objected that, among other things, Prime Minister Salem had failed to explain where he proposed to raise the money for his ambitious development programme.

That had also been the gravamen of the case made by Khalid

Muhyieddin, leader of the National Progressive Unionists, a coalition of left-wing and Nasserist groupings. He could not quarrel with the government's diagnosis of the country's economic woes—'consumption, which devours the greater part of production; inflation; inefficiency of the public sector; non-participation of the private sector; exploitation, speculation, pilfering of the people's daily bread; tax evasion; illicit enrichment. . . .' But the prescription for curing those ills was quite another matter. How could the government call for an investment of £E6,000 million in its forthcoming five-year plan—if it could be called a plan at all—when 'we all know that local savings do not suffice for that'? By what means, in order to finance this investment, did the government propose to achieve a domestic saving of 20 per cent, when this same government had, the previous year, told the Assembly that consumption had outstripped production by 2·5 per cent? Its calculations did not appear to make sense. Its investment target for 1977 was £E1,350 million. It proposed to raise less than half of that, £E627 million, locally; yet even that low proportion exceeded by £E333·1 million the year's anticipated domestic saving of £E293·9 million. In other words, the government presupposed an increase in domestic saving of 113 per cent, and 'the least that can be said about that is that it requires exceptional measures to limit consumption and to direct the surplus revenues to investment purposes'. Also presupposed was an increase in exports of 39 per cent, against only 6 per cent in imports, while, for the five years from 1970 to 1975, exports had been rising by a mere 2·9 per cent a year and imports by 16·4 per cent.

It was not at all clear, Muhyieddin had continued, how this sudden reversal was to be achieved. Of course there *was* a way to raise revenue to finance investment, and that was to raise it from those who could afford it, but that was precisely the way which this government was unable or unwilling to adopt. And yet by its own admission the rich had been getting richer and the poor poorer at a frightening pace. 'The only way to control consumption is equality of sacrifice; and not to demand self-denial from those who cannot even have enough *foul*, *tam'ieh* or white cheese while others spend hundreds of pounds on New Year feasting or buying imported Coca-Cola by the barrel.'[39]

The general verdict on the government programme seemed to be that this, like the 'mobilizations' that preceded the October war, was another performance of the *galla-galla* men, the illusionists, addressing themselves to an infinitely gullible audience. For if the money was not to come from those who could afford it, neither, according to the government's assurances, was it to come from those who could not. Throughout the debate, ministers had promised that the subsidies on basic commodities would remain intact. And that point was made again and again in a series of statements and newspaper articles. On New Year's Day the Prime Minister's plan to stabilize prices had been the lead story in *al-Ahram*. On 3 January *al-Gumhuriyah* had reported that, according to an authoritative source, there would be no rise in the price of basic commodities during the year. On 10 January *Akhbar al-Yaum*'s headlines had proclaimed: 'Sadat insists this generation should not bear all the sacrifices. On the contrary, its burden should be lightened, because it offered much and sacrificed of its own free will.'

The deception was maintained to the end. Even as Dr Kaissouni was announcing the new measures to the People's Assembly, they had already been put into effect. Small wonder that the following day, at a meeting of the Planning and Budget Committee, Dr Muhammad Qadi, an 'independent' deputy, exclaimed: 'The government pledged that it would not touch subsidies without consulting the Assembly; this is the biggest price rise ever.' The 'independent' deputies sent a memorandum to the President saying that 'to take decisions of such critical importance for the destiny of the nation and the life of the masses in the absence of the Assembly, and to put them into effect without laying them before it, is a dangerous precedent which exposes the country to upheavals'.[40]

The President was at the time in Aswan, where he was about to receive President Tito of Yugoslavia. He was apparently suffering from a throat ailment, for a specialist had been flown there aboard his private Boeing. This was reported that morning side-by-side with the news of the price rises. Aswan was perhaps Sadat's favourite resort, but, naturally, many Egyptians were wondering whether, this time, he had repaired there less for rest and winter sunshine than for political convenience. For he must have known what risk he was taking. Along with the rumours that the IMF and the World Bank were pressing for drastic reforms had been others, which appear to have been well-founded, that one of these organizations, the World Bank, had simultaneously warned him of the popular unrest such action might unleash.[41] But Sadat was said to have brushed these fears aside with the confident assertion that 'I know my people'. The situation, he said, was 'under control'.

The people's response, however, was immediate, fierce and nation-wide.

241

The great food riots

The trouble started in Alexandria. Early in the morning of 18 January a delegation of factory workers set out from Mex, a western suburb, towards the city centre. According to eye witnesses, they marched in an orderly manner, carrying with them a petition and a request to meet the authorities. The police attempted to bar their way across a canal bridge on the edge of the city. There was an argument that turned into a heated quarrel. Soon the two sides came to blows. Within minutes people rushed to the scene from all directions, and as news of the riot spread more and more came pouring out of the slums and 'popular quarters', first in hundreds and then in thousands, shouting anti-government slogans and demanding a repeal of the economic measures.

Soon the whole city centre was in turmoil, with an infuriated mob trying to make its way to the Governor's office and to the headquarters of the Arab Socialist Union (ASU). The police reacted brutally, hitting out with sticks and truncheons and, according to some witnesses, firing 'shots in the air', some of which proved fatal. In their turn, the demonstrators took to hurling stones, bricks and every available missile. Finally, upon reaching the ASU building, they set it on fire. They attacked and ransacked restaurants, bars and shops. Another place which did not escape the anger of the mob was the summer residence, in a quiet and fashionable suburb, of *La Vache Qui Rit*, the nickname the rioters bestowed on Vice President Husni Mubarak; his fixed, bland smile reminded them of the laughing cow on the boxes of processed French cheese that had flooded the market in recent years.

The pattern of events repeated itself in the capital. There, about the same time in the morning a similar delegation had made its way to the People's Assembly. It, too, sought an explanation of the government's policy and a defusing of the economic bombshell. Again the police barred the way. But there was no violence; the delegation changed course and headed for Abidin Palace, which Sadat had taken over as an office. By the time the petitioners had come within sight of the palace their numbers had been swelled by workers from the industrial suburbs to the north and south of the city, by commuters who happened to be on their way to shops, offices and universities, and by the loiterers, the ragamuffins and the workless, who forever fill the city's chaotic thoroughfares. The procession, however, was still an orderly one.

242

But the police and security men hurriedly placed barriers across the street that debouches into Gumhuriyah Square, the vast, open space in front of the palace. The leaders, unsuccessfully seeking to present their petition, were commanded to disperse. Meanwhile, more and more people, deserting homes and places of work, were joining the column. Faced with this rebuff, a collective frenzy seized the multitude. Seen from a rooftop vantage point on the edge of Gumhuriyah Square, it was like a vast sea of humanity. Heads bobbed on its surface; of the hands raised in anger, a few brandished copies of that morning's newspapers, the only available token of their indignation. And upon those already assembled bore down yet more and more, like a tidal wave, from Midan al-Tahrir, another great square about half a mile away, and from every other direction. Then suddenly, like the breaking of a dam, the thwarted multitude became a raging torrent, an uncontrollable force which rushed and swirled and eddied through the man-made canyons of the city wherever the impulse took it. For more than thirty-six hours a usually docile people unleashed all their pent-up fury on targets which, for them, symbolized the yawning gap between the haves and the have-nots, the frivolity and corruption of the ruling class, the incompetence and blind insensitivity of the administration.

They singled out the proliferating 'boutiques', where a new plutocracy spent the American dollars they were not supposed to possess on French perfumes and the finest Swiss watches. They invaded the nightclubs and smart cafés where the same small élite spent on a Seven-Up or a sandwich more than a worker earned in a day; on a single meal more than he earned in a week. When they went for the police stations, the offices of the ASU or the Ministry of the Interior, it was not just lust for destruction which drove them. For these were the symbols of the *Sulta*, of Authority—an authority which boasted of its 'freedom and democracy' restored, but which, on taking a decision of such momentous import, did not consult parliament and now denied the people the right of peaceable appeal to it.

And when the rioters set fire to buses and trams all over the city, when they pulled down traffic lights and road signs, it was even less the lust for destruction which drove them, for these were public facilities without which the hardships of their daily life would have been harder still. It was a despairing protest against the unspeakable conditions in which they had to earn their daily bread—and in particular to make their way from home to workplace. Not for nothing did they converge on the Bab al-Luk station, a short distance from the People's Assembly, and tear up the railway tracks between it and the great industrial centre of Helwan ten miles away. For there was no more notorious example of the country's broken-down transport system than this stretch of line. Tens of thousands of factory workers made the journey along it twice a day, packed like cattle inside the carriages or clinging precariously to the roof, the bumpers or the running-boards. There had been the inevitable toll of fatal accidents. A few weeks before as many as seventy people had died when, as two trains passed, they were ripped from their sides.

But the riot was not all looting and smashing and arson. Indeed, after the flood of humanity had passed, it was really rather surprising to discover how little devastation was left in its wake. Those who were later accused of inciting the demonstrations, such as Muhyieddin's National Progressive Unionists, had been quick at the time to condemn the more violent excesses, and many of the demonstrators required no such counsel of restraint to keep them in check. Besides, crueller, and certainly more memorable, than the physical asaults were the verbal ones which accompanied them. The old favourite, '*Ya Batl al-Ubuur, Feen al-Futuur*', 'O Hero of the Crossing, Where is Our Breakfast?', was heard again. But protests of this scale and intensity could not but yield a rich new repertoire of the rhyming slogans, so difficult to render into a foreign tongue, which are so peculiarly, poignantly Egyptian. 'Thieves of the *Infitah*, the People are Famished.' 'Tell him who Lives in Abidin that the People go Hungry to Bed.' Not just Sadat: his wife, too, was singled out—'*Jihan, Jihan al-Sha'ab Ga'an*', 'Jihan, Jihan, the People are Hungry'—with the insulting implication that she, as much as he, was the ruler of Egypt.

More demeaning still was the reminder that neither Anwar nor Jihan would ever command that spontaneous esteem in which, for all his faults, Nasser had been held, and that, seven years after he had gone, he lived on in the minds of the people, a memory which official neglect could not expunge. 'We would rather be ruled by Nasser from the grave than by Sadat from Aswan.' And for the first time since that unforgettable, exhilarating morning of 16 October 1973, when the air had throbbed to the rhythmic tribute of just two syllables, '*Sad*at, *Sad*at,' there burst forth from hundreds of thousands of angry throats, the '*Nass*er, *Nass*er' of bygone days.

The People's Assembly met in emergency session. Ministers sheepishly tried to explain that for months they had been summoning up courage for these belt-tightening measures which had unleashed the tempest swirling around them. But even in that docile forum the deputies retorted that the 'ministers must be commandos to take such steps; they will need armoured cars to brave the wrath of the people'.[42]

Sure enough, the armoured cars did come out. It was the first time since the overthrow of the monarchy that troops had been used to quell civil disturbances. And that was hardly surprising, for not since 1919, when the Egyptians revolted against British rule, had there been such a commotion. It spread throughout the length and breadth of the land. The riot police, with their shields, batons and tear gas grenades, could not cope. On the evening of 19 January a curfew was imposed, and while clashes between demonstrators and security forces continued late into the night in certain areas, by the following morning it was all over. Full casualty figures were never made public, but unofficial estimates put the number of dead at 800, with several thousand wounded. For a few hours the country had seemed to totter on the brink of civil war.

It was not, however, the army which brought to an end the most ominous upheaval in Egypt's modern history. For even if it had been ready—and there was little sign that it was—to turn its guns on the people from whose broad ranks it was drawn, the people, in their desperation, would probably have braved them. It was an ignominious climb-down which saved Sadat and his regime. The President had returned to a capital in tumult. The planned visit of President Tito had been cancelled, ostensibly because of the death of the Yugoslav Prime Minister. Sadat had taken special precautions to avoid recognition by the infuriated mob. According to eyewitness accounts, he used an old taxi cab to get to Aswan airport, and, irony of ironies, the *fellah* from the village of Mit Abul Kom had to 'disguise himself as a *fellah*'.

He himself said nothing on his return, but according to his Vice President he was 'anxious to alleviate the sufferings of the toiling masses'.[43] Simultaneously, the government announced that, 'in agreement with President Sadat', the prices of basic commodities would return to their previous levels. And it took good care to stress that, in cancelling the price rises, it was not touching that other, compensating part of the austerity package—the 10 per cent wage increase and other benefits for public sector employees. In other words it had not merely failed to administer its economic medicine, it had aggravated the disease which it sought to cure.

The climb-down amounted to more than the admission of a mistake; more, too, than an admission that its social and economic policies were misconceived. It meant that something was fundamentally rotten in the state of Egypt.

Red peril over Egypt

It is customary, in the wake of such a crisis, for a leader to address his people, to restore their confidence, and to do so quickly. For it was not against Dr Kaissouni that the masses had revolted. He was just a technician trying to balance his budget, and it was not he who had dictated the means of doing so. In effect, if not, perhaps, in conscious intent, they were revolting against the whole system. Rampaging through the streets until the government withdrew the price rises it had introduced had been the only course left open to them. For such was now the divorce between the system and the people it was supposed to represent.

True, Dr Kaissouni had announced his measures in the People's Assembly, and the Assembly had just been re-consecrated as the centrepiece of Sadat's 'freedom and democracy'. In October the people had gone to the polls to elect what, on paper, was the first multi-party parliament since the Revolution. It had been a landmark in the erosion of Nasser's Arab Socialist Union in favour of a pluralism that Sadat had once called an abomination. The new parliament embodied a rather unusual, arbitrary form of democracy-by-decree. Right up to the elections, Sadat had been arguing that it was still too early for political parties. Instead, he had authorized the formation, within the ASU, of three autonomous 'pulpits' — right, left and centre — and it was as representatives of these pulpits, or as independents, that candidates ran for parliament. The country's main political forces, the *Wafd*, the Moslem Brotherhood, the Nasserists and the communists, were denied any official voice. Most people stayed away from the polling booths, out of apathy or a conviction that elections were always rigged. They certainly were this time, though perhaps less systematically than usual. The centrists, or Egyptian Arab Socialists led by Prime Minister Salem and Sadat's brother-in-law Muhammad Abu Wafia, won an overwhelming majority of the Assembly's 360 seats; they were the unconditional loyalists. The right, or Social Democrats, won twelve seats. The left, Khalid Muhyieddin's National Progressive Unionists, was the only 'pulpit' which could be counted on to furnish a genuine opposition. It had been denied access to the 'free press'. It won two

246

seats. There were forty-eight 'independents'. Many of them were Nasserists, but they could not formally proclaim themselves as such, because, according to official dogma, Sadat was a Nasserist too; he was only correcting his predecessor's mistakes, he was not repudiating all that he stood for. After the elections Sadat decreed that the pulpits should turn themselves into fully fledged political parties. The elections, he said, had been 'the cleanest in Egypt's history'.[44] However extravagant that claim might have been Sadat presumably hoped that, in some small measure, his new parliament would serve as barometer and lightning conductor of popular discontents.

But since, when he announced them, Dr Kaissouni's economic measures had already gone into effect, parliament was no more than a platform for their promulgation. Prior consultation had been confined to a parliamentary committee of the centre party. That should, in theory, have been quite enough to ensure parliament's overwhelming approval, even for measures which were to have a more direct and devastating effect on the masses than anything, including the Crossing, that had happened since Sadat had come to power. In the event, it was not enough, because the people, rioting in the streets outside, usurped the functions of parliament.

Dr Kaissouni, accepting full 'responsibility' for the riots, offered to resign. The centre party expressed its understanding of a popular reaction which its parliamentary committee had failed to foresee. A conclave of the country's 'political and executive leaderships', presided over by Sadat, concluded that it was 'natural' for 'certain sections of the people' to reject the new 'burdens' imposed upon them; the people's 'food and clothes' should not be touched.[45] But —apart from the ignominious retreat from the economic measures themselves—the regime's self-criticism went no further than that.

It was a full two weeks before President Sadat addressed the nation, and when he did the nationwide food riots were no longer the authentic expression of a people's anguish, they were 'an uprising of thieves'. He conceded that his government had made a mistake. 'There is not a regime or a government in the world which does not make mistakes.' Besides, he himself had had nothing to do with it. Indeed, he had foreseen what would happen. Naturally, he said, 'you will be astonished to hear that. But I really did foresee what would happen. Why? I shall tell you why. On 1 January I came and met with my political leadership here and told them: "A tax law, immediately, and a housing law, both on an urgent basis." I said that a tax law must be introduced before anything else. Just look at the newspapers of 2 January. It is written there.' In this way Sadat absolved himself, and endorsed what had, all of a sudden, become the official wisdom: the rich must do their bit as well as the poor. The state must strike 'without mercy' at the profiteers, the so-called 'parasites' of *Infitah*; fair and efficient tax gathering, and a proper control of the real estate market, was the way to go about it.[46] 'When there is a budget I want every citizen to feel there is something in it for him, every complaint to have its answer'—though 'of course', he went on, 'all this complaining, this talk about the government being for the bourgeoisie, comes from the communists and the spiteful.'

The price rises, Sadat explained, had been just the opportunity the communists were waiting for. They

> exploited every little mistake or slip the government made, exploited the atmosphere of freedom and democracy which I built, through the state of institutions, through the people, through you. They exploited it to the utmost. Why? To seize power. To seize it how? By destruction, sabotage, killing, robbing. That is what the 18 and 19 January was all about. They say it was a popular uprising. For shame! It was an uprising of thieves. Protesting against the transport crisis by burning trains and buses; protesting against the supply crisis by ransacking and robbing cooperatives. Is that a national uprising? I say again, it was an uprising of *thieves*.[47]

It had all been an 'odious, criminal plot, and when I say odious criminal plot I mean every word I say'. Although he had all the facts before him, he could not reveal them. 'How can I, while the affair is still *sub judice*? Ours is a state of institutions.' The plot was a communist one. He had his own clemency to thank for it. For with his defeat of the Ali Sabri power centre in May 1971, he had only bothered to 'neutralize the heads', while he should have 'neutralized the tails as well, the hiding-places in the media, the press and all the machinery for influencing the masses. Why? Because almost six years after the 15 May Corrective Revolution, Egypt, for the first time in its history, faces a premeditated plan for its destruction.' True, the communists were only a handful, representing no one but themselves.

> How could they mobilize Cairo, Alexandria, Minia, Assiut, Aswan? Did they have the strength for that? Never! Never! . . . .

248

What they did was to exploit the telexes sent by the National Progressive Unionists. The Unionists are an officially authorized party. We are a state of institutions. It sends telexes to its members all the time. They have 'Arab Socialist Union' written on top. That is legal. . . . Most of the [former] communist leadership had joined the Unionists, so as to preserve two things: freedom of action and legality through the Unionists, and the core of their secret underground operations for sabotage and seizing power. . . . All this is from the dossiers here before me. What I am saying is not imagination, not speculation. No, the dossiers are clear and complete, with names, with everything, with the telexes summoning the meetings, orders from the party to its people to go out and support the opponents of the [economic] decisions. As if they wanted to add fuel to the flames. All this is official, because, as I told you, 'Arab Socialist Union' is written on top, all correct and legal. As I told you, in this conspiracy they got up to things like this. . . . I haven't gone into details. That's not my business. That's the job of the Prime Minister, the Prosecutor General. But, as you can see, conspiracy stares you in the face.

Although the communists bore the brunt of Sadat's anger, the Nasserists were not spared either. For he now went further than ever in his public assault on the man whom, in his lifetime, he had all but deified.

There is no difference between the communists and those who call themselves Nasser's heirs. . . . What did Nasser achieve? Is surveillance what you want, expropriation, detention camps, Arab unity the Nasser way, turning Egypt into a loudspeaker for all the Arabs, dividing them into progressive and reactionary camps, and exploiting the Palestine card. . . . We did better than Abdul Nasser, we fought the October war, and all the Arabs stood by us with the oil weapon, they cut off the oil, not just some of it, but all of it. . . . The difference between me and Nasser is the emergency laws which I abolished completely, which I have refused to employ, and still do so — in spite of this conspiracy.

At which Sadat announced that he was putting just such emergency laws to a referendum. 'Participation in, or intent to establish, organizations hostile to the social system' would become punishable by life imprisonment with hard labour. So would 'demonstrating with intent to destroy public property', participation in, or incitement of, riotous assembly or public disorder', 'obstruction of, or intent to obstruct, the proper functioning of government bodies, public or private institutions or educational establishments by the threat of force', 'planning or participating in a gathering or sit-in which could endanger public security', 'deliberately striking . . . for the achievement of a common aim which could be damaging to the national economy'. And he threw in a commandment that all citizens should pay their taxes. Within three months they had to complete a form recording all property and capital in their possession. Making a false statement would be punishable by imprisonment with hard labour. As for the 'conspirators', Sadat swore that he would track them down, however long it took—even to the end of his life. And 'If I have not dealt with them by then, I urge you, the people, to do so for me.'

By the usual thumping majority—99·46 per cent, to be precise—the people voted in favour of the new laws, or, as the posters put it, they said 'yes to peace, freedom and security', and 'no to blood and destruction'. It earned Sadat the animosity of yet another of his original companions. In a message to the President, Kamaluddin Hussein, a Free Officer well known for his stout anti-communism and a member of the People's Assembly, said that by signing the decrees Sadat had legalized injustice. 'Instead of punishing your government for its stupidity and inefficiency, instead of waiting for the outcome of the trials of the criminals now in your hands, you are punishing the people and the People's Assembly.' The day he signed them, 4 February, was 'a fatal day in Egypt's history', comparable to the 'ignominy' of 4 February 1942, when the British forced Nahas Pasha to accept the Premiership—an acceptance which, it will be recalled, Sadat had considered so treasonable that he tried to assassinate him. The Assembly promptly expelled Hussein 'for contempt of the constitution and the President at a time of crisis and sedition'.

Meanwhile, the police had been losing no time in tracking down the 'conspirators'. By ten o'clock on the morning of 19 January, the Ministry of the Interior had begun broadcasting statements which denounced the demonstrations as communist-led. On 26 January, the Public Prosecutor disclosed that, according to initial investigations, four underground communist organizations had been working 'to bring down the regime' by inciting demonstrations and acts of violence. Four days later, the Prime Minister, Mamduh Salem, spoke of 'a close organic connection between the recent subversive conspiracy' and 'international trends' which he did not identify; he stressed his deep regret that an authorized political party, the National Progressive Unionists, had so 'shamefully involved itself in this abominable national crime'.

Loyalist pressmen wrote elaborate, but curiously undocumented reports about the catastrophe that Egypt had so narrowly escaped, thanks to the vigilance of the authorities. According to *Akhbar al-Yaum*, timing was all in the strategy of the communists, and the regime's determined attempt to solve a grave economic crisis for which 'neither Sadat nor this government and previous ones were responsible' had furnished the perfect opportunity. Their plan was to burn almost everything simultaneously — the police stations of Cairo and Alexandria, Nile bridges, telephone exchanges, factories, cooperatives, and — 'so as to spread hunger' — bakeries too. The communists had no real following, but, if they had chosen their moment well, it would have been quite possible for highly trained and organized activists to accomplish all this. 'It only required one member of the sabotage gang outside each police station. He stirs up the simple-minded and the riffraff in the vicinity. Then he hurls his firebrand. . . .'[48]

In their determination to find any explanation other than the real one for the nationwide riots, the authorities would first magnify the dimensions of the 'conspiracy' and then, realizing where such arguments led, belittle the influence of the 'conspirators'. True, the communist underground had little weight. But the police dragnet, sweeping wide, hauled in more than 3,000 people. Some actually were rioters who had looted and burned. But most were peacable citizens who happened to get caught up in the demonstrations or joined them when they learned what they were about; or they were National Progressive Unionists; or they belonged to that *potpourri* of 'regulars' whom the secret police, delving into its files, rounded up as a matter of course in times of tension: journalists and play-wrights, doctors and lawyers, intellectuals of many political persuasions, some of whom were apprehended in circumstances that tended to cast a particularly farcical light on the whole campaign. Qutb Ahmad Qutb was 'seen' leading a demonstration, even though he was in a hospital recovery room at the time and secured an affidavit to prove it. Muhammad Salmawi, of *al-Ahram*, was charged with taking an active part in the demonstrations although, according to evidence furnished by the newspaper, he spent the whole day in his office. Fatallah Khafagi was held on a charge of setting fire to a sentry box in Minia, even though the Secretary General of the ASU testified that he had been in Cairo attending a training session of the ASU Central Committee.

The Uprising of Thieves was ancient history by the time the 'conspiracy' was reduced to its true, its entirely fictitious dimensions. More than three years were to pass before the State Security Court acquitted all 176 persons who had been formally accused and tried for 'incitement and belonging to secret organizations related to the events of January'. The Egyptian judiciary was thereby showing an independence which it owed more to constitutional uncertainty and its own traditions than to Sadat's 'state of institutions' or his concern for the separation of powers.

Farewell to Arabia

Though essentially economic in inspiration, Sadat liked to say that *Infitah* was political, cultural and civilizational too. Clearly his experiment in political liberalization was now in jeopardy. The only redeeming feature of the new emergency laws was the certainty that he could no more enforce them, in all their rigour, than he could his anti-rumour legislation in the bygone era of 'no war, no peace'. But his economic experiment was in graver jeopardy still.

Still, by jettisoning his whole austerity programme, he had made a point in the Arab world and the West: that there were clear limits to the amount of belt-tightening that he could impose on the Egyptian masses without endangering his regime. The eternal pauper's cry went up again, but more stridently, reproachfully and menacingly than before. Newspapers lamented that Egypt had bled itself white on the Arabs' behalf. Since 1967, calculated *al-Ahram*, the war effort had cost £E16 billion; to that the Arabs had contributed a mere £E1·69 billion. Tawfiq al-Hakim, doyen of Egyptian letters, urged that 'we proclaim it frankly and firmly: any conflagration in our country will cause those who sit on wells of gold to sit on wells of fire. Any conflagration in Egypt, the heart of the Middle East, will expose the whole world to grave dangers.' He proposed that, 'to keep the explosion from their own oilfields', the Arabs should finance four-fifths of Egypt's military budget'.[49]

The Arabs heard the cry. Some of their newspapers called for an emergency summit conference of the oil-producing countries to draw up an Arab 'Marshall plan' for the rescue of the Egyptian economy. The Kuwaiti daily *al-Watan*, often Nasserist in tone, had no particular affection for Sadat. But *al-Ahram* gladly reproduced what it was saying now: that there was one oil producer so rich that, by setting aside one-third of one year's revenue, it alone could pay off all Egypt's outstanding debts.

And, in concert with the West, there was also a more practical response. The United States, rallying to Sadat 'in a real hour of need', promptly showed the way by diverting $190 million, originally earmarked for development projects, to the purchase of commodity imports.[50] The oil Arabs, through GODE, began to commit funds, some $1·9 billion by the autumn, to pay off Egypt's short-term debts. Creditors, including the IMF, now adopted a more lenient view of Egypt's economic aberrations, and its failure, after the subsidy débâcle, to come up with any alternative belt-tightening strategy.

Instead of the £E150 million to which Dr Kaissouni had planned to reduce it, the domestic deficit for 1977 soared to over £E1 billion. In the summer Sadat made things worse by suspending all repayment of Egypt's Eastern Bloc debts and, in consequence, the annual trade agreements through which they were made; it was another blow to industry, since it deprived Egypt of its only serious export market. But greater understanding from Western Arab governments, as well as increased earnings from the Suez Canal, oil revenues and remittances from Egyptians working abroad did help ease the strain. At the most the January riots had bought Sadat time and cash, while the conditions which had provoked them remained fundamentally unchanged.

So, with domestic political pressures building up again, Sadat badly needed to generate movement somewhere, to restore the sense of purpose which, even before the riots, he appeared to be losing. Sadat the actor needed to recapture the centre of the stage. And he needed the dramatic coup, commensurate, at least, with his setback, to put him there. But what?

Who would have imagined [asked the left-wing weekly *Rose el-Youssef*] that, after more than a quarter-century of Egypt's leadership of the Arab nationalist movement—who would have imagined that there would come a day when the Egyptian people returned to those bewildering questions: are they an Arab people or an Egyptian one only? And if they are an Arab people, why do the other Arab peoples treat them as if they were Egyptian only? And if our people are Egyptian only, why do they accept their responsibility as an Arab people? And if they accept their responsibility as an Arab people, why don't the other Arab peoples acknowledge the Arab character of the battle? And if the other Arab peoples don't acknowledge the Arab character of the battle, why don't the Egyptian people acknowledge only its Egyptian character — and accept a unilateral solution?[51]

It was another of Egypt's leading men of letters, Naguib Mahfuz, in whom Egypt's anti-Arab cry of anguish found its most ominous expression. Not that he spared the Egyptians themselves. At bottom, he said, their crisis was a moral one. So they had to mend their ways too. At the same time, however, they must reconsider their place in the world.

Arab nationalism was supposed to have meant more strength and civilization. German nationalism turned artificial polities into a great power. Italian nationalism created a strong state out of a string of comic entities. Why does our nationalism alone have to bring nothing but hunger and internecine strife? With all my strength I urge that we balance our budget, starting with defence, that we forge a natural union with the Sudan, and that we abandon the Arabs if they have decided to abandon us.[52]

If Sadat entertained such revolutionary thoughts, he kept them to himself. Egypt, he insisted, remained true to its Arab brethren. Of the many aims behind the conspiracy,

one of them was to undermine our bargaining power at Geneva . . . and to undermine our Arab position, because if Egypt goes, the whole Arab world goes with it. . . . Itzhak Rabin [the Israeli Prime Minister] says: 'Sadat, you can't frighten us, your people are not with you.' But I say to Rabin: 'No, you're hopelessly wrong.' It's sheer rubbish. That's what they [the Israelis] were saying in 1973. And they believed it. Then came October to prove the opposite. . . .[53]

Given his flamboyant, risk-taking character, however, it is unlikely that Sadat had overlooked the depth of feeling that underlay the bitter attacks on those Arab billionaires, and in all probability he was already contemplating his most extraordinary gamble of all.

6

The Pilgrimage to Jerusalem

To the ends of the earth for peace

There was no sense of expectation when, on 9 November 1977, Sadat addressed the annual opening of parliament. It was just another routine speech; and it proceeded that way until, nearing the end of it, he appeared to depart from his prepared text—in so far as his rambling, interminable discourses ever had one—and informed his audience that he was ready 'to go to the ends of the earth if this will prevent one soldier, one officer, among my sons from being wounded—not being killed, just wounded. I say now that I am ready to go to the ends of the earth. Israel will be astonished when it hears me saying now, before you, that I am ready to go to their own house, to the Knesset itself, to talk to them.'[1] The words came casually, without emphasis, as an afterthought almost. Few of his audience grasped their momentous import. Still, they were dramatic enough to elicit one of those statutory rounds of applause that punctuated all his speeches. The PLO leader, Yasser Arafat, 'a dear and wonderful colleague in our struggle' who had been specially invited to attend, joined in. Either, like most of the audience, he was not paying proper attention, or, if he was, he thought that it was a rhetorical flourish, a daring one no doubt, but hardly a serious declaration of intent. Yet with those words President Sadat had launched a gamble for peace which made his October Crossing pale into insignificance.

The words demanded a response, and a prompt one. Ever since the Jewish State came into being, the Israelis had been insisting on 'direct negotiations' as the only sure indication that the Arabs were really prepared for peace. Only if they met them face to face, looked them squarely in the eye across the negotiating table, could it truly be said that they were ready to recognize their right to exist. The Arabs had adduced many reasons for their refusal to deal directly with their implacable foe, but it was obvious that if most Arab regimes, not just Sadat's, had come to the conclusion that Israel was here to stay, that peace between Arab and Jew was desirable, then, sooner or later, they would have to confer some kind of recognition on it. That was still projected into the indefinite future, however; the end, rather than the beginning, of a long process. And the degree of recognition the Arabs were ready to confer was vague; it was to be the absolute minimum they could get away with in exchange for the achievement of their official aims: the return of the occupied territories and the fulfilment of the legitimate rights of the Palestinians.

Now here was Sadat signalling his readiness to do what had hitherto been unthinkable. He wanted, as a Beirut newspaper put it, 'to show the Israelis that their "extermination complex" is out of date, that the Jewish state can no longer exploit the Arab rejection of its existence to annex territories in the name of secure frontiers. What more spectacular proof of that than the presence in Jerusalem, within the walls of the Knesset, of the leader of the most powerful Arab nation?[2]

Menachim Begin was as sceptical as everyone else. He only heard of Sadat's offer from a BBC newscast the following morning. His bureau chief had wondered whether to alert him that same night, but thinking it was just 'one of Sadat's tricks', he had decided not to bother him. That certainly fitted in with Begin's opinion of the Egyptian leader, for whom he had coined various uncomplimentary nicknames; *Czodak*, the Russian for rascal, was one. Pressed for a public reaction, Begin permitted himself a grudging, disdainful acknowledgement; 'if this is no mere phrase,' he told Israel Radio, he was ready to meet Sadat anywhere he pleased to negotiate true peace. The idea that Sadat really planned to descend on Jerusalem was obviously incredible to him. 'He can come to Geneva,' he told an afternoon newspaper the same day. 'He can present his stand just as we will present ours. Neither side must turn its position into a prior condition.'[3] 'Sadat's speeches are all stratagem,' wrote a Tel Aviv columnist, 'the Egyptian President has come up with a new plum: for the sake of peace he is prepared to go even to Jerusalem . . . that fox knows that he will impress the innocents in America—and that's where we will call his bluff: for how can the man who refused to meet us in Washington come to us in Jerusalem?'[4]

Begin's reflexes, like everyone else's, were conditioned by the prevailing diplomatic circumstances. For the whole thrust of Middle East peace-seeking had been directed towards a reconvening of the Geneva conference, which had lapsed since its inaugural meeting in the immediate aftermath of the October war, when Syria had refused to go, and the PLO had not been invited. Geneva, with all parties in attendance, was now seen as the only possible forum for a 'comprehensive' settlement guaranteed by the superpowers under the auspices of the United Nations. After the reconciliation between Egypt and Syria in October 1976 which had brought an 'official' end to the Lebanese civil war, the two countries had embarked on a joint 'peace offensive' designed to show their 'moderation'. Jimmy Carter, at the outset of his presidency, had called 1977 'the brightest hope for peace that I can recall'. With a show of that high moral purpose with which, after the shabby Nixon era, he had conquered his high office, he had inspired Arab hopes of an American administration which might, at long last, hold its own against the all-powerful Zionist lobby. Acknowledging the Arabs' moderation, he led them to believe that it would earn the response, in the shape of real pressure on Israel, that it seemed to deserve. He outlined his conception of a final peace; but for 'a few minor adjustments', he said, Israel should relinquish all the occupied territories; a 'homeland' must be found for the Palestinian refugees 'who have suffered for many, many years'. 'If this is true', said Yasser Arafat, in an unprecedented tribute to an American president, 'he has touched the core of the problem without which there can be no settlement.'

Like Sadat, the Americans had been dismayed but not outwardly deterred by the greatest upheaval in Israel's domestic politics since the foundation of the state — the victory in the general elections of May 1977 of the right-wing *Likud* party, embodiment of the fanatical, openly expansionist wing of the Zionist movement, led by the one-time *Irgun* terrorist chief, Menachim Begin. As Prime Minister he immediately proclaimed his attachment to Greater Israel; what he called the 'liberated' territories would not be given up in return for the peace settlement which, in the same breath, he urged upon the Arabs. In May 1977 President Carter went to Geneva to meet President Assad, thereby bestowing unprecedented attention upon a country which Israel had always cast as the most bellicose of its neighbours.

Carter wooed the Palestinians, too. Getting them to Geneva in some guise or other that would satisfy the PLO without incurring the inevitable veto of the Israelis was the seemingly insuperable task to which Carter and his peripatetic Secretary of State, Cyrus Vance, devoted Kissinger-like energies throughout the summer and autumn. It carried them into an amazing labyrinth of proposals and counter proposals, each more ingenious and sophisticated than the last, until finally, devising one of those 'procedural' formulae, not too suggestive of substance, which all parties could interpret as they pleased, it began to look as though they might find their way out of the labyrinth. Perhaps the Geneva conference, four years after its first and only session, would reconvene after all.

Egyptian reflexes were conditioned by Geneva too, and, the next day, Sadat's astonishing offer got a confused reception. In spite of his much-vaunted 'free press', editors always sought guidance from on high, with Cairo's three leading dailies frequently coming out with almost identical headlines. This was a Sadat spectacular about which they had clearly not been briefed. *Al-Ahram*, the most sober and authoritative of the three, played safe: 'We are ready to go to Geneva regardless of procedural problems', ran its main headline. A second headline accused Israel of concentrating on procedural at the expense of substantive issues. Only underneath that did *al-Ahram* highlight the Sadat 'challenge': his willingness to go to the Knesset — 'from a position of strength in order to confront Israel with the liberation of land and the rights of the Palestinians'. *Al-Akhbar*, always more sensational, bannered in red: 'Sadat challenges Israel which is running from Peace; We are not Afraid of any kind of Confrontation with Israel now that we have cut it down to its Natural Size.'

Officials in the United States, taken by surprise and preoccupied with Geneva and a 'comprehensive' peace, reacted cautiously. The Arab world, accustomed to Sadat's verbal excesses, appeared not to take him seriously.

But, even had he wanted, what Sadat had so casually begun he could no longer stop. The affair developed a momentum of its own. In the afternoon of Thursday, 10 November, some visiting American Congressmen asked Begin what he thought of Sadat's offer; this time he was more forthright, assuring them that if Sadat really intended to visit Jerusalem he would be received 'with all the honour befitting a President'. Then, on the evening of the next day, in a formal television address, he really threw down the gauntlet to the

Egyptian people. 'Citizens of Egypt! . . . you are neighbours and always will be. . . . Let us say to each other, and let this be the silent vow between our two nations: no more wars, no more bloodshed, no more threats.' It was the first time, Begin said, that he had addressed the Egyptian people directly; but this did not seem to render him any less partisan in the apportioning of historic blame.

> Since the time when the government of King Farouk ordered the invasion of our land, Eretz [greater] Israel, in order to strangle our newly restored freedom and independence, four major wars took place between you and us. In retrospect we know that all the attempts to destroy the Jewish State were in vain . . . and I may tell you, neighbours, that so it will be in future. . . . We wish you well, in fact there is no reason whatsoever for hostility between our peoples. . . . In ancient times, Egypt and Israel were allies — real friends and allies against a common enemy from the north. . . . Your President said two days ago that he will be ready to come to Jerusalem to our parliament — the Knesset — in order to prevent one Egyptian soldier from being wounded. It is a good statement. I have already welcomed it, and it will be a pleasure to welcome and receive your President with the traditional hospitality you and we have inherited from our common father Abraham.

Unlike Sadat's speech, Begin's made world headlines. Obliged to react, the official Egyptian spokesman complained that, while the speech was welcome, it should have been addressed to all the Arab countries, not just to Egypt. The Cairo press was scathing too.

> It would have been better [said *Akhbar al-Yaum*], had Begin addressed his message to the people in Israel. Why has he never made this call for peace since he took power . . . all his behaviour has been characterized by intransigence, expansionism, the establishment of [West Bank] settlements, placing obstacles in the way of the Geneva Conference, refusing to recognize the rights of the Palestinian people . . . and the latest of his deeds has been the insane raids on South Lebanese villages and the slaughter of hundreds of women and children . . .[5]

When Sadat in his turn received the visiting American Congressmen on Saturday, 12 November, he denied that he was laying down conditions for his visit. 'We are ready to go even if we have to spend two or three consecutive days in the Knesset. I am ready to do this and engage in a discussion with all of them . . . but I don't see any sign of welcome.' He had not even received an official invitation.

Conditions or not, Sadat none the less insisted that Palestine was the heart of the problem, and the only way to lasting peace was 'the establishment of a Palestine state in the West Bank and Gaza with a corridor between them'. There could be no separate Israeli–Egyptian deal, he told the Congressmen; nor could there be 'the kind of peace that Mr Begin is talking about, saying that Palestine is their land, that they came back to it and that the situation there, even in the land they took in 1967, is not an occupation of any kind'. As for Palestinian representation at Geneva, this was no longer an obstacle. 'I have solved this problem for the Israelis. As you know, they object to the participation of the PLO; that is in spite of the fact that Mr Begin himself wrote in his memoirs that he was a terrorist and very proud to be one. We are two delegations only. An Israeli and an Arab delegation.' The latter would include an American professor of Palestinian origin. 'Can the Israelis call *him* a terrorist?' he asked. 'We have settled this matter', he claimed, 'and Arafat has agreed.'[6]

On the evening of the same day, Begin told a forest of microphones that 'in the name of the government of Israel, I officially invite the President of Egypt to come to Jerusalem.' '*Ahlan wa Sahlan*', he concluded in Arabic. Welcome.

In the Egyptian press, the invitation was lost among headlines given over to Sadat's 'unmasking of Israel's manoeuvres', the 'corner' he had placed it in, its failure to learn that 'Egyptian statements are not open to interpretation', and its rejection of the Palestinian representative, the American professor, at Geneva. But, in an editorial, *al-Ahram*, addressing itself to the invitation, did tell the Israeli Prime Minister that there were certain 'immutable realities' which he must 'get clear'. The first was that Sadat's readiness to go to the Knesset depended on Israel's readiness to evacuate the occupied territories and permit the establishment of a Palestine state; the second was that Egypt categorically rejected a separate peace, a partial agreement or a third Sinai disengagement.

As the Cairo newsmen, still unbriefed, groped miserably in the dark, others, more illustrious than they, were taking over the limelight. For as it dawned on the outside world that Sadat really did mean what he said, it became the turn of the great American television stars to participate in the making of history. In what one rhapsodic account of the Sadat peace mission called a 'smashing doubleheader',[7] Walter Cronkite, anchorman of CBS, went on his *Evening News* programme to interview separately, by satellite,

Sadat and Begin. From Cairo, Sadat told him that all he now needed was 'the proper invitation'.

'And how would that be transmitted, sir, since you do not have diplomatic relations with Israel?'

'Why not through our mutual friends the Americans?'

Asked about opposition from the Arab world, Sadat said that he had not told 'any one of my colleagues and I didn't ask them to agree or not agree upon this'.

But had not Arafat expressed any opinion? 'Not at all, not at all, because as I told you, Walter, this is my initiative.'

Sadat reiterated that there were no conditions to his visit—except that 'I want to discuss the whole situation with the 120 members of the Knesset and put the full picture and detail the situation from our point of view.' There had never been such a 'suitable moment' to achieve 'genuine peace' as there was now, he said, 'so I want to put the facts before them and in the same time, we want to discuss what will be the other alternative if we can't achieve peace. It would be horrible. Believe me, horrible.'

The scene shifted to Tel Aviv, where Begin confirmed that there were no 'preconditions' on either side and said that he would ask his 'friend', the American ambassador, to use his good offices to pass on the formal invitation to President Sadat.[8]

The Egyptian press finally got the message. What until now had been interpreted with instinctive, baffled caution as another display of Sadat's tactical genius, was now eulogized as the most daring and revolutionary step in the history of the Arab–Israeli conflict—one that put Sadat on the same plane as the giants of the Arab past. A columnist in *al-Ahram* pointed out that the Prophet Muhammad himself, no less, had concluded a peace treaty with the Jews in the earliest days of Islam and that, during the Crusades, Saladin had called on Richard the Lionheart in his headquarters. 'Let us', he urged, 'rally behind the fighter-negotiator in all his boldness.'[9]

The Arab world, or a great portion of it, was aghast. Indeed, disaffection began in Sadat's own immediate entourage. His Foreign Minister, Ismail Fahmi, resigned. 'No longer', said his enigmatic resignation statement, could he 'carry out his duties and share responsibilities under these circumstances.' He was Sadat's third Foreign Minister to fall by the wayside; Murad Ghalib went after the expulsion of the Soviet advisers in 1972 and Muhammad Hassan Zayyat after the post-October lurch into the American camp. But he was not to be the last; indeed, no sooner had Fahmi stepped down than the man appointed in his place, Deputy Foreign Minister Muhammad Riad, did so too. It did not mean that Sadat's regime was beginning to crumble from within, for neither men had any real power base, but it was hardly surprising that the world began to wonder whether Sadat could weather the gathering storm.

The semi-tolerated Egyptian opposition, represented by the National Progressive Unionist party, called on Sadat to forgo his Jerusalem pilgrimage. In a statement that could not be published inside Egypt itself, it declared that it was 'not opposed to a peaceful solution in principle', but explained that 'such a solution depends on building up the Arabs' own strength through which we can force Israel to accept the conditions of peace'. The visit, it went on, would 'legitimize Jerusalem as Israel's own city at a time when all states, including the US, which is Israel's protector, refuses to recognize that right'. It would enable Israel to 'impose what it calls normal relations with the Arab states before the establishment of peace . . . and extend to Israel a kind of full recognition on the international level'. All this was happening 'without anything in exchange or any promise of an exchange'. It would divide the Arabs and increase Israel's intransigence.

In the rest of the Arab world, it was the Syrians who led the hue and cry. Sadat went through the motions of consulting his 'brother', President Assad, paying him a flying visit. But no one could dissuade him now. In fact, just before Sadat left for Damascus, the formal invitation by which he set such store had arrived; he would be in Jerusalem during the *Id al-Adha*, the Feast of the Sacrifice, and he would be 'praying together with the Palestinians' in al-Aqsa mosque, Islam's third most holy place.

Although Sadat was received in Damascus with a 21-gun salute and all the honours due to a head of state, neither he nor his host disguised in their separate airport press conferences the unhappy outcome of their meeting. It was the first time in living memory that two Arab leaders, after so solemn a *tête-à-tête*, had so publicly proclaimed their complete disagreement. The Progressive National Front, the institution through which Syria's ruling Baathists deliver themselves of their most authoritative pronouncements, denounced Sadat's latest and gravest excursion into go-it-alone diplomacy as a 'painful blow to the Arab nation, a defiance and fragmentation of its national solidarity'; it would 'give the Zionist enemy gains which it has been unable to obtain in the past thirty years in spite of all the wars it has waged against the Arabs'.

The PLO Executive Committee, representing all the guerrilla organizations, declared that the Arab nation 'will not forgive any ruler' for an initiative which amounted to 'apostasy against the dearest and most sacred goals of our people and a defilement of the blood of hundreds of thousands of martyrs who died for Palestinian and Arab land.' Al-Aqsa mosque, 'which has been the symbol for the caravan of freedom-fighters and martyrs, can never be the temple of surrender'.

Not even arch-conservative, staunchly pro-Western Saudi Arabia could keep quiet this time. Though it had been Egypt's key ally since the October war, it could not condone this affront to its larger role as the guardian of Arab solidarity. 'King Khalid', said a statement issued by the Royal Court, was 'surprised' by Sadat's determination to go to Jerusalem. The king had conveyed a message to the Egyptian leader 'clarifying the position of Saudi Arabia on this matter in a frank way that brooks no doubt or uncertainty'. Saudi Arabia believed that 'any Arab initiative in regard to securing Arab Middle Eastern aims must stem from a united Arab stand'. It was couched in the discreet and dignified language always employed by the House of Saud, but it was a stern rebuff from Sadat's principal paymaster that meant more than all the ear-splitting outrage emanating from Damascus, Baghdad, Tripoli or the Palestinians.

There was violent protest too. Seventeen people were injured when Arab students stormed the Egyptian embassy in Athens. In Beirut, a guard died when an explosion tore a hole in the embassy there; and a bomb gutted the offices of Egypt Air. Palestinian refugees shouted 'Sadat is an agent, Israel cannot save him'. In posters that went up on the city's walls, Sadat wore a star-and-stripes hat and a Dayan eye-patch under the caption *Shalom*.

There was official support from only three Arab countries. President Numairi of the Sudan congratulated Sadat on 'his great victory in the field of international strategy'. King Hassan threw his diplomatic weight behind a mission which he had secretly helped to prepare. And for what it was worth, unqualified, if patently expedient approval came from the Sultanate of Oman. Only Jordan took a middle position, calling for 'wisdom and patience', and apparently hoping that Sadat would achieve something to which it could eventually subscribe.

There was no such discord in the Israeli camp. True, the Chief of Staff, General Mordechai Gur, obsessed by memories of the Crossing, did warn Sadat that if he was planning another surprise attack in the guise of peace-maker his deception would not work. It was an appalling indiscretion; but fortunately for Israel, this new, infinitely indulgent Sadat did not take offence. Besides, the Israeli public were already at his feet. For them, the sheer excitement, joy and wonder of the event they were about to witness banished all thoughts of the calculations that may have lain behind it. For them, it was a carnival with all the corny, commercial trappings. For $1 they could buy a stick bearing Israeli and Egyptian flags, for $3·50 tee-shirts with a grinning Sadat and Begin clutching a bright red heart and the slogan 'All You Need Is Love'. Jerusalem bakers produced cakes with Peace enscrolled in the icing, plastic roses and pictures of the two leaders. The Shalom Department Store advertised '*Shalom* to Sadat' and knocked 10 per cent off all its prices. The Zion Insurance Company reminded its clients that it once had a branch in Cairo. At thirty-six hours' notice, the Jerusalem Municipal Theatre was turned into a press centre, with free telephone facilities to the rest of the world, for the 8,000 newsmen about to descend on the city. The Israeli army band, with no score to help them, frantically sought to master the Egyptian national anthem. Menachim Begin, once 'wanted for murder' in British-ruled Palestine, had to put off his appointment with James Callaghan at 10 Downing Street that weekend in order to keep a new, altogether more incredible one, in the King David Hotel, Jerusalem.

In the lion's den

Hu higiya. With the Hebrew words for 'he's arrived', commentator Yaacov Ahimeir told three million Israelis that it was not a dream, not a trick, not an optical illusion on their television screens. At 20.01 on the evening of 20 November, after a brief flight from Abu Sweir airbase, the Boeing 707, code-signed Egypt 01, touched down at Bengurion Airport, not far from Tel Aviv. As it taxied into the reception area twelve spotlights illuminated the aircraft with the flag of Egypt painted on its tail. Trumpets sounded. First to emerge, with indecorous haste, was a plump lady whom nobody recognized; she was from Egyptian television and was rushing to transmit a live description of history in the making. Then came Walter Cronkite and a throng of illustrious newsmen. But all eyes were still fastened on the door of the airliner. The suspense was almost unbearable. Someone bristling with medals stepped into view; it was a military aide. Then, a few moments later, a slight, shy-looking man in a light grey suit, his features fixed and tense, appeared at the top of the ramp. In that instant, something indescribable must have tugged at the hearts of countless millions, in Israel, Egypt and the world, as another flourish of trumpets greeted the arrival of Muhammad Anwar Sadat, President of Egypt, in the Land of Israel.

At the foot of the gangway stood President Ephraim Katzir, thickset and austere, and Prime Minister Begin, diminutive and beaming. Historic handshakes. Then more unreality. The Egyptian national anthem sounded through the terminal where the red, white and black colours of Egypt mingled with the blue and white of Israel. A 21-gun salute. The Zionist Hymn of Hope, *Ha-Tikva*. Begin and Sadat stood shoulder to shoulder through it all, a nervous twitching of the eyelids Sadat's only trace of emotion. Others openly wept. 'President Sadat is now inspecting a guard of honour of the Israeli Defence Forces,' gasped an Israeli Radio reporter. 'I'm seeing it, but I don't believe it.'

But there was more to come. Sadat confronted Golda Meir, Prime Minister at the time of the Crossing and the despised 'old lady' of so many of his pre-war speeches. 'Madam', he now graciously addressed her, 'I have wanted to meet you for a long time.' Many reporters, perhaps carried away by excitement, believed that he actually kissed the eighty-year-old matriarch as he stooped to press her hand. For some reason, he asked particularly after General Ariel Sharon and when, somewhere down the long line of dignitaries, he came upon him he had his verbal sally ready. 'I was hoping to trap you over there,' he told the audacious, insubordinate architect of the Israeli counter-crossing, failing to add, of course, what this lighthearted banter was designed to hide perhaps even from himself: that if he *had* trapped him, there would have been no need for him to be greeting him in Jerusalem that day.

President Katzir and his guest mounted the black, bullet-proof limousine specially borrowed from the American embassy, and with Begin and other ministers in cars behind, the motorcade, lights blazing, sirens howling, swept up the broad, steep highway to Jerusalem. As it wound through the streets of the city, thousands lined the pavements to cheer it on its way; mothers held their infants aloft to catch a glimpse of the visitor. Soldiers and police mingled with the crowds; security precautions were unprecedented even in this most security-conscious of countries. Many thousands more, deterred by the sharp, cold air of the hill-top city, remained transfixed before their television screens. The electricity corporation reported record power consumption. The cinemas closed for lack of customers.

At the King David Hotel, the manager welcomed President Sadat with certificates testifying that 180 trees had been planted in his name in the Jerusalem Peace Forest. Watching tourists yelled and clapped their approval. The security men would have preferred the Hilton; it was easier to guard; but Begin decreed otherwise; only the hotel which he had blown up thirty-one years before had the aura and status to match the occasion. He escorted Sadat to the royal suite where President Nixon and Dr Kissinger had stayed before him. The two men were closeted alone for a while. 'You can say that we like each other,' was all that Begin would divulge when he came out. But it was news enough to send reporters flying to their telephones.

The next morning Sadat went to al-Aqsa mosque. It was here, in 1951, that a Palestinian assassin had murdered King Abdullah, grandfather of the present monarch, King Hussein, as a punishment for his secret dealings with leaders of the new-born State of Israel. On this occasion, about 1,500 Israeli and Egyptian security men filled the magnificent interior. If worshippers did outnumber them, it was not by very many. Indeed, just how many Palestinians, ostensible object of Sadat's solicitude, came to pray with him was a calculation that seemed to vary according to the political viewpoint of those who made it. During the service the preacher politely reminded the leader of the most powerful Arab nation that 'from this mosque you can see the misery of the Palestinian people, which has suffered since the Catastrophe'. To abandon Jerusalem, he warned, would be like abandoning Mecca itself.

When Sadat left the mosque, for a quick, ecumenical visit to the Church of the Holy Sepulchre, demonstrators were less polite. While some shouted slogans in his favour, others chanted rhythmically: 'Sadat, what do you want from us? We are against you. We don't want you here.' They shouted Nasser's name, and denounced his successor as a 'traitor', but scattered into the narrow alleys of the Old City as police moved towards them, sub-machine guns at the ready.

Their protest did not match the stream of vitriol pouring from the Arab world. The day Sadat arrived in Jerusalem, Syria went into national mourning. Offices were closed. Traffic stopped for five minutes. Muezzins and church bells sounded all day. A few hours after his wartime ally had prayed in al-Aqsa, President Assad, at the

Ommayyad mosque in the heart of Damascus, heard the preacher condemn him as 'a traitor who had plunged a dagger in the back of the Arab nation'. Zuhair Muhsin, leader of the Syrian-backed Saiqa guerrilla organization (and subsequently to be assassinated in the luxurious apartment on the French Riviera where he used to take time off from the rigours of 'revolutionary' struggle), reached a new pitch of virulence, even for him, with his call to 'spill the traitor's blood, to spit in his face'. In Iraq *Id al-Adha* celebrations were cancelled. Libyan envoys in various capitals ceremonially burned the Libyan flag (still the same as Egypt's) because it had been flown alongside the Star of David. In Beirut, the leading left-wing newspaper *al-Safir* said that

> Sadat has entered history. As of today, his name will be remembered along with those of Herzl, Balfour, Weizmann, Bengurion, Golda Meir and Moshe Dayan as one of the founders of the State of Israel, the consolidators of its existence, the champions of its imperialist dreams. Sadat has entered history — but he will enter it again. The decision rests with the Arab people of Egypt, the Egyptian army, or indeed with any Arab. For he is now the enemy of them all, and it is the right of any one to pass judgement and carry it out.[10]

From the Moslem and Christian shrines Sadat went to the Jewish ones, chief among them Yad Va-Shem, which commemorates the victims of the Nazi holocaust. For the Zionists, this chamber of horrors symbolizes Israel's *raison d'être*. To go through it is a rite which all official visitors are expected to observe. Sadat was no exception. But mindful, no doubt, of the unfortunate impression it would create in the Arab world, he did decline the customary skullcap, and walked bare-headed through the consecrated halls. When United Nations Secretary General Kurt Waldheim had done likewise in 1973 it caused consternation, but this time it raised not a murmur, so eager were the Israelis to preserve their state of enchantment. Sadat said little as he moved from exhibit to grim exhibit; in the visitors' book he wrote: 'Let us put an end to all the sufferings of the human race.'[11]

But the real climax of the visit, where its ceremonial merged with its momentous political import, came in the Knesset. There the atmosphere was both festive and tense — festive on account of the almost miraculous quality of what it was about to behold, and tense for fear that all expectations might simultaneously be hurled to the ground. Special rules of protocol had been devised; for the first time in its history the Knesset would be permitted to applaud a guest. A bugle call proclaimed the entrance of the two presidents. Sadat mounted the rostrum beneath a portrait of Theodor Herzl, founder of Zionism. Unknown to him, a voice stress analyser had been attached to the microphone; it was later established that the needle jumped slightly when he spoke about reconciliation.[12]

Sadat's address was certainly in keeping with his lofty purpose. All war is vanity, he began, and the only vanquished is mankind itself. He harboured no ill-will towards those who had received his announcement, before the Egyptian National Assembly, with 'surprise and amazement. No one had ever imagined that the president of the greatest Arab state . . . which bears the heaviest responsibility pertaining to the cause of war and peace in the Middle East could declare his readiness to go to the enemy with which we are still in a state of war . . .' Again he stressed that he had consulted none of his 'colleagues or Arab brethren'. He bemoaned 'the fruitless discussions on the convening of the Geneva Conference, all showing utter suspicion and absolute lack of confidence'. He had taken his decision after long thought, knowing that it constituted a grave risk, but it was his responsibility before God 'to exhaust every means in a bid to save my Arab people and the entire Arab nation the horrors of new, shocking and terrible wars, the dimensions of which only God himself can foresee'. His mission had a universal significance. For he bore 'the same responsibility towards each and every man on earth, and certainly towards the Israeli people'. He touched the most universal of emotions. 'Any life lost in war is a human life, be it that of an Arab or an Israeli. A wife who becomes a widow is a human being entitled to a happy family life, whether she be an Arab or an Israeli. Innocent children deprived of the care and compassion of their parents are ours. For the sake of them all, for a smile, for a smile on the face of every child born in our land. For all that, I have taken my decision to come to you.'

The warm and personal note deeply moved his rapt, attentive audience. But then, inevitably, the tone changed. Let it not be thought that he had come out of weakness. Harking back to his greatest triumph, he said that, in his speech to the People's Assembly on 16 October 1973, he had called for an international conference to establish a just and lasting peace. He had not been in the position of one who was 'pleading for peace or begging for a ceasefire'. Fate had now decreed that his mission of peace should coincide with the *Id al-Adha*, 'when Abraham, peace be upon him, the ancestor of the Arabs and Jews, submitted to God. I say that when God Almighty commanded it of him, he went forth not out of weakness, but out of devotion, deep spiritual force and freedom of choice, to sacrifice his very own son'. His own mission could be 'a radical turning point in the history of this part of the world, if not in the history of the world as a whole'. He had not, he insisted, come for a 'separate peace' between Egypt and Israel, nor for a 'partial peace' — one that, merely terminating the state of war, indefinitely deferred a final settlement. Nor had he come for a third disengagement in Sinai, a second in the Golan, or a first one in the West Bank, for that would merely 'delay the lighting of the fuse'.

Tension in the Knesset rose. Sadat reverted to a conciliatory note. He conceded that there had been fault on the Arab side.

> You want to live with us in this part of the world. In all sincerity, I tell you that we welcome you among us, with full security and safety. . . . We used to reject you, yes. We had our reasons and our claims, yes. We refused to meet with you anywhere, yes. We used to brand you the 'so-called' Israel, yes. We were together in international conferences and organizations and our representatives did not — and still do not — exchange greetings with you, yes. This has happened and is still happening. It is also true that we used to demand, as a precondition for any negotiations with you, a mediator who would meet separately with each party . . . yes, this happened. Yet today I tell you, and I declare it to the whole world, that we accept to live with you in permanent peace based on justice.

One barrier — Israel's alleged invincibility, and the ability of its long arm to 'reach and strike anywhere' — had collapsed in 1973. Yet there remained another; 'a psychological barrier between us. A barrier of suspicion. A barrier of rejection. A barrier of fear and deception. A barrier of hallucination around any deed and decision.' This psychological barrier constituted '70 per cent of the problem'.

The time had come to break it down. The Israelis had to do their part. Sadat told them roundly what it was. And his audience did not like what it heard. Tension rose again. The Israelis had to 'give up, once and for all, the dreams of conquest, and give up the belief that force is the best method of dealing with the Arabs'. There had to be complete withdrawal from all the occupied territories. And this included Arab Jerusalem. There could be no annexing of the City of Peace. Instead of reviving the prejudices of the Crusaders, the Israelis should emulate the spirit of Omar al-Khatib and Saladin— the spirit of tolerance and respect for rights. He had not come to them 'under this roof' to plead for that. That was axiomatic. Further-more, the Israelis had to recognize what the entire world, what even America, its foremost ally, recognized: namely, that the Palestine cause was the crux of the whole problem. 'If you have found the legal and moral justification to set up a national home on a land that did not belong to you, it is incumbent upon you to show under-standing of the Palestinian people's insistence on establishing once again a state on their land.'

General Ezer Weizmann, the Defence Minister, leaned over to-wards Foreign Minister Moshe Dayan and passed him a note: 'We've got to prepare for war.' Begin's face grew even grimmer. 'That's an ultimatum,' he said in an audible whisper.[13]

President Sadat ended his address on the exalted plane that he began it, quoting a Koranic text to the effect that all 'people of the book', Jews, Christians and Moslems, were equal in God's sight. He had done his part for the peace of the world. In going to the ends of the earth, to the Knesset itself, he had 'set aside all precedents and traditions known by warring countries'. He now awaited the com-mensurate response. He conceded that he could hardly expect it right away, during the visit itself. He had only come 'to deliver a message. I have delivered the message, may God be my witness. . . . Peace be upon you.'

The Knesset, taken aback by the firmness of that message, could only muster half-hearted applause. Begin, General Sharon, and Chief of Staff Mordechai Gur did not applaud at all.

Begin is one of the most forceful speakers in the Knesset. He rarely reads from a prepared text, and since he had not seen Sadat's speech in advance, it was an impromptu reply that he made. It was as spontaneously hard and unyielding as the man himself. Character-istically, it was a speech no less steeped in religiosity, no less insistent on Israel's peace-loving intent, than Sadat's own; but that was mere embellishment for a standard Zionist version of the Palestine struggle that bluntly rebutted Sadat's. 'No sir', he retorted, 'we did not take a foreign country. We came back to our homeland. The link between ourselves and this country is eternal. It was created in the dawn of humanity; it was never severed, never disrupted.' It was a reiteration of the *Likud* party's expansionist orthodoxy, softened a little by the high oratorical style of its delivery and even—though this came hard to a man like Begin—by the tact which the occasion demanded. Everything could be negotiated, he said. There were no preconditions. Yet he effectively posed them himself. For him Israel was *Eretz* Israel, the biblical, God-given land in its entirety. There could be no sundering of what, in 1967, had forever been 'joined together' again, no redivision of Jerusalem. He did not even mention the Palestinians, neither their existence as a people, nor their right to self-determination and statehood. (Although, according to a subsequently released official text, he supposedly did invite 'genuine spokesmen of the Arabs of the Land of Israel to come and hold talks with us about our common future'. If so, it did not add up to a concession of any kind.) It was no good President Sadat trying to make out that, through his act of courage, he had fulfilled his part of a bargain which commanded an automatic *quid pro quo*. For 'President Sadat knows, and he knew from us before he came to Jerusalem, that our attitude is different from his as far as the borders around us, between ourselves and our neighbours, are concerned.'

Begin's speech made as unfavourable an impression upon the Egyptian delegation as Sadat's had on the Knesset. Both sides had stated their well-known positions, and the gulf between them was enormous. But in their final press conference the two leaders glossed over it; before the cameras they were all smiles and cordiality. Besides, said Begin—and Sadat more or less corroborated it—on one point 'momentous agreement' had indeed been reached. It was what Begin had called for in his first, direct address to the Egyptian people: 'no more war, no more bloodshed'. 'That mutual pledge was given in Jerusalem. We are very grateful to President Sadat that he said so in the Knesset, personally to me and today also to my colleagues in Parliament.'

But had Begin given Sadat anything in return for the risk he had taken, a journalist persisted? 'It is not a matter of a kind of compensation,' Begin parried. 'What we wanted to achieve was to make sure we started a serious direct dialogue: peace not only between Israel and Egypt, but all the other states. The key word is continuation. We agreed to continue our dialogue. And, ultimately, out of it will come peace.'

For his part, Sadat did manage, the bonhomie notwithstanding, to stammer out once again his message that if peace was to come it no longer depended on him. 'Let us hope, all of us, that we can keep

271

the momentum in Geneva' — for, in the joint communiqué, Geneva and a comprehensive peace was formally acknowledged as the official aim — 'and may God guide the steps of Premier Begin and the Knesset because there is a great need for hard and drastic decisions. I have already, I mean, I took *my* share in my decision to come here, and I shall be really looking forward for those decisions from Premier Begin and the Knesset.'

Sadat left Israel bearing gifts; from Begin, a signed copy of his autobiography; from President Katzir, three urns from the age of the patriarchs; from Mrs Katzir, a large portrait of a dove; from Golda Meir, 'as a grandmother to a grandfather', a pair of earrings for a granddaughter born to him during his pilgrimage; from 300 schoolchildren letters, like the one from Hanna Muallem, aged eight, asking him 'to make peace so that we can play with your children'.

'Thanks for everything,' he called to the television crews at Bengurion Airport. Theirs had been the greatest gift of all. Just forty-four emotion-filled hours after it had touched down in the Land of Israel, Egypt 01 took off home with an escort of four Kfir jet fighters. *Hu halach.* He had gone. If he really took with him any hope for 'the hard and drastic decisions' he had come to extract, he was soon to be disappointed. Those were a gift that Begin did not intend to bestow.

Prince of Peace

With his descent upon Jerusalem, Sadat achieved a new apotheosis which, in the universality of its impact, surpassed that earlier one, his triumphant proclamation of the Crossing. But with this new, this "psychological" Crossing, it was not in his Arab constituency that he achieved it; it was in the world, especially the Western world, at large. In Europe and the United States the man who had once been depicted as a warmonger was now hailed as a hero of peace. The leaderwriters outdid one another in the superlatives they heaped upon him. Sadat was truly a great man. His pilgrimage was a sublime gesture, a masterstroke, a watershed in history. A newspaper whose pro-Zionist enthusiasms (until the advent of Begin) had always been extravagant, put it this way: 'Statesmanship, dignity, and humility have been movingly blended in everything that President Sadat has so far said and done during his momentous visit to Israel. Venturing like some self-appointed Daniel into the lion's den of the Israeli Knesset, he pleaded and reasoned with his opponents on their behalf and that of mankind as much as on that of his own people.'[14] A famous columnist remarked how petty Sadat had made Nasser seem by comparison. There was an extraordinary euphoria, an unreasoning belief that peace between Arab and Jew—so desirable in itself and so vital to Western interests—was finally at hand. It inspired wonder, reverence and piety, and in no one more than in President Carter who, before watching the Knesset encounter on television with his family, offered a prayer for Middle East peace from the pulpit of Washington's First Baptist Church. He said that rarely in world history had there been a moment when the hearts and minds of all people were so joined together in thanksgiving and prayer. 'No one can predict what will happen,' he intoned with his eyes closed, 'but it is being done in Your name.'

It was certainly on the highest mystical plane that, in retrospective justification, Sadat sought to place his mission. The whole idea had come to him, he recounted, in a train of thought which Carter himself had set in motion. A personal envoy had delivered a handwritten message from the American President. For it was the custom of the two leaders to assess the international situation together. Carter was a 'serious and sincere' person who really wanted to bring peace to the region. In this personal letter, Carter had asked what could be done to get the Arabs together in Geneva. It plunged Sadat into thought. Only after visiting Romania, at the end of October 1977, had he been delivered of his mental strife. He had asked President Ceausescu, the one East European head of state to entertain good relations with Israel, two questions: did Begin really want peace, and, if so, was he strong enough to deliver it? To both questions the answer was a firm yes. 'That', recalled President Sadat, 'was all I wanted to know from the Romanian President. And I couldn't stop thinking. Thoughts assailed me from left to right. I felt that the Arabs were drowning in a flood of words and conflicts . . . and the matter growing more and more confused and complicated.'

From Bucharest Sadat flew on to Teheran.

I don't know whether this thought of the Flood came to me merely because the aeroplane was passing over Mount Ararat where Noah's (peace be upon him) ark came to rest and the dove of peace, released from the ark by our forefather Noah, returned with an olive branch as a sign that the flood waters were retreating and that the shore was near. And I was elated merely to recall the story of

273

the Flood, the ark and the olive branch. And I felt as if all my thoughts were as doves bearing olive branches, and that I had to select one of them. But the abundance of branches in the doves' beaks troubled me greatly.

His first thought was that he should call for a meeting in Jerusalem of the five great powers in order to prepare for the Geneva conference.

But time was short; it was impossible to address such invitations to heads of state at such short notice, for they have engagements for months ahead . . . and I wanted to take Israel by surprise, for surprise is one of the elements in both peace and war. More important, even if the invitation to the Big Five had worked—and that was improbable—it still would not have achieved what I wanted: the demolishing of the psychological barrier, the earthen screen of doubt and misunderstanding between me and Israel. If the demolition of the Bar Lev put an end to feelings of defeat and collapse, then the destruction of this "psychological" Bar Lev would do away with the accumulation of years—thirty years or thirty centuries—of the feeling that there is no other way but strife and bloodshed between us for ever. These thoughts turned in my mind. I isolated myself and pondered . . . and I decided to go to Jerusalem. In the People's Assembly I announced my readiness to go to Jerusalem. Events moved with lightning speed.'[15]

It was also the apotheosis of Sadat the actor. In a sense that it never had been before, the world was now his stage. He had it all to himself, whereas, in earlier acts of the same drama, he had played second lead to Henry Kissinger Superstar. The pilgrimage was a media event *par excellence*, television diplomacy at its most spectacular. True, it was only a symbolic gesture which Sadat had made, but one which, of itself, was expected to generate immense practical consequences. It was supposed to transform the climate of opinion, both inside Israel itself, to whose people he appealed over the heads of its leaders, and in the West, especially the United States, where the public sympathy gained for the Arab point of view would eventually be converted, by due political process, into governmental pressures for an appropriate Israeli response. The transformation would be commensurate with the impact the gesture made; it was therefore vital to secure for it all the exposure, the ballyhoo, the awed and sacramental quality which only the great American networks can bestow. It was perhaps an accident, but certainly a fitting one, that Walter Cronkite, anchorman of CBS and an American institution, should from the outset have become an actor in the drama, a Kissinger of the television screen, while the Administration—its only function the delivery of Begin's formal letter of invitation—was reduced to the role of postman. Sadat knew what he was about. It was only a half-hour flight from Abu Sweir airbase to Bengurion Airport, but, during it, he managed to give exclusive interviews both to Cronkite himself, and the two rival stars of ABC and NBC. He was to grant well over a hundred more in the next few weeks. After Jerusalem, every television company in the world had at least one camera crew in Cairo, the big American ones fielding at least three, with their usual army of extras.

As yet another producer flew in from Burbank, California, he summed it all up: 'You sure have a great President here. He knows the deadlines of every news show in the States.'[16] Begin, well aware that the Arab–Israeli struggle had shifted from the sands of Sinai to the hearts and minds of the American people, was no less obliging— though less effective—than Sadat. Golda Meir, pungent as ever, got it right: 'Never mind the Nobel Peace Prize,' she exclaimed, 'give them both Oscars.'

The West was Sadat's new constituency, but in the Arab world he did strike an authentic chord of popular approval, barely audible though that might have been against the clamour of denunciation orchestrated by party-cum-military dictatorships which monopol-ized the means of communication. It goes without saying that the approval was strongest in Egypt itself. There, of course, the state-controlled press and radio did as much to encourage and dramatize the general enthusiasm as their Arab counterparts did to belittle it; the enthusiasm was very real all the same (and the Arab outrage only served to increase it) for, in addition to a genuine yearning for peace, Sadat was exploiting that deepening strain of Egyptian nationalism which necessarily took an anti-Arab form.

Sadat had correctly divined the mood of his people. Like the Israeli man-in-the-street, his Egyptian counterpart was overwhelmed by the sheer drama of the event itself—plus a pride in the daring of his President and the world's acknowledgement of it—and he did not trouble himself about the conditions which had led to it, or the results, if any, which it had produced. It is true that virtually none of the country's authentic political parties, clandestine or semi-tolerated, formally supported the visit, but it was not to them that Sadat, the unerring populist, was making his pitch; it was to the masses. And set against their response, the objections of the resigning Foreign Minister, Ismail Fahmi, or the criticisms of Khalid

Muhyieddin's National Progressive Unionist Party, seemed at the time a rather pedantic carping. His triumphant return was popular mandate enough.

'More than five million people welcomed me,' became a continuous refrain of his. He had slipped out of Egypt, after dark, from a remote Sinai airbase; he insisted on going back to Cairo International Airport in broad daylight with an escort of Mirage jet fighters. During a solemn, but smiling, reception, the band played the Palestinian as well as the Egyptian national anthem. From then on it was another of those characteristic Cairo carnivals, part spontaneous, part contrived, with lorry and busloads of peasants and workers pouring into the capital to swell the welcoming multitudes. Sadat rode, upright and radiant, in an open limousine through the human colonnade that lined the thirteen-mile, flag-draped route from the airport to his house in the suburb of Giza.

The crowds, already celebrating the Feast of the Sacrifice, acclaimed him with shouts—'in our blood and spirit we shall sacrifice ourselves for you, O Sadat'—with banners—'he has carried the truth, and the voice of the heart into the heart of Israel'—with female ululations and orchestras of tambourines and bedouin flutes. 'Without Egypt there is no Arab world,' insisted a Cairo Radio commentator as he described the scene, 'Cairo is not the capital of Egypt alone, but the centre of the entire Arab world.' *Al-Ahram* dubbed him the 'peace-warrior'. And a spokesman added that the visit had been 'one hundred per cent successful'; 'thirty years of war [had] been eliminated in thirty hours'; 'from the first day', he said, the Israelis had tried to get Sadat to enter into a separate deal; but he had steadfastly refused; Arabs and Israelis were heading for Geneva and Geneva alone.

As for the rest of the Arab world, it might not be true that the pilgrimage generated more grassroots sympathy in Syria than anywhere else outside Egypt. But it is certainly true that the discrepancy between what the public silently thought and what the regime proclaimed in their name was wider there than anywhere else. It was not that the Syrians, traditionally militant for Palestine, enthusiastically endorsed what Sadat had done. It was simply that the Baathists were deeply unloved, that the divorce between ruling and ruled was so great that what the one opposed the other had a perverse impulse to support.

In general, however, the authentic shock and consternation was at least the equal of the furtive satisfaction. The outrage may have come insincerely from governments such as Syria's, which had done their share of mischief at the Palestinians' expense. There was none the less good reason for the gravest misgivings. After all, it was not for nothing that the West had hailed the Jerusalem pilgrimage as the spectacular gesture it was. At a stroke it had shattered the most sacred of Arab taboos. The 'psychological barrier' which Sadat claimed to have breached was indeed formidable. Even in the earliest days, when the 'Zionist menace', as the Palestinians called it, was embryonic, they had refused to confer upon it the legitimacy of direct negotiations. In 1939, during the negotiations that ended the Arab rebellion against British mandatory rule, the Palestinian delegates sat in one room, the Zionists in another, with the British commuting between the two. This foreshadowed the 'indirect negotiations', the 'proximity talks', Dr Kissinger's jet-age 'shuttle diplomacy' and all the ingenuities that peace-makers of the future would dream up. If their fathers and grandfathers refused to recognize the Zionism of their day—before it had even grown to statehood on the debris of the Palestinian community—how much more shocking for their sons to witness an Arab leader dealing with the Zionism of today. And what a Zionism! A Zionism that was led, a prominent Palestinian scholar observed, 'by the last Israelis to be worthy of shaking hands with the head of the largest Arab state'.[17]

It would appear, wrote Sabri Jiryis, that Sadat did not really appreciate the symbolism of the gestures his Israeli hosts invited him to make. One such was his visit to Yad Va-Shem. One of the greatest achievements of Zionism has been to stamp indelibly—but, in the Palestinian view, illogically and unjustly—upon the Western mind the proposition that Israel is the indispensable sanctuary for the victims of Nazi atrocities and the guarantee that no such calamity will ever befall the Jews again. 'Palestinians have not only suffered the wretchedness and bitterness of being displaced to solve a European problem—the persecution of Jews—for which they were in no way responsible, they have also watched in anguish as the State of Israel has used the *historical misery* of the Jews—symbolized by the Yad Va-Shem memorial—to justify maintaining the *present misery* of themselves. . . .'[18]

Now the Palestinians saw not a Western leader, but the head of the most powerful Arab state—the one upon which the ending of their misery most depended—paying homage at Yad Va-Shem. It was not a little ironic, in their eyes, that the Arab leader best known for his one-time Nazi sympathies should be the first to do such a thing. There was also a degree of anti-Semitism in Sadat and some of his entourage that was not to be found in other Arab leaders—Nasser, for example—who none the less used, like him, to deem the 'liberation' of Palestine the highest cause of the Arab nation. It is paradoxical, perhaps, but in no way surprising, that the most ardent apologists of Sadat's 'peace mission' were also the most overtly anti-Semitic. The degradation of the Egyptian press, once the most vigorous and respected in the Arab world, began under Nasser, but Sadat completed the process. Anti-Semitism—indeed, any kind of racist outpouring—came naturally to the vulgar breed of sycophants and opportunists who now expounded Sadat's words and deeds. Exalted among them was Anis Mansur, editor of the weekly magazine *October*. He was so faithful a mouthpiece that his writings could often be taken as an advance text of Sadat's own platform performances. It was Mansur who, shortly before the October war in whose name the magazine was founded, praised Hitler for his extermination of the Jews. For they were the 'enemies' of humanity. 'They have no principles, they respect no religion but their own and they are traitors to the countries which give them shelter. For them all that matters is that Israel should survive even at the price of a world conflagration and the destruction of mankind.' Hitler, said Mansur, was a 'genius'. 'The Nazi tortures are but a pale reflection of the methods used by the Jews in the conquered territories. The world now realizes that Hitler was right and that the gas chambers had their *raison d'être* in the punishing of such contempt for human values, principles, religion and righteousness.'[19] It was Sadat himself who had encouraged these excesses when, a few months before, he said that the Koran proved the 'perfidy' of the Jews.

Till now the Israelis never tired of reminding the world of Sadat's inglorious past. Their propaganda machine kept dredging up the famous Letter to Hitler. But it became politic, for the time being at least, to let these bygones be bygones—and to welcome Anis Mansur as an apparent convert to the Zionist cause, who paid frequent visits to Israel and wrote complimentary articles about it. Only the most benighted of backwoodsmen now persisted in preaching the wickedness of Anwar Sadat—and, characteristically, went to ludicrous lengths in doing so. Thus, in his book *Sadat's Strategy*[20] one Paul Eidelberg makes out that the Egyptian leader, in secret connivance with his Arab enemies, was really putting into effect the 'peace phase' of the Nazi Model of Conquest.

There was some irony, too, in the fact that it was Zionist officials who took Sadat on his tour of Yad Va-Shem. For one aspect of *their* past about which they were a good deal less candid than their guest is that, once upon a time, they too collaborated with Nazi Germany. One group that went further than mainstream Zionism in dealing with Hitler was the *Stern Gang*. Early in 1941, when it appeared that Nazi Germany might well win the war, *Stern* leaders tried to forge a military alliance with Hitler against Britain, which, as the Mandatory power in Palestine, they regarded as the main enemy. The unsuccessful proposal was that Jews in Nazi Europe would be conscripted into an army under the control of *Stern*, which would then make war on Britain in Palestine, creating a fascist Jewish state in league with Nazi Europe.[21] It was a *Stern* leader, Itzhak Shamir, who, as Speaker, introduced Sadat to the Knesset, and sat on one side of the Egyptian leader as he made his speech. On Sadat's other side was Menachim Begin, one-time leader of the *Irgun* terrorist organization.

Not far from Yad Va-Shem is the Kiryat Shaul Hospital for Mental Diseases. The Arab village which it has replaced remains indelibly printed on Arab minds as the most emotive slogan of an unending struggle. Its name was Deir Yassin. At 4.30 in the morning of 9 April 1948, Begin and Shamir ordered a combined force of *Irgun* and *Stern*, 132 strong, to attack the sleeping, virtually defenceless village. By the following afternoon, they had slaughtered some 250 of its inhabitants; they loaded some twenty-five surviving men into lorries, took them on a 'victory parade' through the streets of Jerusalem and then shot them in a nearby quarry.[22] The 'victory' at Deir Yassin—as the Irgunists called it at a press conference—had immense repercussions.[23] As Begin himself recalled, 'Arabs throughout the country . . . were seized with limitless panic and started to flee for their lives. This mass flight soon developed into a maddened, uncontrollable stampede. Of the about 600,000 Arabs who lived on the present territory of the State of Israel, only some 165,000 are still there. The political and economic significance of this development can hardly be over-estimated.'[24]

The Palestinian scholar was being too charitable. President Sadat well understood the symbolism of what he was doing. One of the first indications, after he came to power in May 1977, that Begin intended to set Israel on a more aggressive course had been the open flaunting of what his predecessors officially disclaimed: namely, that Israel was aiding right-wing Christian militias in Lebanon. This drew an indignant response from Sadat. It was with 'sorrow and indignation', he informed other Arab leaders, that he had learned that 'there are parties in Lebanon which are asking for Begin's protection'. Furthermore, it was 'a disgrace to the Arab nation that Begin, who slaughtered Palestinians at Deir Yassin in 1948, should become the ally of a group within an Arab state such as Lebanon'.[25]

For the Arabs, it was not merely the symbolism of what Sadat was doing—though that was troubling enough—it was the context in which he was doing it. Obviously, if the Arabs were ever to make peace with Israel all their leaders would have to do what he had done, but—and this was the vital point of difference—it should have come at the end of the peace-making process, not at the beginning. It would thereby have constituted that full recognition of the State of Israel which the Arabs, formally renouncing a territory they deemed their own, could only confer in exchange for the return of the occupied territories and the establishment of a Palestinian state. It was this that would have marked the consummation of a 'just and lasting' peace in the Middle East. Yet such was Israeli intransigence, with Begin as the quintessential expression of it, that this could only come about through a fundamental change, in the Arabs' favour, of the Middle East balance of power. It had always been Sadat's contention that the Crossing had brought about that change. But, in reality, it had not. On the contrary, the balance of power—the strictly military balance at least—had now shifted dramatically in the opposite direction. It was this which, at bottom, prompted his pilgrimage to Jerusalem. He went there, not—as he and his publicists proclaimed—from strength, but from a position of abject weakness.

He had already come close, in effect, to publicly admitting it. Only a month earlier, he had threatened to go to war. 'If Israel wants to test us', he told a rally at Suez, 'we shall teach her a crueller lesson than before. . . . We seek peace, but if it is not realized then fighting will become imperative.' Egypt was ready to go to Geneva, but not on terms that undermined its achievements or those of 'the Palestinian people, who have chosen the PLO as the instrument of their struggle'. The Egyptian army, Sadat warned, still had its finger on the trigger.[26] A few weeks before that, he had told Israel that he had the capability to wipe out a third of its population. He was in possession of

definite information that the Israelis have nuclear weapons. . . . They put this about from time to time in the hope of weakening the Arab bargaining position. . . . If Israel uses the atom bomb against us, we may lose a million people, but there would still remain thirty-nine million Egyptians. . . . My plan is that we work to destroy one million of them in return for the million Egyptians, and in my opinion that would finish off Israel. As you know, two-thirds of the Israeli people live within the small triangle formed by Jerusalem, Tel Aviv and Haifa. My plan can finish off half of them.[27]

For Sadat to fall back on the language of 'no war, no peace'— language that the October war had supposedly banished for ever— was tantamount to admitting that his 'victory' had been no victory at all. Buffoon though it had made him appear, it had then served his ultimately belligerent purposes. Now it was the language of desperation pure and simple. A full four years had elapsed and nine-tenths of Sinai, not to mention Golan, the West Bank and Jerusalem, still lay in enemy hands, and this time he certainly did not have the means to carry out his threats. According to the *Washington Post*, the Israelis were ready to use the overwhelming superiority which America had conferred upon them. If pushed into a corner, they were ready to fight a war of 'annihilation', whether America liked it or not. A Beirut newspaper neatly caught the Arab—and the American— predicament: 'The Israelis are now hinting to the Americans: don't pressure us or we shall blow up everything—oil, the international balance of power, your friends in the Arab world. We are ready to take you on politically by taking on the Arabs militarily. We are ready to change the political and military map, and convene the Geneva conference the Israel way. . . .'[28]

Sadat publicly contradicted himself. Even as he sprang his plan to visit Jerusalem upon an astonished world, and warned of the 'horrible' consequences he could inflict on Israel if it came to nothing, he was telling American Congressmen a very different tale. Israel was the real threat to peace, he told them, 'the real threat to the Arab world in its entirety, not just to a Palestine state, but to all us Arabs'.[29]

Thanks to you, to your committee [the House Armed Services Committee] and what you have given Israel in the way of the most modern and sophisticated weapons—thanks to this, I fear that one day you will discover that they [the Israelis] are a threat to you, because they can get anything they ask for. They can start a war, and, as the report of your Ministry of Defence [the Pentagon] says, they can carry it on for six months without needing anything new from you.[30]

'The responsibility lies on the shoulders of the American President, Congress and the American people; they must know that they have supplied Israel with everything so that they can threaten America in the matter of peace.'[31]

As for Egypt's nuclear capabilities, they were a figment of Sadat's imagination. Muhammad Heikal, former editor of *al-Ahram* who had been, since his disgrace, one of Sadat's most effective critics, said that it was time the Arab leaders stopped making idle threats about what they would do 'if' Israel introduced nuclear weapons into the area,[32] and, during the visit to Jerusalem, one of Sadat's closest confidants apparently told the Israelis just how hollow the threats were. Mustafa Khalil, then Secretary-General of the Arab Socialist Union, confided to Professor Yigael Yadin and General Ezer Weizmann that 'we know that we would not have a chance of winning a war and we also know that you have the atom bomb. Egypt doesn't have a military alternative and we have to seek a different solution.'[33]

Nor, according to Sadat, was it Egypt's economic plight, exemplified by the nationwide food riots of ten months before, that had forced his 'initiative' upon him.

We do suffer from the economic situation [he conceded], but we are now doing splendidly . . . our Arab brethren are helping us with billions of dollars this year and we have paid all our debts. Even great countries like Britain are far worse off than us. . . . We are not seeking peace at any price. Not at all. You don't know my people.

As for the food riots, he reiterated that they were just 'an uprising of thieves . . . the same thing happened in New York when there was an electricity breakdown. . . . We had a popular plebiscite (after the riots) which produced 10,100,000 votes for and 5,600 against. Can you imagine that?'[34]

In Jerusalem, however, his newly appointed Acting Foreign Minister, the scholarly and serious Butros Ghali, painted a grim picture of Egypt's social and economic woes. 'Did you know', he asked his hosts, 'that every year one million babies are born in our country, and that today one million Egyptians—from professors to prostitutes—are working in other Arab countries?'[35]

If Sadat, thus exposed, had any bargaining power, it lay in his readiness to take Egypt further down the road which—with his unilateral ceasefire, Kilometre 101, the first Sinai disengagement, the premature lifting of the oil embargo, the unscheduled re-opening of the Suez Canal, the second Sinai disengagement—he had already taken it. It lay in the completion of that go-it-alone diplomacy whose premise was that the more Egypt detached itself from the Arab world, the more it could expect to get for itself. When, therefore, Sadat told Walter Cronkite that he had consulted none of his fellow Arab leaders, that the Jerusalem pilgrimage was entirely his own initiative, he was telling the plain truth. To his American audience, if this conveyed any impression at all it was probably one of disarming candour. But for the Arabs, and especially their leaders, the implications were shattering. It was public confession of his own duplicity. For the consulting of colleagues lay at the heart of the concept of Arab solidarity, a concept which Sadat himself, ostentatiously setting himself apart from his late predecessor, had largely pioneered. If Egypt and Saudi Arabia had been the two great adversaries in the ideological struggles of Nasser's day, Saudi–Egyptian reconciliation underpinned the community of Arab purpose in Sadat's. Just a week before he dropped his bombshell in the People's Assembly, Sadat had been in Saudi Arabia. But of his plan to take the gravest single step in the modern history of the Arab nation he had breathed not a word. 'He came here,' recalled Crown Prince Fahd, 'and I stayed up with him until three in the morning and he said nothing except that he was dead set on the Geneva conference.'[36] He had not told the Saudis, Sadat himself said later, because his decision was 'above their level of comprehension'.[37]

It made complete nonsense of the Unified Political Command set up by Assad and Sadat, under Saudi auspices, less than a year before to launch their combined 'peace offensive'. To an Arab world all-too-familiar with Sadat's backslidings the mere failure to consult meant that he was up to no good, but this *announced* failure to do so, and on so momentous an issue, meant that he was up to no good on a momentous scale. It was not what he said in the Knesset that mattered—for that, by and large, was an unimpeachable presentation of the standard Arab position—it was the circumstances in which he had said it. Syria and the PLO, the parties most directly threatened, immediately announced the formation of a 'unified front', and then, at a summit conference in Tripoli, three other so-called 'radical' Arab states, Libya, Algeria and South Yemen, joined them in the Front of Steadfastness and Confrontation, which resolved to foil the consequences of Sadat's 'treason', to 'freeze' political and diplomatic relations with the Egyptian government and boycott any meetings of the Arab League at its Cairo headquarters.

Representing the most uncompromising opposition to Sadat, the

Front was gravely weakened from the outset by its failure to win the adhesion of Iraq, which did not consider it uncompromising enough; behind this holier-than-thou 'rejectionism' lay altogether less exalted motives, not least a hatred of the rival Syrian Baathists, who were 'accomplices in the crime of capitulation'.[38] Others, though distinctly reserved about Sadat's initiative, refrained from condemnation. King Hussein, who made a futile attempt to mediate between Damascus and Cairo, said that his main preoccupation was to prevent a 'disastrous' split in Arab ranks. Speaking for the so-called 'silent' Arabs, Crown Prince Fahd said that 'in our opinion, inter-Arab divisions are more dangerous than wars'.[39] All, reacting in different ways, had one fear in common—that Egypt, the largest Arab state and the lynchpin of concerted Arab strategies—was heading for a 'separate peace'.

Nor was it just the Arabs whom Sadat had failed to consult. It was the Americans too. (Although it has been suggested that President Carter knew about, if he did not actively encourage, Sadat's initiative.[40]) Relations between him and President Carter were so close, he claimed, that 'we [were in the habit of] exchanging our assessment of the political situation at all times'. On this occasion, however, 'Carter had the most violent surprises'.[41] Sadat was determined to make Egypt the principal bastion of American interests in the Middle East, and he habitually insisted that, in the search for peace, America held 99 per cent of the cards. None the less, his descent on Jerusalem had to be a *fait accompli* for America too, for he feared that it might not like the idea. It appears that the former Israeli Prime Minister Yitzhak Rabin had asked to meet Sadat during a secret visit to King Hassan of Morocco in the summer of 1977. But Sadat would not oblige, at least not yet, for Dr Kissinger had strongly advised him against it, fearing as he did that once Israelis and Egyptians started talking to each other the United States would lose control of events.

The unexpected triumph of Menachim Begin in the May 1977 elections, and his adroit use of an Israeli intelligence coup, helped encourage Sadat's independence of the Americans. According to the West German magazine *Stern*, Mossad agents reckoned to have uncovered a plot by Colonel Gadafi to assassinate President Sadat on 23 July 1977, the twenty-fifth anniversary of Nasser's revolution. The terrorists were said to be training at an oasis 20 miles from the Egyptian frontier. Given this information, Begin felt helpless. 'What have we done before with such material?' he asked his predecessor.

284

Told that they used to pass it on to the CIA, Begin replied that this time Israel would let Sadat know directly. 'No harm in showing him our good will.' The information was passed to Hassan Tuhami, Vice Premier and one of Sadat's closest friends. Sadat ordered a six-day frontier war against Libya—and sent his thanks for the tip-off.

There followed a secret meeting on 27 August in Romania between Begin and Sayyid Marei, the President of the People's Assembly, but it was Foreign Minister Moshe Dayan who made the decisive breakthrough. On 16 September he flew to Brussels to meet General Alexander Haig, commander-in-chief of NATO. In the afternoon he was due to go to New York, but only his wife Rachel actually arrived there, for just before the plane took off a black Citroën raced up and Dayan, wearing two enormous goggles and with the brim of his hat down over his nose, was bundled into it and spirited to another runway to board a Moroccan plane for Tangiers. There he met Tuhami, who conveyed Sadat's readiness for a meeting. The only condition was Israel's withdrawal from Sinai. The next day Dayan was spotted in Paris. He flew back home to see Begin, and on 18 September he was on his way to New York to catch up with his wife. At a stop-over in Zurich he told an Egyptian emissary that Israel had agreed to the Sinai withdrawal. The CIA, unable to give the White House any explanation for Dayan's peregrinations, was puzzled. It managed to track down his diversion to Tangiers. 'Probably to see King Hassan', was its conclusion. But that was all. Sadat's bombshell of 9 November was indeed something that even President Carter had not 'anticipated'.[42]

The Americans—or at least their more far-sighted policy-makers—did not want a 'separate peace' any more than the Arabs. They were aware of its disruptive consequences for the Arab world, and, eventually, for their own interests in the area. It is true that, after what the Palestinians regarded as a promising start, President Carter began to exhibit that vacillation which was later to exasperate even his closest European allies. During the run-up to Geneva Yasser Arafat had responded to American overtures with a flexibility which brought his followers close to revolt. He had offered to accept a suitably amended version of Security Council Resolution 242—holy writ to the peace-makers—which, as it stood, referred to the Palestinians as mere 'refugees' rather than as a people with national rights,[43] but to no avail. Carter bowed to the pressures exerted by the all-powerful Zionist lobby. In October there came the joint Soviet–American communiqué on the Middle East, which even the 'rejectionist' Popular Front for the Liberation of Palestine found 'interesting'. Surrender to the virtual Israeli *diktat* was swift and ignominious; the President of the world's most powerful nation and his Secretary of State closeted themselves with Israeli Foreign Minister Moshe Dayan in a long, late-night emergency meeting; in the 'working paper' which these consultations produced, the United States abandoned positions taken earlier in the Palestinians' favour, such as their need for a 'homeland' and respect for their 'legitimate rights'. None the less, in spite of that, the US was still officially bound for Geneva and a 'comprehensive' settlement. In the opinion of the resigning Egyptian Foreign Minister, Ismail Fahmi, 'the great powers don't like surprises', and if President Carter 'hadn't brought such a bunch of amateurs into the White House', the Americans would never have allowed Sadat to go ahead with a 'television initiative' which wrecked their whole peace-seeking strategy.[44]

Sadat's pilgrimage to Jerusalem had set in motion a process which neither he, nor the Arabs nor the Americans could stop. He expressed it in his own quaint, vainglorious metaphor.

There are some who blame me for my 'thundering initiative'. Why? Because normally in politics someone rides on a horse and expects the others to follow him. But I am riding a rocket. And all the knights of politics are panting behind me. They beg me for an opportunity to get their breath back. But I know that my Egyptian people are out ahead of me. . . . Indeed, it is they who are urging me onwards, faster and faster. The world sees me racing and can't catch up with me. I see my people racing and I try to catch up with them. Our people repeat five words that mean everything: let's have done with it![45]

In the end, of course, the rocket was to go out of control, propelling him where he had sworn he was not going—to a separate peace which, even after he had concluded it, he continued to swear it was not. For when his gesture failed to work its hoped-for psychological magic, when Begin obdurately remained what he had always been, the embodiment of Zionism at its most expansionist and extreme— then Sadat was to find himself at the end of his diplomatic tether. Stage by stage, he alienated Egypt from almost the entire Arab world, 'moderates' and 'radicals' alike.

The Americans who, at first, had tried to slow him down acquired such a vested interest in his mission that they ended up hastening him recklessly onward. It took fifteen months of unseemly haggling and harassment, of tantrums and reconciliations, an eleven-day summit in the seclusion of Camp David and President Carter's final, astonishing descent on the Middle East to snatch agreement from the jaws of disastrous failure—but in the end Sadat was to capitulate all along the line.

My friend Shylock

No sooner had Sadat got back from Jerusalem than, justifying his 'initiative' before the People's Assembly, he dropped another bombshell. He invited 'all parties to the conflict'—the two super-powers, the United Nations, Syria, Jordan, Lebanon and the PLO—to attend a conference in Cairo to prepare for Geneva. Israel promptly accepted. The UN was lukewarm. Dr Waldheim agreed to send a representative, the Chief Co-ordinator of the UN Peace-keeping Operation in the Middle East, but, given his commitment to a full-dress conference at Geneva, he described Sadat's proposal as 'a little premature'. After embarrassed hesitation, the United States announced that it would send a rather low-level representative to attend, in the shape of its Assistant Secretary for Near Eastern Affairs. Everyone else turned the invitation down. Sadat well knew that they would—so well, in fact, that that must surely have been his intention.

For with his Jerusalem pilgrimage he had sabotaged the Geneva conference at the very moment when, according to him (though Israelis and Palestinians contested it), he had finally solved the crucial problem of PLO representation via an American professor of Palestinian origin. It was this sabotaging of Geneva, and with it all hope of preserving unity of Arab ranks, that prompted Ismail Fahmi, unconsulted by his master, to submit his resignation. But more had been lost than Geneva and Arab solidarity. According to Fahmi, Sadat and Colonel Gadafi had been on the point of spectacular reconciliation; as a token of good will Gadafi had agreed to supply Egypt with 500 tanks (plus five squadrons of jet fighters and a gift of several million dollars according to other sources) in order to strengthen her bargaining position in Geneva. It was Yasser Arafat, that indefatigable mediator, who had achieved this feat; and his special invitation to attend the 9 November opening of parliament had come as a kind of 'reward' for his labours. 'Now', lamented Fahmi, 'in my opinion everything is finished.'[46]

Sadat virtually admitted it. It was true, he said, that President

Carter had tried to postpone the pre-Geneva Cairo conference in a bid to win Arab support for it. However, in spite of Carter's 'thorough grasp' of the Middle East problem and the 'delicate calculations' of his advisers, he and they did not understand 'the nature of certain Arab regimes'.

> I noticed that in the short time between my journey to Jerusalem, my return to Cairo and my speech to the People's Assembly there was movement in the Arab world. The Syrian Baath will not go to Geneva; and if it did, the picture would be as follows. The Soviet Union has put Syria in her pocket, and Syria has put the Palestinians in hers. In Geneva, we would get bogged down in what we have completely freed ourselves from, legalistic and semantic quibbling, and procedures and the titles of the functional, positional, and geographical and historical committees . . . and the whole bag of tricks we know so well from the Syrian Baath party. And the result would be that the Geneva conference would add enormously to our stock of despair—I know this. . . . Was it necessary to complain to President Carter that the Arabs won't agree? Was it necessary to complain to him about the Arabs . . . that is, to complain to him about myself? Then to ask him to rescue me from myself? From my family? From my brother Arabs? My experiences in the matter are very numerous and well-known, declared and recorded. I have announced it tens of times. I am convinced that the Syrian Baath and its hangers-on don't want peace. Neither they nor the Soviet Union. For this reason I have taken an Egyptian decision, and a destiny-shaping one to boot.[47]

The fact is that Sadat did not really want the Geneva conference at all—or rather the Russians' and the Syrians' participation in it, which would reduce his own importance. He had been jealous of American wooing of President Assad, and although the Soviet–American communiqué on the Middle East, with its American acknowledgement of the rival superpower's right to a share in the peace-making, greatly strengthened the general Arab position, he had given it a lukewarm reception. He knew that the balance of power had shifted so far against the Arabs that, if they relied on themselves, they could not hope to secure a 'comprehensive' settlement; and, with Carter's retreat from the joint communiqué, he had just been given an object lesson in the futility of relying on the Americans to redress the balance on their behalf. So, with his pilgrimage to Jerusalem, he made a virtue out of self-inflicted necessity; while he became a pariah in the

Arab world, he regained for himself that central place on a broader stage that more than made up for it.

No sooner had he issued the invitation to the Cairo conference than, in yet another interview with American television, he issued a virtual ultimatum. 'It is for everyone to decide for himself. If only the Israelis come, I will start the conference.' Egypt and Israel alone? 'Yes, yes, like I visited Jerusalem alone.' Of course, he added his ritual caveat. Any agreement that was reached would be 'part of a whole settlement. I am not after a separate settlement.'

But wasn't he? For even before the conference opened he joined his faithful press pundits in hinting that he was. He was under growing pressure from the Egyptian people, he told the Kuwaiti newspaper *al-Siyasah*,[48] 'to proceed in a way that will guarantee Egypt's regional interests while ignoring the Arab cause'. In the People's Assembly, a key loyalist deputy, Elwi Hafiz, told the new Foreign Minister that 'if you don't get Arab support for Egypt's efforts for a comprehensive settlement, come to us in parliament and we are prepared to give you a mandate to conclude a separate peace with Israel'.[49]

If ever there was a remote possibility that his Arab adversaries would show up in Cairo, he ensured that they would not by launching violent tirades against the very people he was inviting. Whereas, after the second Sinai disengagement agreement, Sadat and his propaganda machine had generally confined themselves to attacks on Syria's ruling Baath party, now they went for President Assad in person. 'The rejectionists have lost everything and the biggest loser is Hafiz Assad, who has lost Egypt and lost me.' He ridiculed the 'children' who had foregathered in Tripoli to set up their Front of Steadfastness and Confrontation. Even President Boumediène, on whom he used to lavish extravagant praise, was not spared. Using what was now to become, by a long way, his favourite word of abuse, he said that Boumediène had 'grown small in my sight—he is but a dwarf in the company of that other dwarf, Gadafi'. His adversaries had become no more than 'mice or monkeys which the Soviet Union juggles with. The Soviet Union is the conjuror blowing on his fiddle and, hey presto, everyone twists to right and left, ready to creep in any direction. And the direction is pointed by the Soviet Union—against Egypt.'[50] The Cairo press enlisted academic authority for the view that most Arab leaders were mentally unstable. Dr Adel Sadek argued that Arabs who opposed Sadat's peace initiative required psycho-therapy. 'One of the greatest catastrophes at present is that several Arab leaders are either psychopathic, paranoid or schizophrenic.'[51] President Sadat broke off diplomatic relations with the members of the Steadfastness Front as well as 'rejectionist' Iraq; he closed down Palestinian offices in Cairo and the Cairo-based Voice of Palestine radio station. Officially, his invitations still stood, but at the same time, 'No one enters Egypt who slights and insults, whatever his position in his own country.'[52]

With Syria the schism was complete. No longer was it merely a question of 'cutting Assad down to size', as it had been after Sinai Two, it was a question of overthrowing him. Sadat began to forecast upheavals in Syria, implying that he could be instrumental in bringing them about, with Lebanon, still a potential arena of Arab civil war by proxy, as the ever-ready platform for the purpose. As for the Syrians, they left no doubt about it: this time, Sadat had to go.

Towards the Palestinians Sadat was ambivalent. It was mainly for their sake, after all, that he had gone to Jerusalem. From now on there were to be good Palestinians and bad—those who understood that salvation lay with him, and those who danced attendance on their Syrian and Soviet masters. He never formally repudiated the PLO as the 'sole legitimate representative' of the Palestinian people, but if he had any hopes of the 'dear and wonderful' friend, Yasser Arafat, in whose presence he had proclaimed his 'initiative', or a pro-Egyptian faction within the PLO, they were soon to be dissipated. In his Knesset address he failed to mention the PLO by name, and in his first speech on his return to Cairo, he mentioned it only once, and then—in what was certainly an uncorrected, if not actually a Freudian, slip—he called it the 'Israeli Liberation Organization'. He likened the PLO to 'a ball in a stadium, with every player kicking it around as he wished'.[53] In going to the Tripoli summit the PLO leaders had 'committed the biggest mistake of their lives'. If they had trusted him and come to Cairo instead 'their recognition would have been automatic in that they would have sat together round the same table. But they didn't'.[54] No one had pushed harder, at the Rabat summit conference in 1974, to secure Arab, and in consequence international, recognition of the PLO; spurned by it, he now sought to exclude it from the peace-making altogether, or, at least, to frighten it with the spectre of an alternative Palestinian leadership. This he hoped to conjure out of the occupied territories, traditionally more moderate than the Palestinian diaspora. But with one exception all the mayors of the West Bank and Gaza, expressing solidarity with the PLO, rejected an invitation to go to Cairo for consultations. In the end, no one of any real stature went at all. Those who were ready to go, and a group of Gazans who actually did, were, in the words of the Israeli daily *Haaretz*, 'third-rate personalities', or, in the words of the mayor of Ramallah, did not 'even represent their wives'.[55] When this tactic failed, Sadat tried another. He sought to re-assign to King Hussein the role which, at Rabat in 1974, he had persuaded other Arab leaders to divest him of, suggesting that the Palestinians should transfer their loyalty from Arafat to Hussein. But the Palestinians would not; nor was the king going to make any attempt to persuade them to do so.

In turning against the PLO, Sadat gave the signal for a propaganda campaign that fed on, and excited, Egyptian chauvinism. It was not the first of its kind, of course, but it took an altogether cruder form than usual. Directed against the Arabs in general, it was the Palestinians who tended to bear the brunt of it. Thus, taking its cue from Sadat's own words, the weekly *Rose el-Youssef* featured a well-dressed 'rejectionist' standing outside a night-club and saying to a friend: 'Excuse me while I go in there and do some struggling.' That Palestinians were particularly addicted to the *dolce vita* was always a theme of these campaigns.

After the assassination in Nicosia of Yusif Sibai, chairman of *al-Ahram*, and Sadat's impetuous, disastrously bungled and wholly unnecessary attempt to do an Israeli-style 'Entebbe' rescue operation at Larnaca Airport the campaign reached its furious climax. The assassins *were* Palestinians. But the PLO denounced the murder as a 'criminal and cowardly deed'. That was not good enough for Sadat. Without any proof, he and his propaganda machine insisted on blaming the PLO and Yasser Arafat, who now figured in newspaper cartoons with hands dripping with blood. It looked as though Egypt was preparing to withdraw formal recognition of the PLO. At the funeral of Egyptian commandos, there were calls for vengeance. The press warned that what it called the popular mood might be translated into official action. Only Arafat himself could now head off the worst, wrote the Palestinian affairs correspondent of *al-Ahram*. 'Spontaneously, with suffering and pain, the Egyptian people went out into the streets and shouted "no to Palestine after today". Before official Egypt responds to the anger of the masses we ask: where are you heading for, Palestinian leaders? I fear that official Egypt will act on the anger of its sons. I fear that the blow dealt at Egypt was dealt at Palestine. Who can save Palestine?'[56]

It certainly did not look as though Egypt could. That Israeli response to his 'initiative', the 'hard and drastic decisions' he had pleaded for in Jerusalem, failed to materialize. For Begin was well aware that 'weakness, even desperation' drove Sadat.[57]

He was unbending from the outset. And why not, asked one of the most irreverent critics of Zionist orthodoxy? 'For him', wrote Uri Avneri, 'this visit was a gift from Heaven. It was handed to him free, on a silver platter. It was Sadat who initiated it and paid the full price for it, endangering his life and his regime, and gave Israel an invaluable prize—full recognition of her existence and her legitimacy. What did Begin pay? Nothing at all, not even a piastre with a hole in it.'[58]

Begin and the ruling establishment were well aware that Sadat had opened up the most alluring possibilities. A columnist was frank where the politicians tended to be discreet. 'Everyone is avoiding the word "separate peace" as if it was something shocking. For myself, with all respect for the politicians who took part in this, I disagree. A separate peace is a legitimate expression, not a dirty word: the wedge we have promised not to drive into the Arab world exists, and it would be stupid to ignore its existence.'[59] The Israelis knew that, at the very least, they were now in a position to eliminate or reduce the role of those—Russians or Americans, 'radical' or 'moderate' Arab states—who could influence the negotiations on the PLO's behalf. 'Why deny it? Sadat's Egypt is today making a huge diplomatic concession to Israel. . . . Israel asked for negotiations without the PLO and Egypt has in fact accepted this demand.'[60] It was apparently at Moshe Dayan's suggestion that Sadat failed to mention the PLO in his Knesset address.[61]

If Egypt had not bowed to Israeli ultimatums, the pre-Geneva conference in December would not even have convened. When the Israeli delegation arrived at Mena House Hotel, next to the Pyramids, they noticed, among the plaques reserved for the absent invitees, one bearing the words Palestine Liberation Organization. Eliahu Ben-Elissar, the head of the delegation, asked that it be removed. The Egyptians refused. Ben-Elissar was adamant. The Egyptians proposed a compromise: just the word 'Palestine'. 'If you put that name on the table', said Ben-Elissar, 'we are not going to enter the hall.' In the end, after a whole day's argument that had to be referred to Sadat, it was decided that there would be no plaque at all. Then the Israelis noticed a 'strange and unknown' flag flying alongside all the others. So the Palestinian colours, in turn, had to be lowered, along with those of all the non-attending parties.[62]

The Cairo conference was a side-show which Begin turned into an irrelevance when, even as it was meeting, he suddenly took off for Washington to win approval for his plan for Palestinian 'autonomy' or 'self-rule'. He realized that he had to give something in return for Sadat's gesture, and this was to be it. It was a *Likud* formula which, for all practical purposes, ensured that control of all the 'liberated' territories of Greater Israel was retained without their formal annexation, a so-called 'functional' solution which preserved the essential gains of occupation—military bases, immigration, settlement and economic domination—while passing the burdens of civil administration to the local inhabitants or, in part, to Jordan. The occupation would acquire permanent *de facto* legitimacy. It was hoped that, with immigration and settlement, the Jews would eventually become a majority. The West Bank and Gaza would be markets for Israeli products and springboards for economic penetration of the Arab hinterland. Arab manpower would furnish Israel with cheap labour. With time and economic neglect, educated Palestinians, finding no livelihood, would gradually be forced to emigrate. There would be no right of return for the Palestinian diaspora. In short, as Israelis put it, 'autonomy' would enable the Palestinians 'to determine the placing of sewage pipes in Hebron',[63] or, as Arafat put it, it was Israel's Bantustan.

In private, even Dr Brzezinski, President Carter's National Security Adviser, exclaimed to an outraged Begin that 'that's like South Africa. You are taking away the right to vote from the people.'[64] True, the last of the plan's twenty-six points stipulated that the whole would be 'subject to review after five years'; but that was just a subterfuge to draw Egypt into a separate deal without a final decision on the West Bank and Gaza. As for Sinai, Begin assured the Knesset that, even under a peace treaty with Egypt, Israel would retain the settlements in the Rafah salient, linked to it legally and administratively and defended by its army.

Normally, Sadat spent his birthday, 25 December, in Mit Abul Kom, where, in peasant simplicity, he liked to 'sit alone and commune with [himself]'.[65] But on Christmas Day 1977, the eyes of the world were on the Canal Zone town of Ismailia. Here Begin, the first Israeli Prime Minister to set foot on Egyptian soil, had repaired for the second Israeli–Egyptian summit meeting, bringing with him his plans for 'autonomy' and the future status of Sinai. But Sadat had other ideas. He wanted a 'declaration of principles' on the Palestine problem that would satisfy the Arab world.

The talks went badly. 'You want an Arafat Palestine state,' said

Begin. 'I am not talking about Arafat,' Sadat rejoined, 'the subject is self-determination for the Palestinians ... It is in your interest that I continue to be the leader of the Arab world. I can finish Arafat off in two weeks. We must have something in hand, otherwise they will stone me.' He fared no better on the bilateral front. 'If I tell my people that Begin wants to leave his settlements in the Sinai and that the Israeli army will protect them, they will stone me. Begin's proposal is not enough for me, especially when I face the whole Arab world.'[66] So Sadat did not get his 'declaration of principles', nor even a joint communiqué, but only an agreement to form two committees, a political one, headed by foreign ministers, which would meet in Jerusalem, and a military one, headed by defence ministers, which would meet in Cairo.

Sadat's Arab adversaries ridiculed the Ismailia summit as a total failure. Sadat's concessions, said the Damascus daily *Tishreen*, were only breeding more concessions, while a Beirut columnist remarked that the danger of riding on rockets was that they sometimes crashed as fast as they took off. The Arabs pointed out that Begin had not even agreed to withdraw from Sinai, a barb that really drew blood when, a few days later, a spokesman announced that he and his wife had joined the Neot Sinai settlement and would retire there in a bungalow 'with a magnificent view of the Mediterranean'. Further disclosures followed about the 'strengthening of settlements' in the Yamit area.

Sadat owed it to himself and to Egypt to preserve his serenity. From the outset he had pledged that if his 'initiative' failed he would do the honourable thing. 'I told Hafiz Assad that I am putting history in one scale and my initiative in the other; if it fails, I shall tell Assad that he was right and I was wrong and I shall submit my resignation to the People's Assembly immediately.'[67] He always kept his nerve, he told Anis Mansur, editor of *October* magazine, and it was because they could not stand the strain that he had lost men like General Shazly during the October war, and now Foreign Minister Fahmi in the struggle for peace that was 'tougher than fighting and war'.[68] 'I saw a film recently about journeys into space. I saw the scientists ... they record every breath the astronauts take, telling them when to eat, drink or tie a shoelace. These scientists sit there completely calm before their machines and electronic minds ... the captain of the ship of peace must not be like the waves and the storms, he must be solid like the shore.' Besides, Sadat was the ruler of Egypt, and 'while the Egyptian citizen may not be educated, he is the heir to a civilization which is thousands of years old. Ancient Egypt fathered all human progress and values; even the stones it turned into mighty pyramids. Civilization has made the Egyptian peasant and city-dweller proud of his history, his glories, and his superiority over all mankind.'[69]

Initially, Sadat may really have felt the confidence he publicly expressed. 'The price Israel is willing to pay is this,' he told the Rome daily *Il Tempo*, on 19 December, 'to withdraw from the territory occupied in the war and to resolve the Palestinian problem, recognizing the right of the Palestinian people to a homeland and a state.... This programme can be realized now, right away ... there can be no half-measures.' On the eve of the Ismailia summit he told Anis Mansur: 'True, I gave something away, but I shall get something in return. This is for sure.' When he got nothing, he remained outwardly philosophical. Mansur observed that, though he had given up his anniversary for affairs of state, he had had no cake, no candles lit for him, 'no gift either symbolic or political'. 'No,' he replied, 'the Suez Canal Authority offered me a cake. But we had other things to do, and I instructed others to eat it....' There was no profit in talking about concessions. 'That's a word the other side uses.' The important thing lay elsewhere.

> It is the first time since Israel came into being that the Jews have put forward a plan.... They used to make very sure that everything was like a jelly, shrouded in fog, so that you could see neither the beginning nor the end, neither head nor tail. This time they came so that we could discuss together. I say my opinion, they say theirs ... this in itself is positive ... Begin said everything is negotiable. This is alien to his thinking. He is the hawk of hawks.[70]

But then, suddenly, Sadat did lose his composure. He threw the first of his tantrums. It was the Sinai settlements which really seemed to have infuriated him. 'I emphasize from now that I will not agree to any Israel settlement on my territory. Let them plough them up.'[71] A newspaper cartoon depicted Begin flying over the Pyramids on his way from Ismailia, with an official looking down on them and saying: 'That would be a good spot for building a Jewish settlement.' The Cairo press warmed to old themes, turning on the Israelis with a violence which, of late, it had reserved for Arabs and Palestinians. Begin was a Shylock demanding his pound of flesh. The Jews will bargain even with the angel of death. To sit with the Jews is to sit with the world's speculators of every generation. An indignant Begin himself regaled the Knesset with a list of these insults, which came of course from the self-same pens that had been most extravagant in praising Sadat's 'initiative'.[72]

Warnings accompanied the invective. 'You are contradicting yourselves,' the editor of al-Ahram told Begin. 'First you used to accuse us of wanting to throw you into the sea, trumpeting this argument round the world and, the moment we say that we shall recognize you, you say you do not need our recognition.' None the less, the Israeli people desired peace. Ali Hamdi Gamal was certain of that. It was only the 'arrogance and conceit' of their leaders which denied it to them. In an open letter to 'Israeli youth', another al-Ahram columnist said that in men like Begin 'bloodthirstiness still prevails over dreams for peace, and I fear that it will conquer them altogether. . . . Tell your leaders . . . not to let this opportunity pass. . . . Otherwise, instead of flowers we shall bear arms . . . and we shall curse the day we ever entertained hopes that so quickly faded.'[73]

Suddenly, Sadat himself was agreeing with his Arab adversaries. 'Begin has offered nothing. It is I who have given him everything. I offered him security and legitimacy and got nothing in return. This peace initiative is not the King David Hotel which Begin blew up when he was young. He cannot blow up the initiative without destroying himself and others for hundreds of years.'[74] The Egyptian delegation, led by Foreign Minister Ibrahim Kamil, was recalled from Jerusalem only two days after it had arrived there for the first session of the 'political committee' decided upon at the Ismailia summit.

But Sadat was not admitting failure. He was not resigning. The 'door to peace' was not yet closed. For it was now up to the international community, having seen what it had seen, to shoulder the burden which he had first taken up. 'The Egyptian initiative is no longer just Egyptian, it has become an historic act which the whole world acclaimed . . . and no one can erase it from the history of the world.'[75]

Camp David

Essentially, the world meant the United States. It was there that President Sadat now repaired, in February 1977, for the support and solace he so badly needed. He had already been transformed into something of an American hero. *Time* magazine had named him Man of the Year. For its cover photograph he posed, a twentieth-century

Pharaoh in flawless pin-striped elegance, before the Pyramid of Cheops. An American committee had proposed him as its candidate for the Nobel Peace Prize. President Carter had called him one of the bravest men on earth, and 'the world's foremost peace-maker'.

But Sadat needed more than accolades, gratifying though they were; he needed practical assistance for promoting the kind of 'comprehensive' settlement he could sell to the Arab world. For despite all his threats to do so, he could not openly go after a separate peace or wash his hands of Palestine.

Certainly, there were signs that Sadat was getting results. His pilgrimage to Jerusalem had been calculated to engender an historic shift in American perceptions of the Arab–Israeli conflict and, by the time he arrived in Washington, such a shift was under way. Those instant guides to the nation's mood, the public opinion surveys, recorded it. In February a *Newsweek–Gallup* poll which asked 'Which country has been the more willing to compromise?' produced an astonishing 45-to-26 response in favour of Egypt. The May/June issue of the magazine *Public Opinion* registered a thirteen-point slide in sympathy for Israel over a six-month period; it was the 'sharpest, deepest and fastest drop' of its kind in the history of the Middle East conflict. A month later, the magazine released the results of its 'Great Decisions' seminar. This recorded that a full 60 per cent of its sample poll voted either to 'approve', or 'to go along without enthusiasm with', the view that the United States should use its influence to persuade Israel to accept 'a Palestinian homeland to be created out of territories now occupied by Israel'. In the personality contest Sadat trounced Begin. Being Palestinian in origin, Dr Hisham Sharabi, President of the National Association of Arab Americans, had no illusions about the unwelcome consequences of Sadat's 'initiative', but he conceded that he had 'changed the image of the Arab in the United States and Western Europe'.[76]

It was not merely the American public at large which Sadat so strongly impressed. The Jewish community itself was showing signs of division and disenchantment; for the first time since the State of Israel arose, many Jews came out openly against its policies.

American commentators perceived the change, but, at the same time, they wondered whether it was a temporary aberration in the Arabs' favour or a much deeper stirring in the nation's outlook, whether it had gone far and fast enough to produce a commensurate change in those quarters—particularly the White House and Congress—where Israel's domestic extension, the Zionist lobby, still exerted such a powerful influence. Was true 'even-handedness'—which had provoked such an uproar when proposed, ten years before, by Senator William Scranton—finally in the offing?

It did look as though it might be. President Carter was angry with Begin, there was no doubt about that, and it was the question of Jewish settlements in occupied territories—the West Bank as well as Sinai—on which both he and his advisers were least prepared to hide their irritation. They were the most obvious, provocative indicators of Israeli intransigence. Carter considered Begin devious and deceitful. On 10 February, only two days after Sadat left Washington, Secretary of State Cyrus Vance issued the bluntest warning yet. The settlements, he said, were 'contrary to international law and should not exist'. Referring to the 'intertwined Palestinian question', he told reporters that 'these two problems must be overcome if we are going to make progress in these negotiations . . . the continued settlement activity by Israel creates an obstacle to peace and must be faced up to and dealt with in order to make progress.' There was also a dispute over the interpretation of Security Council Resolution 242. The Americans had condemned the PLO for rejecting it. How could they overlook the fact that Begin, in effect, had now reneged on Israel's original acceptance of it? For it was impossible to reconcile his 'autonomy' plan with the territorial withdrawal for which the resolution called.

In the event, however, it was not to be. Carter and his Administration took the easy course which the Sadat 'initiative' had opened up. For them, after the first, stunned hesitation, the Jerusalem pilgrimage had become a godsend to be exploited, the opportunity for a facile foreign policy triumph that could reverse the rapid decline in their own popularity. Like Sadat himself, the United States continued to insist on the need for a 'comprehensive' peace. It expressed the pious hope that other Arab parties would rally to his 'initiative'. Secretary of State Vance had been the first of many emissaries to travel to the Middle East in a bid to win them over. He had been told in Damascus that Sadat had 'wrecked the chances of Middle East peace', and one of his entourage had conceded that there were 'deep wounds in the Arab world which it is going to take time to heal'.[77] But such warnings—and the misgivings of the State Department—tended to fall on deaf ears in circumstances where realism in foreign affairs took second place to the electoral imperatives of domestic politics. Thus it was Carter himself who, after a New Year whistle-stop tour of key bastions of Western influence in the Middle East, had summed up his impressions with an optimism which, even without the benefit of hindsight, could only be described as fatuous: 'The Shah will be supportive, the Saudis were very encouraging about the future, and Hussein and we completely agree. I don't think I would be violating any confidence to say that all Arab leaders with whom I met said they supported Sadat unequivocally.'

The Americans had profited from Sadat's descent on Jerusalem to vindicate those retreats from stated policy which, even before it, the Zionist lobby had forced upon it. Vance had said that he thought that Geneva was no longer necessary, and won the emphatic approval of his predecessor, the architect of step-by-step diplomacy, who still exerted a powerful out-of-office influence on the direction of American foreign policy; as a negotiating forum, said Henry Kissinger, Geneva was dead, and 'just as well'. President Carter had said that, because of its 'completely negative attitude', the PLO had forfeited its right to participate in the peace-making. He thought that Begin's 'autonomy' plan—or at least as originally presented to him in December—was a 'realistic starting point for negotiations' and showed a 'great deal of flexibility'. He did not believe in 'self-determination'—which Begin had told him would lead to a Palestinian state—but rather that the Palestinians should 'participate in determining their own future'. He was against the creation of a 'radical, new, independent nation' for the Palestinians; 'any homeland ought to be tied at the very least in a very strong federation or confederation' with Jordan. His National Security Adviser Zbigniew Brzezinski had set the seal on this American retreat with a flippancy which seemed unbecoming—and not just to the Palestinians—in a man of his stature. The United States, he told *Paris Match* on 28 December, had failed to persuade the PLO to 'moderate' its policy so it was 'bye-bye PLO'.

Much of this was displeasing to President Sadat and, for all his continued insistence on Carter's high integrity, he felt constrained to say so. In Washington he was seeking American support for Palestinian 'self-determination'; he wanted the United States to become a 'full partner in the establishment of peace' and not just a 'go-between'; in other words he wanted American pressure on Israel. At the same time he wanted 'equal treatment' in the furnishing of arms; he needed them to make possible the role of Western gendarme that he was so anxious for Egypt to play. Of course, he was not going to use them to attack Israel, 'but if there are persons in this region who think that arms can make them reach everything, then I say that

I am bearing responsibilities and obligations that transcend this region to cover the whole of Africa'.[78] It was Israel's American-supplied arsenal that made it so intransigent in the peace-making. Sadat was demanding, 'officially and for the first time, that Egypt be armed with everything Israel has'. In Washington, he told Congress that he would 'raise hell' if he did not get the latest F-15s and F-16s.

Yet, despite the favourable impression he had made on public opinion, Sadat did not get what he wanted from Carter, whose senior officials said that they were not going to support his call for 'self-determination'. If negotiations resumed, it was intimated, the Israelis might acknowledge the Palestinians' 'legitimate rights'. As for arms, all that Sadat could get—and not even that without a fierce Zionist rearguard action against it—was his paltry share of a wider Middle East 'package'. The Israelis got seventy-five F-16s, and fifteen F-15s to supplement the twenty-five they already had, along with all the extras—such as Sidewinder missiles and long-range fuel tanks—which ensured their full, 'offensive' capability. The technologically backward but politically safer Saudis got sixty F-15s without the extras. Sadat had to be content with fifty obsolescent F-5Es, which he himself had scorned as 'tenth-rate'.

Sadat told the National Press Council in Washington that, in spite of Israel's return to the 'vicious circle of arguing over every single word and comma' and its 'hiding behind fanatic groups who are beating the drums of war in their feverish campaign to build these settlements'—in spite of this, he was still 'committed to the cause of peace' and 'willing to give the experiment every possible chance until I reach the conclusion that enough time has elapsed without achieving any tangible progress'.

So it was that, after Sadat's first tantrum, a reconciliation of sorts was arranged; but now, instead of direct negotiations, there would be a return to the American-sponsored 'shuttle' diplomacy of old.

The shuttles—conducted by Alfred Atherton, appointed for the task as Ambassador-at-Large with Special Responsibilities for the Middle East, Secretary of State Vance, and Vice President Walter Mondale—went on through the summer of 1978 in a climate of rock-like Israeli inflexibility, deepening American pessimism and a President Sadat alternating between despairing frustration and brave assertions that, in spite of everything, he was not giving up his 'sacred mission'.

Begin was in Washington six weeks after Sadat. One newspaper described his visit as a 'diplomatic disaster'. Vance said it was absolutely essential that Israel accept Resolution 242, agree to abandon the Sinai settlements, and offer the West Bank a degree of self-determination. Begin was unbending on all three counts. Relations between America and Israel reached their lowest ebb since 1956, when President Eisenhower had forced Begin's old rival, David Bengurion, to withdraw his army from Sinai after the tripartite invasion of Egypt.

On 16 April, the Israeli cabinet did at least re-affirm its acceptance of Resolution 242. But this did not signify any change in Israeli policy, a spokesman said. The Egyptian Foreign Minister, Ibrahim Kamil, called it a play on words, and the day after that Secretary of State Vance said that 'if the peace process remains deadlocked, the inevitable regression towards conflict will be difficult to halt—with the most profound consequences for us all'.

On 10 May, President Sadat offered another concession. He said he wanted to 'make it easy' for Begin by proposing that Israel return the West Bank to Jordan and Gaza to Egypt. He told the *New York Times* that while negotiations on security matters and the eventual status of the occupied territories were in progress he 'did not care' how internal affairs were handled or whether Begin applied his 'autonomy' plan or not. What mattered was that the Palestinians should 'get rid of Israeli occupation'. Begin 'utterly rejected' the latest offer.

Between this propitiatory gesture and a belligerent one to come, Sadat engineered another of those sudden, sweeping 'corrections' of his own, much-vaunted 'freedom and democracy' in a way which showed how insecure he was feeling at home. Lack of progress in the peace-making merged with the familiar, but ever-growing socio-economic hardships to produce a renewal of domestic unrest, or what Sadat called a 'licence in press and parliament that resulted in open attacks' on his leadership and members of his cabinet. With another referendum, yielding a 98·29 per cent vote in his favour, he secured a virtual *carte blanche* to exclude from public life almost anyone he liked.

The belligerent gesture came, appropriately enough, on the tenth anniversary of the 1967 war whose consequence he had still so signally failed to eliminate. He reverted yet again to the language of 'no war, no peace'. The second Sinai disengagement agreement was due to expire in October, and if there was no progress by then, he warned, Egypt would repudiate it. He told troops in the Canal Zone that if Israel persisted in failing to understand the spirit behind his 'initiative', they would be called upon to 'complete the battle of liberation'. If there was any threat to Egypt's territorial integrity, 'I shall give you the order, as I did in October.'[79]

Begin retorted that Sadat had broken the 'no more wars' pledge which he had made in Jerusalem, a pledge that was 'completely unconditional'.

Propitiation followed. In July Egypt worked out a new peace formula, which Western diplomats considered more flexible than ever, and this was what its Foreign Minister, Ibrahim Kamil, laid before his Israeli counterpart, Moshe Dayan, at Leeds Castle, England, in the presence of Cyrus Vance. This, too, was spurned. Kamil declared that Israel's security philosophy, based on expansion, contained the seeds of a new war. In Cairo, President Sadat declared the talks at a standstill; there could be no resumption of them without Israel's 'official agreement' to withdraw from occupied territories. President Carter, he said, was still a man of 'ethics and principles'; Sadat did not want to embarrass him; but the United States should play the role of 'full partner' and not just 'mediator'. Kamil made the point more forcefully. 'Frankly', he said, 'I am not happy with the American position.' For its part the United States was 'very disappointed' with Egypt's new stand. American officials saw Sadat at another war-or-peace crossroads.

Then, in early August, Vance returned to the Middle East in what at first appeared to be a last despairing bid just to get the two sides talking again. But in reality he came bearing two letters, written in President Carter's own hand and sealed with red wax: one for Begin, the other for Sadat. When the two leaders had accepted the invitations the letters contained, it was announced in Washington that on 5 September they would join President Carter at Camp David, Maryland 'to seek a framework for peace in the Middle East'. The idea was that they would remain closeted in the sylvan seclusion of the presidential retreat until something was achieved; for if nothing could be achieved there, away from the attentions of the media and the posturing and point-scoring they engendered, then nothing ever would. After all the stratagems—from 'indirect negotiations' to 'proximity talks', and from 'shuttle diplomacy' to the 'electric shock' of Sadat's descent on Jerusalem—that had been applied to the world's most dangerous and intractable conflict, this summit of summits was surely the ultimate procedural resource.

The *Washington Post* described it as 'an almost desperate gamble'. It was a White House decision. When they first heard about it State

Department officials were not happy—quite the reverse. Indeed, some White House staff cautioned against it too. The stakes were too high. The President was placing all his prestige on a single card. His popularity was low enough, and failure would probably wreck his hopes of re-election. His critics would ridicule it as the crowning blunder of this inexperienced peanut farmer from Plains, Georgia. But Dr Brzezinski said that the summit was necessary not because peace prospects were good, but precisely because they had grown so much worse. And Carter himself had no illusions. As his helicopter took off from the White House, he said that the 'chances of complete success are very remote. The disagreements are deep. Four wars did not lead to peace in that stormy region, and there is no cause for undue optimism—but neither is there a reason for despair.'

But, in addition to his willingness to take risks, the summit was just the kind of enterprise which appealed to Carter's unsophisticated sense of mission, his evangelical zeal. And it was in that spirit that the conference opened. At Mrs Carter's request, the three delegations called on 'people of all faiths to pray with us that peace and justice may result from these deliberations. We place our trust in the God of our forefathers from Whom we seek wisdom and guidance.'

President Sadat went to Camp David in the hope that he could get Carter to exert more pressure on Egypt's behalf than he had ever done before, that America's obvious exasperation with Begin's intransigence would at last find practical expression. For Carter was going to make 'constructive' suggestions; the United States was at last going to assume the role of 'full partner' in the negotiations that Sadat had long urged upon it. The Egyptians billed it as a make-or-break occasion, the 'last chance' for peace. It would, Sadat told *al-Ahram*, 'determine the fate of the region for many generations, either by peace or endless struggle'.[80]

Sadat's hopes were Begin's fears—that the 'constructive' suggestions would turn into ultimatums. To accept them would be an historic betrayal of the Jewish people, to reject them would turn Israel into a universal pariah. But Begin sought to mask his anxieties. Whatever happened, the summit was but another landmark, albeit an important one, in the long road to a final settlement. If anyone—that is to say, Sadat—described the meeting as a 'fateful one, we will not agree with him. . . . Our nation has existed thousands of years before Camp David and it will continue to exist for thousands of years after it.' And after all, he believed, America and Egypt had just as much cause for concern as Israel did. 'What is Sadat's alternative—war?

Will he drop the Americans and return to the Soviets? Who will save him—Assad, Brezhnev, Gadafi?'[81] He was taking no new plan with him; the one he had presented to Sadat at their last encounter in Ismailia was 'very good as it stands'.

For the Arab world as a whole, Camp David was a momentous event. For pro-Western regimes, such as Saudi Arabia, it was the last chance to vindicate the strategy which they had tried to sell to all the Arabs, and which Sadat had now bought with greater enthusiasm than even they had bargained for: namely, that their salvation lay with the Americans rather than the Russians. For so-called 'radical' regimes it was Sadat's final 'striptease' that would demonstrate, however it ended, the bankruptcy of his go-it-alone diplomacy. For Syria, in particular, the 'Camp David conspiracy' was already making itself felt in an all-too-familiar, Lebanese form: yet another 'round', which promised to dwarf all earlier ones, was in the making between Syrian 'peace-keeping' forces and Israeli-assisted right-wing Christian militiamen. Both Egypt and Israel, from their rather different standpoints, saw the Syrian engagement in Lebanon as the unfolding of a Soviet grand design.

From the moment the summit got under way it seemed to hover on the brink of calamity. Not that anyone really knew for sure. For none of the world's press got anywhere near that clearing among the chestnut, oak and hickory trees where—Carter in Aspen Lodge, Begin in Birch and Sadat in Dogwood—the three leaders and their principal advisers were to be confined for the next thirteen days. Even CBS anchorman Walter Cronkite had to do his 'stand-up' beside the wooden gate that said 'Camp David'—and even he needed an escort to get that far. Hundreds of pressmen milled about in the little town of Thurmont, six miles away. Every day they congregated in its Legion Hall to receive their one and only briefing—from White House press secretary Jody Powell, who would only tell them who met whom and for how long, and refused to 'characterize'—his favourite word—whether the talks were taking a positive or negative turn. Only the Egyptian press, notably Moussa Sabri, conveyed any idea of how things were going, though without revealing anything of substance. As the days lengthened into a week, the dispatches he sent back to Cairo grew gloomier and gloomier.

'Fundamental differences', he reported on 12 September, 'remain unsolved. Begin is still far removed from the just solution, regarding the West Bank and rights of the Palestinian people, on which Egypt insists.' He reported that Carter had so far spent thirteen hours with the Israeli Prime Minister, as opposed to only four with Sadat, in a bid to break down his obduracy. And no fewer than three times now he had summoned Vice President Walter Mondale, known for his Israeli connections, to Camp David in an attempt to bolster his own flagging persuasions. 'I repeat what I said in my last dispatch: the next two days will be decisive. The facts do not suggest that Carter will be able to persuade Begin to change his position. This was expected all along, and that is why we ask Carter to take a courageous political decision. . . . Will he do so?'[82] Two days later he was reporting that the conference was as good as done for, and that America's Zionist organizations were mobilizing for a public relations campaign that would hold Egypt responsible for the failure and portray Sadat as 'a man capable only of striking dramatic and emotive postures who wanted to destroy Israel by bringing pressure on it . . . I say it again: the success of the conference now hangs on a miracle.'[83] And as the summit grew into the longest of its kind since Potsdam in 1945, and as rumour spread that Sadat was about to walk out, even the inscrutable Jody Powell began to imply that things were more negative than they were positive.

It was Moussa Sabri who—to the *cognoscenti* at least—signalled the eleventh-hour breakthrough. Suddenly, after days of unrelieved despondency, he changed his tone entirely. 'Conference Saved From Collapse', ran the bold red headline of *al-Akhbar* on the morning of Sunday, 17 September; and perplexed readers tried to decipher the dispatch which justified it. It was the efforts of President Carter, and yet another intervention from Vice President Mondale, which had done the trick, Sabri explained. There had been a 'surprising development', narrowing the differences to four points which, while 'procedural' in nature, were 'substantive' too. 'I say today that the conference can be saved.'

Sure enough that Sunday evening, the message suddenly went out to the television networks: prepare for a live cast from the White House. The networks had come into their own again, but—after thirteen frustrating days of rigorous exclusion from the summit proper—with a distinct lack of enthusiasm. For that evening happened to mark the formal opening of the most fiercely competitive season in American television history. Scores of millions of dollars had been poured into rival productions. ABC had to black out *Battlestar Galactica*, perhaps the most expensive TV programme ever; NBC was in the final stages of its four-hour showing of Dino de Laurentis's *King Kong*; while CBS was covering the Emmy awards,

TV's Oscars. In place of these 'blockbusters' a tired but triumphant Jimmy Carter staged one of his own: he announced the Camp David agreements to an astonished world. They consisted of two parts, the Framework for Peace in the Middle East and the Framework for the Conclusion of a Peace Treaty between Egypt and Israel. At an emotional ceremony before a cheering audience in the East Room of the White House, he embraced Begin and Sadat in turn, and praised them for their wisdom and courage. A beaming Begin called Sadat his 'friend', but reserved his real praise for President Carter, who had 'worked harder than did our forebears in Egypt building the Pyramids'. He urged that the conference, the most successful since the Congress of Vienna in 1815, should be named 'the Jimmy Carter Conference'. President Sadat, looking drawn and solemn, made no mention of Begin but was equally flattering of Carter. Next day Carter told a joint session of Congress that 'today we are privileged to see the chance for one of the sometimes rare, bright moments in human history'. The summit, he said, had exceeded his expectations. It certainly had—and the worst fears of almost the entire Arab world.

Separate peace

Begin was right. It *was* Jimmy Carter's conference. He came down from the mountain bathed in the ethereal glow of victory. Banished, overnight, was that thickening penumbra of naïveté and ineptitude. His presidency was born again. Gallup recorded a 17 per cent leap in his ratings since early August. Democratic candidates, who had been distancing themselves from him before the mid-term elections, now fell over themselves to proclaim their fealty. Henry Kissinger said that he could not have done better himself. The *Washington Post*, a normally sober journal, asserted that 'it is a marvellous thing that has been done at Camp David.... It was in truth Jimmy Carter's conference. We salute him: he did a beautiful piece of work. He saw possibilities that few others saw, took risks that he did not have to take and set a model of disinterested dedication that let him call for concessions that were simply unforeseen. There will be a richly earned boost to his presidency and to the stature of the United States in the world.'

But Begin, too, had every reason, at the White House ceremony, to wear the smile—and Sadat every reason to look so solemn. Who caved, asked the Washington columnist Joseph Kraft? He did not supply the answer, but a colleague, James Reston, did. Reston attended the news briefings which the two leaders gave after the summit. He drew a startling contrast between an 'almost recklessly confident' Begin and a Sadat so exhausted that at one point he referred to the US Senate as 'the Knesset' and—causing reporters to gasp with astonishment—to Camp David as 'Waterloo'. And Reston recorded this exchange between Sadat and his interrogators: 'Friday, when you called for the helicopter and were ready to leave, President Carter must have said something to you that was rather persuasive.'

'With President Carter, mark this: we shall face the impossible, whatever it is.'

'But how did he prevail upon you to change your mind? What did he say, precisely?'

'Come, come, come. I can't disclose this between two friends. He imposed upon me certain things that I wouldn't agree upon without his imposition. . . .'

'But what led to the breakdown from your view? What happened that made you change your mind?'

'I shall never tell you.'

'Was it that bad?'

'Yes. Because you know I don't lose my patience easily. But Carter proved to have more patience than me.'[84]

The circumstances of Sadat's cave-in remain a mystery. He lost yet another Foreign Minister, Ibrahim Kamil, in the process. The resignation, submitted during the summit, was not divulged until it was over. The Israeli delegation noticed that Sadat spent much of his time alone, shaking off his aides, barely consulting Kamil, or even allowing him to open his mouth at conference sessions.[85] It was apparently on the seventh night of Camp David that, sleepless and tormented by the unilateral concessions he was expected to endorse, Kamil woke up his cabin-mate, Boutros Ghali, and announced: 'I've had enough . . . I've decided to resign.' Before Ghali had time to reply, he got in touch with Sadat and did so.[86] 'I forgive him', Sadat said later, 'because he could not stand the terrible pressure on his nerves.'[87] Unlike his predecessor, Ismail Fahmi, Kamil shed no light on his motives.

'The peace agreement which Israel is to negotiate with Egypt within three months looks like a separate Israeli–Egyptian peace, feels like a separate Israeli–Egyptian peace, and smells like a separate Israeli–Egyptian peace, but is not a separate Israeli–Egyptian peace. At least, that is what Prime Minister Begin does not want the Israeli press to call it because "it would weaken and embarrass President

Sadat." ' That was the opening passage of a report in the *Jewish Week* on Begin's meeting with Hebrew-language newspapers the day after the summit ended.[88] Israel's dream of dividing the Arab world, of getting its most powerful member-state to withdraw from the struggle for Palestine, was well on the way to fulfilment—and, more incredible still, it was happening under the auspices of the most extreme and chauvinistic leadership it had ever had.

Camp David was the consummation of a bargain that had been implicit in Sadat's go-it-alone diplomacy from the outset: Israel gives up Sinai in return for retaining the West Bank, Gaza and the Golan. It would appear that, throughout the conference, Begin had fought like a tiger even for the retention of Israeli settlements in Sinai, but since they were not located on what he considers to be the God-given territory of Eretz Israel, he had decided to put the matter to the Knesset, where the deputies, recognizing a bargain when they saw it, voted by an overwhelming majority in favour of yielding 'land for peace'. The territorial bargain was, of course, reinforced by all the juridical guarantees—'normalization', United Nations forces, de-militarization, and so on—of the peace treaty. There was no 'linkage'; the implementation of the treaty, so desirable to Israel, was not contingent upon progress towards a 'comprehensive' peace, so vital for the Arabs.

There was, of course, an attempt to furnish the 'comprehensive' cover. But in all essentials the Framework for Peace in the Middle East was just an elaboration of the 'autonomy' plan which Begin had put forward nine months before. A 'self-governing authority' was to be established for a five-year 'transitional' period, by the third year of which negotiations would begin 'to determine the final status of the West Bank and Gaza and to conclude a peace treaty between Israel and Jordan'. The formula bristled with conditions, and neither Begin—disobeying his own injunction—nor the Hebrew press had many inhibitions in elucidating them. They made for an 'autonomy devoid of meaning', which would 'add nothing to what [the inhabitants of the West Bank and Gaza] already had.' Autonomy would never signify sovereignty, and 'if one day the administrative council of the autonomous region declares the creation of an independent Palestinian state, it will be its first and last proclamation. We shall go in and dissolve it.'[89] The Israeli army would remain essentially where it was. And the programme of immigration and settlement on expropriated Arab land would continue unabated. As for East Jerusalem, Israel could press ahead with the Judaization of its 'capital city' as it pleased. The exchange of letters on the subject, with Sadat and Begin each informing Carter of their respective official positions, and Carter informing them of his, out-Kissingered Kissinger in the boldness of its sophistry. It was left to Moshe Dayan, with his habitual candour, to size up the whole Camp David transaction. It would not be advisable, he said, to hold a public debate on Palestinian 'autonomy' because 'if the Egyptians understand Israel's real intentions on this matter they would not sign the peace treaty'.[90]

Sadat returned home to the usual hero's welcome. The 'battle of liberation' was now over, he said, and a 'new era, the battle of reconstruction' had begun. After an emergency session the Cabinet hailed Egypt's 'most marvellous victory in modern times'; it was bound to 'bring welfare and prosperity ... after years of bloodshed and destruction'. It was, of course, a victory for the Arabs too. In its first report on the Camp David agreement, *al-Ahram* devoted its entire front page to headlines, the upper two-thirds of them listing 'Palestinian gains' and the lower third 'Egyptian gains'. *Al-Akhbar* was categoric: 'Israel will withdraw from the West Bank and Gaza.'

The Arabs did not agree. They immediately saw through the 'comprehensive' cover. This time it was to be much easier for the Syrian-led bloc of Arab states to rally the non-committal ones in a broad pan-Arab coalition designed to stop Sadat—and the Americans too. For President Carter had immediately dispatched his Secretary of State to Amman and Riyadh. This was a *démarche* that merely underlined the obvious. These two capitals could exert a key influence for or against the Camp David accords—Jordan because, the cockpit of the Arab–Israeli conflict, it had been formally invited to participate in the Egyptian-led negotiations, and Saudi Arabia because of the unique authority, rooted mainly in immense wealth, which it commanded in inter-Arab counsels. While the Americans recognized one obvious fact, they failed—or at least behaved as if they had failed—to recognize another one: namely, that these so-called 'moderate', pro-Western countries could not possibly throw their weight behind Camp David, and that, even if they did, that would not be enough to bring the Arab world into line. They failed to recognize that there would come a point, somewhere down Sadat's lonely road, when, for their own security and ultimate survival, they would have to put their Arab obligations ahead of their American ones. That point had now been reached. To be sure, for them to make such a choice was dangerous in itself. But that merely served to underline a third obvious fact: that, by forcing them to make it, the Americans were doing a great disservice to their own friends and allies and, by extension, to their own interests in the area. Even before Vance arrived, both countries formally rejected Camp David; they deemed it a violation of the principles which, as a broad Arab consensus defined them, should underlie any 'comprehensive' settlement. Whereas King Hussein had found redeeming features in the pilgrimage to Jerusalem—notably its effect on world opinion—he found none in Camp David. As for the Saudis, they saw it as a body blow to their position as the guardian of Arab solidarity.

Others felt likewise. Indeed, the record showed that every Arab country from Bahrain to Mauretania passed some sort of judgement on Camp David—and that only one could be described as favourable. Of the three countries which had backed the Jerusalem pilgrimage, Sudan now confined itself to an ambivalent statement, seeming to approve and disapprove at the same time. Morocco reiterated its support for the Rabat summit conference of 1974, which had recognized the PLO as 'the sole, legitimate representative of the Palestinian people'. Only Oman remained faithful, and Sadat owed this lonely and hardly decisive tribute to the fact that the Sultanate was more beholden to a tottering Shah than to anyone else. For the first time in modern history, Egypt stood in one trench and virtually the entire Arab world in another.

Sadat's first response to the Arab outcry was a mixture of wishful thinking and weird arithmetic. 'Egypt alone is forty million; if we add President Numairi and the Sudan, that is twenty million; King Hassan and the people of Morocco another twenty million; and if we add Saudi Arabia, the United Arab Emirates, Somalia and *all the others* that means that more than 90 per cent of the Arab world supports us.' He also contended that he had the backing of the people most directly concerned. During the Camp David summit, he said, he 'could hear the same cries of our Arab women that I heard when I visited Jerusalem last November'. In any case, he would press on regardless, because he was determined to 'remove the suffering of those people under occupation'.

But then Sadat reverted to insults—insults which, this time, were more extreme and indiscriminate than ever. For all their disarray the Arabs, from the arch-conservatives of Saudi Arabia to the Marxist–Leninists of South Yemen, achieved a greater community of purpose, in their opposition to Camp David, than he or the Americans had expected. In Lebanon, the Israeli-assisted right-wing

Christian militias and the Syrian 'peace-keepers' fought another, desperate 'round', which the Saudis only succeeded in bringing under control with a supreme exertion of their inter-Arab diplomacy. Then the Iraqi Baathists, the one-time 'radicals' who were now the Saudis' closest collaborators, put in a bid for the Arab leadership which Sadat was throwing away. To this end President Saddam Hussein abandoned at a stroke long-held Baathist sanctities—such as the rejection of Security Council Resolution 242—and, in a spectacular easing of that most vicious of inter-Arab feuds, invited the rival Baathist leader, President Assad, to Baghdad, where he was greeted with a golden key to the city and proposals for a fresh attempt at Syrian–Iraqi unity.

Iraq hosted a plenary Arab summit in Baghdad. It was the first ever held in the absence of Egypt. Hitherto it had been Palestine—the more or less permanent emergency of Palestine—which had generated and perpetuated the theory and practice of collective Arab action, with Egypt as its mainstay. But with Egypt's threatened defection from the Arab world, the priority for everyone else was no longer the recuperation of Palestine—however the Arab consensus of the moment might define that evolving concept—it was the recuperation of Egypt. The 'common denominator' round which the participants managed to unite was a remarkably moderate one. President Sadat was not condemned as a traitor who had placed himself irrevocably beyond the pale. Syria would have liked that; but Saudi Arabia and Iraq would not have it. The conference sought to save Sadat from himself. It solemnly called on the 'government of Egypt to abandon these [Camp David] agreements and not to sign a peace treaty with the enemy'. If Sadat ignored the warning, political excommunication, and massive economic reprisals, would surely follow. If he heeded it, he could expect a rich reward. A special fund for 'front-line' Arab states would be set up; out of a total of £4·5 billion a year, Egypt would get £2·5 billion. The conference dispatched a special delegation to Cairo to tell him so.

The oil-rich Arabs had never questioned their obligation to preserve their most powerful but impoverished 'sister-state' from economic collapse. They did sometimes question the amount of cash that obligation entailed, the channels through which it was delivered, and the uses to which it was put. When relations with them were good Sadat would praise their generosity, when they were bad he would arraign them for their meanness. Egypt had certainly paid a high price to sustain the Arab 'war effort'. It did not really lend itself to precise calculation, but it tended to grow with every outbreak of anti-Arab propaganda. After Camp David it reached astronomical dimensions. According to *al-Akhbar*, Egypt had lost 100,000 men on the battlefield; 20 per cent of its financial resources went on the army and 36 per cent on the repayment of debts. The 1967 war and its consequences had cost Egypt no less than 60 billion dollars.[91]

Sadat's relations with his Arab paymasters were now worse than ever. Offered aid on a scale he had never been offered before, he turned it down with a fine show of outraged honour. He sent the summit emissaries packing. 'I welcome them', he announced, with heavy sarcasm, to the People's Assembly,

> but they won't meet me or any official . . . what counts with Egypt is morals and values. Egypt is not like other countries with a hundred million dollars making it decide one way, a hundred million another. . . . No, not a thousand million, not two thousand or hundreds of thousands of millions of dollars . . . can buy the will of Egypt. . . . They came from Baghdad thinking I was like Hafiz Assad, who can be bought with cheques, as you all know . . . or Hussein, who also is bought with cheques . . . our ears are closed to the hissing of vipers and we stand aloof from the antics of dwarves.

For King Hussein had now joined the 'dwarves'. He had failed to 'shoulder the responsibilities' which Camp David had laid upon him. Another epithet favoured by Sadat was 'paralytic'. And it pained him to see that not just King Hussein, but Crown Prince Fahd of Saudi Arabia and Sheikh Jabir Ahmad of Kuwait were putting themselves in the company of such 'paralytics' as Assad, Boumediène and Gadafi. The oil rulers were 'war profiteers who think that money is everything'. They put it in Jewish banks—for it was no secret that the Jews controlled the world's economy, newspapers and television—and 'I have to go and borrow your Arab money at twelve or fifteen per cent and pay the interest to the Jews.'[92] But they could not 'isolate' Egypt, because Egypt was the 'mind, heart and arm of the Arab nation'. On the contrary, it was Egypt which would isolate the others.[93]

Maybe the Arabs could not 'isolate' Egypt, but, trapped in his own logic, Sadat was isolating Egypt from the Arabs. For how could Egypt, with its '7,000 years of civilization', identify itself with people whose minds were 'sick', 'ossified', 'sunk in the middle ages', and 'incapable of rising to the spirit of the age'? Instead, it was identifying itself with the West. Unlike the Arabs, Sadat said, Egypt had benefited from a close relationship with Europe that reached way back into the nineteenth century. It was true that Egypt needed money for the 'battle of reconstruction', and, spurned by the Arabs, it was to that 'giant, that man of principles and integrity', President Carter, that he would turn. 'I want to tell you something... I shall ask President Carter for a Carter Plan, on the lines of the Marshall Plan, and I shall ask him openly, before the whole world, the Senate and the Congress.' According to *al-Ahram*, Sadat was looking for up to $15 billion-worth of economic aid from the United States in the five years following the signing of the treaty; it 'would perform miracles for the country'. And if Carter were not forthcoming?

> Shall we die.... You don't know Egypt at all.... If their crust is divided up into a million pieces the Egyptians are the happiest of people.... We despise with all our hearts those who have no values.... We don't respect the rich just because they are rich.... We shan't starve.... But we shall rely on our own exertions.... Our strength is here.... God be praised, we have land, water, sun, peasants and knowledge. We've got everything ... all we need is a little sweat and toil.[94]

Of necessity, Egypt was also beginning to identify itself with Israel. It was Anis Mansur who now argued that 'the peace treaty between Egypt and Israel is very much like a marriage in which the couple comes together for better or for worse'. The real problems always begin after marriage. Egypt and Israel would not be friends overnight; nor in ten years. The peace treaty was a declaration of good intentions which would inevitably be followed by differences and quarrels. But inter-Arab differences were much worse than those between Egypt and Israel. 'At least', Mansur argued, 'Egypt and Israel are trying to agree to understand each other, while the Arabs are doing their utmost to disagree with each other. It is not strange that the enemies of yesterday become the friends of tomorrow.' And the self-confessed admirer of Hitler's gas chambers went on to say that 'the Israeli in no way resembles the image of the puny, bald, hook-nosed Jew who would sell everything, even his honour, for a profit. This false picture was deliberately introduced into Egyptian culture to mask the Israeli problem.'[95]

Sure enough, the quarrels soon began—indeed, the very day after Camp David ended. At first it was more Begin versus Carter than it was Begin versus Sadat. It was the old story: those settlements in occupied territories. The peace treaty was due to be signed by 17 December. So when Begin assured his own public that the most he had agreed to at Camp David was to 'freeze' the establishment of new settlements until then, Carter immediately stepped in to set the record straight. Settlement activity was not merely to be 'frozen' for three months, but for a full five years until the 'final status' of the West Bank and Gaza had been decided, and, even after that, it would require the approval of all parties, including the Palestinians, to resume it. The Begin rejoinder was, as usual, swift and sharp; but he graciously promised to consult his own foreign and defence ministers. 'I will respect their better memories.' Nothing was heard of this consultation, but Moshe Dayan's views on settlement were: 'We must seize more land through the intermediary of the military government. The Prime Minister must give the order to the Minister of Defence, who, for his part, must order the sealing-off of the necessary areas. And if the Egyptians and Americans object? Well, we are not ready to sign a peace treaty which suits them alone. If they refuse to sign, too bad. What can they do? Kick us out?'[96]

The Israeli government contented itself with a 'thickening' of existing settlements for three months—and elaborated a five-year programme for the establishment of eighty-four new ones, accommodating 27,000 Jewish families at a cost of 54 billion Israeli pounds.[97] The Administration did nothing to stop it, although it was 'deeply disturbed' about this 'very serious matter'. Carter insisted that he had a 'very clear understanding' of what had been agreed. It seemed, however, that there had been 'an honest difference of opinion'. And he did not think that President Sadat would 'let any single element of a West Bank–Gaza settlement prevent the conclusion of a peace treaty'.

The Americans were less indulgent towards the PLO. After the Jerusalem pilgrimage it had been Zbigniew Brzezinski's 'bye-bye PLO'. Now Carter told a Pittsburg audience that the PLO reminded him of the Ku Klux Klan, the Communist party and the Nazis. 'There are many groups like this that cause us concern. . . . It would be nice for us if they would just go away.'

But in due course, the dispute turned primarily into an Israeli–Egyptian one. In response to Arab outrage, President Sadat had to establish that clear interdependence between the Israeli–Egyptian treaty and a 'comprehensive' peace that was missing from Camp David. If there was no linkage between Israeli withdrawal and the future of the West Bank and Gaza, he said on 20

November, that would constitute a separate peace, and he would never agree to it. He wanted a definite timetable for the establishment of 'autonomy' and while, at Camp David, it was agreed that full diplomatic relations should be established after the interim Sinai withdrawal—that was to say, nine months after the signing of the treaty—he now wanted a firmer tie-up between that and 'autonomy'. He also began to draw a distinction between the West Bank and Gaza, that little corner of Palestine which, until the 1967 war, fell under Egyptian administration, and insisted that 'if the treaty is not linked to Gaza at least, then it will not be acceptable to us'.[98] For their part, the Israelis insisted that the peace treaty should supersede all Arab alliances, to which, technically at least, Egypt remained a party.

Essentially, the Americans took Egypt's side. 'There is no doubt in my mind', said Carter on 9 November, 'or President Sadat's, or Mr Begin's, that one of the premises for the Camp David negotiations was a comprehensive peace settlement that includes not just an isolated peace treaty between Egypt and Israel, but includes a solution for the West Bank, Gaza and the Golan Heights.' On 16 December, he praised Sadat's 'generosity' and said that he had agreed to establish diplomatic relations with Israel as soon as it completed the interim Sinai withdrawal. Only the exchange of ambassadors would be delayed, and he described this schedule—which Israel had rejected—as 'reasonable'.

The deadline for the signing of the treaty, 17 December, came and went without the signing—which made Begin's collection of his Nobel Peace Prize just a week before, rather more ironic than it already was. At the ceremony in Akershus Castle in Oslo, he took his share of the joint award; at £40,000, it was some £10,000 more than the price that the British authorities, thirty years before, had put on his head as the most wanted terrorist in Palestine. Sadat refused to go to Oslo. He was piqued. He could hardly say so himself, though his press did. 'We refuse absolutely this incomprehensible sharing of the peace prize.' It was 'humanity's duty to acclaim President Sadat's courage and heroism. This duty was fulfilled, but, alas, so badly.'[99]

As for President Carter, he no longer disguised an exasperation that was directed squarely at Begin and the Israelis. In February 1979 the Egyptian Prime Minister Mustafa Khalil met Moshe Dayan at Camp David but what was left of 'the spirit of Camp David' the Israelis all but finished off with their rejection of Egyptian proposals that were favoured by the Americans. Carter then invited Begin to come

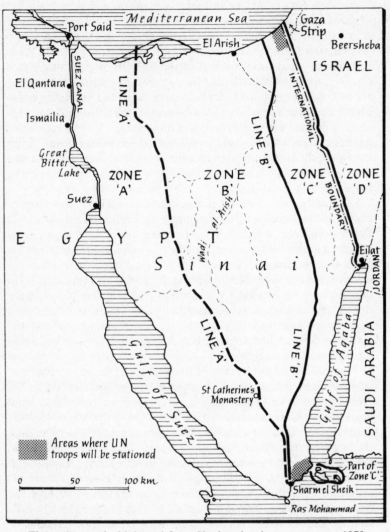

Three phases of withdrawal from Sinai under the peace treaty, 1979

to Camp David too. But since Sadat was not going, he would not do so either, for everyone knew that Khalil was only nominally his equivalent in rank. 'Why should I go?' he demanded of colleagues who suggested that he should, 'so I can say to the President of the United States, no, no, no, no! Why do I have to be the one to say no to Washington, when I can just as easily do it from Jerusalem?'[100] There had been no progress in the Khalil–Dayan talks, he asserted. 'A more extreme position' had been presented by the Egyptian delegation which 'nullified' the meaning of the peace treaty.

Carter publicly disagreed, and described the whole Middle East peace-making as 'one of the most difficult, frustrating and discouraging experiences' that he had ever had. 'It is most disgusting that we are that close and can't quite get it. We have come so close to the consummation of a peace agreement and we still have some absolutely insignificant difficulties that are now creating apparently insurmountable experiences.'

Begin agreed to see Carter, if he was not expected to see Mustafa Khalil too. He came to Washington in belligerent mood; the talks were in 'deep crisis', he said, and Israel would not be pushed into any 'sham treaty'. The deadlock was complete. The one great triumph of Carter's presidential career was about to collapse in ruins about him.

Something had to be done and, suddenly, on 4 March, it was. Carter put to Begin what American officials described as 'important and significant' new proposals. Begin instantly acknowledged that they were 'different' from earlier ones, and expressed the opinion that if they were accepted by Egypt then 'we shall be on our way to signing a peace treaty'. No sooner had Begin given his approval than the White House announced that President Carter himself would be leaving for the Middle East in two days' time. He was going to Egypt and Israel at the invitation of their leaders for 'talks that will focus upon the peace process, regional security and bilateral relations'.

This time, surely, it really had to be the ultimate procedural resources of Middle East peace-making; the ultimate gamble with the destiny of nations and their leaders. This time, apparently, not just the State Department, but most of the White House were against it. The risks of failure were simply too great. But Carter apparently reckoned he no longer had anything to lose. The Arab world instantly saw it as the last, despairing attempt to salvage a fundamentally bankrupt policy from the collapse it deserved. 'Acrobatics', 'exercise in futility', 'theatrics', 'a gamble with the prestige of the Presidency of the United States', clamoured Beirut newspapers of all political persuasions. To sustain this 'moveable Camp David'—as one promptly dubbed it—Carter was clearly counting on President Sadat and another eleventh-hour cave-in of the kind which saved the original one.

President Sadat welcomed the visit as a 'true reflection of American ethics and dedication to peace'. But he knew what was coming. The faithful Moussa Sabri reflected his views. Since Camp David, he said, Begin had tried every trick to escape from 'the cage of peace'. At the same time he was conducting an

odious campaign to ruin Carter's reputation, warning him day after day that the Zionist forces can vanquish him even in the White House, robbing him of his second presidential term; while the American administration has accustomed us to acting, growing enthusiastic and going the whole way with us . . . and then just as surely retreating step by step in the face of Zionist terrorism. For this reason I received the news of Carter's visit to Egypt with great caution, especially after Begin announced that he had agreed . . . to new American proposals. . . . When Begin agrees to proposals, it means that he thinks that they will fulfil his dreams of clinging to the land, that he reckons that Egypt will make a separate peace with him, that he imagines self-rule for the Palestinians will become a word without substance.

It was true that Carter had done all in his power for peace. But 'the enemy lurking in Israel has not yet risen to the responsibilities of peace, not yet shed worn-out ideas that cause it to believe that it can set the whole world ablaze for the furtherance of its ambitions. It still exploits the Zionist octopus in America, Europe and the Soviet Union to hinder all steps towards peace.'[101]

Upon his arrival in Egypt on Thursday, 8 March, Carter laid his proposals before Sadat. 'Linkage' had been frayed to the flimsiest of threads—incorporated in yet another of those non-contractual appendices, a joint letter from Begin and Sadat to Carter, which Begin could ignore if he chose, and which Sadat knew that he could ignore. The timetable for 'autonomy' no longer really was one at all. Within a month of the exchange of instruments of ratification, Egypt and Israel would begin negotiations for setting up an 'elected self-governing authority' in the West Bank and Gaza. They 'set themselves the goal' of completing them within one year so that elections could be held 'as expeditiously as possible' thereafter. Thus Israel was

318

under no *obligation* to complete the negotiations on time, while 'as expeditiously as possible' was at the mercy of its interpretation of the possible. The letter also 'confirm[ed] our understanding that the United States Government will participate fully in all stages of the negotiations'—which meant that the only leverage Sadat now commanded was that which the Americans cared to exert on his behalf.

Sadat made a last, pathetic stand for his proposal that, should 'autonomy' prove impossible on the West Bank, it should be established in Gaza first, and that Egypt should set up a 'liaison office' there. He still balked at fully fledged diplomatic recognition independent of progress on the 'comprehensive' front. And he put his foot down over Israel's new and outrageous demand—prompted by the fall of the Shah and the consequent drying up of Iranian oil supplies—that Egypt pledge itself, under the treaty, to grant it special access to Sinai oil.

When, on Saturday, 10 March, President Carter went on to Jerusalem, he put up *his* last, pathetic stand on Sadat's behalf. And it was pathetic. Begin was unbending to the end. 'Why does Sadat want to establish a liaison office in the Gaza Strip all of a sudden?' he demanded. 'This is nothing less than a clear violation of the Camp David agreements.' The Israelis' opinion, in the words of General Ariel Sharon, was that 'from such a liaison office a Palestine state will grow within a month.'[102] Begin continued to insist on preferential oil supplies.

The following morning President Carter was invited to chair a meeting of the Israeli cabinet, an honour never before bestowed on a visiting foreigner. The most hectic days of Carter's career, and among the most critical for the future of the Middle East, and perhaps for the world, were replete with flatteries of the kind—and by public utterances whose banality, insincerity and grandiloquence were matched only by the acrimony of the behind-the-scenes wrangling. It was the ghastly, tasteless climax of shuttle-cum-television diplomacy.

During that cabinet meeting, it appears that Carter all but lost his temper.

The chances of peace were slipping away in front of his eyes. Frustration and disappointment were clearly registered on his face. 'I cannot return from Israel empty-handed. You must sign,' pleaded Carter angrily. His tone surprised the ministers. There was silence for a second and then Begin spoke. 'Mr President, you will

319

excuse us, but we must tell you that we will only sign what we want to sign and that we will not sign what we do not want to sign.'[103]

At a state banquet that night, which opened with a performance of Beethoven's Spring Sonata for violin and piano, Israeli President Itzhak Navon proposed a toast to Carter's 'sincerity, nobility and warm personality'. Then it was Begin's turn to speak. 'It is my duty to say', he declared, 'that we have serious problems to solve before we can sign this peace treaty.' Some Israeli politicians, reported the *New York Times*, 'gasped aloud as he spoke', and 'Mr Carter's face turned grim and ashen. He looked as pained as if he had been struck.'[104] It seemed to be all over.

Carter was due to leave the next day, Monday, 12 March. The airport was being prepared for his departure. The guard of honour had already arrived. He himself was on the way back from the Knesset to the King David Hotel to pack his bags. But then it happened once more. One of those last-minute changes of plan. A personal initiative by Moshe Dayan and he agreed to stay an extra day. Yet again, that Monday night, it seemed to be all over. Presidential spokesman Jody Powell said that Carter would be leaving Jerusalem without an agreement, returning via Cairo to brief President Sadat. For CBS, Walter Cronkite reported from the King David that the great gamble had failed. John Chancellor and Barbara Walters did likewise for NBC and ABC. Next morning, Tuesday, 13 March, as Air Force One left Bengurion Airport, hundreds of journalists continued to assume that he was going home a deeply disappointed man. And in Cairo the newspapers were full of gloom and foreboding. 'If peace is not born', said *al-Gumhuriyah*, 'the whole world and the US in particular should give chase to the culprit who committed this crime against humanity.'

What no one knew was that Cyrus Vance and Zbigniew Brzezinski had woken Carter up at three o'clock on Tuesday morning to show him the latest formulations they had worked out with the Israelis: Egypt agrees to exchange ambassadors immediately after the interim Sinai withdrawal; the Gaza 'liaison' office will be among the subjects to be discussed between Egypt and Israel in the 'autonomy' talks; the United States guarantees to sell Israel oil for fifteen years if Egypt refuses to do so. And over breakfast five-and-a-half hours later, Carter and Begin had clinched the deal.

The meeting between Carter and Sadat took place at Cairo Airport. It lasted two-and-a-half hours and as it drew to a close television cameramen were invited in to witness Carter speaking to Begin on the telephone. When the two leaders emerged, they strode down a long red carpet. Carter said that he had 'an extremely important' announcement to make. He was quite expressionless as he made it. Begin and Sadat, he said, had both accepted the latest American proposals for resolving outstanding issues. 'I am convinced that now we have defined all of the main ingredients of a peace treaty between Egypt and Israel and which will be the cornerstone of a comprehensive peace in the Middle East.' As Carter spoke, Sadat stood silent at his side and then, still without a word from the Egyptian leader, the two advanced a few more paces down the carpet, stood to attention for the national anthems and reviewed an Egyptian guard of honour.

A peace treaty it was. The *Washington Post* waxed even more lyrical—if that were possible—than it had over Camp David: 'an extraordinary—and humbling—achievement' reached by Carter's 'transcendent vision and steadiness'. But a 'cornerstone of a comprehensive peace in the Middle East' it definitely was not. Through sheer will-power and ruthless fixity of purpose, Begin had stripped it of every ingredient that might have made it one, and, in that final, humiliating airport bargain, Sadat had abdicated every position but one: Egypt's right to dispose as it saw fit of its own natural resources, of the produce of a few paltry, half-exhausted Sinai oilfields.

On the wan, wintry afternoon of Monday, 26 March 1979, Anwar Sadat and Menachim Begin met on the White House lawn to sign the historic treaty. President Carter appended his signature as witness. For some reason President Sadat failed to read page seven of his prepared address. It contained a passage that called for justice for the Palestinians. It was an appropriate omission. The betrayal of the Palestinians lay at the heart of this separate peace which he swore he would never sign.

7

Epilogue

The Arab boycott of Egypt

According to President Sadat, of course, it was not a separate peace. However, almost the entire Arab world concluded that it was. Indeed, it was perceived as an historic calamity, the lineal descendant of those earlier ones—the Sykes–Picot Agreement, the Balfour Declaration, the rise of Israel and the 1967 war—which had befallen the Arabs in the twentieth century. It put the very concept of an Arab nation in jeopardy. For here was Egypt, the great power of the Arab world, opting out of it altogether, allying itself with the Zionist intruder and enormously enhancing its ability to disrupt what was left of the existing Arab order.

The Arabs could not but react with all the vigour at their command. At the Baghdad summit in November 1978 they had served warning on Sadat. Now they re-assembled in the Iraqi capital to make that warning good. Once again the Americans tried to keep their Arab friends in line, to prevent the so-called 'moderates' from joining the 'radicals' in outright opposition to the peace treaty. President Carter's National Security Adviser, Zbigniew Brzezinski, descended on Amman and Riyadh. King Hussein openly accused him of 'arm-twisting'. 'I don't think', he said, 'there has ever been in the past a misunderstanding like the one that exists now between Jordan and the United States.' Even the devoutly anti-communist Saudi press likened American behaviour to the aggressive European colonialism, the gunboat diplomacy, of the nineteenth century.

To the consternation of Egyptians and Americans, the Saudis threw their formidable weight behind sanctions which excommunicated Sadat and attempted to reconcile maximum damage to his regime with minimum hardship for the Egyptian people. All aid of an official nature was suspended. Diplomatic relations were severed. Egypt was expelled from the Arab League and specialized institutions such as the Arab Organization of Petroleum Exporting Countries and the Arab Fund for Economic and Social Development. The Arab Organization for Industry, the Egyptian-based armaments corporation financed by the oil-producers, was disbanded. Saudi Arabia withdrew the funds it had promised for Egypt's purchase of American fighter aircraft.

There was much opposition to the peace treaty inside Egypt itself. True, the People's Assembly overwhelmingly approved it. But that had been a foregone conclusion. For since his pilgrimage to Jerusalem Sadat had pushed through—by referendum—yet another re-organization of his 'freedom and democracy'. A challenge to his authority had arisen from the resurgent *Wafd*, the pre-revolutionary nationalist party; he had struck back with such crippling restrictions on its activities that it had decided to disband itself altogether. He had also decreed the formation of a brand-new loyalist party, the National Democrats, and then asked some of its members to 'volunteer' for service in what he called his 'honest opposition', the Socialist Labour Party. So parliament was now even more unrepresentative than it had been at the time of the Uprising of Thieves.

More significant than parliament's massive vote in favour was the dissent of a small minority. Mumtaz Nasser, a former *Wafdist* and respected legal authority, led thirteen deputies, representing various political persuasions, in opposition to the treaty. It *was* a separate peace, they insisted. It deprived Egypt of sovereignty over Sinai. As for the presence of an Israeli embassy in Cairo before the full withdrawal of enemy troops from Egyptian territory, that was 'reminiscent of the position of the British High Commissioner in Egypt'. They refuted the government's contention that the treaty would spare Egyptian lives and ease the burden of military expenditure. The government itself had announced the dispatch of military missions to eight African countries; military spending had continued to rise; resources that should have been invested in development projects had been diverted to the army; and of the $1,800 million in American aid which the treaty had brought with it $1,500 million would go towards 'keeping the army happy'.

The real test of opinion lay outside parliament altogether. And there, insofar as they could make their voices heard at all, every leading politician, party, faction or group raised them against the treaty. Moslem fundamentalists, declaring that any peace with Israel was 'contrary to Islam', called for a *jihad* against the 'usurpers'. The *Wafd* opposed it because, among other things, it had not been put to the people for proper scrutiny and debate. The Nasserists called on Egyptians to confront 'those who are leading us down a blind alley in the name of peace, prosperity and stability'. The communists denounced this 'shameful surrender to American imperialism and its Zionist ally'. Among the most important of the many tracts and manifestos which could not find their way into the state-controlled press was one from four surviving Free Officers—Zakariah Muhyieddin, Kamaluddin Hussein, Abdul Latif Boghdadi and Hussein Shafi—who accused their former comrade-in-arms of sacrificing both Egyptian sovereignty and the Palestinian cause, severing Egypt from its Arab environment, aspiring to play the role of gendarme for the United States, and bringing the Egyptian economy under the thumb of international Zionism. In short, they said, Israel had got 'absolutely everything' and Egypt 'absolutely nothing'. Never had Islam and the Arab nation known 'so grave a crisis as that which we face today'.

Confronted with this opposition President Sadat had little choice but to press ahead regardless on three main fronts—to persist in the contention that he really had laid the basis of a just peace for the Palestinians, to bring 'prosperity' to the Egyptians, to defy, denigrate and divide the Arabs, and, above all, to put his faith in the Americans.

No voice louder than the peace

Camp David would of course remain incomplete until the second of its two components, the Framework for Peace in the Middle East, had been filled in to the satisfaction of Arabs and Palestinians. In principle, at least, President Sadat acknowledged this. That it would be, provided everyone showed the necessary good will and common sense, he doggedly insisted; that it could not be was a possibility he refused to admit. And he sought to sustain the illusion by the simple expedient of denying anyone the right to challenge it.

Prime Minister Mustafa Khalil prepared the ground for him when, upon the publication of the text of the treaty in Egypt, he told parliament that to call it a separate peace was a downright lie. It was a triumph for Egypt and the Palestinians. The Israelis would evacuate Jerusalem and all the occupied territories, and dismantle their illegal

324

settlements; the Palestinians would establish a state in their place.

'Dr Khalil,' came Mr Begin's disdainful rejoinder in the Knesset next day, 'I inform you that Israel will never return to the borders of 4 June 1967. Dear and honourable Dr Khalil, please note this: Jerusalem, the united, the one and only, is the eternal capital of Israel. It will never be divided, and this is how it will remain for generation upon generation. Dr Khalil, a state called Palestine will never be established in Judea, Samaria and Gaza.' Autonomy was for the inhabitants only, not for the territories on which they lived. The settlements would continue—ten new ones were announced on the eve of the treaty signing—because Israel had 'a perfect right to settle anywhere in the land'. And just in case Begin had not made himself sufficiently clear, his government subsequently spelled it all out in a twenty-point statement, laying down, among other things, that Israel would retain control of public land, water, internal security and all the major economic functions such as taxation and customs.

President Sadat could not silence Mr Begin, or his Arab adversaries, but he could and did try to silence his domestic critics. This required yet another referendum. On 19 April, the people were asked to say yes or no to peace. According to the official count, 90·2 per cent of the electorate turned out to do so, and of those 99·95 per cent said yes. There is no doubt that the treaty did enjoy much popular support. Peace held the promise of a better life; it was a supremely emotive issue; it lent itself to demagogy and manipulation; in offering it, Sadat had a built-in advantage over all those who, however cogent their reasons, rejected it. It is therefore not impossible that had Sadat consulted the people in an open, authentically democratic fashion, he would have triumphed over his detractors. But it was no such consultation. Even if the referendum results had not been falsified— and those who took an interest in such matters reckoned the turn-out at no more than 10 per cent—not much confidence could be placed in one measure of public opinion when another one, the attitude taken by almost every political party and personality in the land, yielded such contrary results. Not content merely with the extra-parliamentary mandate which the referendum furnished, Sadat also used it to punish an Assembly which, with those thirteen 'no' votes, had 'exploited democracy, undermined democratic rule, dragging the country back to autocratic rule and domination by power centres'. Accordingly, in the same referendum, the people were asked whether the Assembly should be dissolved—two years ahead of schedule and just after it had overwhelmingly endorsed the treaty; 99·9 per cent said it should. In the election campaign that followed, it was forbidden to debate the treaty on the ground that all but 5,000 out of 40 million people had already approved it. Anything resembling an authentic opposition was yet further emasculated. Only one of the thirteen nay-sayers, Mumtaz Nasser, was re-elected. Illegally harassed and hounded, the National Progressive Unionists lost their last two seats. But in a press conference afterwards, the party's leader, Khalid Muhyieddin, was able to point out that, though he had lost, in his constituency alone he had secured twice as many votes as had supposedly been cast against the treaty in the country as a whole.

Sadat was not entirely secure from domestic attack. The critics found various, sometimes quasi-legal means of making their opinions known. But he felt secure enough to press ahead with the 'peace process' as if he really did believe that it could be brought to a successful conclusion. So Egypt entered into negotiations to attain the unattainable, a Palestinian autonomy which, with wonderful sophistry, Camp David took away even as it conferred it. The negotiations began on 26 May 1979, making 26 May 1980 the 'target' date for their completion.

To no one's surprise, the Palestinians, in whose name they were conducted, stayed away. Sadat took this in his stride. 'I am custodian for the West Bank and Gaza. Why? Because these poor people don't have a custodian. . . . The PLO is composed of ten or twenty groups each accusing the other of treason, so it cannot be custodian. . . .' As for Jordan, though officially entitled under Camp David to join the autonomy talks, it had disqualified itself by its 'betrayal' of the Palestinians. Syria? Sadat was not even ready to talk about it. 'Never! Not with those dirty Alawites and Baathists in power . . . famous for their envy, spite, impotence and ignorance', who had 'sold the Golan'.[1] The opposition of the Arabs in general he likened to the 'idolatry and polytheism faced by the prophets of olden times'.[2]

So, with the United States as their 'partner', the Israelis and Egyptians negotiated alone. The talks limped along, staggered, fell, picked themselves up. There was no discernible progress. To every Egyptian proposal of which they disapproved—that the 'self-governing authority' should have legislative powers, that the inhabitants of East Jerusalem should participate in elections to it, that Egypt should set up a 'liaison office' in Nablus and Gaza—Begin and his autonomy negotiators had a standard retort: 'Camp David did not provide for that.' They were right. It did not. By August, the chief Egyptian negotiator, Prime Minister Mustafa Khalil, was complaining that, at this rate, 250 sessions would be needed to reach ageement; Foreign Ministry officials spoke of the 'hundred years negotiations'. Sadat himself complained from time to time that the Israelis were not playing the game, that Begin was sabotaging his peace mission, that he wanted 'to stop in the middle of the road'.[3] On this at least he had public opinion behind him. For while sentiment might still be running in favour of peace, there was diminishing forbearance, in both official and popular quarters, of this obstinate, ungrateful enemy with whom it had been made. As 'normalization' proceeded, things Israeli were spontaneously shunned. Dr Butros Ghali, the Minister of State for Foreign Affairs, complained to a friend that he spent most of his time receiving Israeli visitors 'because no other Egyptian official wants to deal with them'.[4]

Yet, for all his impatience, Sadat would always fall back, magnanimous and serene, on his philosopher-statesman's pose. His traditional birthday broadcast from Mit Abul Kom was an appropriate occasion for that. On Christmas Eve 1979, he assured his people that he was 'optimistic' about the autonomy talks. All issues would be settled on time. If, to a sceptical public, that sounded more like faith than optimism, al-Ahram hastened to confirm that that, indeed, is what it was. It was 'the voice of faith . . . and the voice of faith is stronger than all obstacles'. Had people forgotten Sadat's last Christmas message? Did they not remember that then, too, they had been pessimistic because the peace treaty had not yet been signed, though the deadline for doing so had passed? That Sadat had none the less assured them that all would be well in the end? 'A man of faith knows his way and defines his objectives with precision. . . . Sadat's statements came true. The peace treaty *was* signed in March . . . three months after the deadline.'[5] Perhaps, the sceptics suggested, even the faithful al-Ahram was being ironic.

Sadat would praise the Israelis as often as he admonished them. In the midst of one particularly violent tirade against the Arabs, he said that they had 'honestly and faithfully' fulfilled their treaty obligations.[6] If, in fact, they had, it was only because, pressing ahead with 'normalization', Egypt was sticking to its part of the Camp David bargain. In this, however, Sadat had found reason to go faster, and offer more, than the treaty required of him, in accordance with the principle, enunciated before the autonomy talks began, that 'for every step Israel takes, we shall take two, to encourage her'.[7]

If Sadat had had his way ambassadors would have been exchanged, and frontiers opened, well ahead of schedule. Only bureaucracy and the dissuasions of his Foreign Ministry had prevented it. It was during a visit to Haifa in September 1979, aboard what was once King Farouk's yacht, that Sadat made his most generous offer. In expansive mood, he tilted again his cornucopia of concessions, and into Begin's lap there fell agreement to sell Israel 2 million tons of oil a year to compensate for the loss of the Sinai oilfields it had been exploiting for twelve years. Sadat would also ensure the rapid development of economic and cultural relations. And he invited the 250,000 inhabitants of Haifa to visit the port city of Alexandria with which they had been 'twinned'.

Back home, Egyptians were astonished. But there was more to come. In a bout of uncontrollable affection for the people of Haifa—he was later to confide that he had fallen in love with them—he told a group of Israeli newspaper editors: 'I am planning to bring the Nile water—this is the sweetest of the four big rivers of the whole world—to Sinai. Well, why not send you some of this sweet water to the Negev Desert as good neighbours? Sinai is on the border with the Negev. Why not? Lots of possibilities, lots of hope.'[8] For Egyptians the Nile is more than just their most precious natural resource, it is the giver of life, enjoying since ancient times a sacred, almost god-like character, and for Sadat to lavish its bounty on the mortal enemy of yesterday seemed more than presumptuous, it was blasphemous. Not a word was said about it on the radio or in the 'free press', but all politically minded Egyptians rely heavily on foreign radio stations anyway, and by the time Sadat's plane touched down in Cairo, a campaign of protest was underway. Proving much less pliant than expected, Sadat's own 'honest opposition', the Socialist Labour Party, took a prominent part in it; its weekly newspaper al-Shaab warmed to the patriotic theme, 'The Nile is threatened', with hardly less vigour than the semi-clandestine broadsheets, manifestos and, later, the full-length book which rehearsed Zionist designs on the river since the turn of the century.

Sadat enlisted Anis Mansur, the editor of October magazine, in an attempt to still the protests. Mansur's approach was to raise the whole issue to a higher, religious plane that was in keeping both with the 'peace mission' and the sanctity of the Nile. Ignoring the offer to irrigate the Negev—just rumours, officials were saying—Mansur reported that what Sadat had actually done was to propose, 'in the name of Egypt and the holy al-Azhar [Cairo's great centre of Islamic learning] that the Nile water should become a Zemzem [the sacred well in Mecca] for the faithful of the three religions. It would be one more proof of Egypt's commitment to peace.'[9] Sadat embroidered on that theme in his Christmas message; what he really wanted, he explained, was to send the Nile up to Jerusalem as a means of bringing the Israeli and the Palestinian people together 'so that we can all live in peace'.[10]

Jerusalem—whose ultimate status Camp David had, in effect, simply ignored—overshadowed the autonomy talks as the target date approached. In March Sadat warned that if the talks were not finished on time it would create 'a new situation'.[11] In May, another round of talks proved so barren that even Sol Linowitz, the American negotiator and a career optimist, conceded that it was 'not inaccurate to say that President Carter is not wholly satisfied'. Then, on 12 May, reacting to what he considered to be a Begin ultimatum, Sadat suspended the talks indefinitely, only to say five days later, under pressure from the Americans, that, although 'the gulf is very wide', he would allow them to resume, because 'nothing would please Begin more than for me to say I don't want to negotiate'.[12] Even as he was saying that, in the course of a four-hour keynote address to the nation, deputy Geula Cohen, a nationalist fanatic, was introducing a bill, adopted by the Knesset, that would declare Jerusalem Israel's united and indivisible capital. Sadat suspended the talks again. But on 26 May there was no sign of the new situation he had warned of in March. On the contrary, he considered that the peace process had become irreversible. 'It will never collapse', he told the *Washington Post*, 'for the very simple reason that between Egypt and Israel there is a treaty now, there are good relations, there is good neighbourliness, there is a table around which we sit . . .'[13]

Taking over the premiership himself, Sadat appointed a Foreign Minister for the first time since Ibrahim Kamil had resigned the post during Camp David. This was Defence Minister General Kemal Hassan Ali. Hitherto responsible for normalization, he had proved himself even more flexible than Butros Ghali and a Foreign Ministry team which, having carried on where so many others had given up in despair, could hardly be taxed with intransigence. The Americans confidently assured the Egyptians that they had 'reason to believe' that the Knesset vote on Jerusalem would be quietly shelved for the time being.[14] In the company of General Ali and his Israeli counterpart, Sol Linowitz announced in Washington on 3 July that the talks would be resumed in the form of specialized committees. President Carter then received the trio in the Oval Room of the White House. Television recorded the scene. For it was hardly a secret: the purpose of resuming the talks was less to achieve a highly improbable breakthrough in the Middle East than to secure Carter's re-election.

Then, on 30 July, within a fortnight of their resumption, the Knesset solemnly voted the Jerusalem bill into 'fundamental law', provoking Arab outrage, a Saudi call to *jihad* and worldwide condemnation. In a letter to Begin, Sadat said that the law deprived the talks of all meaning, and he suspended them for the third time. But so great was Carter's need of proof that his one great foreign-policy triumph had life in it yet now Sadat was prepared, overruling even the accommodating General Ali, once again to oblige him. He let the talks resume on the understanding that, re-installed in the White House, Carter would convene another Camp David.

American elections are not Egyptian referendums, and, decidedly, Sadat was unlucky: first Nixon, then Ford, and now Carter. Sadat felt no loss as deeply as this one. He had to start all over again with Ronald Reagan. This time the talks really were indefinitely suspended. And then he suffered another setback at home. In early 1981, his 'honest opposition', which had hitherto given its conditional support to the peace treaty, now withdrew it altogether on the ground that Israel had annexed Jerusalem and was continuing to establish settlements on occupied territory.

But Sadat could not risk any threat to the one great objective of his separate peace: Israeli withdrawal from Sinai. In August 1981, in Alexandria, he met Begin for the eleventh time. According to the latter, it took the two men thirty seconds to agree on an eventual resumption of the talks. They had not even consulted the Americans. Sadat also agreed to facilitate the process of normalization in those areas, such as tourism, where, according to the peace treaty, he had no hard-and-fast obligation to produce results. Sadat's compliance had not been engendered by concessions from the other side—far from it. Re-installed as Prime Minister after general elections in June, Begin had formed a coalition government whose programme laid down that after Palestinian autonomy had run its pre-ordained five-year course (if it ever did) Israel would claim sovereignty over the West Bank and Gaza. Begin had gone to Alexandria amid hints that, if Sadat did not do all that was expected of him, Israel might renege on the third and final phase of the Sinai withdrawal, due to be completed by April 1982.

Sadat's only consolation was to indulge his penchant for symbolic projects in keeping with the higher spiritual significance of his peace mission. Not that he had much success with these either. They were all associated with Mount Sinai or, as Jewish tradition calls it, Mount Moses. He had hoped that the Pope and the world's spiritual leaders would attend the signing of the peace treaty there, or subsequent commemorations of it. But he had been disappointed. Even Begin had declined; it was not certain, he said, that Moses really did receive the Ten Commandments there, and in any case he was not going to climb the mountain 'on a donkey'.[15]

Sadat set his heart on a tri-confessional complex at the foot of Mount Sinai combining mosque, church and synagogue all in one. But the plans for it, and for the accompanying 'tourist village', are still at the drawing-board stage. The cost of this ecumenical temple of peace is estimated at some $60 million, and he had to launch a 'world appeal' for funds.[16] One project that *has* been completed was the brainchild, not of Sadat, but of a Belgian artist whose peculiarity is that he can only express himself creatively on a gigantic scale. Describing himself as 'a man of the soil and the word', as 'peasant and writer', who considered 'the earth the source of all life', Sadat enthusiastically supported Jean Verame's ambition to paint Sinai blue.[17] So the Plain of Hallaoui, all 25 square miles of it, is now the largest painted surface on earth. Using 3 tons of undercoat and 10 tons of finishing, Verame and his three assistants have covered whole rock masses in the colour of heavenly peace, with black and occasional red thrown in, and 'marked' others with various motifs— dashes, circles, whorls and parallel lines—isolated or in series, from 1 inch in size to 10 yards. The artist hopes that the special non-biodegradable paint, acrylic, will withstand sun and sand for 150 years. As for himself, Sadat established the latest of his 'resthouses' on Mount Sinai, where he frequently repaired for prayer and meditation. This hallowed spot was also intended to be his final resting place; for it is there that he moved the tomb which he had originally constructed for himself in Mit Abul Kom.

Peace but no prosperity

Not only during the elections to the new Assembly had it been forbidden to discuss the peace treaty; issues affecting 'national unity and social peace' had also been placed under ban. Rigorously interpreted, that had removed from public scrutiny economic and social policies which, with the 'national' issue now resolved, assumed pre-eminent importance. Just as Sadat had made sure that parliamentary opponents of the treaty were all but eliminated, so, too, he disposed of the only 'legal' party, the National Progressive Unionists, likely to present a systematic challenge to the theory and practice of *Infitah*.

Other oppressive enactments followed. The most remarkable was the so-called Law of Shame, drafted, upon Sadat's express instructions, to 'protect the rights of the people and the political, economic, social and moral constituents—including the genuine traditions—of the society of the Egyptian family'. Among the 'crimes' punishable under this law were 'advocating any doctrine that implies negation of divine teachings or which does not conform with the tenets thereof'; 'allowing children or youth to go astray by advocating the repudiation of popular, religious, moral or national values or by setting a bad example in a public place'; 'broadcasting or publishing false or misleading news or information which could inflame public opinion, generate envy and hatred or threaten national unity and social peace'; 'broadcasting or publishing gross or scurrilous words or pictures which could offend public sensibilities or undermine the dignity of the state . . .' Endangering public property, squandering public funds, abusing power, directly or indirectly influencing the prices of basic commodities and accepting bribes also fell into the category of 'shameful' crimes. The Socialist Public Prosecutor, a kind of Grand Inquisitor appointed by the President and answerable to the People's Assembly and its Committee of Values, had exclusive jurisdiction over the investigation and indictment of offenders. He was empowered to bar them from public life, from engaging in economic activity or managing their own property; he could condemn them to internal exile or prohibit them from leaving the country. These penalties were applicable for five years, or, in the case of backsliders, ten.

In passing this law on 29 April 1980, the People's Assembly had also approved other amendments to the constitution which established the *Shari'a*, or Islamic jurisprudence, as the source of all legislation, created a 132-member *Shoura*, or consultative council, one-third appointed by Sadat and two-thirds elected by the Assembly, with final say over matters of internal policy, and made Sadat President for life. A nationwide groan went up when it was announced that the amendments were to be endorsed by yet another referendum. According to the official count, 98·56 per cent of the electorate said 'yes' to all they were asked to approve. This was even more miraculous than usual. For, apart from the loyalist majority which ensured its automatic passage through parliament, everyone, including the 'honest opposition', had denounced the Law of Shame as 'an act of shame'. Virtually the entire Christian community (three million by official reckoning but seven million and more according to the church authorities) was known to be uncompromisingly opposed to the Islamicization of the legal system. It could safely be said that the political opposition, the judiciary, the intelligentsia and much of the public at large objected to life presidency for Sadat. They also objected to the whole concept of the referendum, or Sadat's incessant resort to it as a means of lending spurious popular legitimacy to his own arbitrary, and increasingly autocratic rule.

In May 1980 an impressive, non-partisan body of leading citizens charged Sadat with superseding his own constitution. 'The style in which Egypt is governed today' [their manifesto declared], 'is not based on any specific form of government. While it is not outright dictatorship, nazism or fascism, neither is it a democracy nor even a pseudo-democracy. It has become pointless to discuss any decision, whether it is to support or criticize it, for no sooner is a random decision taken in one direction than it is replaced by another in a different direction.' Referendums and other arbitrary practices had

> paralyzed the country's constitutional bodies, disrupted the apparatus of government, rendered support or opposition irrelevant, stripped the people of their supervisory function, opened the door to exploitation, laxity and shirking of responsibility and created a climate of anxiety, confusion and instability. The state, with the vast machinery of government at its disposal, has become unable to think, plan or implement.... We consider that this style of government must cease forthwith.[18]

It was not surprising that Sadat kept his 'freedom and democracy' under so tight a rein. He continued to face alarming problems, not the least of which was the growth of Islamic fundamentalism, as well as friction between Christians and Moslems, which, though it had been exaggerated and exacerbated by the regime for its own purposes, was threatening to get out of hand. In mid-June 1981 scores of people were killed and injured, dozens of houses destroyed and three churches set ablaze during confessional disturbances in three Cairo suburbs. Two-and-a-half months later President Sadat ordered the biggest round-up of his opponents since he came to power. Moslem fundamentalists bore the brunt of it. At least 1,500 people according to the official figure—far more according to unofficial reports—were arrested, including Omar Talmasani, the 'supreme guide' of the

Moslem Brotherhood, Sheikh Abdul Hamid Kishk, a blind, fiery and very popular preacher, and hundreds of like-minded militants. For balance, Sadat withdrew his 'recognition' of the Coptic Pope, Shenoudeh III, banished him to a desert monastery and arrested several bishops and priests. In a snap referendum the people were asked whether they were for or against his 'measures [including sentences for up to life imprisonment or hard labour for membership of an illegal religious party] to safeguard national unity and social peace'.

The confessional strife was the unmistakable symptom of a deeper malaise. The causes were familiar enough. With the peace treaty signed, the people had been assured that, this time, the long-promised prosperity, the economic Crossing, really was at hand. Sadat himself had been as specific as he had been emphatic. There were going to be 'radical' solutions, he said, to those two most urgent of problems: food and housing. 'It is not enough to say that we shall reclaim 20,000 *feddans* a year, or 50,000. No. It must be 300,000 *feddans*, with the most up-to-date technology.... It is not enough to build 100,000 units a year; it must be a million.' The two problems had to be solved 'for ever' within five years.[19] Yet, except on a superficial reckoning, prosperity remained as remote a prospect as ever.

Needless to say, press and radio obeyed instructions to produce tangible evidence of the fruits of peace; they said that Western aid was coming in; that Arab visitors had not been deterred; and that the world was jostling at the door to invest in Egypt. While it is true that there were positive developments, on the whole these were easy, automatic achievements which owed as much to good luck as to good management. The gross national debt continued to rise, but, for the first time since the early years of the Revolution, Egypt escaped the crippling burden of a more or less permanent balance-of-payments crisis. The drying up of Arab funds was offset by the sudden influx of others, largely as a consequence of peace. Apart from Western aid—running at about $2 billion a year—there fell into this category four main hard-currency earners. The recovery of the Sinai oilfields, and the high prices which Egypt could command, raised oil revenues from $312 million in 1976, when the country first became a net exporter, to $2·85 billion in 1980. The Suez Canal, expanded to accommodate supertankers, and tourism brought in $700 million each. Ironically, however, the most remarkable windfall was not merely unrelated to the peace, it was the Arabs who made it possible. Their own insatiable need for imported labour as much as their concern for the welfare of the Egyptian people meant that, in punishing Sadat for his separate peace, the Arabs had done nothing to stem the flow of Egyptian manpower from the Delta to the boom towns of the Gulf. In the long run, the continuing exodus, unprecedented in the history of uniquely sedentary people, could not but inflict further damage on the social and economic fabric of the country, but, undeniably attractive as a short-term palliative, it yielded a revenue in remittances which had risen from a mere $189 million in the first year of *Infitah* to $2·7 billion in 1980. Naturally, over the same period, Egyptian imports had soared too, from $1·4 billion to more than $8 billion. But in 1980, government economists could boast what, a couple of years before, would have seemed a wildly improbable accomplishment, an authentic balance-of-payments surplus.

Sounder finances, fortuitously achieved, did not necessarily mean a sounder economy. They could and should have. They should have furnished a breathing space in which to carry out those structural reforms which alone could generate real, enduring, all-round progress. In the event, they seemed only to have furnished a breathing space for deferring them. Sadat refrained from 'biting the bullet' as Western economic orthodoxy would have had him do in spite, or because, of the relatively favourable conditions for doing so. He did not cut back on consumption. He took neither from those who could afford it nor from those who could not. The fair and efficient taxation which, in the aftermath of the great food riots, he had made his top priority proved so illusory that, at the end of 1980, tax evasion in Cairo alone was officially estimated at £E500 million a year.[20] He did not reduce subsidies—hardly surprisingly, since, according to the Minister of Finance, 40 per cent of their principal component, the wheat allocation, was continuing to disappear or fall into the wrong hands;[21] on the contrary, he raised them, so that, at £E1·5 billion in 1980, they were nearly three times what they had been when, in January 1977, he had attempted to cut them in half. In any case, whatever remedial policies he might have adopted, a system so gangrenous could not have been enforced. So it was more of the same, more drift and *laissez-aller*, punctuated, when things were manifestly deteriorating, by bouts of presidential interventionsim as ineffectual as it was impetuous and theatrical.

The year 1980, Sadat had never tired of forecasting, would see 'the end of all our troubles'. But less than halfway through it, he apparently realized that it would not. Suddenly, in April and May, he began talking about the 'appalling problems' the people faced, the 'food shortages' and the 'soaring prices'. The first part of 1980 had in fact witnessed bread shortages for the first time in living memory and an overall inflation rate officially estimated at 30 per cent. 'Everything, everything', Sadat lamented, 'is being absorbed in higher prices.' He promised that on 15 May, the ninth anniversary of his corrective Revolution, 'the battle to come to grips with all our problems will begin'. He would be 'merciless in punishing those who are exploiting the people' and by the beginning of July 'You will find everything is available at reasonable prices in the new cooperatives.'[22]

Accordingly, on 30 April, in the first of a hasty series of propitiatory hand-outs, he announced a special bonus for certain public sector employees; on 11 May he announced swingeing cuts in import duties on a variety of goods ranging from basic foodstuffs to video cassette recorders; on 13 May he announced a 10 per cent pay rise for all public and private sector employees and an increase in the minimum wage from £E15 to £E20. He then took over the premiership himself, promising to devote 95 per cent of his time to economic affairs, to accomplish in one month what the previous government had only managed in a year and a half, to 'correct the course which Egypt has been following for the past hundred years'.[23] *Al-Ahram* explained that the last time Sadat had made himself Prime Minister was when Egypt was 'busy preparing for the glorious October offensive'. He was doing so again because 'the situation, though different, [bears] resemblances to what it was in March 1973. . . . The battle for prosperity [is] no less dangerous than military action on the same scale. . . . One might say it is even more serious—for our daily problems seem to be increasing while our capacity to meet the needs of day-to-day living is diminishing.'[24] A week later the new government announced price reductions on 124 items, few of which, from canned fruit to camel hair cloth, ever appeared on an 'exploited' family's shopping list.

The price of things that mattered continued to rise as fast as ever. It was clear that no ministry could make good the promises which Sadat, apparently without planning or consultation, had made in their name. The loyalist *al-Akhbar* proposed the establishment of a Ministry of Unfulfilled Promises. That summer it was the rise in the price of meat which outstripped all others. A kilogram of the 'best cut' cost, at £E5, a quarter of the new minimum wage. There came another impromptu edict from on high. These price increases were 'criminal', Sadat said, and—citing the cases of a butcher who paid a

million pounds cash-down for a building and a merchant who tried to
sell a cargo of imported Israeli eggs for three times the regular price—
he banned the sale of meat for a month; and thus precipitated an
immediate, galloping increase in the price of anything that qualified
as protein, so that, by the end of the month, the best cuts were
fetching up to £E10 a kilogram. Meanwhile, letters to newspapers
were asking: when will the government stop the import of putrefied
meat? The Minister of Supply was finally obliged to assure parlia-
ment that steps would be taken to deal with 'greedy importers whose
only concern is to amass wealth even at the expense of the people's
health'.[25] Who were these importers? people asked. Would they be
punished? Such questions, others replied, were naïve. That type of
'criminal' was never punished. They were too high up for that.

President Sadat remained his own Prime Minister, fighting 'the
battle of prosperity'. According to his 1980 year-end report, he had
secured '70 per cent control over prices', and the national income was
being equally distributed while 'the petrodollar earners go to the
casinos, gambling tables and nightclubs, buying up real estate in
Europe, America and all over the world'. It was the least of his claims.
'I can say that the last ten years have corrected and made up for
everything that went wrong in the previous hundred and one years.'[26]

This, however, was not the view of the opposition, 'honest' or
otherwise. On the contrary, they were saying, if anything Sadat was
taking Egypt *back* a hundred years. At the beginning of 1981 he told a
meeting in Aswan of the Consultative Group of Western Creditors
that Egypt was ready to mortgage revenues from its oilfields and the
Suez Canal in order to secure an immediate $3 billion loan which it
needed for development projects. He could not wait, he told the
international bankers, for two or three years until newly discovered
oilfields came into production. An outraged *al-Shaab* newspaper,
mouthpiece of the Socialist Labour Party, likened such economic
policies to those of the Khedive Ismail who, a century before, had
auctioned off Egypt's shares in the Suez Canal and ended up
'destroying Egypt's independence'.[27]

By the tenth anniversary of his May 1971 Corrective Revolution
Sadat was growing tired of this 'honest opposition' of his own
creation, and apparently planning to do away with it on the ground
that 'there is no opposition in Egypt, only twenty spiteful persons out
of 40 million Egyptians'.[28] His opportunity came with the crackdown
on the Moslem Brotherhood. For the round-up encompassed not
merely the religious opposition, but all those whom he accused, in the

most vague and arbitrary fashion, of 'riding the wave of religious extremism'. In addition to such prominent figures as Muhammad Heikal, the journalist of international renown, and Fuad Serageddin, the venerable leader of the *Wafd*, Sadat ordered the arrest of several SLP leaders and the closure of *al-Shaab* newspaper. He would not ban the party, he said, but any individual who 'went astray' would be brought to justice. The day before the referendum to endorse his purge, he told foreign correspondents, summoned to Mit Abul Kom for an angry lecture on the way they had been 'distorting' the true nature of Egyptian democracy, that he forecast a 99·99 per cent vote in favour. According to the official count, however, it was only 99·45 per cent.

Those dwarves, the Arabs

The scale and intensity of the Arab retaliation to the peace treaty undoubtedly came as something of a shock to President Sadat. But attack was his best form of defence. He withdrew his remaining ambassadors in the Arab world before the Arabs withdrew theirs from Cairo, and put on a fine display of his indifference and contempt, and his conviction that nothing the Arabs could do would harm Egypt, or deflect him from his chosen path.

The Arabs, he asserted, needed Egypt more than Egypt needed them. Without Egypt they were 'zero'.[29] 'I don't claim to be the leader of the Arab and Islamic worlds, but neither I nor anyone else can deny that Egypt, with its people, civilization, heritage, will, knowledge and al-Azhar [university], is such a leader.'[30] Relying on the sneers and insults which had now become his stock-in-trade, he directed them against a target, Saudi Arabia, which had hitherto been spared his full fury. 'It is the strangest thing; Saudi Arabia and the other Gulf states learn the results of the referendum, with 40 million—except for 5,000—saying yes to the treaty and the very next day Saudi Arabia pushes Kuwait and all the others to break off relations. . . .'

It was the defection of this key conservative Arab power that disturbed him most, and there was more rage than reason in his explanation for it. Saudi Arabia, he maintained, was trying to usurp the leadership that rightfully belonged to Egypt. But

doesn't the House of Saud know that King Faisal—God rest his soul—always used to tell Assad to his face 'You sold the Golan.' Aren't they the same ones who are now running after these Arabs

338

to break relations with Egypt? So who is Saudi Arabia working for? For the Alawites of Syria, for the Takritis of Iraq (an extraordinarily high proportion of the Iraqi Baathist leadership comes from the small town of Takrit) who drag bodies through the streets . . . for the mad boy of Libya, for the Soviet Union? . . . At the Baghdad conference, the Syrian President told the Saudis: 'I'll take the battle into your bedrooms.' They didn't even get angry . . . I mean, you would have expected that they would have protested for their honour's sake.[31]

Nothing would come of all the sound and fury, Sadat prophesied, because, in spite of Baghdad, the Arab states were divided among themselves and racked by domestic troubles. Egypt was 'the island of peace, the island of love, the island of democracy'.[32] Stripped of characteristic embellishments, the prophecy was to prove accurate enough. For it was largely self-fulfilling anyway. He made it with particular confidence during his stately, sea-borne descent on Haifa. That was appropriate. Every Arab convulsion had its local causes, it is true, but if there was one great upheaval central to them all, it was the separate peace with Israel. None felt it more keenly than the wartime ally who was now Sadat's most implacable enemy. President Assad's was a regime besieged. Afflicted by terrorism and insurgency at home, bogged down as 'peace-keeper' in the morass of Lebanon, his ruling Baathists stood virtually alone against an Israel which, with Egypt *hors de combat*, could now throw perhaps six times the military weight against the 'Eastern front' that it could during the October war.[33]

When his prophecies showed signs of coming true, Sadat lost no time in exultingly pointing that out. In November 1979 religious fanatics staged a sensational, 22-day siege of the Grand Mosque in Mecca. It enabled Sadat to pour scorn on Saudi Arabia's supposed pretentions to regional leadership. Naturally, he said, Egypt condemned this desecration of 'our holiest of holies'. But it should not be forgotten that 'the matter is a political one . . . a question of the regime in Saudi Arabia . . . we could have broadcast the statement put out by those who seized the mosque, about Saudi Arabia, about the regime there, about corruption, and all that they were saying over loudspeakers in the mosque . . . but we did not exploit this opportunity to stab Saudi Arabia in the back.' The fact was, however, that 'the Saudi ruling family [had] been shaken to its foundations for ever'. They lived in terror of Ayatollah Khomeini and his

339

Islam of blood, of mad, yellow vengeance, this bigoted Islam. . . . America was the first to announce that there was a battle in the Grand Mosque . . . immediately Khomeini jumped in and said America was behind it. No Saudi leader had challenged him. They claim leadership but they are afraid of it. None of them can say to Khomeini 'Stop, stay where you are.' Because they are all trembling in the Gulf. . . . No Moslem raised its voice except Egypt. Egypt said: 'This is not Islam.' How can they face up [to him] without Egypt?[34]

As for the rest of the Arab world, Sadat invited his people, on the twenty-eighth anniversary of the Revolution, to look around them.

In Syria, we find a clique called Alawites representing less than 10 per cent of the population who rule with fire and steel . . . they made a law that any member of the Moslem Brotherhood is automatically sentenced to death . . . tanks surround Aleppo . . . assassinations every day . . . the Alawites have called in the Russians to save their skins, but the Alawites have the whole Syrian people against them and the Russians can't exterminate the whole Syrian people. . . .[35]

The truth was, Sadat said, that he got on much better with Begin than he did with Assad. 'The difference between the Syrians and the Israelis is very great—like the difference between ignorance and knowledge, clowning and seriousness.'[36] According to Sadat, other countries—Iraq, for example—were in no better shape.

You all know how Saddam Hussein the bloodthirsty hanged twenty-two of his friends in the government, strung them up before his own eyes. Lebanon. Lebanon is heading for a great calamity, and not just Lebanon, but the whole Arab world. The Phalangists and their allies want to break up the Arab world with their Christian state. . . . Is this Arab solidarity, is this what they achieved by isolating Egypt? They only isolate themselves.[37]

In September 1980 the Iraqi–Iranian war broke out. Sadat branded Iraq the aggressor, but pronounced the conflict to be an excellent opportunity to bring down Khomeini and Saddam Hussein together. He had every ground for satisfaction. The war had dealt the *coup de grâce* to the anti-Egyptian coalition. Its principal sponsor, Iraq, had now in a sense defected from the Arab world in Egypt's wake. Iraq has always had a tendency towards 'isolationism'. Its present ruler has tried to settle the country's perennial 'eastern problem' either by conciliation—the 1975 Algiers Pact—or, as now, by war. In either case, the result tended to be similar: the neutralization of Iraq as an effective contributor to the Arab cause. On the eve of the eleventh Arab summit conference in Amman, Sadat could justly exclaim: 'Fifteen months ago, these countries formed a united front. Today, Iraqis and Iranians are killing each other; Baghdad has broken with Damascus and Tripoli; Saudi Arabia has broken with Gadafi. Which of them can sit down with the other?'[38]

The greater the Arab disarray, the greater Sadat's chances—or so he seemed to think—of re-admission to the Arab fold, or what was left of it. At one time, he entertained special hopes of Saudi Arabia. 'I know that they are with me a hundred per cent. They have no choice, neither they nor any other state.' He was ready, he said, 'to board an aircraft immediately to go to Saudi Arabia'.[39] But he never received an invitation. On the contrary, abandoning the restrained and dignified tone in which they habitually address the world, the Saudis called Sadat a liar, and, referring to the insults he put in the mouth of the late King Faisal, they said that 'he even lies about the dead'. The more the Saudis rebuffed him, the more furiously he upbraided them.

Obviously, a hostile Arab world divided upon itself was less of a menace than a united one. But anything more positive than that, a restoration of Egypt's old influence and prestige, Sadat could never attain. True, he scored an occasional breakthrough of sorts. But these were less indicative of his own impending rehabilitation than of the extremity to which a particular adversary had been reduced. Thus, when President Saddam Hussein was desperately short of ammunition for his war against Iran, Sadat agreed to supply his vital needs, thereby helping to prop up that 'bloodthirsty' tyrant whom, in his earlier view, the world could well have done without. Iraq was still the 'aggressor', Sadat insisted, and recalled that at the Baghdad summit Saddam had led the hue and cry against him; but still, he said, Egypt was grateful for the role Iraq had played in the October war; it had sent a squadron to fight over Sinai and supplied Egypt with Soviet ground-to-ground missiles free of charge. 'I would like to have given them everything for nothing', Sadat said, 'but unfortunately that was not possible.'[40]

It was bizarre and contradictory. But then, since the peace treaty, his whole policy had been steeped in contradictions which, far from trying to disguise or make light of, he had paraded and magnified with a kind of maniacal glee. The Arabs were 'dwarves and igno-

ramuses', their minds were 'putrid and corrupt', and they inter-
preted Arabism as 'the starving of the Egyptian people', but Egypt would
fly to help them if ever help were sought—and even if it were not .[41]

The Americanization of Egypt

It was in collaboration with the United States that Sadat would aid
his brother-enemies. America's task was Egypt's tool. There was no
salvation outside America. That was now his credo. An exchange
with President Carter summed it up. 'I don't agree with you', said
Carter, 'that America holds 99 per cent of the cards in the [Middle
East] game.' Sadat corrected himself. 'My dear Jimmy,' he said, 'you
are right; it is not 99 per cent, but 99·9 per cent.' The two men
laughed.[42] If Egypt could not survive and prosper without the United
States, Sadat was determined that the United States should find in
Egypt the worthiest of protégés, an indispensable ally in the defence
of the West and its vital interests in the turbulent, tormented Middle
East. While ostensibly denying his anxiety to secure the role of
regional gendarme, he was none the less most fearful of losing it, and
these emotions, in a nature already so ingratiating, brought forth a
sycophancy that was often comical in its excess.

More than just friendship and cooperation, Sadat offered as well
complete subservience to American purposes, real or imagined, and
complete dedication to and identification with American 'values' as
he perceived them. In declared intent at least, the Americanization of
Egypt was to be more far-reaching than anything the Shah had tried
to foist on Iran. It began at the top. If imitative regimes can be said to
reveal themselves by their celebrations as much as by their official
policies, then, like the Shah with his gaudy homage to '2,500 years of
Persian monarchy' at Persepolis in 1971, Sadat staged a particularly
revealing one six months after the peace treaty. Unable to organize
his 'world peace festival', with the religious ceremonies on Mount
Sinai seasoned by profaner entertainments in Cairo, the 'event' he
finally did preside over was certainly as close in spirit to the regime's
real nature as the grander solemnities he had originally envisaged.
'This week', wrote the *New York Times*, 'a bunch of beautiful people
have created their own island of conspicuous opulence in a sea of
Egyptian poverty'—a jet-setters' gala in the shadow of the Pyramids
that marked Sadat's enthronement as an illustrious patron of
international café society.[43]

The party coincided with the ninth anniversary of the death of

President Nasser and, for the first time, Sadat absented himself from the service of commemoration. It was starkly symbolic of the distance he had now put between himself and those Egyptian 'values' he had once so grandiloquently exalted in the person of his 'immortal leader'. Historian Desmond Stewart can be forgiven his deadly irony.

Egypt is henceforth part of the American cosmos! The bills were paid by Revlon Inc., the cosmetic giant till then excluded from the Egyptian market because of its Israeli connections.... Over four hundred party goers jetted in from the West, many of them from the same rich-raff previously photographed at Persepolis. Others had more serious intentions. The man in charge was Michel C. Bergerac, the Revlon chairman, whose publicized purpose was to raise funds for Mrs Sadat's favourite charity. But parties charging half a million in expenses make charity ambiguous. The guest of honour, the elderly crooner Frank Sinatra, was claimed by his PR man, Lee Solters, to be paying the expenses of his six key musicians besides his own. But 'a well placed insider' told the *New York Times* that the gala paid Mr Sinatra's bill for a private jet to Cairo. The standard ticket cost the equivalent of nine years' wages for an ordinary Egyptian—$2,500—and paid for the evening's fun, a hotel room with meals and visits by air-conditioned bus to the pharaonic museum and a make-up session in a beauty salon set up by Revlon. A larger price—$30,000—secured an Egyptian minister who could advise visitors in their assault on the local market, with a table for six. These expensive tables were all taken. Their patrons included senior executives of Philip Morris, Pan-Am, TWA and Mobil Oil. After Sinatra had sung to the Sphinx, the action moved to the pool of Mena House Oberoi where Revlon had decreed an 'Ivoire' theme. Women were commanded to wear ivory, black or gold. Jihan Sadat, her daughter and daughter-in-law, allowed themselves to be made up in the ivory look, though one intimate observer told me it made little difference to their normal appearance. Pierre Balmain, a couturier who enjoys a link with Revlon, displayed his personal collection. 'His mannequins marched round the pool in white overcoats with padded shoulders and matching jackboots, then in soft dresses and pyjamas, some of which were made with Egyptian cotton, and finally in a few gold, fig-leaf bikinis.' The party culminated in a dinner for specially important guests at a cinema club in Giza: the host, Mr Alfred Atherton, the US ambassador.[44]

343

Sadat seemed to have America on the brain. He undertook no project for which he failed to discover an American inspiration or vindication. This was as true of the trivial as of the grandiose, the production of eggs or the furtherance of civilization.[45] He got many of his ideas from his evening recreation. Addressing a gathering of his National Democratic Party faithful, he told them: 'I watch a lot of American movies and you will have noticed that as soon as an American policeman comes and arrests someone he tells him: "Every word you say I shall use against you and you have the right to speak only in the presence of a lawyer." Why? Because this is the American Declaration of Human Rights.'[46] And did not America have his Law of Shame under another name?

> In America [he told the *Los Angeles Times*] you have a legal provision punishing anything prejudicial to Americans; I can't remember its text, but it covers anything to do with the ethics of behaviour. Actually, I learned about this in an excellent film I saw recently. It was the life story of Clark Gable. Perhaps you remember, he has relations with a certain artist, Carole Lombard, I think. They were deeply in love. They wanted to punish him, you see, because he had these relations and he was a married man. They charged him with violating the American code of ethics. Because in a case like this the judge can dismiss a man from his post if he is in the government or annul his contract of employment with a company.... This concerns the morals of the American people. I am not doing anything new here in this country. You have such a law. You have more—a law that defends your system.[47]

President Sadat's doubts about his own true and lasting value to the United States were well-founded. In the first place, that other, traditional, self-appointed candidate for the gendarme's role, Israel, had no intention of ceding its special relationship with the United States to a *parvenu* like Sadat. Fearing that peace would mean a downgrading of its importance in American eyes, Israel preached its own virtues as a strategic Western asset in a propaganda campaign which was suitably adjusted to the new realities. In a typical formulation, General Chaim Herzog, the former Israeli ambassador to the United Nations, said that 'the best thing the United States could do today would be to encourage the incorporation of Israel within the NATO treaty agreement. This would mean we would become part of the Western defence element in Europe and the Western Levant against the expansion of the Soviet Union.' And once the treaty with Egypt was signed the new alliance 'could reach down there as well'.[48]

President Sadat more than agreed about the Soviet menace. 'Many quarters', he observed, had always said that he was 'more of a strategist than a tactician'. They were 'quite right', and it was his duty to warn that 'the situation around us is becoming alarming, really alarming'. The greatest threat to world peace lay in the Middle East. But it was no longer the Arab–Israeli conflict which posed it. Now 'the Israelis cross the Sinai by car'. No, the threat came from 'the struggle between the dreams of the Soviet Union to reach the warm waters and ... Western civilization, which is threatened because whenever Europe is deprived of the energy it needs for its factories and the tools of its civilization everything will collapse'.

In the 1950s, it will be recalled, Sadat used to describe the Soviet Union as 'an imaginary foe' of America's making, which lay 'thousands of miles from the region'. Now the Soviet Union was 'more dangerous, much more dangerous' than Hitler had ever been. The Shah had fallen and the Russians had 'captured Afghanistan in broad daylight'. They were also entrenched in South Yemen, Ethiopia and Libya. They were 'only miles' from the Gulf. Besides, there were moral as well as strategic considerations. Sadat understood Soviet villainy, as he did American virtue, from his own personal observations.

> One day I was in West Berlin. As I was going through the gate into East Berlin, I came across an old woman. . . . She looked just like my grandmother. When I asked why an old lady like that was sweeping the streets so very early in the morning, they said, 'Well, this is communist doctrine, and those who do not work do not eat,' or something like that. Ever since then I have felt that the whole thing was repulsive. If my grandmother was alive, believe me, I would do everything in the world to provide her with dignity and security, everything. Not to have to get up early in the morning so as to sweep the streets. Really, the Soviets are vicious.[49]

Sadat faced another, more serious dilemma. In bidding for the gendarme's role he had gone so far, through his separate peace, that he had simultaneously incapacitated himself for it, wrecking the very goal which, since the October war, he had been pursuing so assiduously. Egypt, he had told the Americans, is the 'gateway' to the Arab world; win Egypt's friendship, and you will have the friendship of the Arab world. You will no longer need a gendarme at all. The strategy had made sense. His own pendulum swing from the loveless embrace of one superpower into the welcoming arms of another had been only the most libertine expression of a general shift of affections from which no friend of the Soviet Union, certainly not Syria, had been entirely exempt. But Egypt had now placed itself beyond the pale, almost as much an apostate as Israel itself. There was therefore a danger that the Americans, eventually grasping that the whole Camp David formula was misconceived, would pay more attention to those, the Saudis and the Jordanians, who had told them so from the outset. At best, they would demote Sadat from the privileged position he enjoyed in their Middle East strategies; at worst, considering him to be hopelessly discredited, they would heed Arab advice that it was time for him to go.

Sadat's response was the compulsive one of offering more and more to the Americans—on the Arabs' behalf. He thrust himself upon the United States half in collaboration, half in competition with the rival, aspirant gendarme. For, on the one hand, he was tempted to go the whole hog, not merely to make peace with Israel, but to join it and the United States in a fully fledged military alliance which, with Camp David on its escutcheon, would bludgeon the rest of the Arab world into sullen acquiescence. After one of his many *tête-à-têtes* with Begin, the two leaders were reported to be formulating common policies to face common enemies, with Baathist Syria apparently at the top of the list. The Israeli press hinted at an 'unwritten military alliance'.[50] On the other hand, in the hope even now of being restored to Arab favour, Sadat, backing away from such an extreme commitment, would take refuge in the traditional thesis that Israel was inherently unqualified for the gendarme's role. There could be no strategic cooperation, he said, until, with the establishment of Palestinian autonomy, Israel had fulfilled the 'comprehensive' part of the Camp David bargain. But whether he offered his services in collaboration or competition with Israel, the Arabs were unimpressed. He persisted all the same.

At the end of 1979, in that casual way he sometimes had of announcing seismic decisions, Sadat disclosed that he was ready to give the United States military 'facilities' on Egyptian soil. His purpose, he told *October* magazine, was 'to defend all the Arab countries'.[51] His would-be Arab protégés showed such little desire for his protection that, a month later, he gave one of his more apoplectic public performances. Did they think they were more self-reliant, more independent than Egypt itself? The hypocrisy of it!

All those sheikhdoms on the Gulf, Saudi Arabia included, know perfectly well that their protection comes from America.... I announced that if any Arab country in the Gulf is exposed to a foreign threat and asks America to go in and rescue it—I announced that I would give America facilities before America asks, and even before those dwarves and ignoramuses who want to starve the Egyptian people ask themselves. But here comes this upstart leader [Crown Prince Fahd] and, even after my own announcement, says that Saudi Arabia will not give facilities, bases or anything else. 'For shame, for shame,' he shouted, and an accusing finger stabbed the air.[52]

The Saudis could bury their heads in the sand if they chose. As for himself, he was positively 'running after' the United States to supply those 'facilities'.[53]

The Americans *were* impressed. Here was a key Third World country, which in the 1950s had led the struggle against Western-imposed pacts and military entanglements, now actively soliciting them or, beneath the plausible rhetoric, something closely resembling them. It was very timely; shaken by the downfall of the Shah, the Americans were casting about for ways and means of enhancing their land-based military power in the whole 'zone of crisis'. Publicly at least—for in private they sought written agreements—they tactfully acknowledged that it was not 'bases' that Sadat was offering, that he was not taking Egypt back to the era of colonial domination. But many Egyptians failed to grasp the distinction. For *al-Shaab*, mouthpiece of the 'honest opposition', these were bases all right, and it condemned them in its own and the Egyptian people's name.

Bases or facilities, Sadat was determined to lock Egypt into the Western defensive system. And America, at least, seemed willing to have him. In the matter of arms supplies, Egypt still did not get the special treatment America reserved for Israel, but it was catching up. As its reward for making peace, it got $1·5 billion in military aid on the same easy credit terms as Israel. A year later it was promised a further $3·5 billion, spread over three or four years, for the purchase of the most up-to-date weaponry—including the F-16 fighter—which America had hitherto withheld from it in deference to the Israelis.

When Sadat made his offer of facilities, he was only ratifying an existing reality. AWACS reconnaissance planes were already flying missions out of Qena airbase 280 miles south of Cairo. Then, in April 1980, Qena had served as a staging-post for the abortive attempt to rescue the diplomats held hostage at the American embassy in Teheran. In the summer, another airbase, Cairo West, was put at the disposal of the American airforce, which sent a squadron of F-4 Phantoms with 300 personnel to undertake much-publicized joint manoeuvres with the Egyptian airforce. In November 1,400 American troops, accompanied by tactical fighters, joined the Egyptian army in desert training exercises. Towards the end of the year, the Americans were well on their way to securing their greatest prize, the development of Ras Banas airbase on the Red Sea as a key facility for their new-born Rapid Deployment Force. They expected to spend hundreds of millions of dollars on what was described as the Pentagon's biggest construction job since the Vietnam war. The runways would be upgraded to receive long-range bombers, freight and refuelling aircraft. There would be installations to accommodate a division of troops to be airlifted there whenever the need arose. The port would also be modernized to take American warships. Difficulties developed because the Americans were loath to embark on such an expensive undertaking without the formal agreement that Sadat, sensitive about bases, was reluctant to conclude. But in the end he devised a solution; he offered the Americans the use of Ras Banas in a letter to which President Reagan was enjoined not to reply—and that, according to the magazine *Mayo*, the latest of Sadat's mouthpieces, did not constitute a formal agreement.[54] It was during the argument over Ras Banas that Sadat made his most daring proposition yet in his seduction of America. Once again he vouchsafed it via *October* magazine. 'Personally', he said, 'I would not be at all afraid to join NATO, because the [Soviet] danger would be the same.' The United States did not pose a threat to anyone's sovereignty. 'Although the United States has big bases in Britain, we never read in the British newspapers that America is occupying Britain.'[55]

Clearly, Sadat needed to promote a climate of cold war, confrontation and general emergency in order to sustain his *raison d'être*. He needed threatened Western interests to defend, tottering oil sheikhs to prop up and the Soviet demon against which to launch his crusade. He often had to admonish the Americans for their failure to grasp the full dimensions of the peril, or to take forceful enough action to meet it. They still had not got over their 'Vietnam complex'. Their 'negative' policies enabled the Soviet Union to 'infiltrate' the Middle East by stealth. Their 'timidity' over Afghanistan had been 'very dangerous'. Their 'credibility' among the people of the area was in decline. Europe was 'going soft' too.[56] On the outbreak of the

Iraqi–Iranian war, Sadat exhorted the United States to take this opportunity to plot Ayatollah Khomeini's overthrow. 'This time, for God's sake, don't offer everything to the Soviet Union on a golden platter.'[57] When, after fourteen-and-a-half months of captivity, the American hostages were finally set free, Sadat expressed his disappointment at the weakness of American leadership, and the opportunity it had missed 'to send a message to the world'. After all, he said, 'America loses 55,000 people a year in car accidents and the hostages are less than one per cent [sic] of that figure.'[58] Nor did Sadat confine his advice to Middle Eastern issues. The United States, he argued, should help the Chinese as much as they could. For 'they have 5,000 years of civilization behind them'. Unlike the Soviets, 'they keep their word'.[59]

Despite the grievous blow which Jimmy Carter's electoral débâcle dealt to the 'peace process', there were compensations for Sadat in a cold warrior like Reagan. The two leaders, Cairo commentators hastened to point out, would have no difficulty in agreeing on the gravity of the Soviet peril. The new Administration stepped up military aid to Egypt. When the new Secretary of State, Alexander Haig, came to the Middle East in April 1981 in search of 'strategic consensus' against the Soviet Union, it was not in those traditional anti-communist bastions, Jordan and Saudi Arabia, that he found strongest support for it. There, starting once again on that wearisome business of 'educating' a new Administration, they told him that yes, indeed, there was a Soviet threat, but nothing contributed more to it than America's failure to bring about a just and lasting settlement of the Palestine problem. He found the strongest support in Israel and Egypt. 'We agreed on everything,' said Sadat. What a pity that Saudi Arabia, 'sleeping duck' that it was, continued to ignore the dangers that beset it.[60]

In the footsteps of the Shah

President Sadat did not go unrewarded in his devotion to America and the West. The American investment in him and what he stood for was enormous. Symbolic of the relationship is the new seventeen-storey American embassy, complete with ceremonial entrance-way and reflecting pools, which is still under construction. It will accommodate a staff that has risen from six in 1973 to 872 today, and constitutes America's largest single diplomatic mission. As a recipient of all-purpose American economic—as distinct from military—aid, Egypt is, at the time of writing, now second only to Israel. The result is one of the most ambitious programmes of the kind since the Marshall Plan. The aid, running at about $1,100 billion a year, is being disbursed faster than Egypt can absorb it on a vast array of projects ranging from the construction of wheat silos to the dispensing of birth control devices.

At least as gratifying, for Sadat anyway, was the evidence of the immense respect and affection in which he was held. Few world leaders have been the object of honours, awards, panegyrics and public triumphs on the scale that he was. When they used words like great, noble, courageous, generous and wise the columnists and leader-writers were being ordinary and uncontroversial. For Sadat was a subject who excited quite dithyrhambic eloquence.

> Though he is an emotional man standing now at the pivot of history, Sadat maintains an almost metaphysical serenity. Neither displeasure nor impatience, seldom even the fits and starts natural to frustration can be discerned in his utterances. . . . Performer, politician, poet, prophet—the man is all four sides. They form a geometry as pure in its logic and mystical in its inspiration as the Pyramids. And when studying Sadat, just as when contemplating the Pyramids, one can never quite distinguish between the side one is looking at and the side one has just seen.

In this reverent, but not exceptional, tone did one Gail Sheehy attempt to solve 'The Riddle of Sadat' for the readers of *Esquire* magazine. But perhaps it was his 'good friend Henry' who, admitting that he had once considered him a clown, was to pay him the most gratifying compliment of all: 'Sadat', said Dr Kissinger, 'is the greatest since Bismarck, extraordinary.'[61]

Of President Sadat's final exploits, none excited more admiration in the West than the hospitality he pressed upon the deposed Shah of Iran. He called it an act of 'Islamic compassion'. Remorselessly pursued by the Ayatollah's Islamic Republic, ditched by his Western friends, driven from one hole-in-the-corner asylum to the next, only Anwar Sadat, in superb defiance of much of the Moslem world, would take this dying fugitive in and bury him in a funeral fit for a King of Kings. It was meant to impress the American public, and it did. But for those who remembered that earlier encounter with the Shah, the scathing verses of Rabat (see p. 100), his action seemed to be prompted less by compassion than by the theatrical potentialities it offered. It certainly lent a dramatic edge to the nagging question which some were asking: was there, would there one day turn out to be more in common between the two men than Sadat cared to contemplate? His own emphatic answer to that question had a familiar, statistical ring. He said that 99·9 per cent of his people were behind him and if the percentage fell below that, he would step down of his own accord.[62]

Americans usually put the question in the context of another: was their own, too obvious presence in the country a liability, rather than an asset, for Sadat? Or, as the expression has it, was their visibility too high? Numerically—at some 5,000—that presence remained small compared with the 40,000–50,000 who lived in Iran during the last years of the Shah, or something approaching that number who now live in Saudi Arabia. But that was partly because the business and direct military involvement did not keep pace with the enormous political one. Hermann Eilts, American ambassador during the five hectic years that metamorphosed Egypt's foreign relations, said that 'all of us remember Iran, and while this is nothing like Iran, it could get out of hand. It is a mistake.'[63] A junior diplomat of Arab origin called it 'putting all our eggs in one bastard'.[64] But the degree of American visibility begs the real question, which is whether it identified with a man whose policies were right and achievements real.

It has been said of the Shah that, fearing and despising his own people, he craved in compensation the admiration of the rest of the world. Sadat undoubtedly possessed such a 'foreign complex' and in his own, very special way, he alienated himself from his natural environment as inexorably as the Shah did from his. At bottom, the Shah had only one constituency; that was co-terminous with the territorial frontiers of his realm, however much influence he might have exerted beyond them. By contrast, any Egyptian ruler can be said to have two constituencies, a primary one, Egypt proper, and a secondary one, the Arab world, to which, as its largest single component, Egypt is indissolubly bound by ties of history, religion, language and culture. Doubtless the second is less important than the first, but it is very important none the less. President Sadat had, by the time of his death, all but lost this constituency. Damaged equally were his relations with regimes which, many of them, are no more popular than his own and his relations with the peoples who may eventually dispatch the regimes. True, Sadat was not solely responsible for this. Egypt's decline began under his predecessor, with the suppression of liberties, the shortcomings of 'Arab socialism', the break-up of the

Syrian–Egyptian union, the misadventure in the Yemen, the defeat of 1967—and the survival, growing confidence and accumulating oil billions of the conservative Arab regimes. Furthermore, it was the Arabs themselves, especially, perhaps, those who call themselves 'revolutionary', who helped push Egypt down a path which, under its crushing burden of poverty, it was bound to be the first to take—if any country did. All the same, it required a Sadat, with all his peculiarities, to do what Sadat finally did, to conclude his separate peace and reduce the influence of the Arab world's 'great power' to the nadir at which it now stands. Having lost the Arabs, all that Sadat could do, characteristically, was to cover them in racist contempt.

It was more difficult—but none the less easier than in the case of the Shah—to measure Sadat's standing in his primary, his Egyptian constituency. For he headed a system which, though autocratic, was altogether less tyrannical than that of the Shah. Paradoxically, he first stood to gain in his primary constituency by losing in his secondary one. For the assertion of a specifically Egyptian national-ism, with anti-Arab and pro-Western overtones, appealed to an authentic strain in the Egyptian psyche. Naturally, Sadat rejected any suggestion of subservience. Egypt was worthy of, if not actually superior to, the new company it was keeping. 'We are the source because we've got 7,000 years behind us. Today we can hold up our heads with England and America. With all the Western democracies. France, Germany. Because we are a democracy like them. . . . And 7,000 years old.'[65]

Sadat was not the first Egyptian ruler to link himself, for security and self-aggrandizement, with contemporary centres of world power and prestige. Khedive Ismail presided over the grand opening of the Suez Canal with the slogan that Egypt was henceforth a part of Europe not Africa, bankrupted himself in the fêting, and emulating, of European royalty, and offered to send troops to fight French colonial wars. All things considered, however, Sadat outdid Ismail, a nineteenth-century potentate of alien extraction, in the extravagance of his 'foreign complex'. In the virulence with which he attacked the Arabs and the sycophancy with which he befriended the Americans, Sadat mocked his own *fellah* origins, his nationalist past and the spirit of the age. In due course this was bound to offend the Arab in his people more than it gratified the purely Egyptian, kindling in them the same kind of native resentment that they once harboured against the dynasty of Muhammad Ali. The portents were there. One of the most interesting has been the re-publishing of books and writings that date back to the 'golden age' of Egypt's struggle for independence. This is an ingenious way of circumventing censorship and 'codes of ethics'. An enterprising publishing house recently revived three such works in English: *Spoiling the Egyptians—A Tale of Shame* by J. Seymour Keay; *How We Defended Arab* by A. M. Broadley; and *The Secret History of the English Conquest of Egypt* by William Blunt. They are angry, anguished accounts of Europe's encouragement of Khedive Ismail's headlong rush to Europeanize Egypt; his crippling indebtedness; the imposing of humiliating Anglo–French controls over Egyptian finances; the rise of Colonel Ahmad Arabi's 'Egypt-for-the-Egyptians' nationalist movement; and the complete loss of independence to which, with the British invasion of 1882, this chain of events finally led.

Sadat may not have lost his Egyptian constituency as a whole, but he certainly lost large, representative segments of it. One by one he fell out with quarters which once lent him their support or at least their passive acceptance. Those who stuck by him, in parliament, the press and other areas of his 'state of institutions', could fairly be described, with few exceptions, as compliant, not to say abject, extensions of his will. If, as seems to have been the case, his characteristic response to opposition was to deride and vilify it, then he knew how widespread it really was. Although he did not deride the Egyptians *qua* Egyptians, he came perilously close to it by treating all who disagreed with him, not as critics with a legitimate right to do so, but as miscreants, as traitors to 'the Egyptian family' of which he deemed himself 'the father'. And the ruler who could persistently call the spontaneous, nationwide food riots of January 1977 an Uprising of Thieves mocked the anguish of an entire people.

Having lost the Arabs, and deeply unsure of the Egyptians, President Sadat had only one real constituency left: America and the West. There was surely something wrong with policies and achievements which only commanded admiration in faraway places, something wrong with a leader who deliberately looked for it there because he knew he could no longer command it closer to home. If there was one critical moment when things began to go wrong in the career of Anwar Sadat, it was precisely the moment when, on the face of it, they were beginning to go spectacularly right. The day of his only true, his Arab, apotheosis, was the day of his ultimate undoing. For when, on that afternoon of 16 October 1973, he stood on the rostrum of the People's Assembly and presented his glorious Crossing to the world, the Israelis had already begun that calamitous counter-crossing from which all his subsequent actions can be traced. From that moment on, behind the statesman's, the strategist's pose, he must be seen as more the plaything than the shaper of events.

Clearly, the more an individual, as opposed to the institutions over which he presides, is the maker of policies, the more personal psychology is likely to impinge, in their making, on objective political reality. Sadat was by no means the world's most absolute ruler, but his career illustrated, in a remarkable way, how far the personal can predominate over the political and, when the personal is as peculiar as it was in him, what perversities, in the name of policy, can then ensue. Sadat the man had certain shallow gifts. He was an actor. He had the gambler's flair. But, above all, he was the consummate opportunist. For, as we have seen, there was no deity that he would not dethrone, no principle that he would not abjure, no direction change, friend abandon, enemy embrace. He struck no attitude of which, in his real self, he was not the antithesis. He was constant only in his inconstancy. The politics changed, and out of recognition; only the person, his rhetoric, his very words—intemperate, demagogic, alternately abusive and obsequious—remained opportunistically, mendaciously the same. Examples are legion. Nasser—undoubtedly his primordial complex—was once his demi-god; ultimately he could hardly bring himself to pronounce his name, he ostentatiously boycotted the official ceremonies commemorating his death and sent police to break up unofficial ones. Once it was all the gold of America which could not buy Egypt's will, then of Russia, and finally of the Arabs. In the 1950s Secretary of State John Foster Dulles was 'the cowboy from Texas'; in the 1970s President Carter, being a 'farmer' like himself, was honest and god-fearing.

But *fellah* is one thing that Sadat certainly was not. So what, then, was he? If it is possible to classify him at all, he was surely a *fahlawi*. He fitted almost to perfection this scholar's definition of a uniquely Egyptian concept.

The term, *fahlawi*, is originally a Persian term used . . . exclusively in Egyptian colloquial. A similar term, *bahlawan*, may be found in all good Arabic dictionaries to mean: a clown, a rope dancer, a circus performer, etc. Both the term, *fahlawi*, and the word, *bahlawan*, are derived from the Persian root, *pahlaw*, which has among its various meanings (the majority of which are either place designations or heroic in connotation) the idea of non-productive, vain, futile and wasteful action or deportment. The Egyptian usage of the word . . . is an extremely colourful one. . . . The *fahlawi* is an individual who is happy-go-lucky, hail-fellow-well-met. He is a blusterer who loves his pomp. . . . Generally jovial, the *fahlawi* likes to be liked. He is characterized by an Epicurean approach to life— pain avoidance and pleasure-seeking. Among his phobias is the fear of responsibility, the word itself being extremely distasteful to the *fahlawi*. As for his outward appeal, few actively dislike the *fahlawian* individual, and few would dare trust him. Insofar as the *fahlawi*'s concept of manhood and honour are concerned, they are generally idyllic and chivalric. This lends to his whole personality a complexion very nearly summarized in the English allusory adjective, 'quixotic' (highly caricatured romanticism; a pitifully inane, post-heroic chivalry coupled with a plague of fanciful and usually innocent self-delusion; a benign (if diminutive) messianic insanity). . . . Among other traits, the *fahlawian* personality is characterized by a perennial search for the shortest and quickest means to a particular end, means which avoid the mundane discomfort of expending the energy usually required to overcome the obstacles in the way. The concern of the *fahlawi* is not to complete the work as best as possible, but merely to be done with it and achieve his end in order that it may not be said of him that he was not able to do it or that things 'didn't break his way'. What is important is that he complete the task in a way which enhances his public image. The traditional *fahlawian* behaviour patterns make us unable to accept truth and reality in a manner commensurate with the demands for quick action which times of crisis impose. They force us to hide results, failures and shortcomings in order to preserve appearances and save face. One of the distinctive traits of the *fahlawian* personality . . . is its propensity for sudden excite- ment, violent audacity, underestimating the initial difficulties, and finally fizzling out into listlessness when it appears to the *fahlawi* that the matter calls for perseverance, steadfastness and organized work whose results show only slowly and cumulatively. . . . There are other traits characteristic of the *fahlawian* personality such as an excessive desire for self-affirmation and a penchant for making a show of being able to manage affairs. This is well illustrated by magnanimous, much-promising types when they say: 'Consider the matter solved; I'll put it to the minister myself'; or 'Think no more about it, leave it to me, and I'll take it on my own responsibility', or 'Consider it done! I'll hear no more about it!' and so on. One of the characteristics of the *fahlawian* self-affirmation is to jeer at others, cut them down and pose one's self as being of surpassing ability in managing affairs. The *fahlawi* suffers from a real inferiority complex, a complex which he cannot confess to because he values shame and fear of scandal more than realism, objectivity and the need to frankly recognize inferiority in order to treat it and overcome it. . . .[66]

Egypt and the man who rules it occupy a pivotal place on the world stage. America and the West recognize that, but that they could have reached conclusions about Sadat so sharply at variance with the Arabs' and Egyptians' own, that a formidable scholar-statesman such as Henry Kissinger could call him 'the greatest since Bismarck', that so stylish a writer as Gail Sheehy could discern in him an 'almost metaphysical serenity', raises far-reaching questions about international relations, about the ability of one society to understand another, about the qualifications of the Western media which, for all their massive coverage of the man, ended up with such an unreal portrait of him. How could the leading democracy of the West bring itself to stake so much on so unworthy a protégé? It is more than just a case of putting one's trust in a regime which, like the Shah's, was politically unviable and morally disreputable; more than just apathy or ignorance of foreign affairs which make this possible. There is but one reason why Sadat won such honour in the West: he made peace with Israel. It is essentially that, and not the quality of the peace, which counted, that which caused the West to ignore, minimize or excuse flaws of character and conduct which it would find repugnant in its own leaders. The infatuation for Anwar Sadat therefore represented the crossing of yet another threshold of irrationality—an irrationality which, the outgrowth of its love affair with Israel, has forever caused the West to pursue Middle East policies which run counter to its own interests. Each new threshold brings greater dangers than the last, but now they are taking on a climactic quality. For the Middle East bids fair to be the Balkans of the last quarter of the twentieth century. Of all the troubles which afflict it, its instability and fragmentation, its vulnerability to the machinations of East and West, its possession of vast reserves of oil in an oil-thirsty world, the most dangerous is—as it always has been—the implacable conflict between Arab and Jew. A civilized settlement of that conflict has always been acknowledged as very difficult to achieve. It has yet to be acknowledged that, with Camp David as its basis, Sadat made it impossible. That by which he was judged one of the great men of the age, his 'sacred peace mission', was in reality a disservice to Arab and Jew, East and West, the eventual scale of which we do not venture to prophesy.

Notes

1

1 *Al-Hamishmar*, 10 May 1973.
2 *Maariv*, 5 June 1973.
3 Moussa Sabri, *Documents of the October War* [Arabic], al-Maktab al-Misri al-Hadith, Cairo 1974, p. 28.
4 *Sunday Times* Insight Team, *The Yom Kippur War*, André Deutsch, London 1975, p. 112.
5 Muhammad Heikal, *The Road to Ramadan*, Collins, London 1975, p. 33.
6 *The Yom Kippur War*, pp. 145–6.
7 Heikal, p. 41.
8 *Al-Nahar* (Beirut daily), 11 October 1973.
9 *The Yom Kippur War*, p. 147.
10 Amnon Kapeliouk, *Israel: La Fin des Mythes*, Albin Michel, Paris 1975, p. 201.
11 ibid., p. 203.
12 *L'Orient—Le Jour*, 8 October 1973.
13 Kapeliouk, p. 210.
14 Heikal, p. 40.
15 *Al-Ahram*, 12 October 1973.
16 ibid.
17 *Al-Akhbar*, 8 October 1973.
18 Gamal Abdul Nasser, *The Philosophy of the Revolution*, Government Printing Office, Cairo, n.d., p. 54.
19 ibid., pp. 51, 52, 59.
20 ibid., pp. 12, 13.
21 *Africasie*, 24 January 1972.
22 *Le Monde*, 16 February 1970.
23 *Al-Akhbar*, 28 July 1970.
24 *Al-Ahram*, 15 August 1970.
25 ibid., 22 August 1970.
26 ibid., 24 August 1970.

27 Heikal, p. 100.
28 *Al-Ahram*, 17 October 1973.
29 ibid.

2

1 Anwar Sadat, *In Search of Identity*, Collins, London 1978, p. 17.
2 ibid., p. 16.
3 ibid., p. 8.
4 ibid., p. 7.
5 ibid., p. 14.
6 ibid., p. 2.
7 Sabri, *Documents of the October War*, p. 29.
8 Sadat, *In Search . . .*, pp. ix, 314.
9 ibid., p. 13.
10 ibid.
11 ibid., p. 17.
12 ibid., p. 7.
13 ibid.
14 ibid., pp. 6, 7.
15 ibid., p. 12.
16 ibid.
17 ibid., p. 15.
18 ibid., p. 17.
19 *Akhir Sa'a*, 23 July 1958.
20 Anwar Sadat, *Révolte sur le Nil*, Pierre Amiot, Paris 1957, pp. 36–42.
21 Sadat, *In Search . . .*, p. 20.
22 ibid., pp. 19, 20.
23 ibid., p. 18.
24 ibid., p. 21.
25 ibid., pp. 27, 28.
26 Sadat, *Révolte . . .*, p. 79.
27 Sadat, *In Search . . .*, p. 29.
28 ibid., p. 30.
29 See Ahmad Hamroush, *The Story of the 23 July Revolution* [Arabic], The Arab Institute for Studies and Publishing, Beirut 1977, vol. I, p. 95.
30 Sadat, *Révolte . . .*, pp. 90–6.
31 Sadat, *In Search . . .*, pp. 39, 40.
32 ibid., p. 42.
33 ibid., p. 46.
34 ibid., p. 49.
35 ibid., p. 57.
36 Nasser, pp. 32–6; see also Sayed Muhammad Ashmawi, 'History of Egyptian Political Thought 1945–1952', doctoral thesis [Arabic] unpublished, Cairo University, 1977, p. 286.

37 Sadat, *Révolte . . .*, p. 108.
38 ibid., pp. 135, 136.
39 ibid., p. 168.
40 ibid., pp. 106, 107.
41 ABC, 19 December 1974.
42 Sadat, *In Search . . .*, pp. 59, 60.
43 ibid., p. 62.
44 Sadat, *Révolte . . .*, p. 137.
45 Sadat, *In Search . . .*, pp. 58, 59.
46 Muhammad Naguib, *My Words for History*, pp. 16, 17, cited in Ashmawi, p. 289.
47 Hamroush, vol. I, p. 113; see also Ashmawi, p. 289.
48 Sadat, *In Search . . .*, pp. 104, 105.
49 ibid., p. 113.
50 ibid.
51 *Egyptian Gazette*, 10, 13 June 1948.
52 Sadat, *In Search . . .*, p. 92.
53 Naguib, pp. 16, 17.
54 Sadat, *In Search . . .*, p. 70.
55 ibid., pp. 73, 74.
56 ibid., p. 75.
57 ibid., p. 86.
58 ibid., p. 95.
59 ibid.
60 ibid., p. 97.
61 ibid., p. 86.
62 ibid., p. 97.
63 ibid., p. 91.
64 *Egyptian Gazette*, 14 June 1948.
65 Sadat, *In Search . . .*, p. 98.
66 ibid., p. 99.
67 Sadat, *Révolte . . .*, p. 123.
68 See P. J. Vatikiotis, *Nasser and His Generation*, Croom Helm, London, 1978, pp. 107, 108.
69 Sadat, *Révolte . . .*, p. 185.
70 ibid., p. 177.
71 Anwar Sadat, *The Full Story of the Revolution* [Arabic], Dar al Hilal, Cairo, n.d., pp. 88–90. There are, in effect, at least three sub-versions of Version One; the Arabic, in particular, differs from the French and English ones.
72 Sadat, *Révolte . . .*, pp. 213, 214.
73 Jean Lacouture, *Nasser*, Seuil, Paris 1971, p. 321.
74 *Al-Ahram*, 29 September 1971.
75 Sadat, *The Full Story . . .*, pp. 47, 48.
76 *Al-Ahram*, 29 September 1971.
77 ibid.
78 Sadat, *The Full Story . . .*, pp. 8, 17, 25, 34, 37, 177.

79   Arfan Library, Cairo, n.d., p. 178.
80   ibid., p. 31.
81   ibid., pp. 70, 75, 80, 171.
82   ibid., p. 72.
83   ibid., p. 178.
84   ibid., p. 72.
85   ibid., pp. 97, 98.
86   ibid., p. 142.
87   ibid.
88   ibid.,.p. 173.
89   ibid., p. 132.
90   ibid., p. 161.
91   ibid.
92   ibid., p. 165.
93   ibid., p. 161.
94   ibid., p. 153.
95   ibid.
96   ibid., pp. 117, 118.
97   ibid., p. 52.
98   ibid., p. 192.
99   *al-Mussawar*, 18 September 1953.
100 Sadat, *In Search . . .*, p. 136.
101 ibid., p. 162.
102 ibid., p. 21.
103 ibid., p. 100.
104 ibid., p. 101.
105 ibid.
106 ibid., pp. 147, 163.
107 ibid., pp. 119, 120.
108 ibid., pp. 157, 190, 208–10.
109 ibid., p. 102.
110 ibid., p. 122.
111 ibid., pp. 146–8.
112 ibid., p. 162.
113 Ali Saber, *Nasser en Procès*, Collections Points de Vue, Paris 1968, p. 165.
114 Sadat, *In Search . . .*, p. 163.
115 Vatikiotis, p. 238; Robert Stephens, *Nasser*, Penguin Books, London 1971, p. 293.
116 Vatikiotis, p. 162; Muhammad Heikal, *Le Sphinx et Le Commissar*, Editions Jeune Afrique, Paris 1980, p. 176.
117 Nassereddin Nashashibi, *al-Hibr Aswad . . . Aswad* [Arabic], al-Nahar Press Services, Beirut, n.d., p. 96; see also *Jeune Afrique*, 5 September 1965.
118 Vatikiotis, p. 62.
119 Stephens, pp. 415, 416.
120 *Washington Post*, 24 February 1977.

121 *Guardian*, 26 August 1965.
122 Sadat, *In Search* . . ., p. 180.
123 Abdul Maguid al-Farid, *From the Minutes of Nasser's Arab and International Meetings* [Arabic], Institute for Arab Studies, Beirut 1979, pp. 292–3, 300–301.
124 Marvin and Bernard Kalb, *Kissinger*, Little, Brown, Boston 1974, pp. 190, 191.
125 ibid., p. 289.
126 *Al-Ahram*, 27 September 1969.
127 UPI, 21 December 1970.
128 Sadat, *In Search* . . ., pp. 196, 197.
129 See al-Farid, pp. 214–24; see also Heikal, *Le Sphinx* . . ., p. 97.
130 *al-Jeel*, Beirut, November 1980.
131 Sadat, *In Search* . . ., pp. 202, 203.
132 ibid., p. 203.

3

1 *Al-Ahram*, 19 October 1970.
2 Raymond William Baker, *Egypt's Uncertain Revolution Under Nasser and Sadat*, Harvard University Press, Massachussetts, 1979, p. 123.
3 *Al-Ahram*, 19 October 1970.
4 ibid., 14 October 1970.
5 ibid., 1 December 1970.
6 ibid., 5 January 1971.
7 ibid., 5 February 1971.
8 Muhammad Heikal, *The Road to Ramadan*, p. 116.
9 ibid., pp. 116, 117.
10 *Al-Ahram*, 8 March 1971.
11 ibid., 2 May 1971.
12 ibid., 30 April 1971.
13 ibid., 6 May 1971.
14 ibid., 2 May 1971.
15 Heikal, *The Road to* . . ., p. 128.
16 Sadat, *In Search of Identity*, p. 207.
17 Sabri, *Documents of the October War*, pp. 17–28.
18 Nabil Raghib, *Sadat, Pioneer of the Intellectual Reformation*, Dar el Marif, Cairo 1975, p. 68.
19 ibid., p. 69.
20 Sadat, *In Search* . . ., p. 139.
21 ibid., p. 206.
22 Moussa Sabri, *The May Documents*, Akhbar Publishing House, Cairo 1977, p. 120.
23 Sadat, *In Search* . . ., p. 223.
24 *Al-Ahram*, 2 May 1971.

25 Sabri, *Documents of the October War*, p. 123.
26 Sabri, *Documents of the October War*, p. 173; Sadat, p. 223; Heikal, *The Road to . . .*, p. 133.
27 *Al-Ahram*, 15 May 1971.
28 ibid.
29 Sabri, *Documents of the October War*, p. 228.
30 Heikal, *The Road to . . .*, p. 179; *Al-Ahram*, 4 June 1971.
31 Raghib, *Sadat the Pioneer*, p. 97.
32 *Al-Ahram*, 22 May 1971.
33 *Le Monde*, 1 June 1971.
34 Sadat, *In Search . . .*, p. 222.
35 *Guardian*, 26 May 1971.
36 Sadat, *In Search . . .*, p. 225.
37 ibid., p. 229.
38 *Al-Ahram*, 3 June 1971.
39 ibid., 6 June 1971.
40 ibid., 24 July 1971.
41 ibid., 13 October 1971.
42 ibid., 21 November 1971.
43 *Guardian,* 1 January 1972.
44 *Al-Ahram*, 14 February 1972.
45 Sadat, *In Search . . .*, p. 227.
46 *Le Monde*, 20 January 1971.
47 *Al-Ahram*, 26 January, 17–18 February 1972.
48 ibid., 26 January 1972.
49 Sadat, *In Search . . .*, p. 228.
50 *Guardian*, 9 February 1974.
51 *Al-Ahram*, 17–18 February 1972.
52 ibid., 7 April 1972.
53 ibid., 25 April 1972.
54 Heikal, *The Road to . . .*, p. 166.
55 Sadat, *In Search . . .*, p. 227.
56 *Al-Ahram*, 15 May 1972.
57 Heikal, *The Road to . . .*, p. 171.
58 *New York Times*, 31 July 1972.
59 Heikal, *The Road to . . .*, p. 176.
60 *International Herald Tribune*, 21 July 1971.
61 *Guardian*, 21 July 1972.
62 Heikal, *The Road to . . .*, p. 120.
63 Edward Sheehan, *The Arabs, Israelis and Kissinger*, Reader's Digest Press, New York 1976, p. 22.
64 Sadat, *In Search . . .*, p. 230.
65 *Al-Ahram*, 25 July 1972.
66 *Guardian*, 16 August 1972.
67 Saad Shazly, *The Crossing of Suez*, Third World Centre for Research and Publishing, London 1980, pp. 116, 117.
68 Sadat, *In Search . . .*, pp. 235–6.

69 Shazly, p. 125.
70 ibid., p. 130.
71 *Al-Ahram*, 29 December 1972.
72 ibid., 1 February 1973.
73 Sabri, *Documents of the October War*, p. 192.
74 *Al-Ahram*, 27 March 1973.
75 *Newsweek*, 9 April 1973.
76 Sheehan, p. 42.
77 *Akhbar al-Yaum*, 24 March 1973.
78 Heikal, *The Road to . . .*, p. 181.
79 *Al-Ahram*, 29 September 1973.

4

1   *Sunday Times* Insight Team, *The Yom Kippur War*, pp. 337–46.
2   Third World Centre for Research and Publishing, London, 1980.
3   Shazly, *The Crossing of Suez*, p. 127.
4   ibid., pp. 164, 180.
5   Quoted in *al-Safir* (Beirut daily), 16 April 1974.
6   *The Yom Kippur War*, p. 380.
7   *Al-Nahar*, 23 October 1973.
8   *Al-Akhbar*, 8 October 1973.
9   *The Yom Kippur War*, p. 401.
10 Sabri, *Documents of the October War*, p. 635.
11 Sadat, *In Search of Identity*, p. 262.
12 Sabri, *Documents of the October War*, p. 632.
13 *Al-Ahram*, 24 July 1974.
14 Sabri, *Documents of the October War*, p. 646.
15 Sheehan, *The Arabs, Israelis and Kissinger*, p. 51.
16 ibid., p. 50.
17 *International Herald Tribune*, 18 March 1974.
18 Sabri, *Documents of the October War*, p. 33.
19 Sheehan, p. 49.
20 Sadat, *In Search . . .*, pp. 260, 261.
21 ibid., pp. 263, 264.
22 13 December 1973.
23 Sheehan, p. 72.
24 Interview with *al-Gumhuriyah*, 22 November 1973.
25 Shazly, p. 199.
26 Sheehan, pp. 79, 80.
27 ibid., p. 50.
28 ibid., p. 108.
29 ibid.
30 Matti Golan, *The Secret Conversation of Henry Kissinger: Step-by-Step Diplomacy in the Middle East*, The New York Time Books Co, New York 1976, p. 142.

31 *Guardian*, 19 January 1974.
32 Sheehan, p. 112.
33 ibid.
34 Nixon *Memoires*, cited in Marwan R. Buheiry, *US Threats of Intervention Against Arab Oil: 1973–1979*, Institute of Palestine Studies, Beirut 1980, p. 13.
35 Shazly, p. 194.
36 ibid., p. 116.
37 Sheehan, pp. 148, 149.
38 *Al-Nahar*, Beirut, 16 January 1975.
39 *Al-Ahram*, 30 March 1975.
40 Sheehan, p. 192.
41 ibid., p. 190.
42 *Al-Ahram*, 29 September 1975.
43 ibid., 30 October 1975.
44 16 August 1975.
45 *Al-Ahram*, 5 September 1975.
46 See *Guardian*, 14 September 1975.
47 Roger Morris, *Uncertain Greatness*, Quartet Books, London, 1977, pp. 253, 261.
48 *Al-Ahram*, 19 October 1975.
49 *Al-Hawadith*, 6 February 1976.
50 *Al-Anwar*, Beirut, 30 December 1976.

5

1 *Al-Ahram*, 27 August 1974.
2 Sayyid Marei, *Akhbar-al-Yaum*, 19 April 1975.
3 John Waterbury, *Egypt, Burdens of the Past, Options for the Future*, Indiana University Press, Bloomington and London 1978, p. 207.
4 *Al-Ahram*, 27 August 1974.
5 Muhammad Heikal, *Les Documents du Caire*, Flammarion, Paris 1972, p. 306.
6 *October* (Cairo weekly), January 1978; see also *Akhbar al-Yaum*, 23 February 1980.
7 *New Yorker*, May 1979.
8 See *Akhbar al-Yaum*, 23 February 1980; *Time*, 2 January 1978.
9 *Playgirl*, June 1978.
10 *Time*, 22 November 1977.
11 Waterbury, p. 213.
12 See *Financial Times*, July 1980.
13 Waterbury, p. 244.
14 ibid., p. 245.
15 *The Financial Post Magazine*, June 1977.
16 ibid.

17 *Al-Ahram*, 29 August 1977.
18 Waterbury, pp. 287, 289.
19 See ibid., p. 247.
20 *Guardian*, 10 July 1979.
21 Waterbury, p. 286.
22 ibid., p. 245.
23 ibid., p. 231.
24 ibid., p. 290.
25 *Financial Times*, 15 June 1976.
26 ibid., 15 January 1976.
27 Waterbury, p. 248.
28 See *Observer Foreign News Service*, 15 April 1975.
29 *Guardian*, 29 April 1979.
30 *Al-Ahram*, 28 March 1976.
31 *Al-Hawadith*, 20 March 1975.
32 *Al-Siyasah* (Kuwait daily), 8 January 1976.
33 *Al-Ahram*, 27 July 1976.
34 Waterbury, p. 302.
35 ibid., p. 308.
36 *New York Times*, 9 September 1976.
37 *Al-Akhbar*, 22 January 1977.
38 ibid.
39 *Observations of the National Progressive Unionist Grouping on the Prime Minister's Statement and Their View of the Problems* [Arabic], Cairo, January 1977.
40 Hussein Abdul Razzaq, *Egypt on 18, 19 January* [Arabic], Dar-el-Kalima, Beirut 1979, p. 75.
41 MERIP Report, Washington, No. 56, 1977.
42 *Al-Ahram*, 19 January.
43 ibid., 20 January 1977.
44 ibid., 4 February 1977.
45 *Al-Akhbar*, 24 January 1977.
46 ibid., 31 January 1977.
47 *Al-Ahram*, 4 February 1977.
48 *Akhbar al-Yaum*, 21 January 1977.
49 *Al-Ahram*, 20 January 1977.
50 *Washington Post*, 3 February 1977.
51 *Rose el-Youssef*, 31 January 1977, p. 16.
52 *Al-Ahram*, 24 January 1977.
53 ibid., 4 February 1977.

6

1 *Al-Ahram*, 10 November 1977.
2 *L'Orient–Le Jour*, 18 November 1977.

3   Eitan Haber, Zeev Schiff, Ehud Yaari, *The Year of the Dove*, Bantam Books, New York 1979, p. 24.
4   ibid., p. 25.
5   12 November 1977.
6   *Al-Akhbar*, 13 November 1977.
7   George Carpozi, *Anwar Sadat, A Man of Peace*, Manor Books, New York 1977.
8   ibid., pp. 158–60.
9   *Al-Ahram*, 16 November 1977.
10 *Al-Safir*, 20 November 1977.
11 Haber et al., p. 66.
12 ibid., p. 67.
13 ibid., p. 69.
14 *Daily Telegraph*, 21 November 1977.
15 *October*, 11 December 1977.
16 *Daily Telegraph*, 28 November 1977.
17 Sabri Jiryis, 'The Arab World at the Crossroads', *The Journal of Palestine Studies*, No. 26, Beirut 1978, p. 39.
18 ibid., p. 37.
19 *Al-Akhbar*, 19 August 1973.
20 Dawn Publishing Company, Quebec 1979.
21 Jiryis, p. 38.
22 David Hirst, *The Gun and the Olive Branch*, Faber and Faber, London 1977, pp. 123ff.
23 *Jewish Newsletter*, New York, 3 October 1960.
24 Menachim Begin, *The Revolt*, W. H. Allen, London 1951, p. 164.
25 *Al-Ahram*, 16 June 1977.
26 ibid., 25 October 1977.
27 *Guardian*, 8 July 1977.
28 *Al-Anwar*, 28 October 1977.
29 *Al-Akhbar*, 16 November 1977.
30 ibid., 13 November 1977.
31 ibid., 17 November 1977.
32 *Al-Anwar*, Beirut, 12, 15, 19, 22 June 1977.
33 Haber et al., p. 73.
34 *Al-Akhbar*, 17 November 1977.
35 Haber et al., p. 73.
36 *Al-Nahar*, 15 July 1980.
37 *Al-Ahram*, 29 January 1980.
38 *Al-Jumhuriyah*, Baghdad, 24 November 1977.
39 *Al-Riyadh*, Riyadh, 21 December 1977.
40 See *Le Monde*, 25–6 March 1979.
41 *October*, 11 December 1977.
42 *New York Times*, 5 December 1977.
43 *Guardian*, 3 January 1978.
44 *Al-Hawadith*, 30 December 1977.
45 *October*, 25 December 1977.

46 See Jiryis, p. 45; *al-Mustaqbal*, Paris, December 1972.
47 *October*, 25 December 1975.
48 *Al-Siyasah*, 10 December 1977.
49 *Guardian*, 12 December 1977.
50 *October*, 11 December 1977.
51 *Al-Ahram*, 2 January 1978.
52 *October*, 11 December 1977.
53 *Al-Sisayah*, 10 December 1977.
54 *October*, 18 December 1977.
55 See *Arab Report and Record*, London, December 1977, p. 1,024.
56 *Guardian*, 21 February 1978.
57 Haber et al., p. 42.
58 *Haolem Hazeh*, 23 November 1977.
59 Schmuel Schnitzer, *Davar*, 25 November 1977.
60 *Davar*, 20 November 1977.
61 Haber et al., p. 69.
62 ibid., p. 93.
63 ibid., p. 108.
64 ibid., p. 110.
65 *October*, 1 January 1978.
66 Haber et al., pp. 125, 128.
67 *October*, 11 December 1977.
68 ibid., 1 January 1980.
69 ibid., 11, 25 December 1977.
70 ibid., 1 January 1978.
71 ibid., 8 January 1980.
72 *Guardian*, 24 January 1978.
73 ibid.
74 *October*, 15 January 1978.
75 *Al-Ahram*, 22 January 1978.
76 See Mark A. Bruzonsky, *Middle East International*, London, August 1978.
77 *Guardian*, 15 December 1977.
78 *Al-Ahram*, 22 January 1977.
79 ibid., 7 June 1978.
80 ibid., 4 September 1978.
81 Haber et al., p. 218.
82 *Al-Akhbar*, 12 September 1978.
83 ibid., 14 September 1978.
84 *International Herald Tribune*, 24 September 1978.
85 Haber et al., p. 245.
86 *Al-Hawadith*, 12 January 1979.
87 *October*, 8 October 1978.
88 See Fayez Sayegh, 'The Camp David Agreement and the Palestine Problem', *Journal of Palestine Studies*, No. 30, 1979.
89 Amnon Kapeliouk, *Le Monde Diplomatique*, Paris, January 1979.
90 ibid.

91 *Al-Akhbar*, 26 September 1978.
92 *Al-Ahram*, 9 November 1978.
93 ibid., 5, 9 and 16 November 1978.
94 ibid., 8, 9 November 1978.
95 *October*, 11 October 1978.
96 Kapeliouk, *Le Monde Diplomatique*.
97 ibid.
98 *Al-Ahram*, 15 November 1978.
99 *Journal d'Egypte*, 29 October 1978.
100 Haber et al., p. 292.
101 *Al-Akhbar*, 9 March 1979.
102 Haber et al., pp. 297, 300.
103 ibid., p. 299.
104 *New York Times*, 13 March 1979.

7

Epilogue

1 *Al-Ahram*, 2 May 1979.
2 ibid., 29 January 1980.
3 *International Herald Tribune*, 9 April 1980.
4 *Middle East Reporter*, Beirut, 29 December 1979.
5 *Al-Ahram*, 26 December 1979.
6 ibid., 29 January 1980.
7 ibid., 2 May 1979.
8 *International Herald Tribune*, 7 September 1979.
9 *October*, December 1979.
10 *Al-Ahram*, 26 December 1979.
11 *Haaretz*, 13 May 1980.
12 *Al-Ahram*, 15 April 1980.
13 *International Herald Tribune*, 26 May 1980.
14 UPI, 21 June 1980.
15 *Le Monde*, 27 March 1979.
16 *Al-Ahram*, 7 August; 30 October 1980.
17 *Paris Match*, January 1981.
18 Unpublished statement, 12 May 1980, distributed to the press.
19 *Al-Ahram*, 16 May 1979.
20 *Egyptian Gazette*, 24 December 1980.
21 *Economist*, 1 December 1979.
22 *Al-Ahram*, 1, 2 May 1980.
23 See *Middle East Reporter*, Beirut, 14 May 1980.
24 *Al-Ahram*, 15 May 1980.
25 ibid., 6, 7 December 1980.
26 ibid., 26 December 1980.

27 *Al-Shaab*, 27 January 1981.
28 *L'Orient–Le Jour*, 23 May 1981.
29 *Al-Ahram*, 16 April.
30 ibid., 29 January 1980.
31 ibid., 2 May 1979.
32 *International Herald Tribune*, 7 September 1979.
33 See interview with General Saad Shazly, *Guardian*, 7 April 1980.
34 *Al-Ahram*, 29 January 1980.
35 ibid., 23 July 1980.
36 *October*, 26 April 1981.
37 *Al-Ahram*, 23 July 1980.
38 See *L'Orient–Le Jour*, 18 November 1980.
39 Reuter, 9 July 1980.
40 *Al-Ahram*, 1 April 1981.
41 ibid., 29 January 1980.
42 *October*, 19 March 1979; *al-Ahram*, 10 March 1980.
43 *International Herald Tribune*, 28–9 September 1979.
44 *New Statesman*, 9 May 1980.
45 *Al-Ahram*, 16 May 1979.
46 ibid., 24 April 1979.
47 ibid., 10 March 1980.
48 See the *Guardian*, 10 February 1979.
49 *Al-Ahram*, 10 March, 16 April 1979.
50 *Maariv*, 13 July 1979.
51 *October*, 30 December 1979.
52 *Al-Ahram*, 29 January 1980.
53 ibid., 3 September 1980.
54 *Mayo*, 10 August 1981.
55 *October*, 25 April 1981.
56 *Reader's Digest*, French edition, August 1980.
57 *Al-Nahar*, 26 September 1980.
58 *Al-Ahram*, 19 January 1981.
59 *Reader's Digest*, French edition, August 1980.
60 *October*, 25 April 1981.
61 *Esquire*, 30 January 1979.
62 *Washington Post*, 26 May 1980.
63 *International Herald Tribune*, 15 May 1979.
64 ibid., 31 March 1980.
65 *Al-Ahram*, 15 May 1980.
66 Lewis R. Scudder, *Arab Intellectuals and the Implications of the Defeat of 1967*, American University of Beirut, 1971, pp. 232–43.

Bibliography

Ashmawi, Sayed Muhammad, *History of Egyptian Political Thought 1945–1952*, doctoral thesis (Arabic), unpublished, Cairo University, 1977.

Baker, Raymond William, *Egypt's Uncertain Revolution Under Nasser and Sadat*, Harvard University Press, Massachussetts, 1979.

Buhairi, Marwan, R., *US Threats of Intervention against Arab Oil, 1973–1979*, Institute for Palestine Studies, Beirut 1980.

Begin, Menachim, *The Revolt*, W. H. Allen, London 1951.

Carpozi, George, *Anwar Sadat, A Man of Peace*, Manor Books, New York 1977.

Desjardins, Thierry, *Sadat, Pharaon d'Egypte*, Editions Marcel Valtat, Paris 1981.

Eidelberg, Paul, *Sadat's Strategy*, Dawn Publishing Company, Quebec, 1979.

al-Farid, Abdul Meguid, *From the Minutes of Nasser's Arab and International Meetings*, (Arabic), The Institute for Arab Studies, Beirut 1979.

Golan, Matti, *The Secret Conversations of Henry Kissinger: Step-by-Step Diplomacy in the Middle East*, New York Times Book Co., New York, 1976.

Haber, Eitan, Zeef Schiff, Ehud Yaari, *The Year of the Dove*, Bantam Books, New York, 1979.

Hamroush, Ahmad, *The Story of the 23 July Revolution*, (Arabic), The Arab Institute for Studies and Publishing, Beirut 1977.

Heikal, Muhammad, *Les Documents de Caire*, Flammarion, 1972.

Heikal, Muhammad, *The Road to Ramadan*, Collins, London 1975.

Heikal, Muhammad, *Le Sphinx et le Commissar*, Editions Jeune Afrique, Paris 1980.

Hirst, David, *The Gun and the Olive Branch*, Faber and Faber, London 1977.

Hussein, Mahmud, *La Lutte des Classes en Egypte*, Maspero, Paris 1970.

Jiryis, Sabri, *The Arab World at the Crossroads*, The Journal of Palestine Studies, No. 26, Beirut 1978.

Kalb, Marvin and Bernard, *Kissinger*, Little, Brown, Boston 1974.

Kapeliouk, Amon, *Israel: La Fin des Mythes*, Albin Michel, Paris 1975.

Lacouture, Jean, *Nasser*, Seuil, Paris 1971.

Morris, Roger, *Uncertain Greatness*, Quartet Books, London 1977.

Nashashibi, Nassereddin, *al-Hibr Aswad ... Aswad* (Arabic), al-Nahar Press Services, Beirut, n.d.

Nasser, Gamal Abdul, *The Philosophy of the Revolution*, Government Printing Office, Cairo, n.d.

Raghib, Nabil, *Sadat the Pioneer of the Intellectual Reformation* (Arabic), Dar al-Maarif, Cairo 1975.

Razzak, Hussein Abdul, *Egypt on 18, 19 January*, Dar al-Kalima, Beirut 1979.

Sadat, Anwar, *The Full Story of the Revolution* (Arabic), Dar al-Hilal, Cairo n.d.

Sadat, Anwar, *My Son, This is your Uncle Gamal* (Arabic), Arfan Library, Cairo, n.d.

Sadat, Anwar, *Révolte Sur le Nil*, Pierre Amiot, Paris 1957.

Sadat, Anwar, *In Search of Identity*, Collins, London, 1978.

Saber, Ali, *Nasser en Procès*, Collections Points de Vue, Paris 1968.

Sabri, Moussa, *Documents of the October War* (Arabic), The Modern Egyptian Library, Cairo 1974.

Sabri, Moussa, *The May Documents* (Arabic), Akhbar Publishing House, Cairo 1977.

Sayegh, Fayez, *The Camp David Agreement and the Palestine Problem*, The Journal of Palestine Studies, No. 30, 1979.

Scudder, Lewis R., *Arab Intellectuals and the Implications of the Defeat of 1967*, MA thesis, American University of Beirut, 1971.

Shazly, Saad, *The Crossing of Suez*, Third World Centre for Research and Publishing, London 1980.

Sheehan, Edward, *The Arabs, Israelis and Kissinger*, Reader's Digest Press, New York 1976.

372

BIBLIOGRAPHY

Shoukri, Ghali, *Egypte Contre-Révolution*, Le Sycomore, Paris 1979.
Stephens, Robert, *Nasser*, Penguin Books, London 1971.
Sunday Times Insight Team, *The Yom Kippur War*, André Deutsch, London 1975.
Vatikiotis, P. J., *Nasser and his Generation*, Croom Helm, London 1978.
Waterbury, John, *Egypt, Burdens of the Past, Options for the Future*, Indiana University Press, Washington and London 1978.

Index

375